Forget Me Not

1

ORIGINAL STORY:
Mag Hsu

ART:
Nao Emoto

1

CONTENTS

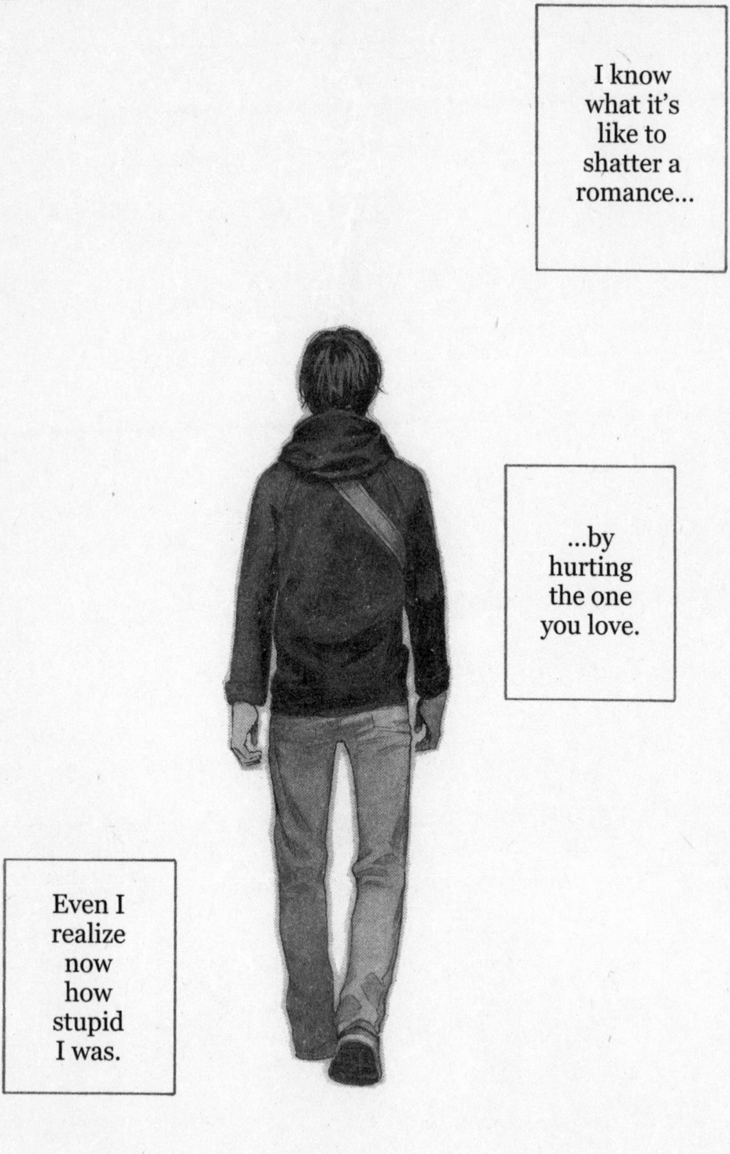
I know what it's like to shatter a romance...
...by hurting the one you love.
Even I realize now how stupid I was.

CHAPTER **1**:
Nobuta

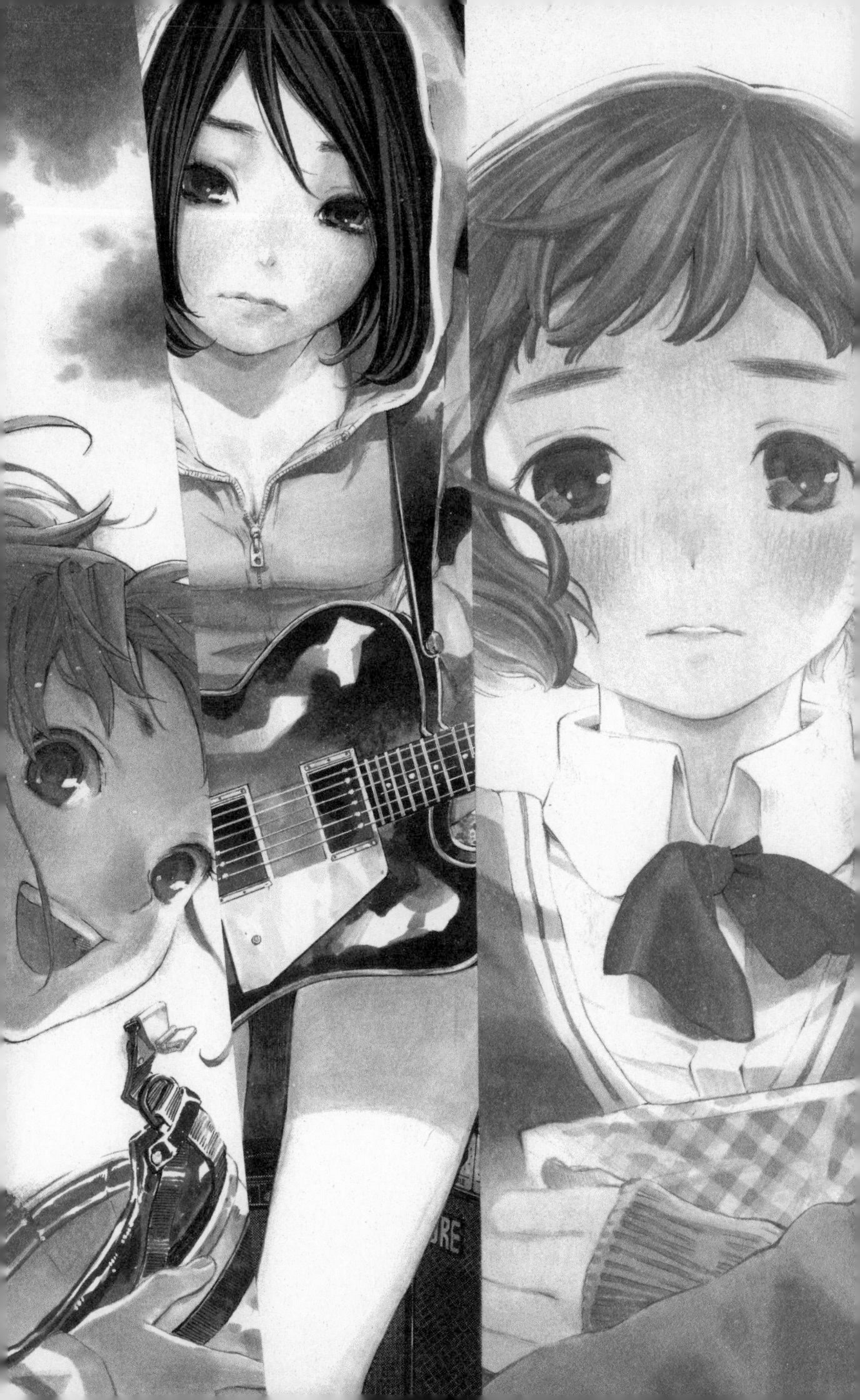

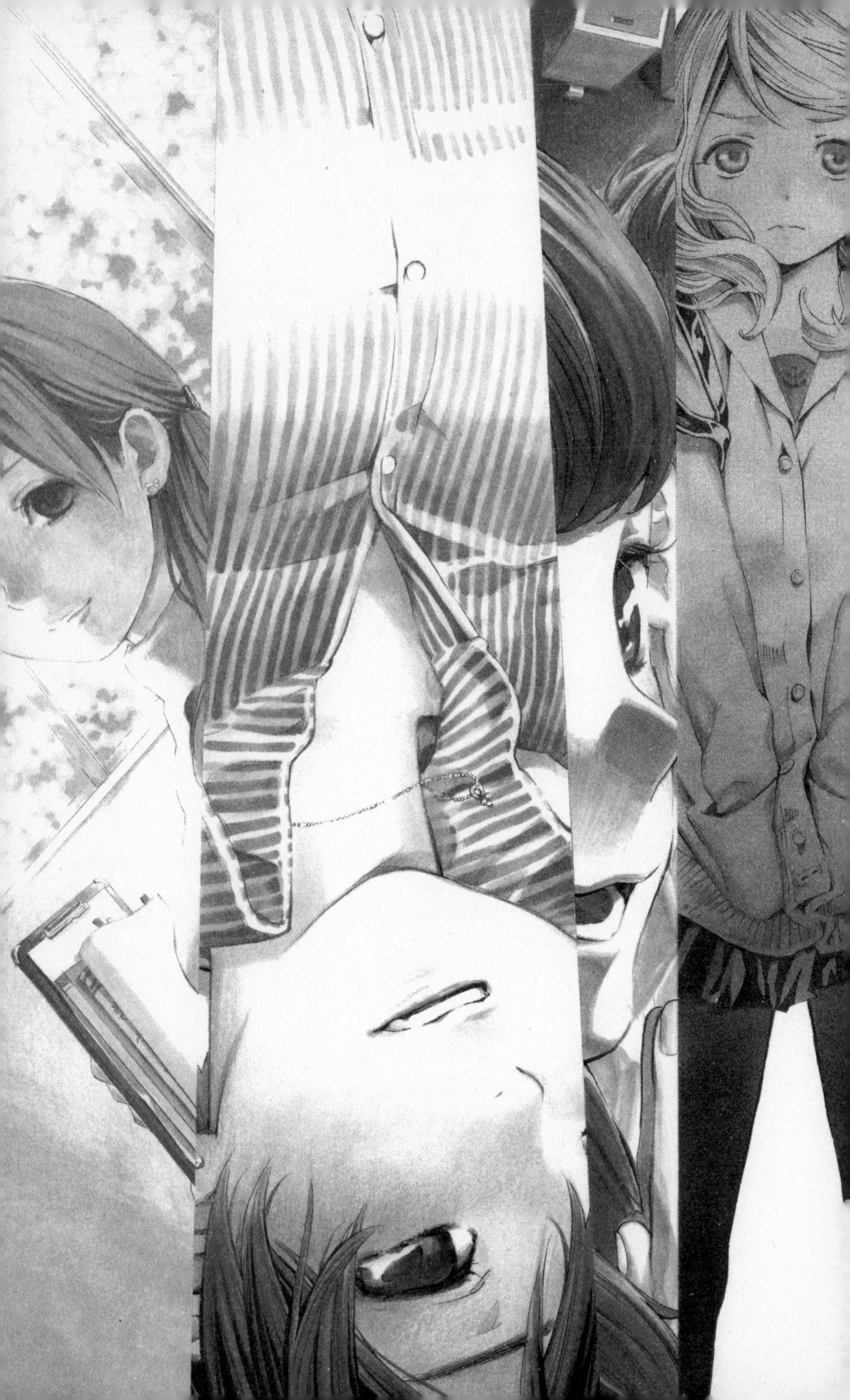

Forget Me Not

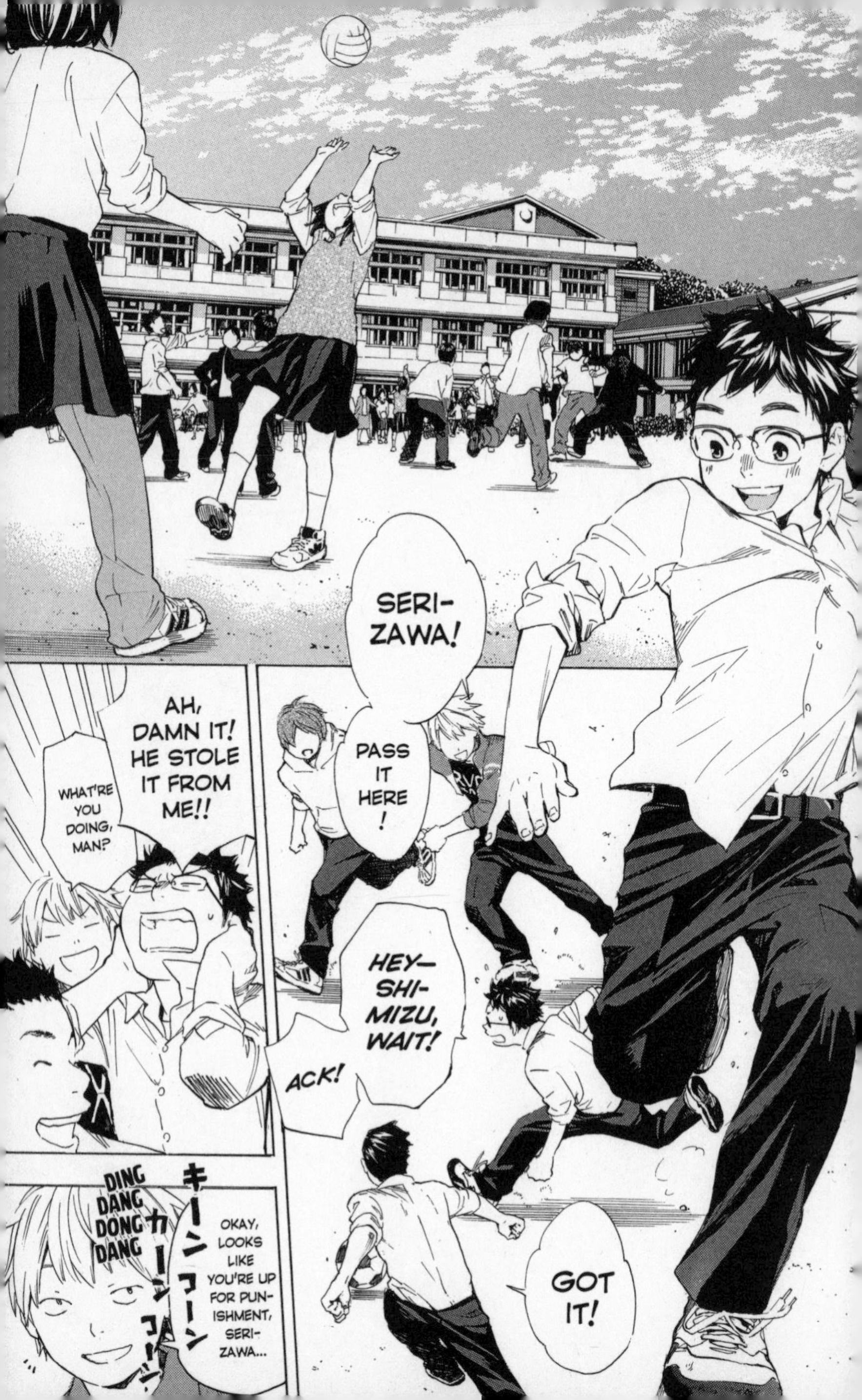
SERI-ZAWA!
PASS IT HERE!
HEY—SHI-MIZU, WAIT!
ACK!
GOT IT!
AH, DAMN IT! HE STOLE IT FROM ME!!
WHAT'RE YOU DOING, MAN?
DING DANG DONG DANG
キーン カーン コーン
OKAY, LOOKS LIKE YOU'RE UP FOR PUN-ISHMENT, SERI-ZAWA...

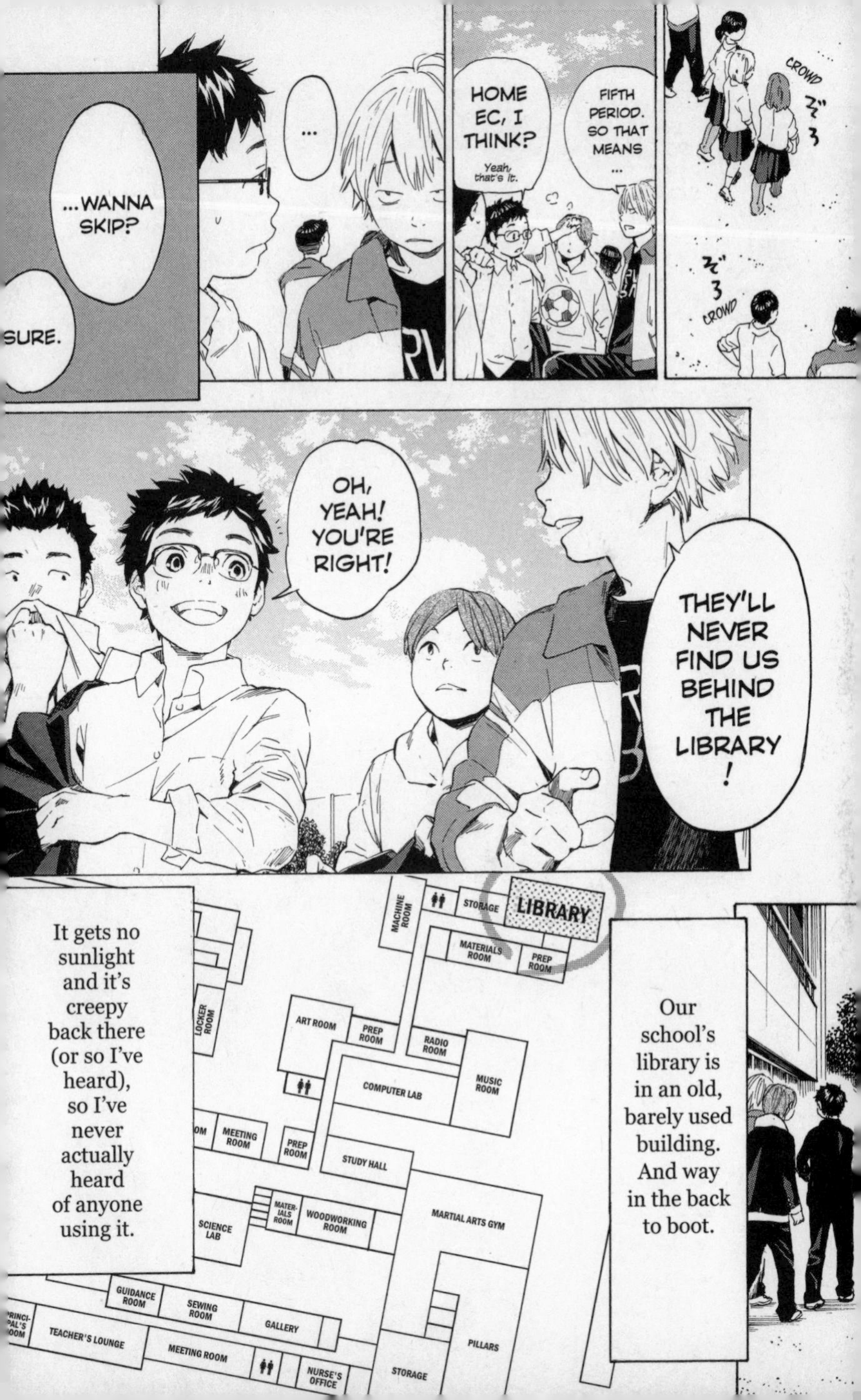
CROWD
ぞろ
ぞろ
CROWD
FIFTH PERIOD. SO THAT MEANS ...
HOME EC, I THINK?
Yeah, that's it.
...
...WANNA SKIP?
SURE.
THEY'LL NEVER FIND US BEHIND THE LIBRARY!
OH, YEAH! YOU'RE RIGHT!
Our school's library is in an old, barely used building. And way in the back to boot.
LIBRARY
STORAGE
MACHINE ROOM
MATERIALS ROOM
PREP ROOM
ART ROOM
PREP ROOM
RADIO ROOM
LOCKER ROOM
COMPUTER LAB
MUSIC ROOM
MEETING ROOM
PREP ROOM
STUDY HALL
MATER-IALS ROOM
WOODWORKING ROOM
SCIENCE LAB
MARTIAL ARTS GYM
GUIDANCE ROOM
SEWING ROOM
GALLERY
TEACHER'S LOUNGE
MEETING ROOM
NURSE'S OFFICE
STORAGE
PILLARS
It gets no sunlight and it's creepy back there (or so I've heard), so I've never actually heard of anyone using it.

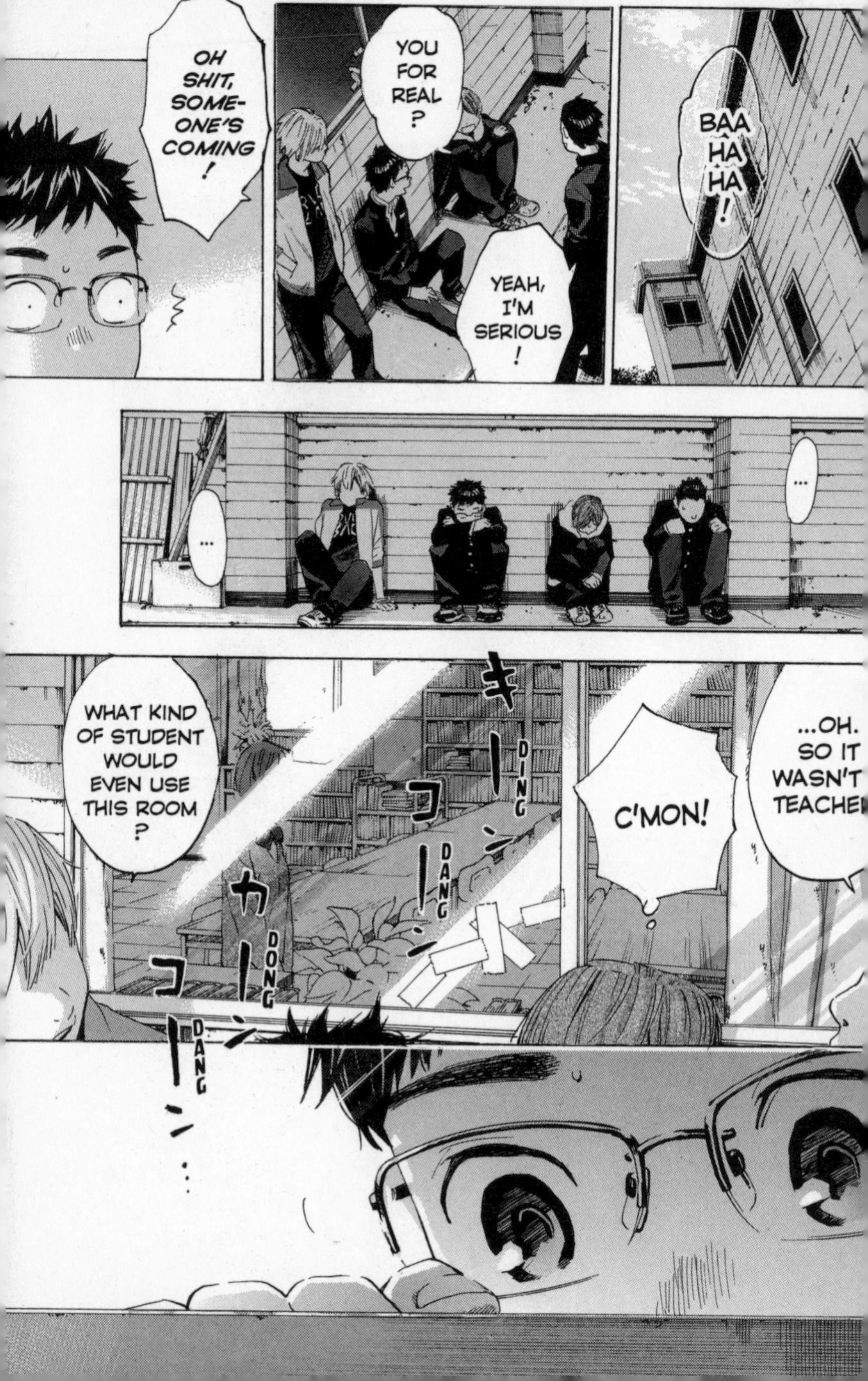
BAA HA HA!
YOU FOR REAL?
YEAH, I'M SERIOUS!
OH SHIT, SOMEONE'S COMING!
...
...
...OH. SO IT WASN'T TEACHE
C'MON!
WHAT KIND OF STUDENT WOULD EVEN USE THIS ROOM?
DING
DANG
DONG
DANG

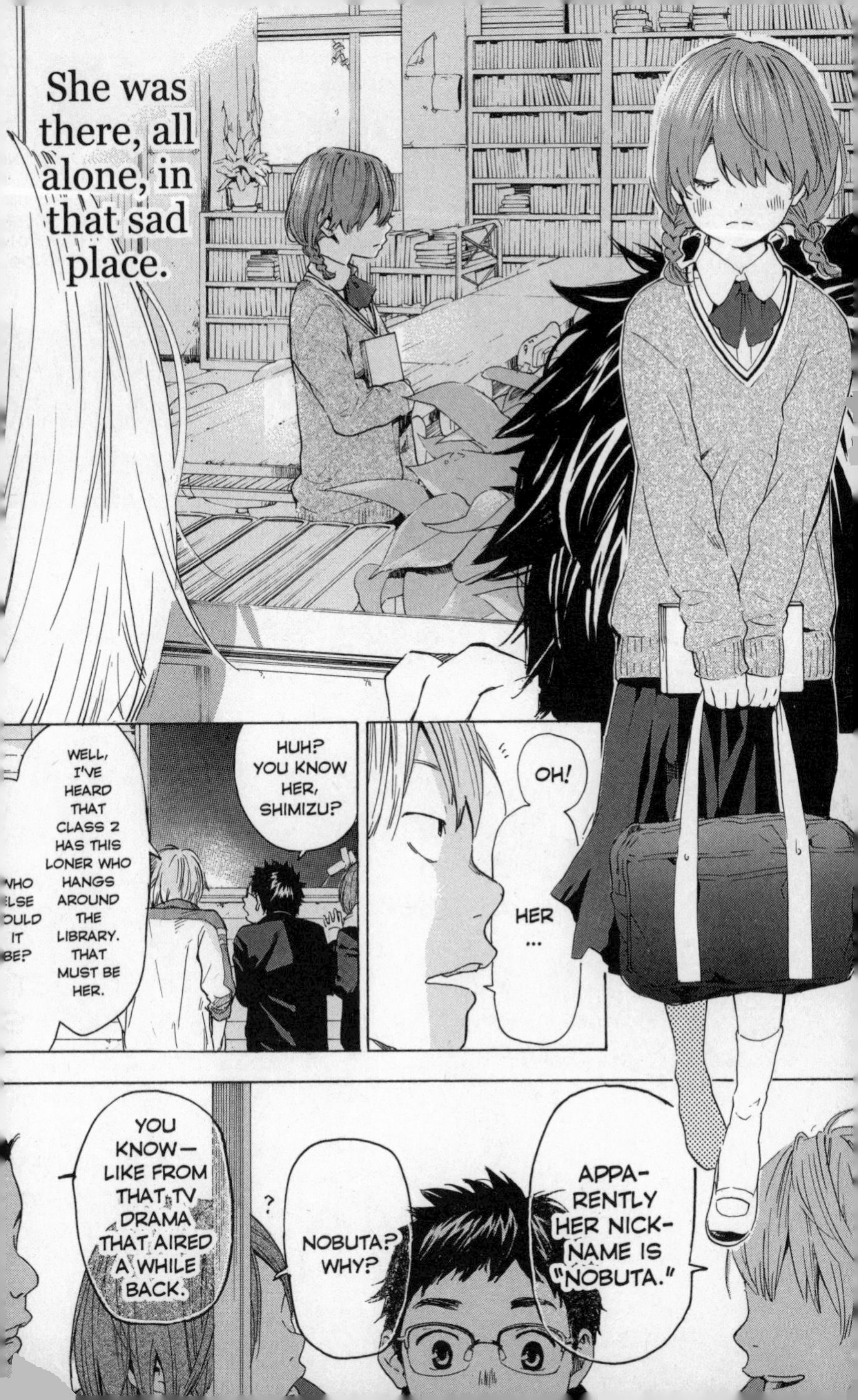
She was there, all alone, in that sad place.
OH!
HER ...
HUH? YOU KNOW HER, SHIMIZU?
WELL, I'VE HEARD THAT CLASS 2 HAS THIS LONER WHO HANGS AROUND THE LIBRARY. THAT MUST BE HER.
APPA-RENTLY HER NICK-NAME IS "NOBUTA."
NOBUTA? WHY?
?
YOU KNOW—LIKE FROM THAT TV DRAMA THAT AIRED A WHILE BACK.

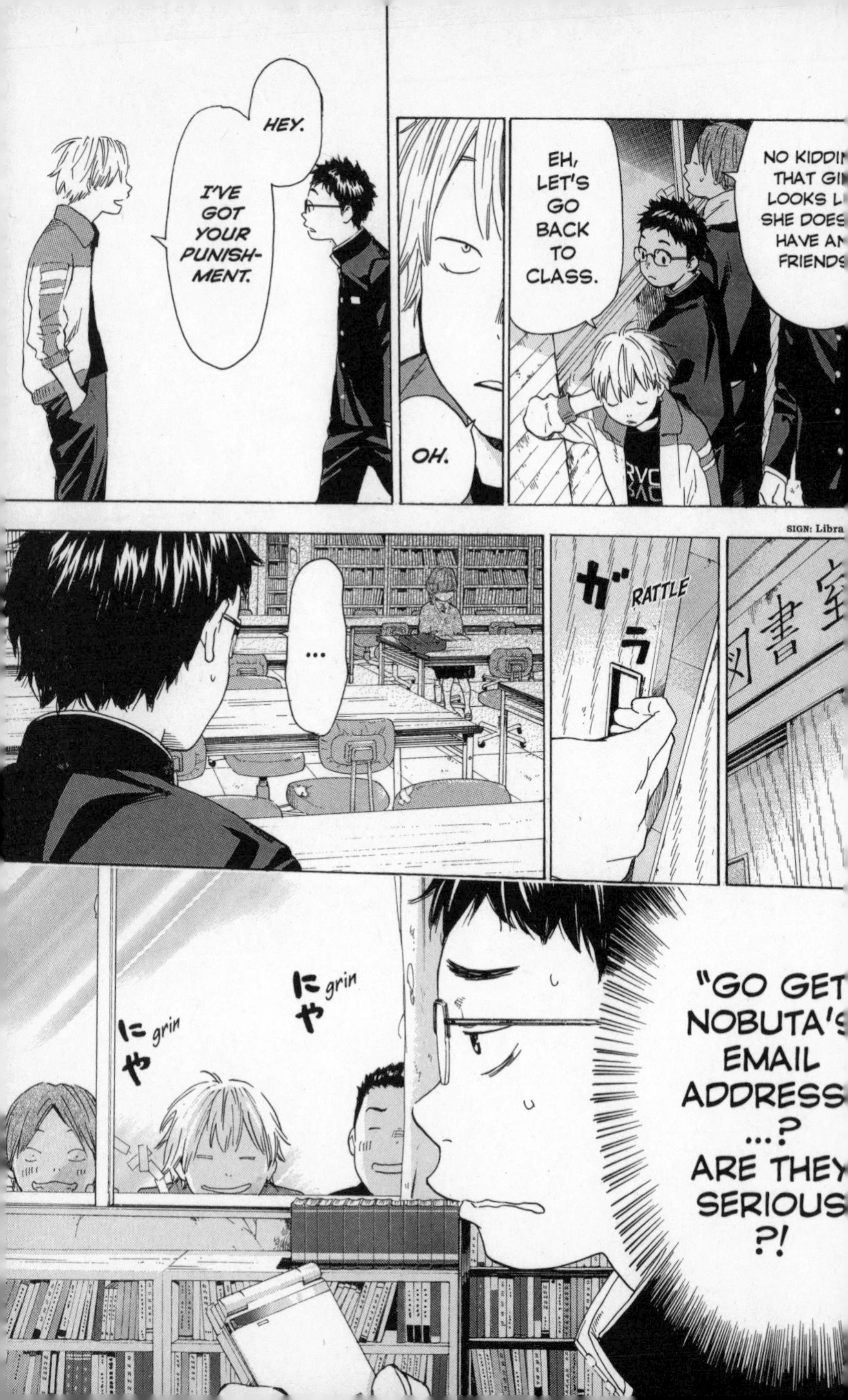
NO KIDDIN THAT GI LOOKS L SHE DOES HAVE AN FRIENDS
EH, LET'S GO BACK TO CLASS.
OH.
HEY.
I'VE GOT YOUR PUNISHMENT.
SIGN: Libra
図書室
ガラ RATTLE
...
"GO GET NOBUTA'S EMAIL ADDRESS ...? ARE THEY SERIOUS ?!
にや grin
にや grin

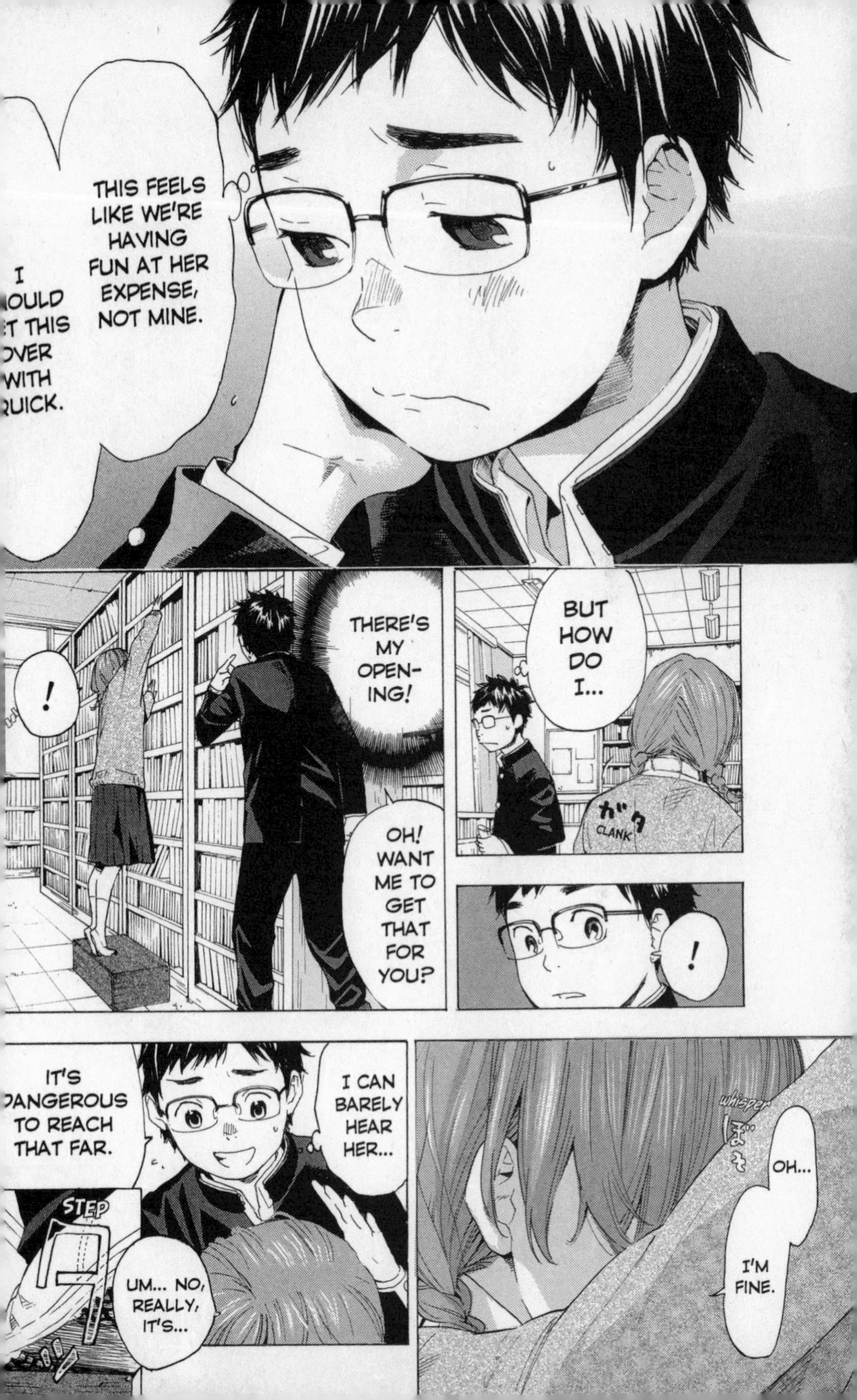
THIS FEELS LIKE WE'RE HAVING FUN AT HER EXPENSE, NOT MINE.
I OULD T THIS OVER WITH UICK.
BUT HOW DO I...
ガタ
CLANK
!
THERE'S MY OPEN-ING!
!
OH! WANT ME TO GET THAT FOR YOU?
whisper
OH...
I'M FINE.
I CAN BARELY HEAR HER...
IT'S ANGEROUS TO REACH THAT FAR.
STEP
UM... NO, REALLY, IT'S...

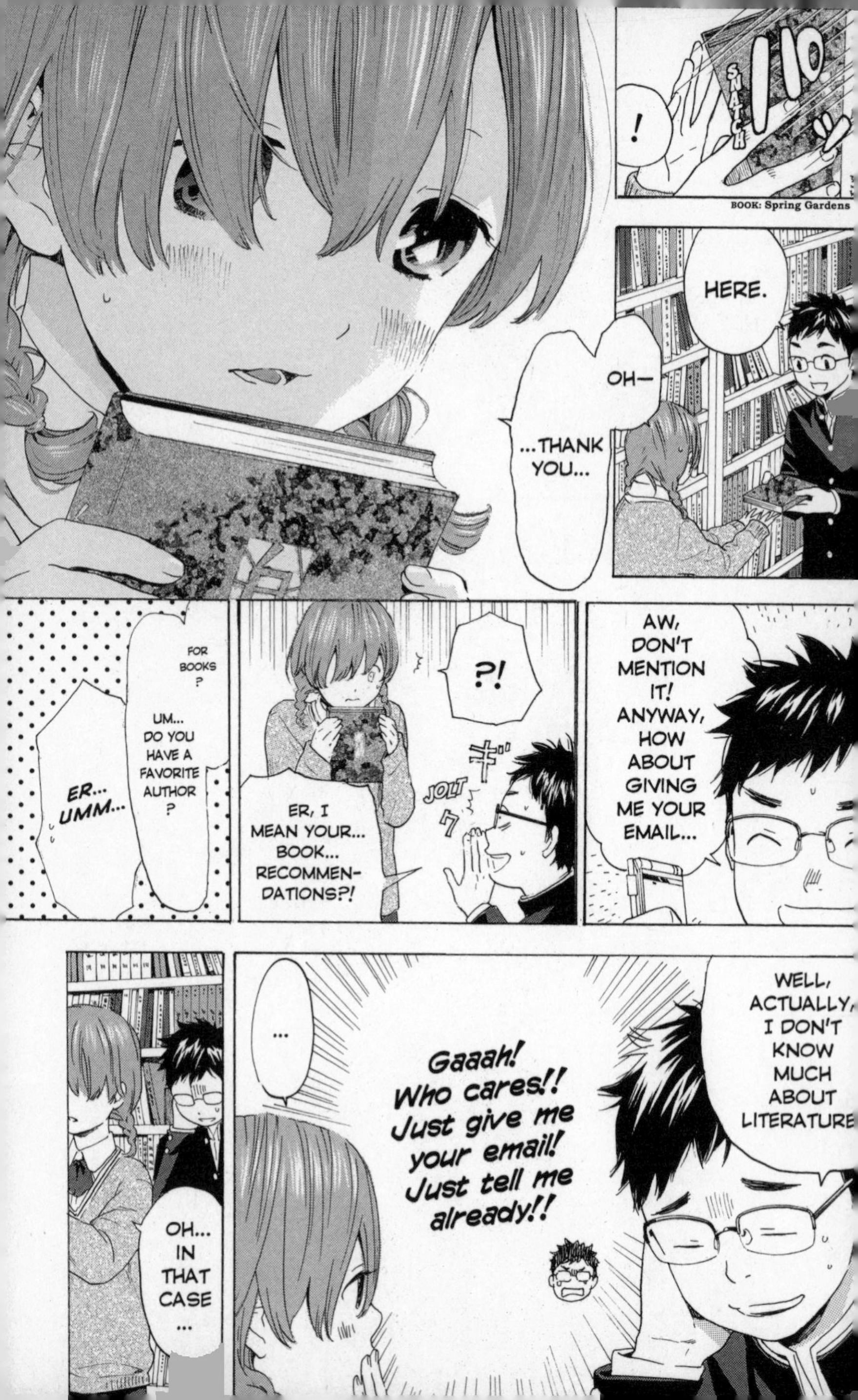
SNATCH
!
BOOK: Spring Gardens
HERE.
OH—
...THANK YOU...
AW, DON'T MENTION IT! ANYWAY, HOW ABOUT GIVING ME YOUR EMAIL...
?!
JOLT
ER, I MEAN YOUR... BOOK... RECOMMENDATIONS?!
FOR BOOKS? UM... DO YOU HAVE A FAVORITE AUTHOR?
ER... UMM...
WELL, ACTUALLY, I DON'T KNOW MUCH ABOUT LITERATURE
Gaaah! Who cares!! Just give me your email! Just tell me already!!
...
OH... IN THAT CASE...

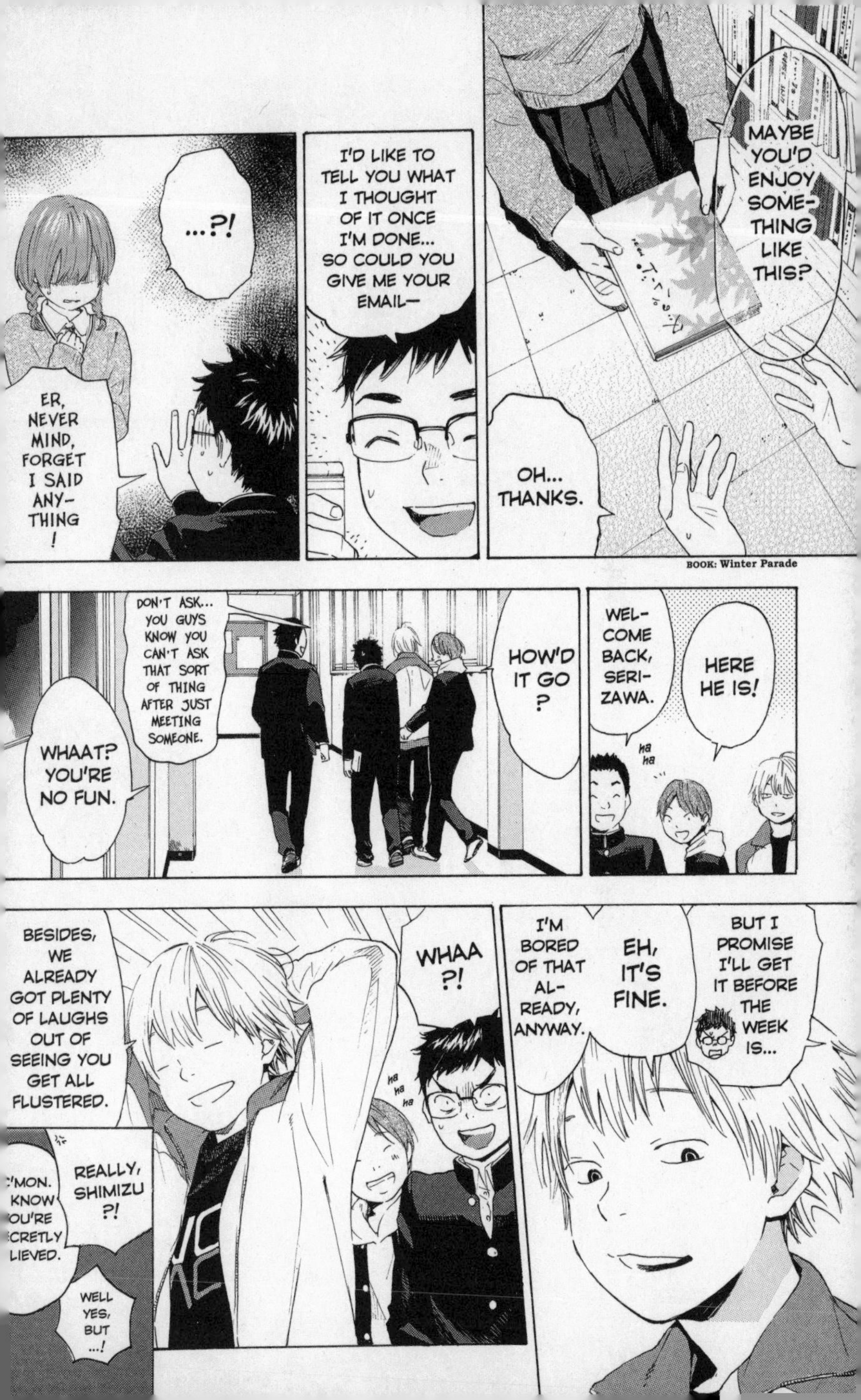
MAYBE YOU'D ENJOY SOME-THING LIKE THIS?
OH... THANKS.
I'D LIKE TO TELL YOU WHAT I THOUGHT OF IT ONCE I'M DONE... SO COULD YOU GIVE ME YOUR EMAIL—
...?!
ER, NEVER MIND, FORGET I SAID ANY-THING!
HERE HE IS!
WEL-COME BACK, SERI-ZAWA.
ha ha
HOW'D IT GO?
DON'T ASK... YOU GUYS KNOW YOU CAN'T ASK THAT SORT OF THING AFTER JUST MEETING SOMEONE.
WHAAT? YOU'RE NO FUN.
BUT I PROMISE I'LL GET IT BEFORE THE WEEK IS...
EH, IT'S FINE.
I'M BORED OF THAT AL-READY, ANYWAY.
WHAA?!
BESIDES, WE ALREADY GOT PLENTY OF LAUGHS OUT OF SEEING YOU GET ALL FLUSTERED.
ha ha ha
REALLY, SHIMIZU?!
'MON. KNOW OU'RE CRETLY LIEVED.
WELL YES, BUT ...!

BOOK: Winter Parade

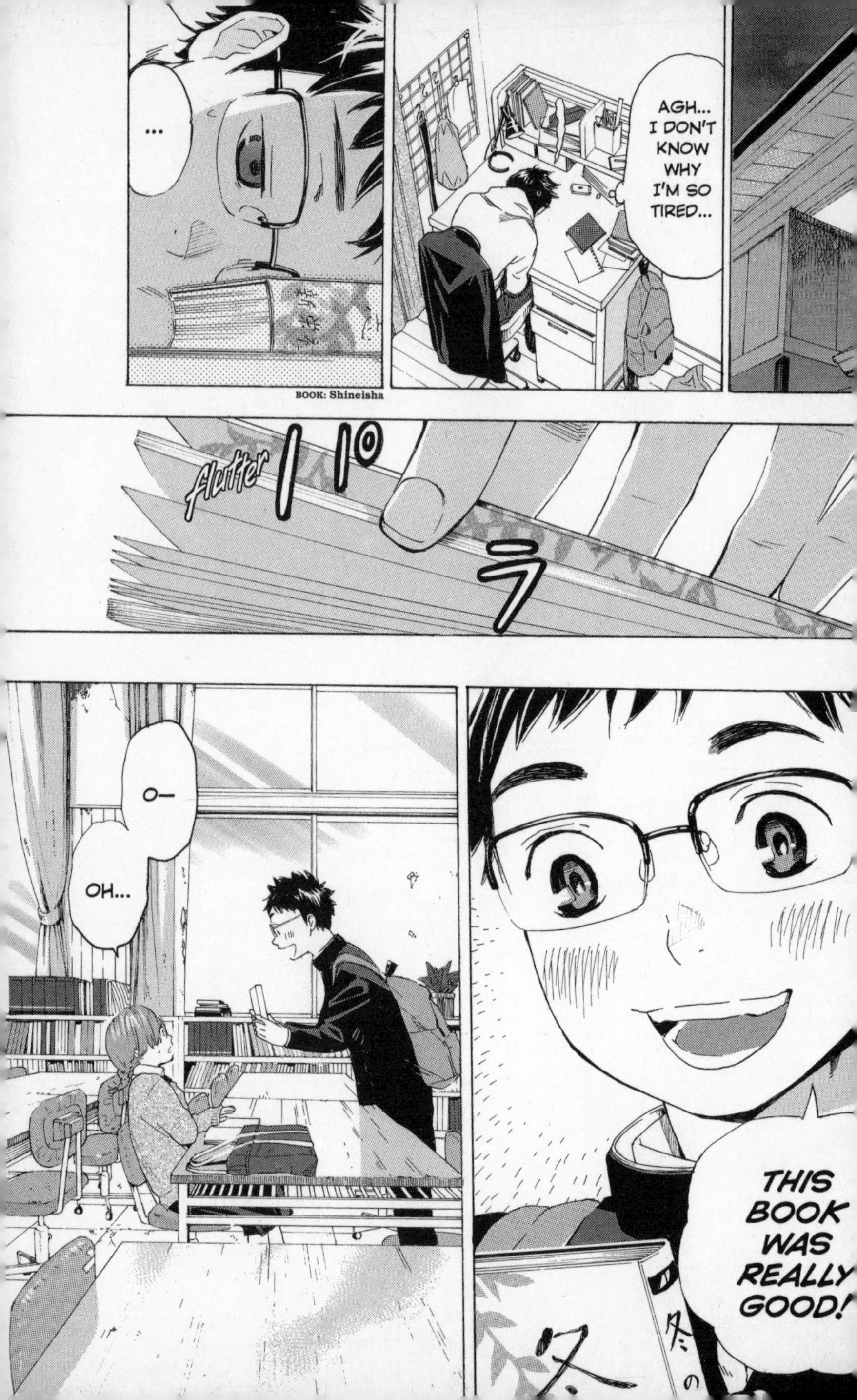
AGH... I DON'T KNOW WHY I'M SO TIRED...
...
BOOK: Shineisha
Flutter
パラ
THIS BOOK WAS REALLY GOOD!
O–
OH...

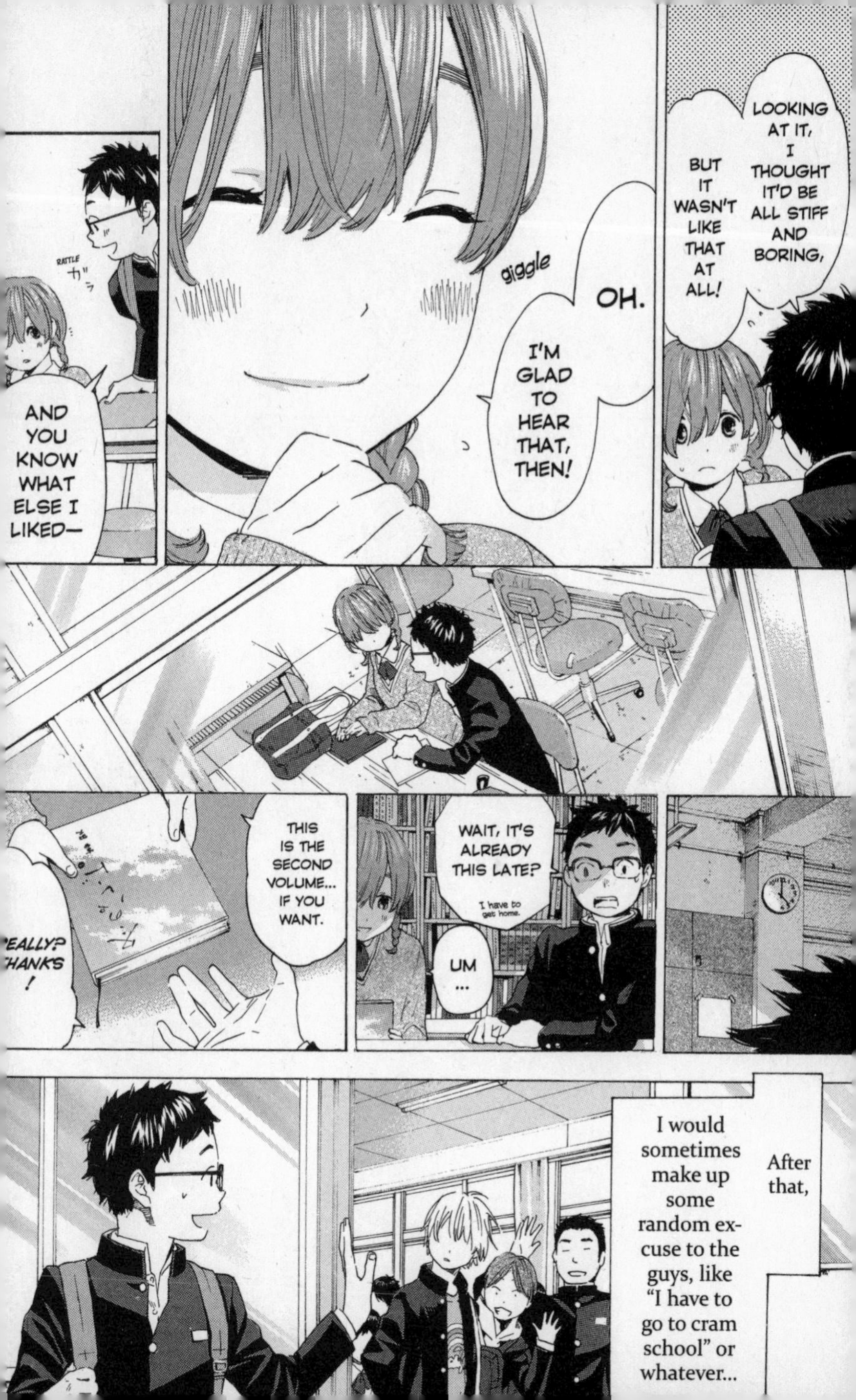
LOOKING AT IT, I THOUGHT IT'D BE ALL STIFF AND BORING,
BUT IT WASN'T LIKE THAT AT ALL!
OH.
giggle
I'M GLAD TO HEAR THAT, THEN!
RATTLE
AND YOU KNOW WHAT ELSE I LIKED—
WAIT, IT'S ALREADY THIS LATE?
I have to get home.
UM ...
THIS IS THE SECOND VOLUME... IF YOU WANT.
EALLY? HANKS !
After that,
I would sometimes make up some random excuse to the guys, like “I have to go to cram school” or whatever...

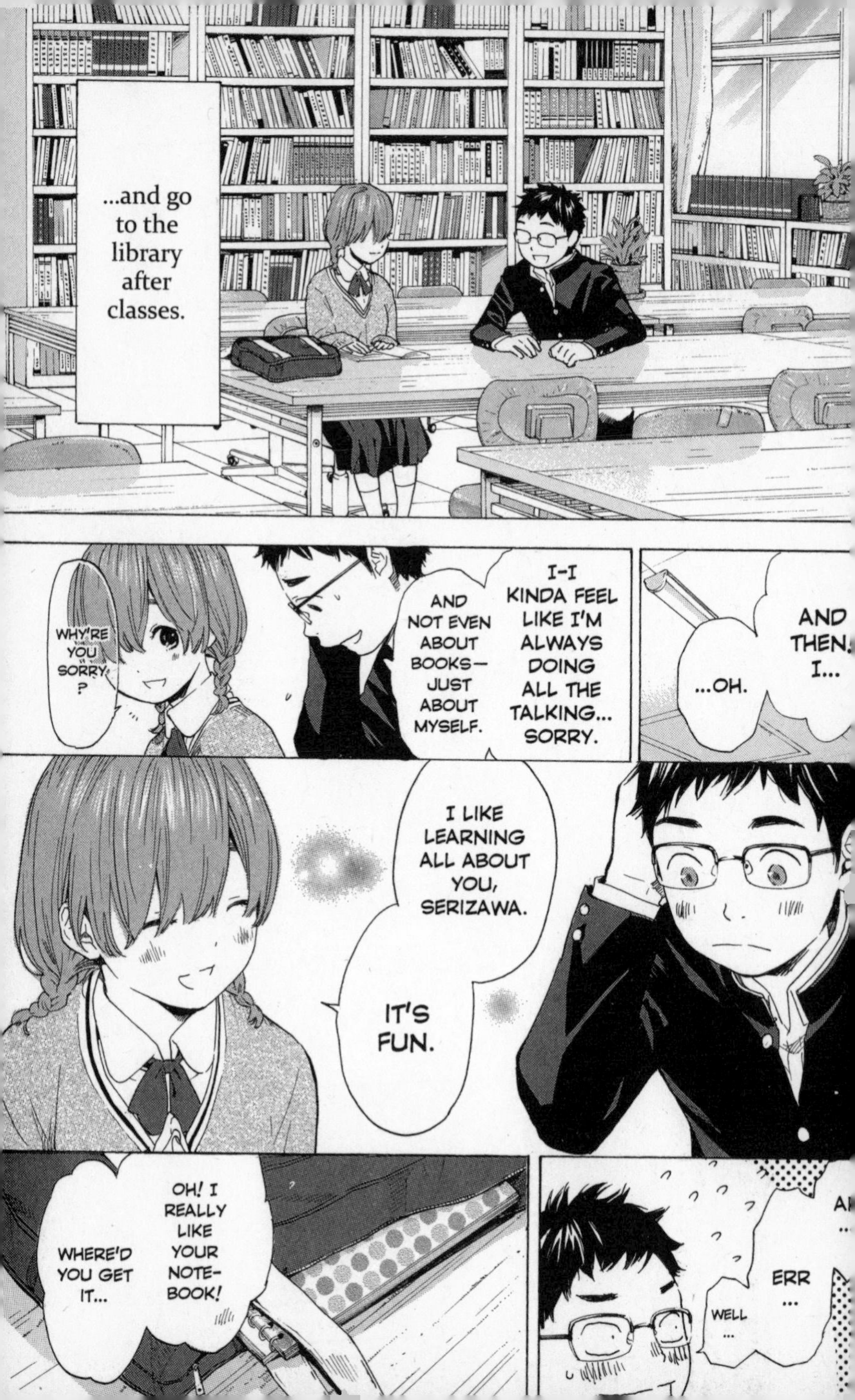
...and go to the library after classes.
AND THEN, I...
...OH.
I-I KINDA FEEL LIKE I'M ALWAYS DOING ALL THE TALKING... SORRY.
AND NOT EVEN ABOUT BOOKS—JUST ABOUT MYSELF.
WHY'RE YOU SORRY?
I LIKE LEARNING ALL ABOUT YOU, SERIZAWA.
IT'S FUN.
A...
ERR...
WELL...
OH! I REALLY LIKE YOUR NOTEBOOK!
WHERE'D YOU GET IT...

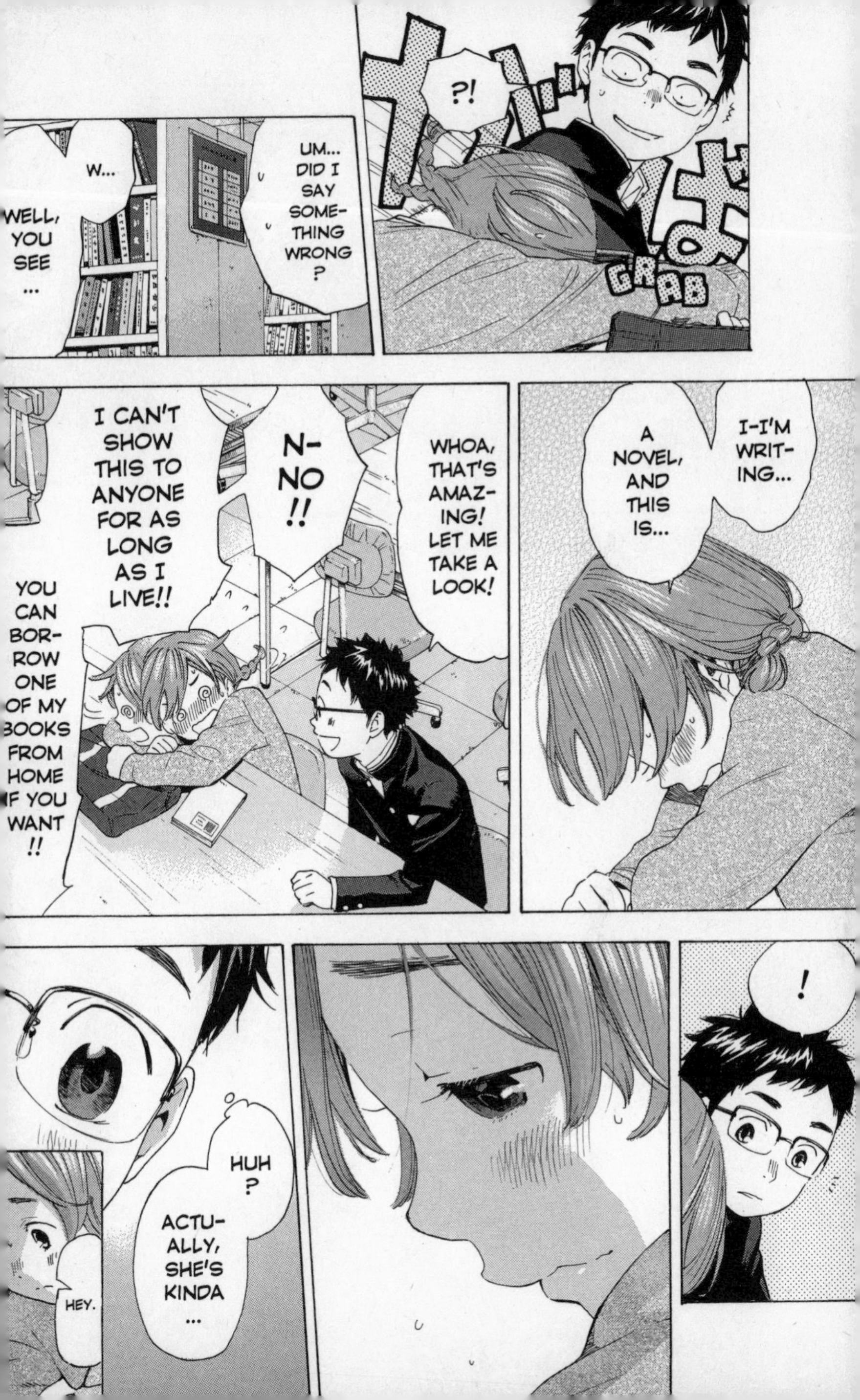
?!
GRAB
UM... DID I SAY SOME-THING WRONG?
W...
WELL, YOU SEE...
I-I'M WRIT-ING...
A NOVEL, AND THIS IS...
WHOA, THAT'S AMAZ-ING! LET ME TAKE A LOOK!
N-NO!!
I CAN'T SHOW THIS TO ANYONE FOR AS LONG AS I LIVE!!
YOU CAN BOR-ROW ONE OF MY BOOKS FROM HOME IF YOU WANT!!
!
HUH?
ACTU-ALLY, SHE'S KINDA...
HEY.

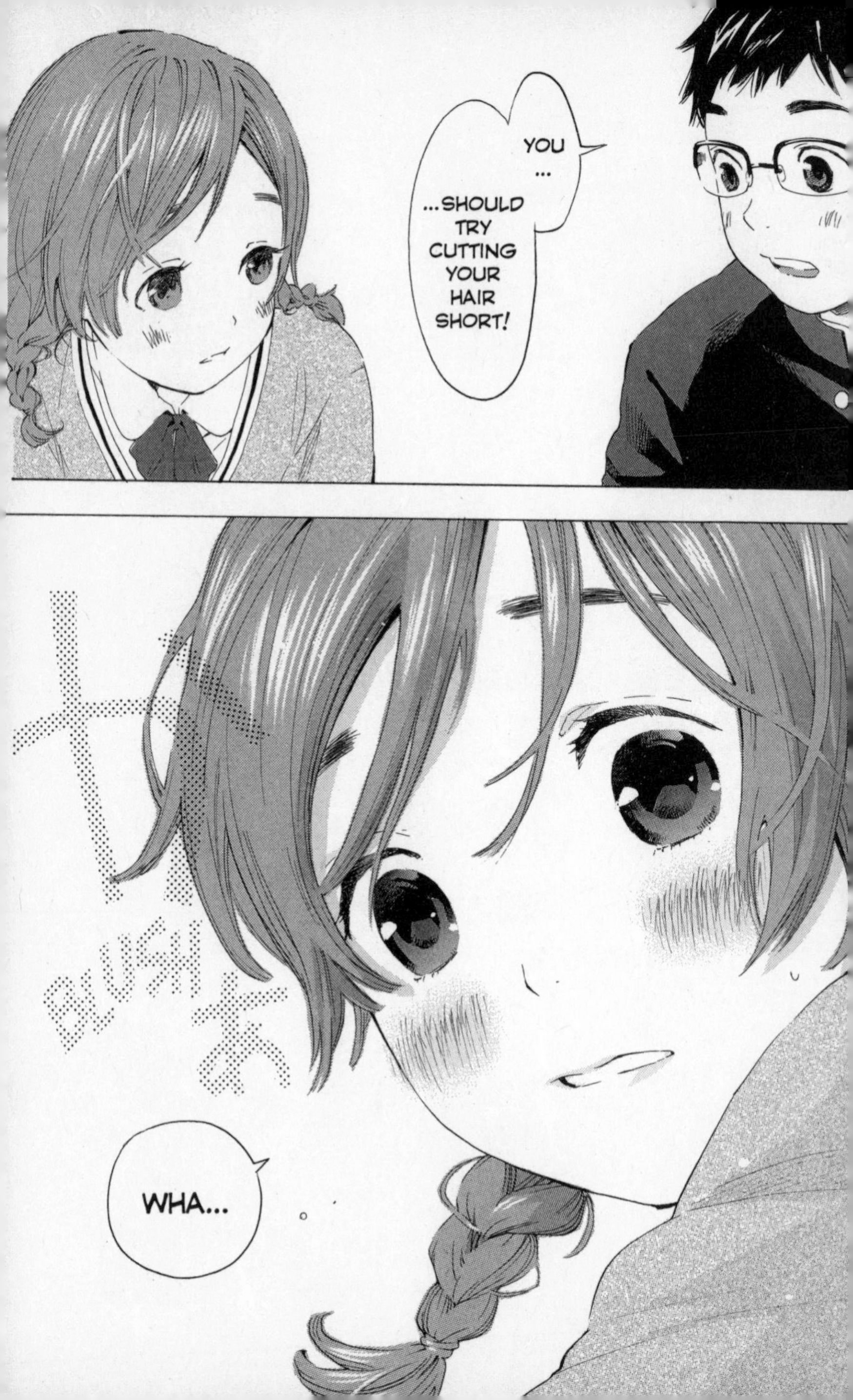
YOU ...
...SHOULD TRY CUTTING YOUR HAIR SHORT!
BLUSH
WHA...

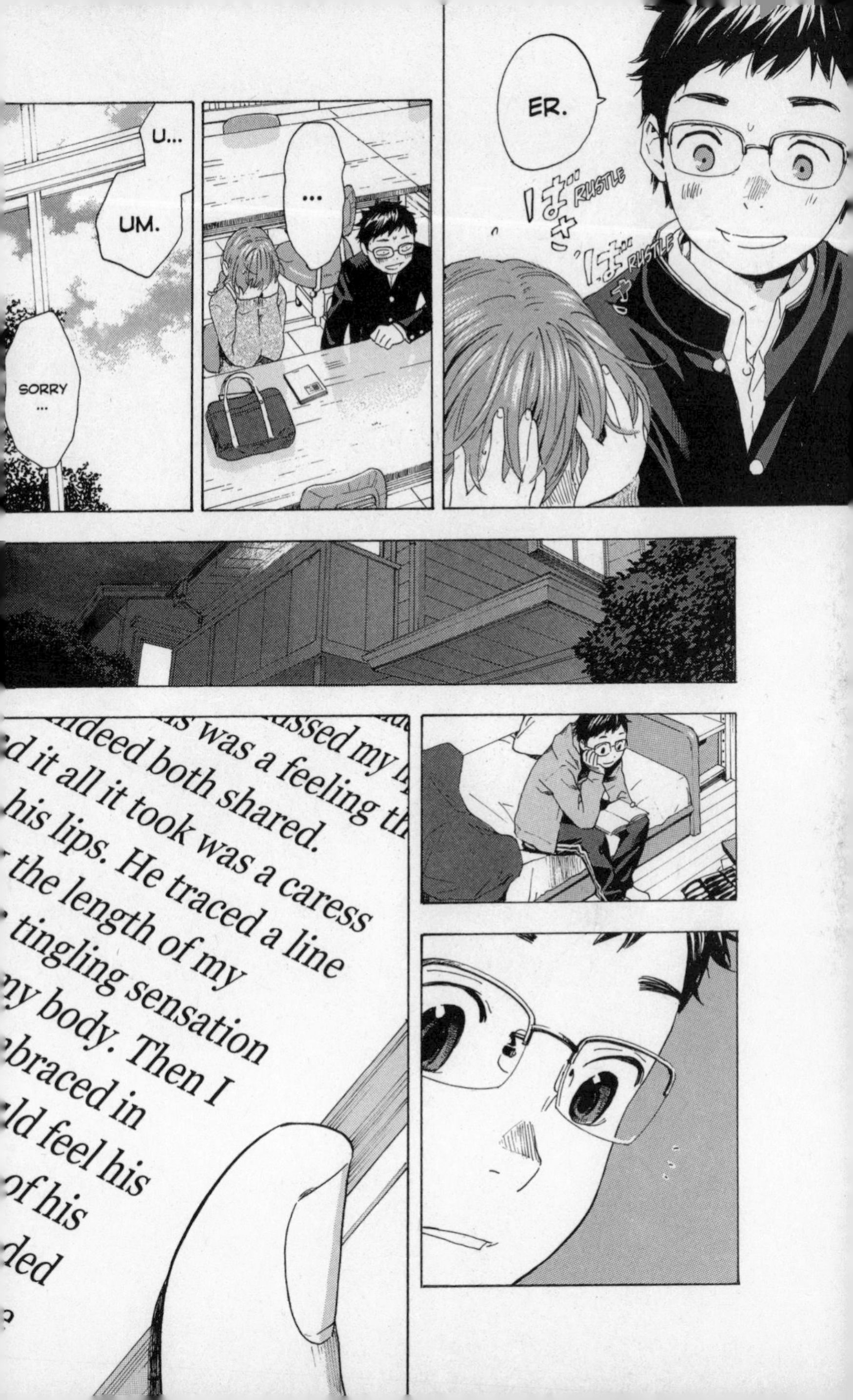
ER.
ばさ RUSTLE
ばさ RUSTLE
...
U...
UM.
SORRY ...
was a feeling
indeed both shared.
it all it took was a caress
his lips. He traced a line
the length of my
tingling sensation
body. Then I
braced in
feel his
of his

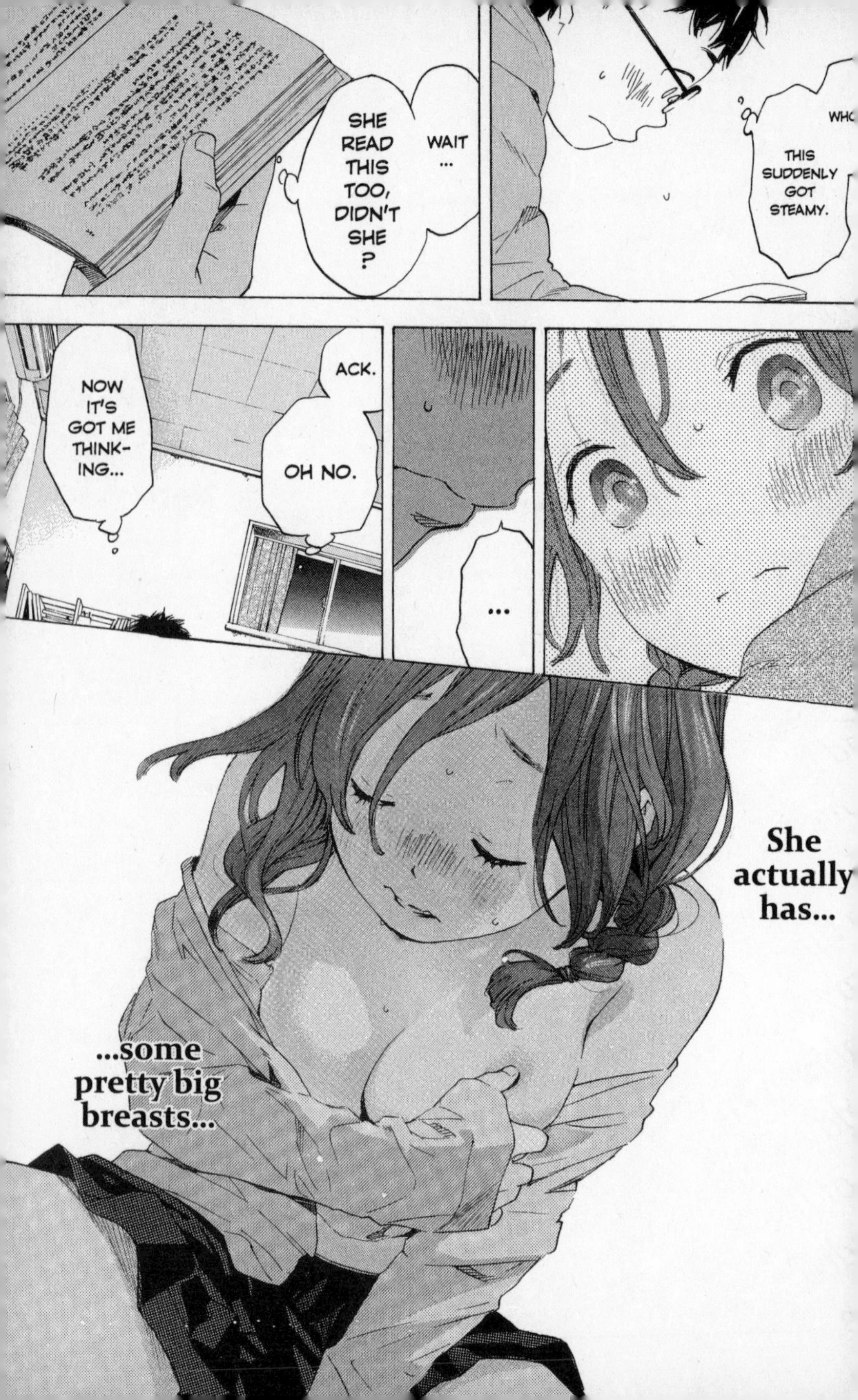
WHO
THIS SUDDENLY GOT STEAMY.
WAIT ...
SHE READ THIS TOO, DIDN'T SHE?
...
ACK.
OH NO.
NOW IT'S GOT ME THINKING-ING...
She actually has...
...some pretty big breasts...

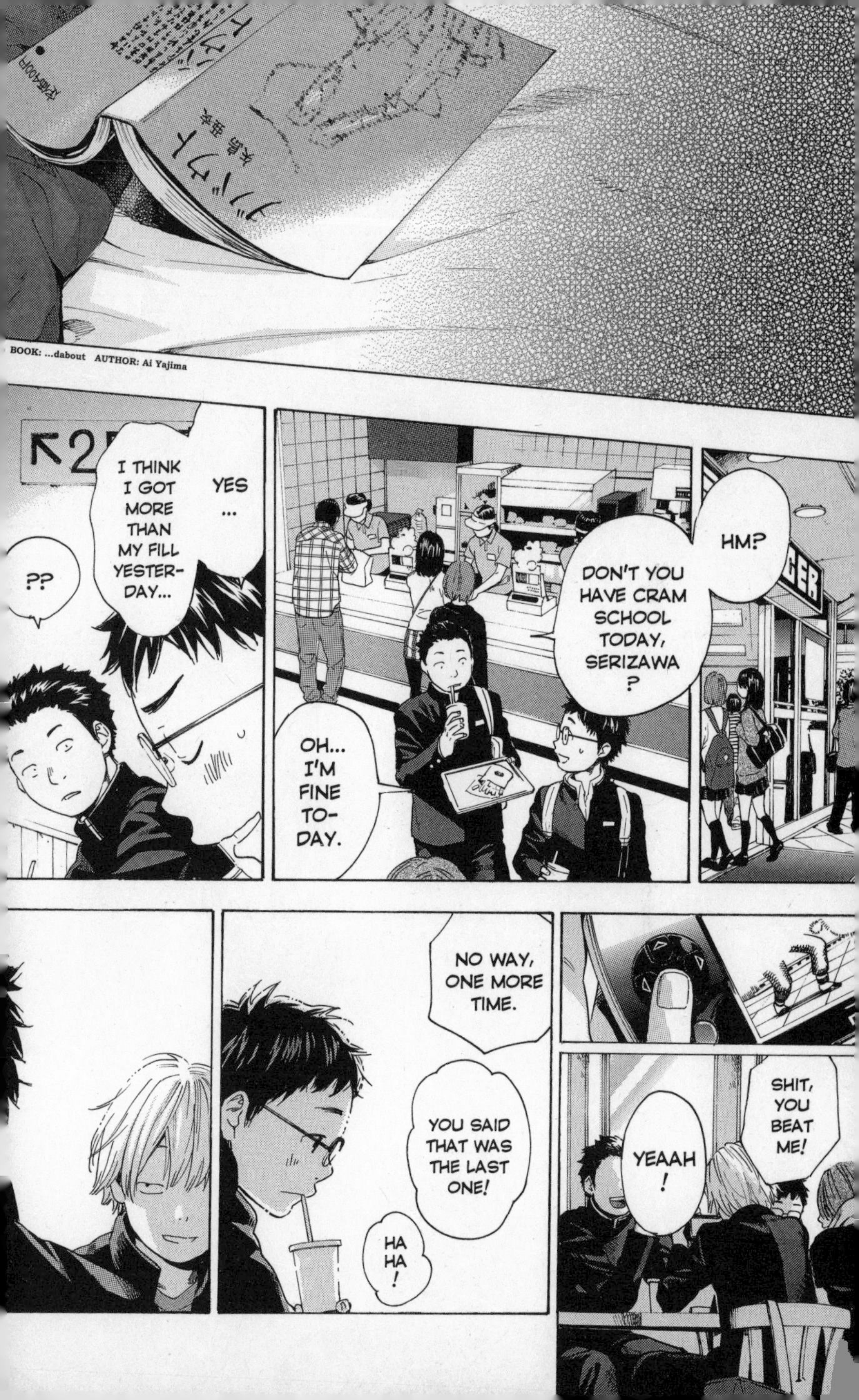
BOOK: ...dabout AUTHOR: Ai Yajima
HM?
DON'T YOU HAVE CRAM SCHOOL TODAY, SERIZAWA?
OH... I'M FINE TO-DAY.
YES ...
I THINK I GOT MORE THAN MY FILL YESTER-DAY...
??
SHIT, YOU BEAT ME!
YEAAH!
NO WAY, ONE MORE TIME.
YOU SAID THAT WAS THE LAST ONE!
HA HA!

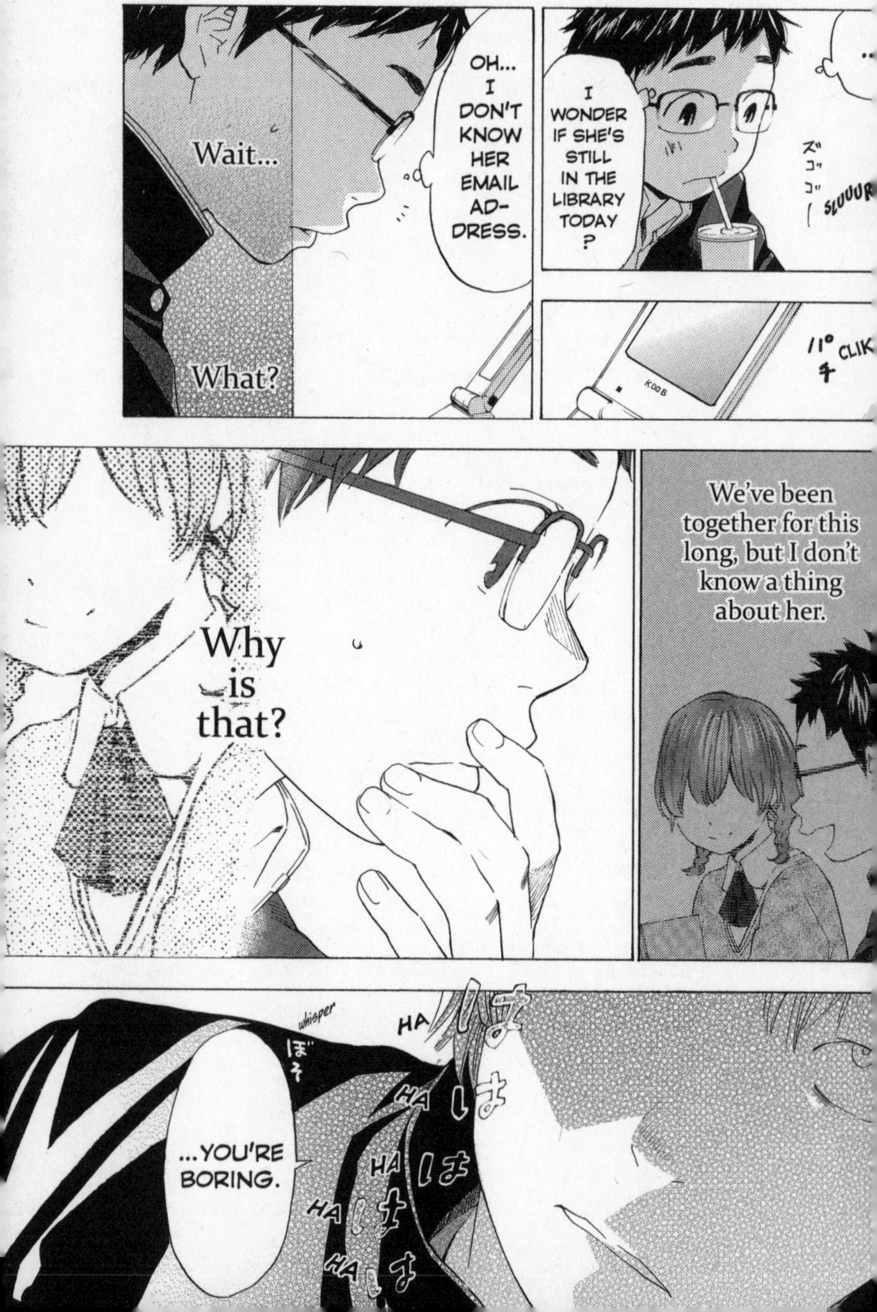
...
ズゴゴ
SLUUUR
I WONDER IF SHE'S STILL IN THE LIBRARY TODAY ?
パチ
CLIK
OH... I DON'T KNOW HER EMAIL AD-DRESS.
Wait...
What?
We've been together for this long, but I don't know a thing about her.
Why is that?
HA は
HA は
HA は
HA ま
HA ま
whisper
ぼそ
...YOU'RE BORING.

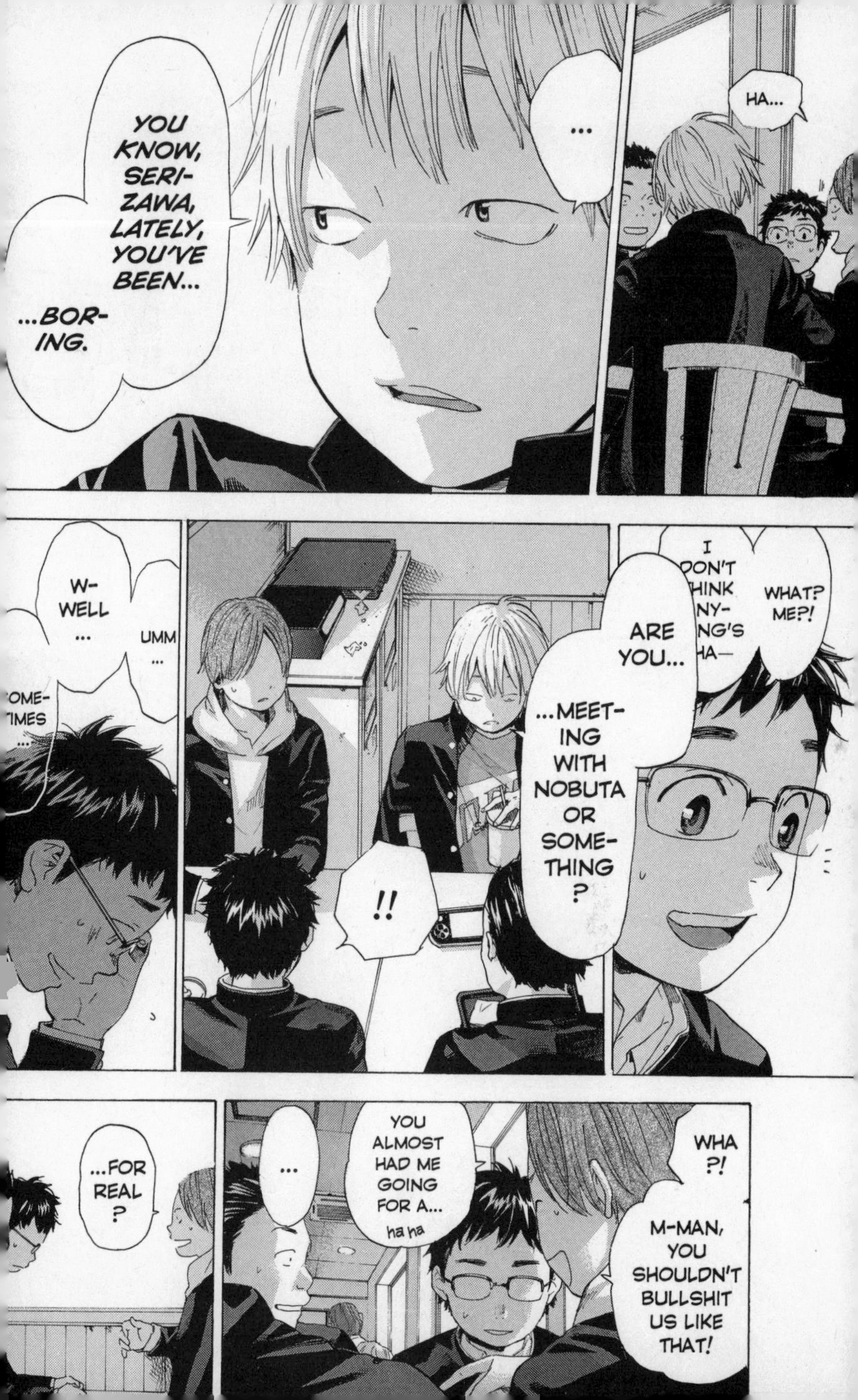
HA...
...
YOU KNOW, SERI-ZAWA, LATELY, YOU'VE BEEN...
...BOR-ING.
WHAT? ME?!
I ON'T HINK NY- NG'S HA—
ARE YOU...
...MEET-ING WITH NOBUTA OR SOME-THING?
!!
W-WELL ...
UMM ...
OME-TIMES ...
WHA?!
M-MAN, YOU SHOULDN'T BULLSHIT US LIKE THAT!
YOU ALMOST HAD ME GOING FOR A...
ha ha
...
...FOR REAL?

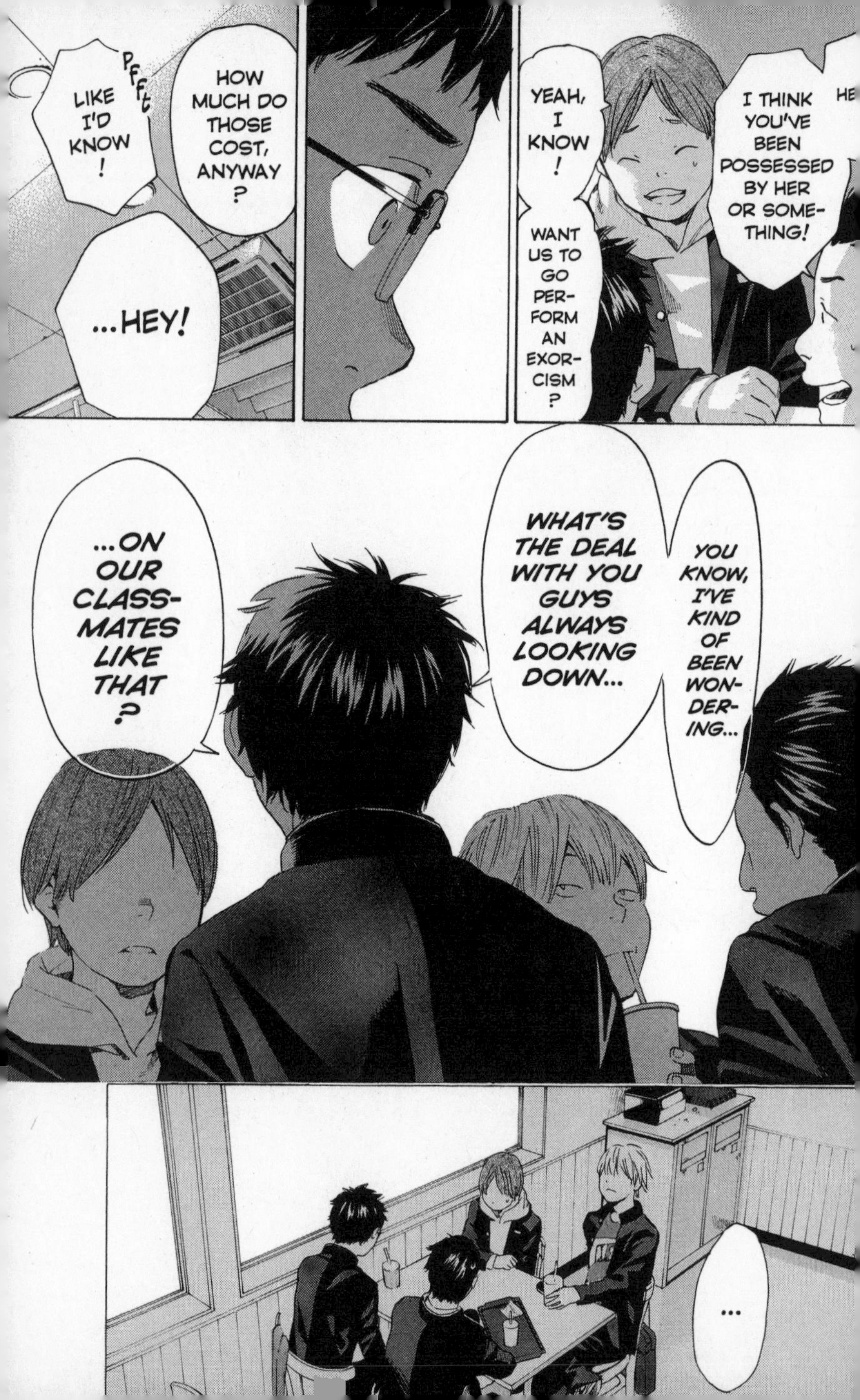
HE
I THINK YOU'VE BEEN POSSESSED BY HER OR SOMETHING!
YEAH, I KNOW!
WANT US TO GO PERFORM AN EXORCISM?
HOW MUCH DO THOSE COST, ANYWAY?
Pffft
LIKE I'D KNOW!
...HEY!
YOU KNOW, I'VE KIND OF BEEN WONDERING...
WHAT'S THE DEAL WITH YOU GUYS ALWAYS LOOKING DOWN...
...ON OUR CLASSMATES LIKE THAT?
...

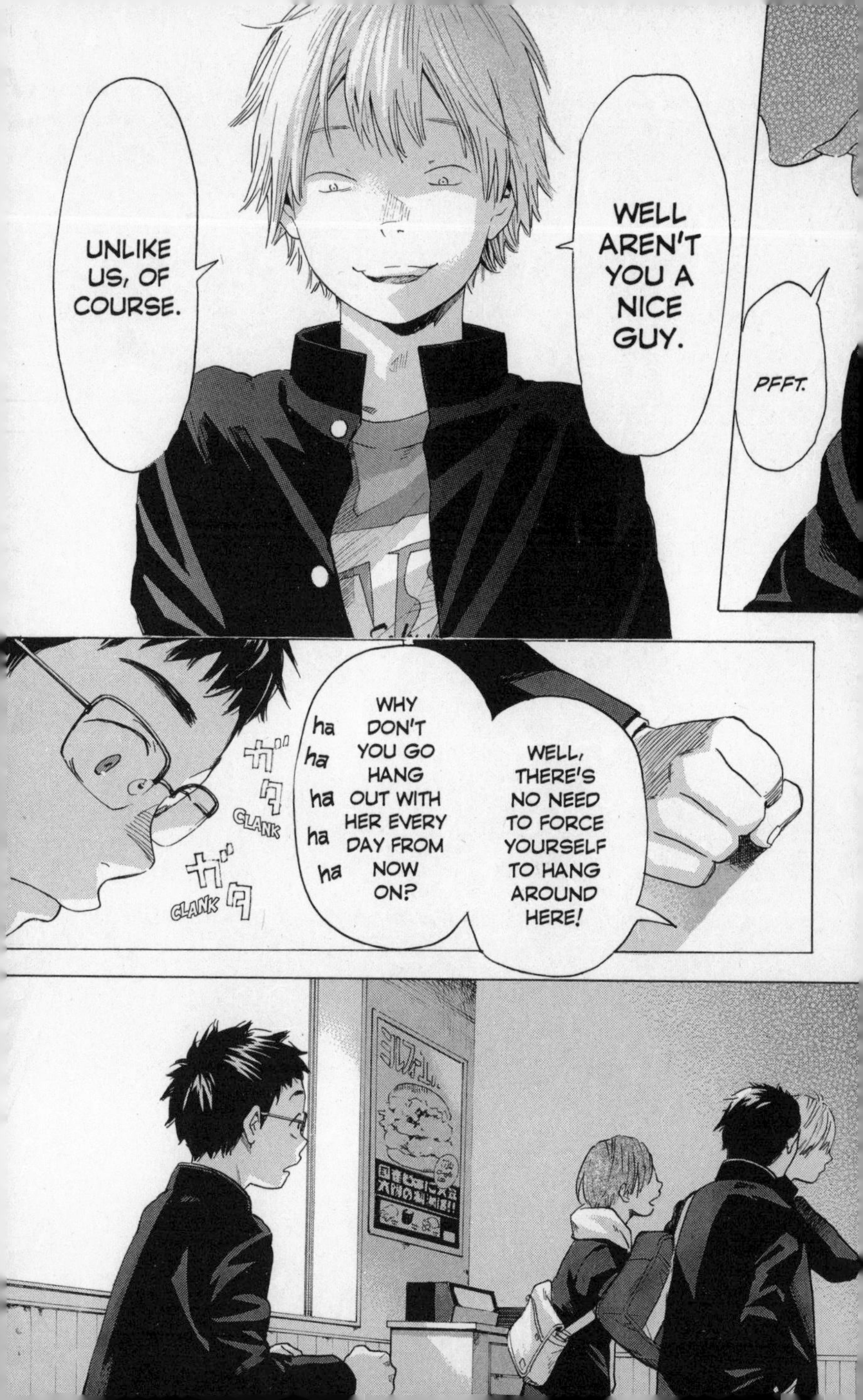
PFFT.
WELL AREN'T YOU A NICE GUY.
UNLIKE US, OF COURSE.
WELL, THERE'S NO NEED TO FORCE YOURSELF TO HANG AROUND HERE!
WHY DON'T YOU GO HANG OUT WITH HER EVERY DAY FROM NOW ON?
ha ha ha ha ha
ガタ CLANK
ガタ CLANK

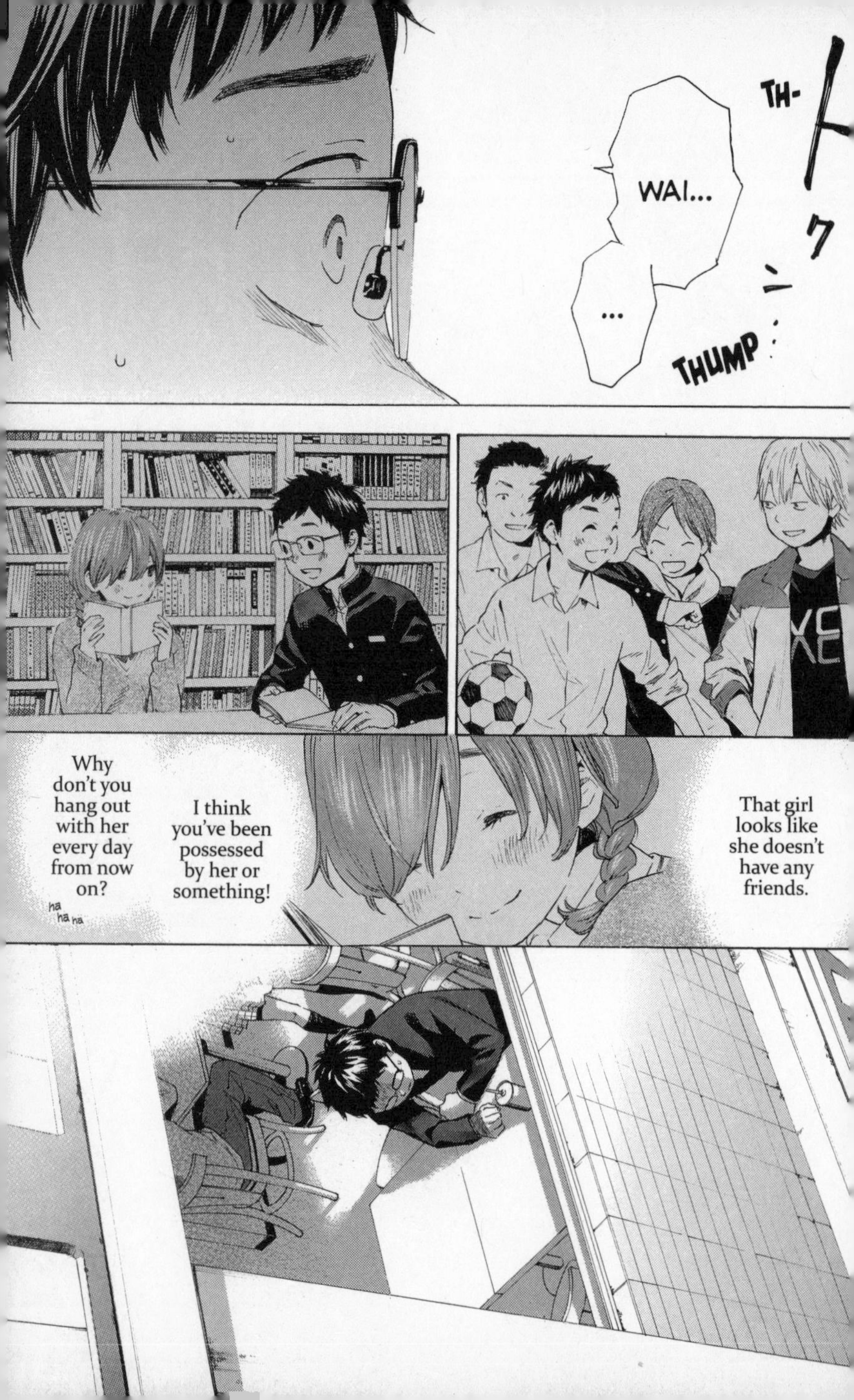
TH-
THUMP
WAI...
...
That girl looks like she doesn't have any friends.
I think you've been possessed by her or something!
Why don't you hang out with her every day from now on?
ha ha ha

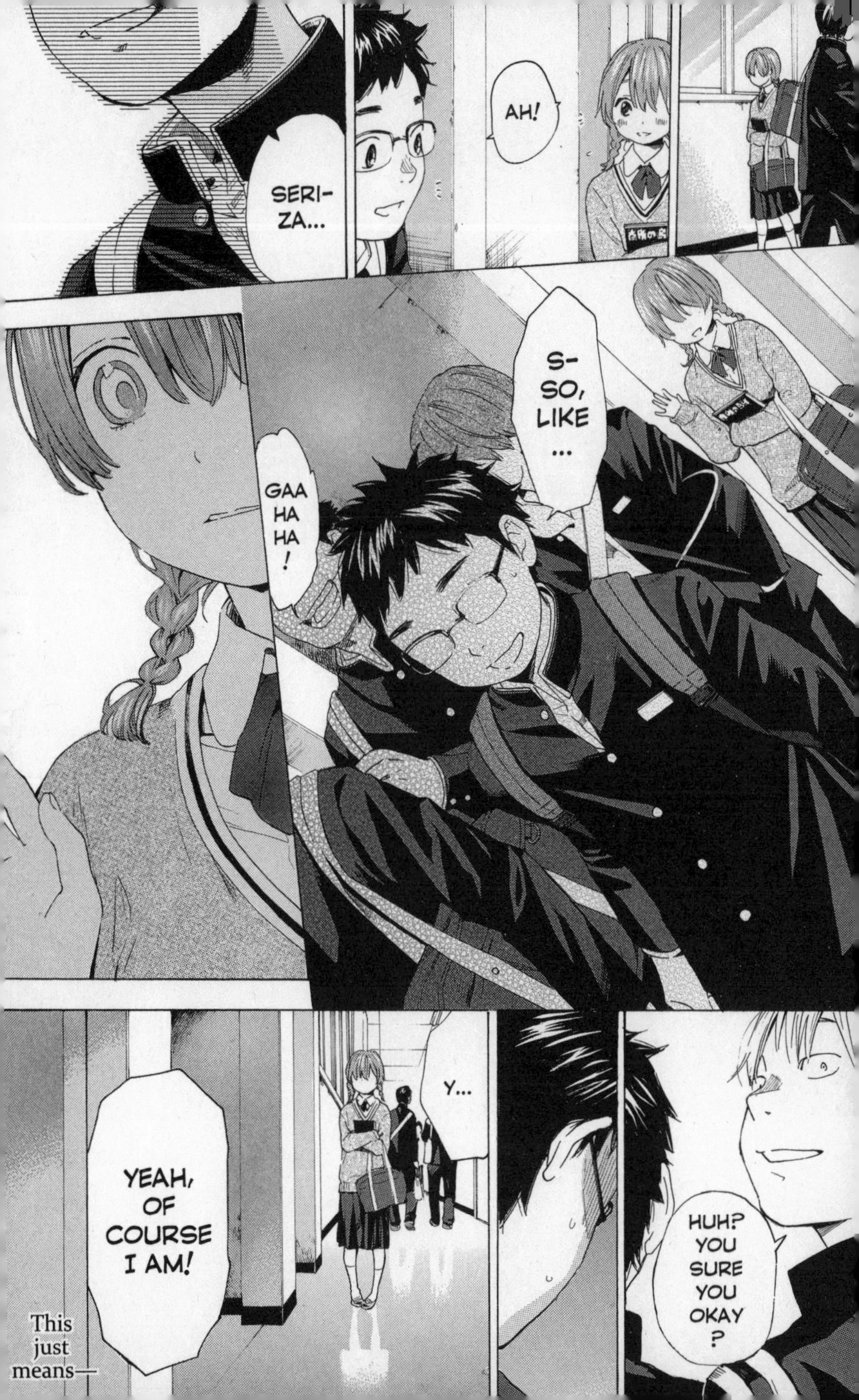
AH!
SERI-ZA...
S-SO, LIKE...
GAA HA HA!
HUH? YOU SURE YOU OKAY?
Y...
YEAH, OF COURSE I AM!
This just means—

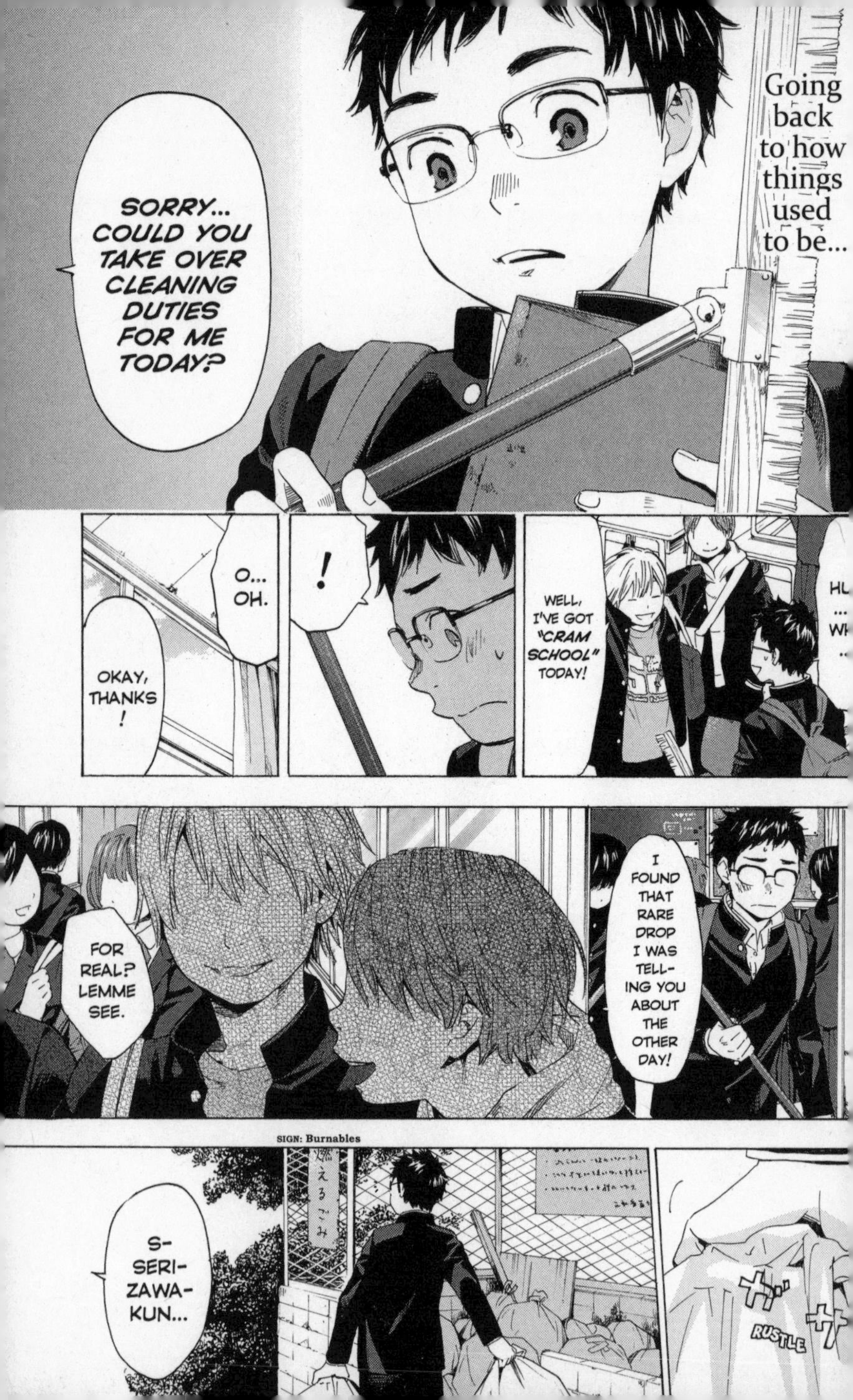
Going back to how things used to be...
SORRY... COULD YOU TAKE OVER CLEANING DUTIES FOR ME TODAY?
WELL, I'VE GOT "CRAM SCHOOL" TODAY!
!
O... OH.
OKAY, THANKS!
I FOUND THAT RARE DROP I WAS TELLING YOU ABOUT THE OTHER DAY!
FOR REAL? LEMME SEE.
SIGN: Burnables
RUSTLE
S-SERI-ZAWA-KUN...

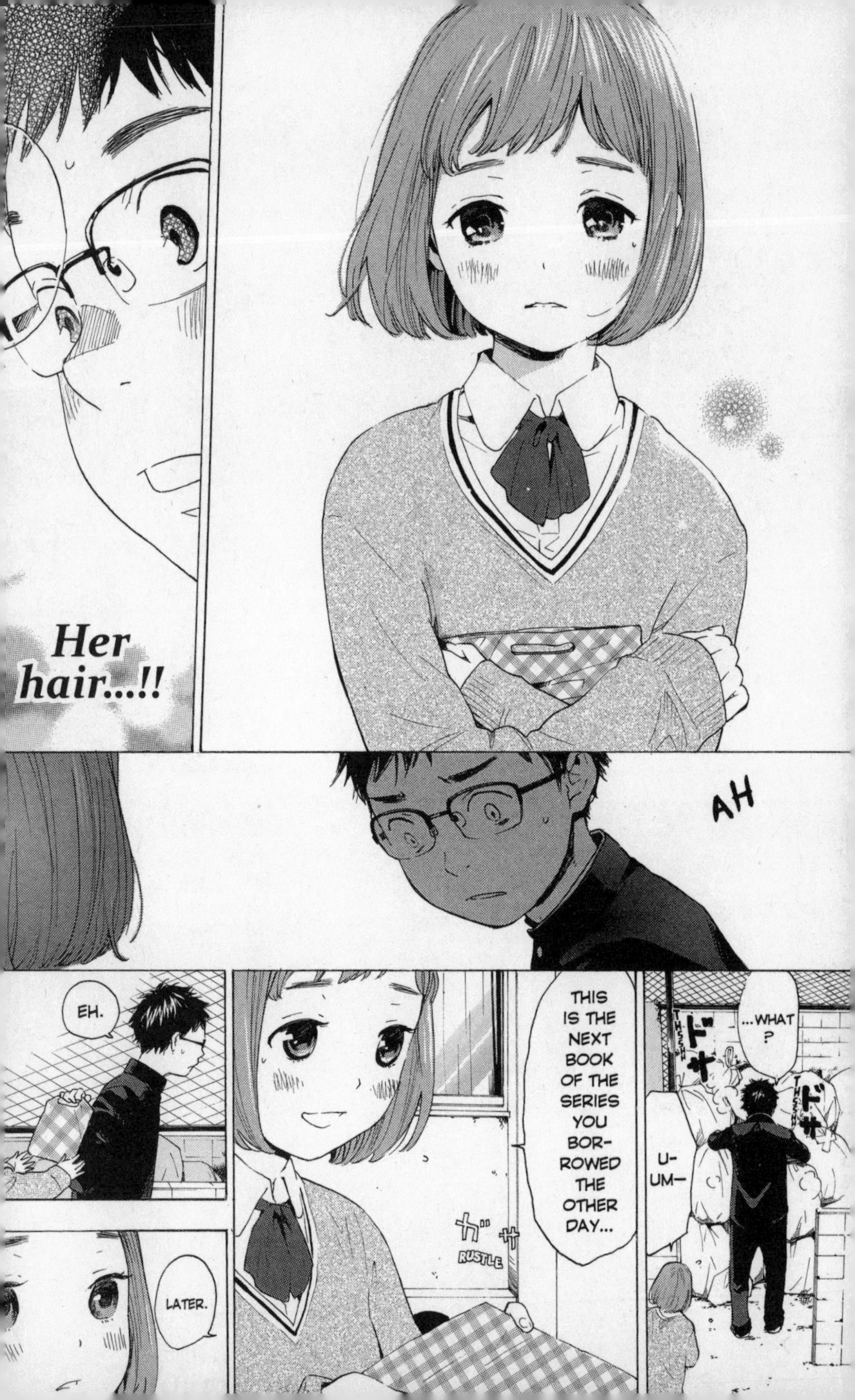

Her hair...!!
AH
...WHAT?
THSSH
THSSH
U-UM—
THIS IS THE NEXT BOOK OF THE SERIES YOU BOR-ROWED THE OTHER DAY...
RUSTLE
EH.
LATER.

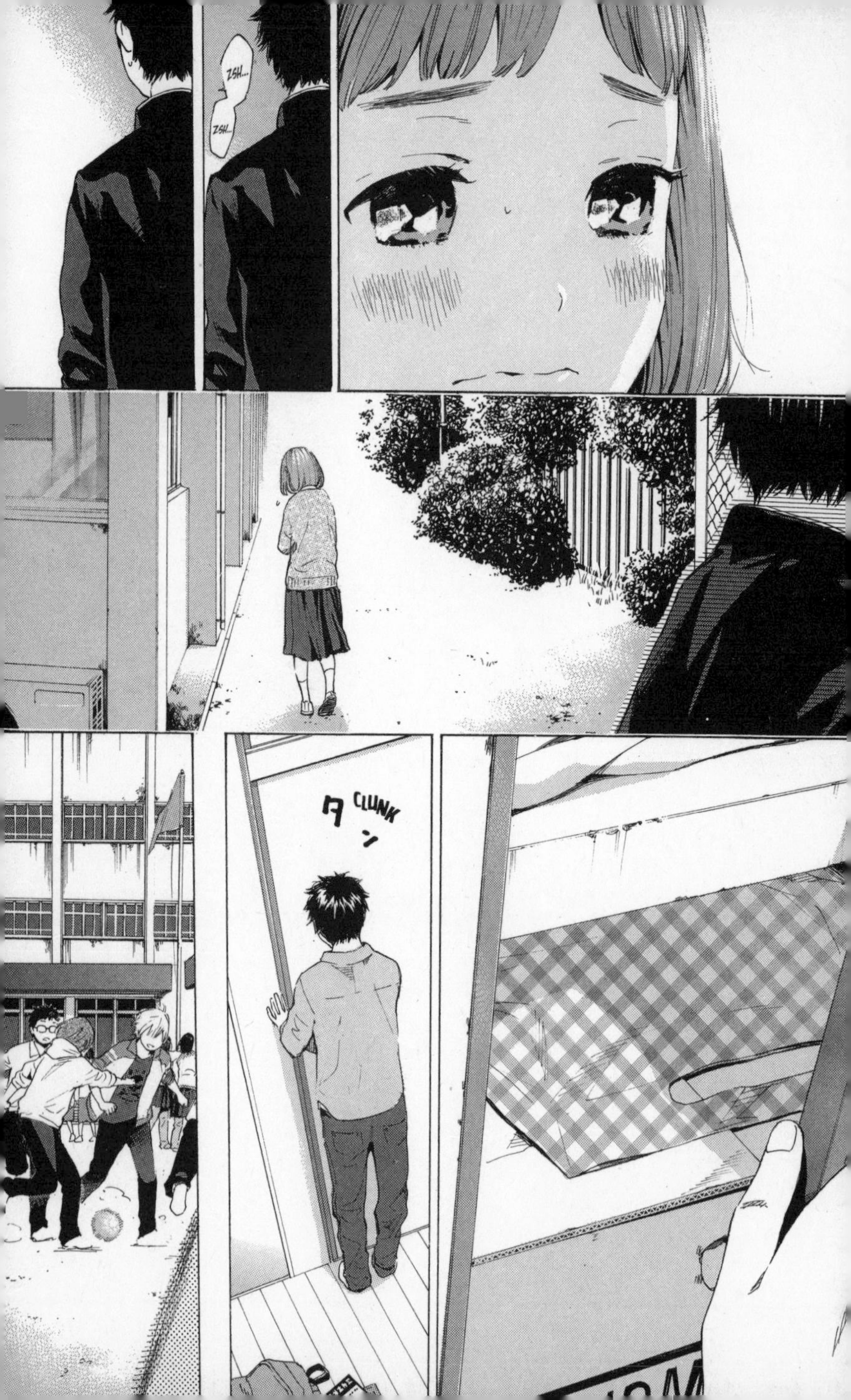
ZSH...
ZSH...
タン
CLUNK

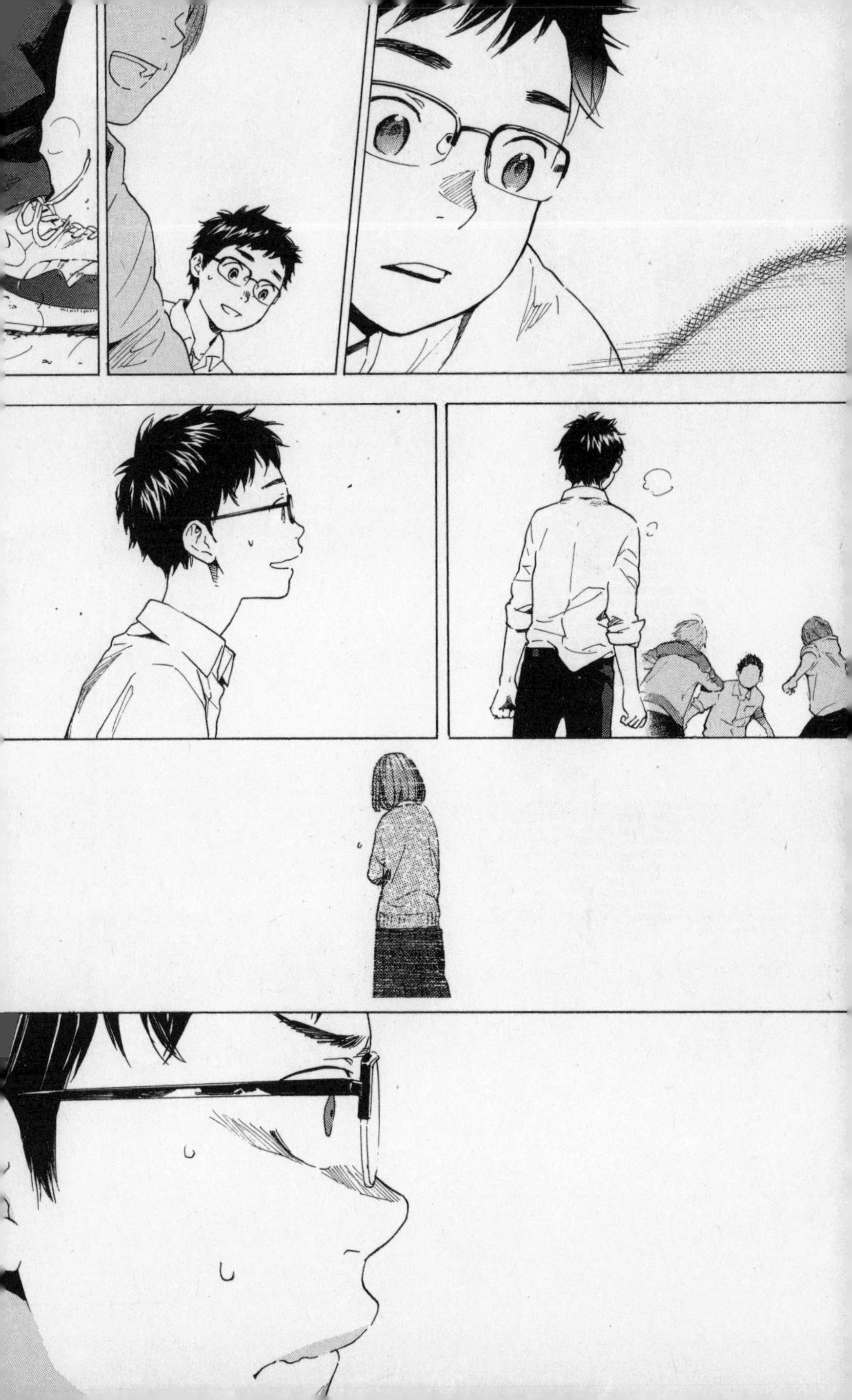

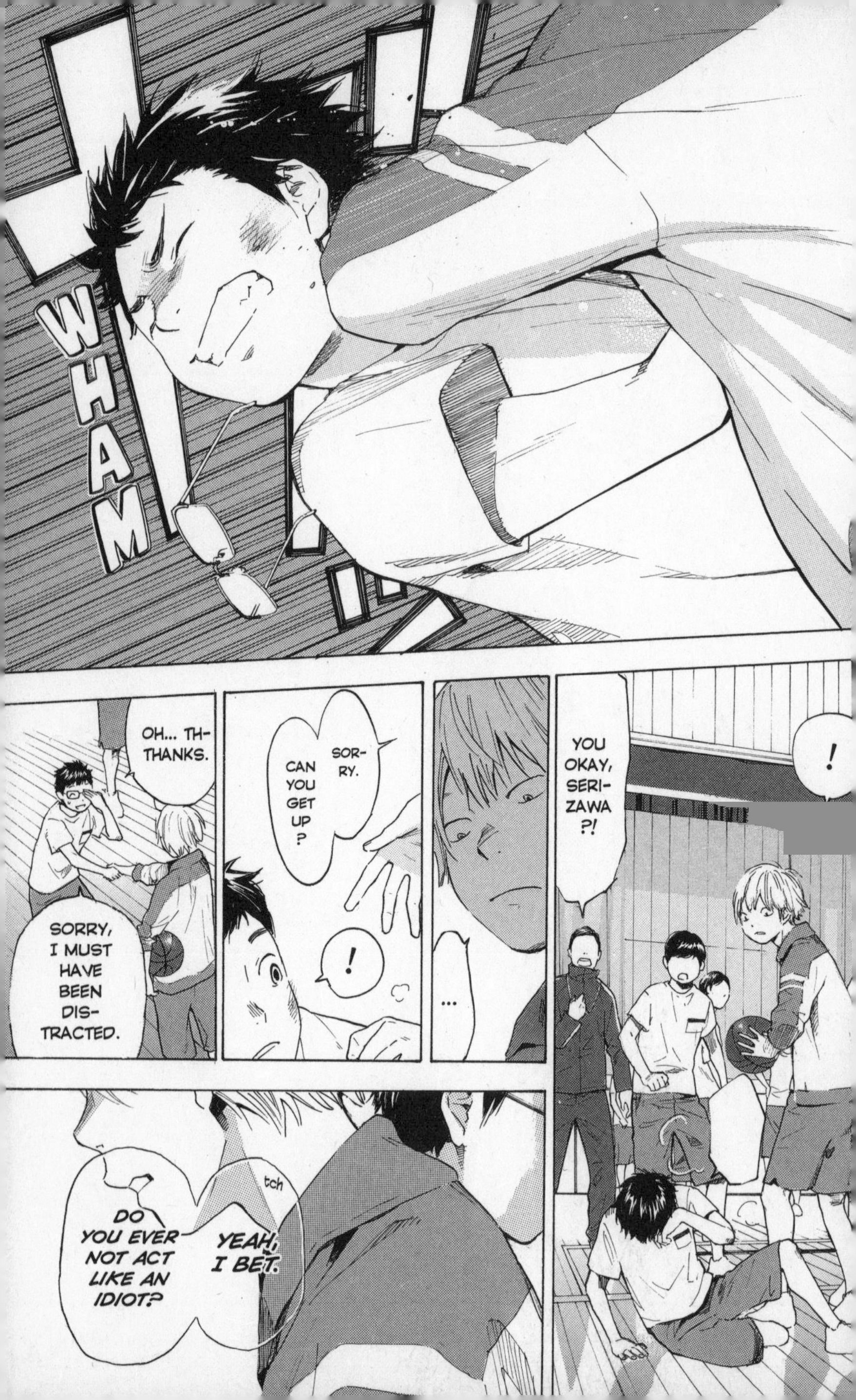

WHAM
!
YOU OKAY, SERIZAWA?!
...
SORRY. CAN YOU GET UP?
!
OH... TH-THANKS.
SORRY, I MUST HAVE BEEN DISTRACTED.
tch
YEAH, I BET.
DO YOU EVER NOT ACT LIKE AN IDIOT?

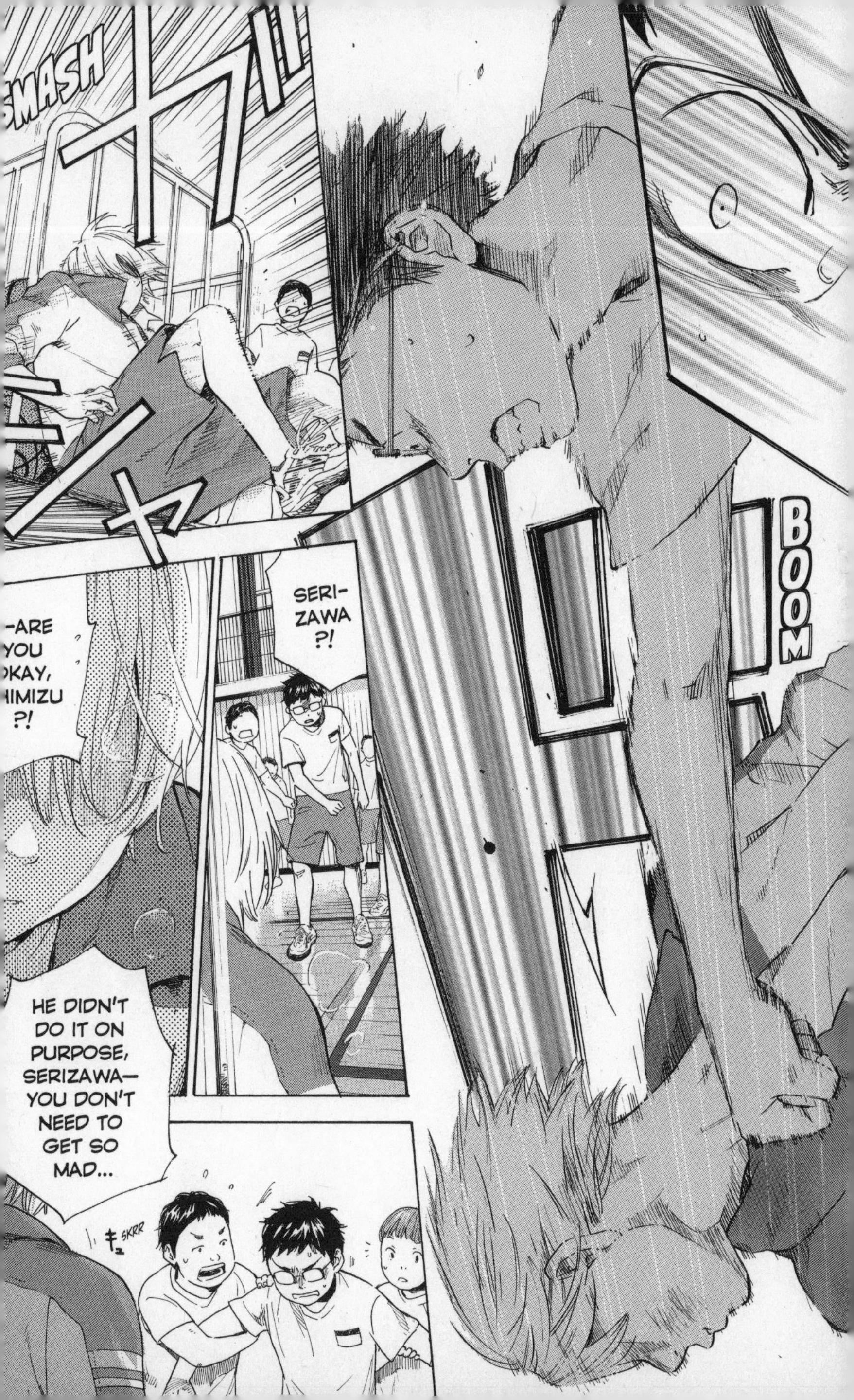
SMASH
BOOM
SERI-ZAWA?!
-ARE YOU OKAY, HIMIZU?!
HE DIDN'T DO IT ON PURPOSE, SERIZAWA— YOU DON'T NEED TO GET SO MAD...
SKRR

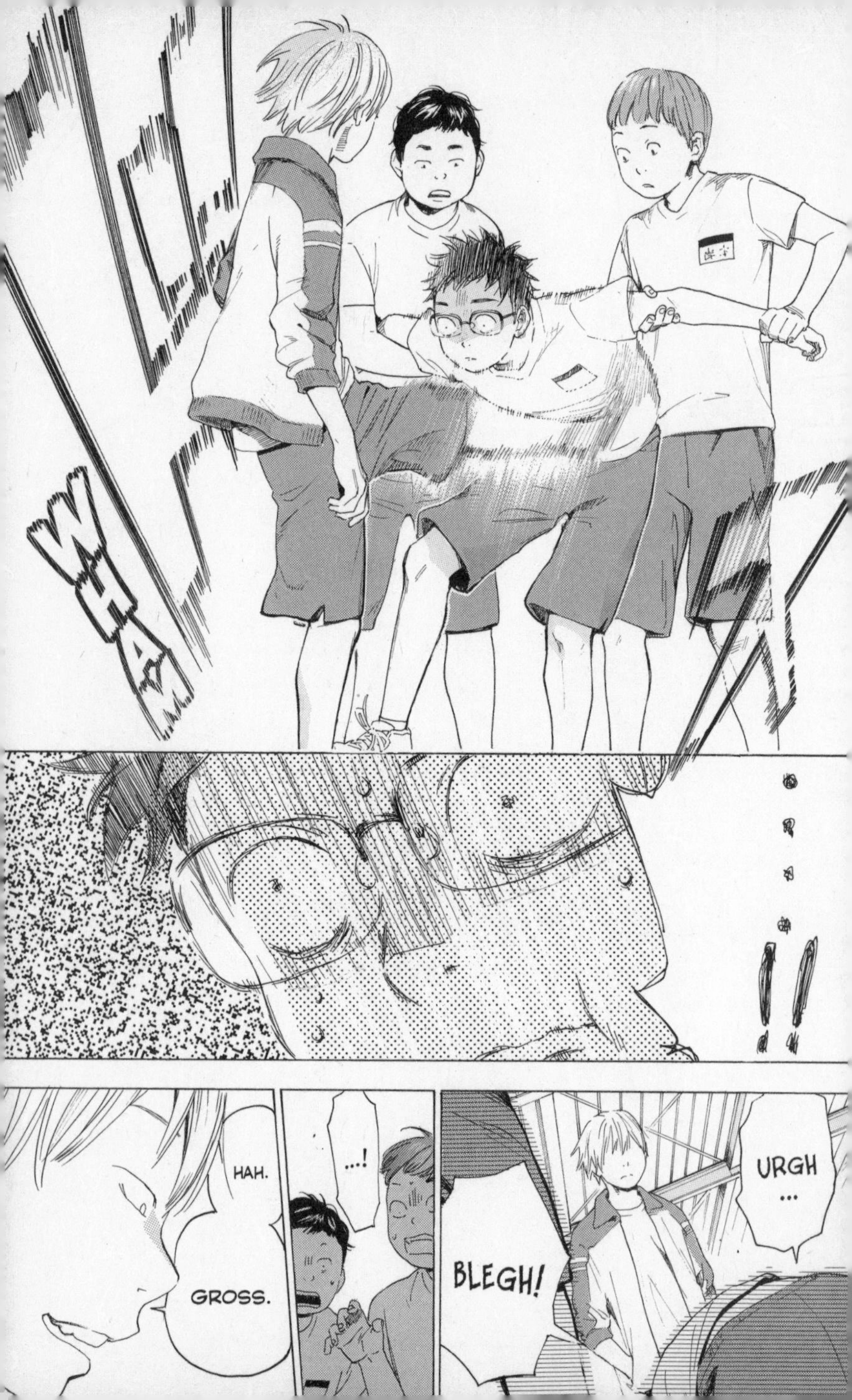
WHAM
URGH ...
BLEGH!
...!
HAH.
GROSS.

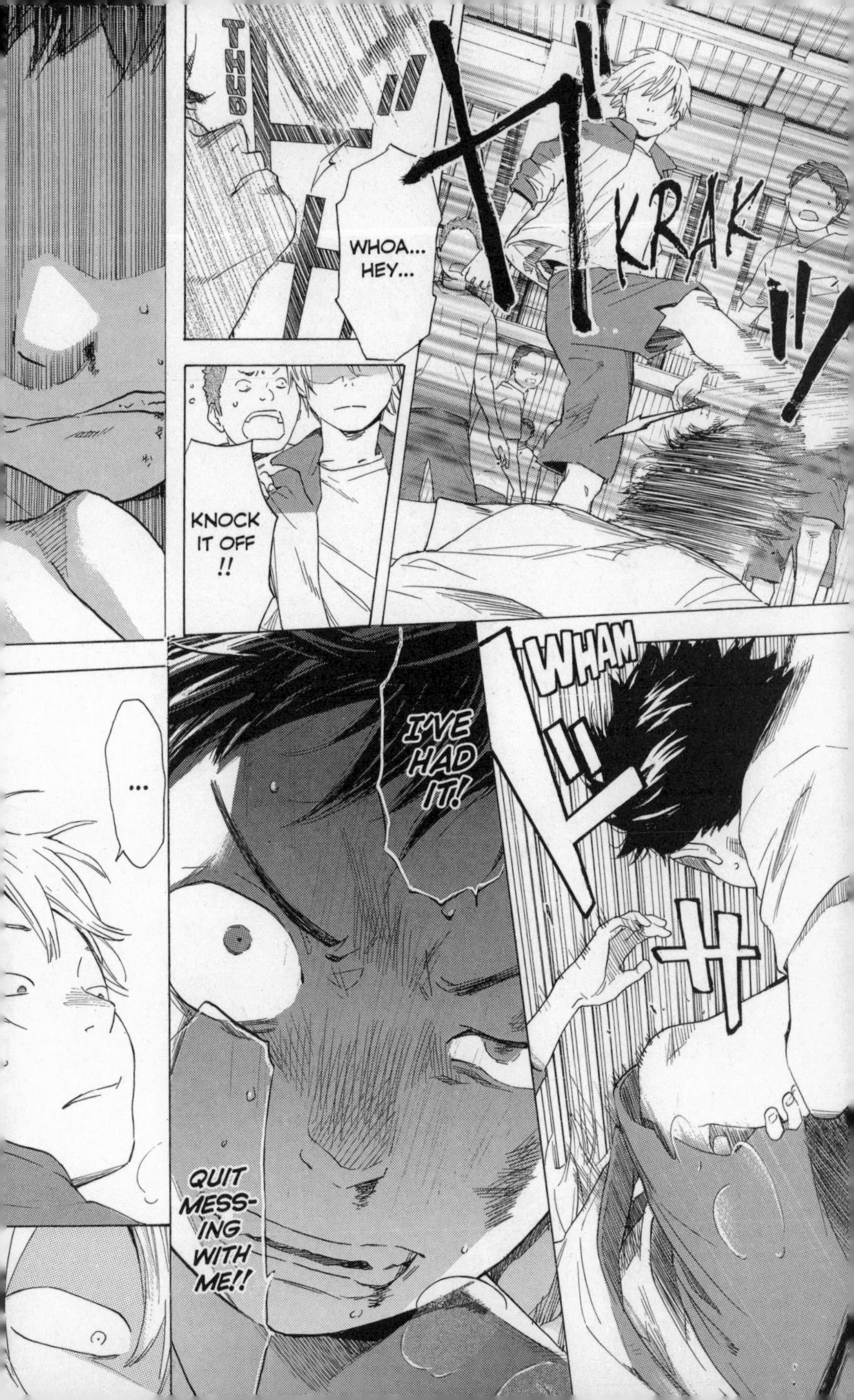
KRAK !!
THUD
WHOA... HEY...
KNOCK IT OFF !!
WHAM !!
I'VE HAD IT!
QUIT MESS-ING WITH ME!!
...

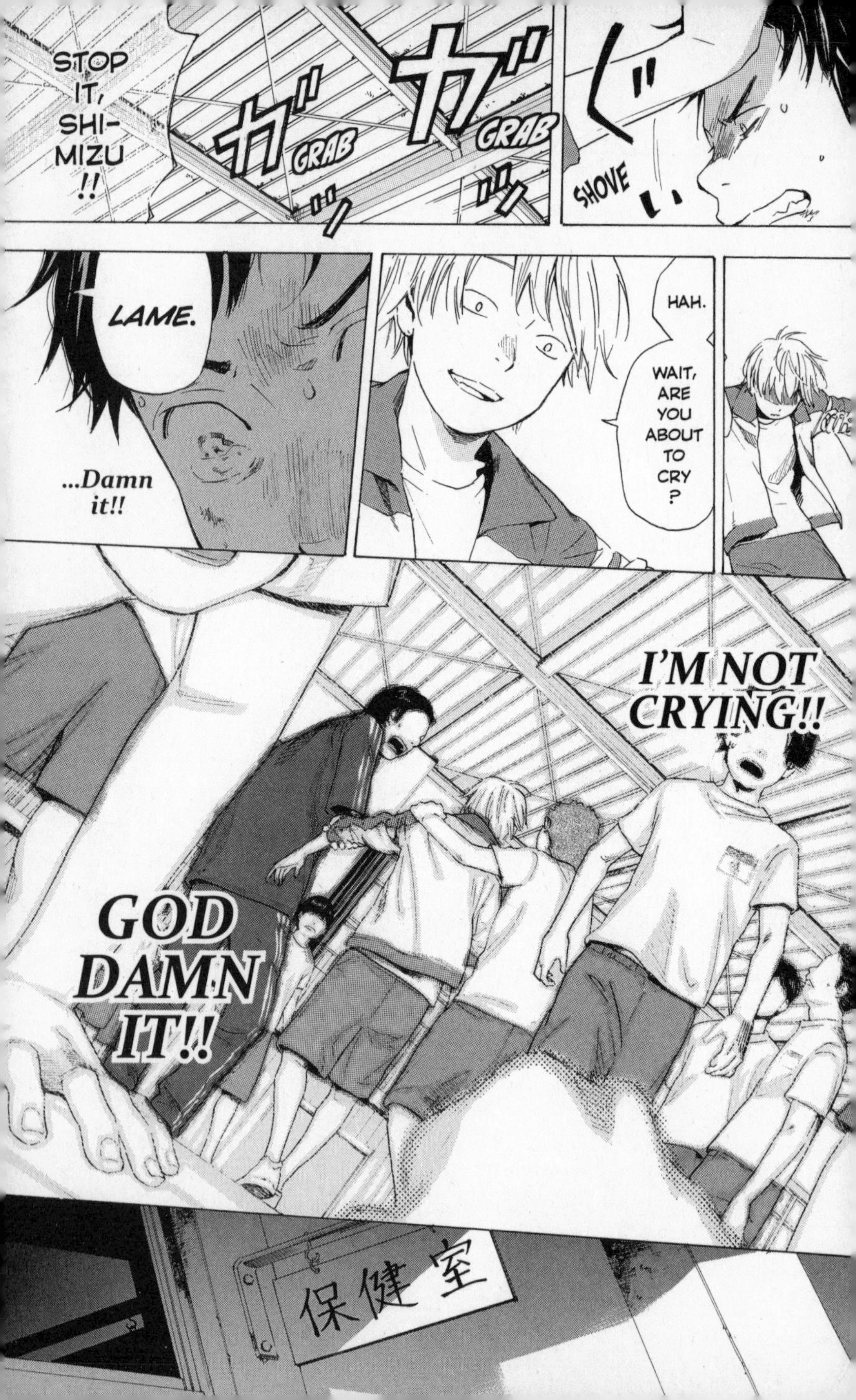
SHOVE
STOP IT, SHI-MIZU!!
GRAB
GRAB
HAH.
WAIT, ARE YOU ABOUT TO CRY?
LAME.
...Damn it!!
I'M NOT CRYING!!
GOD DAMN IT!!
保健室

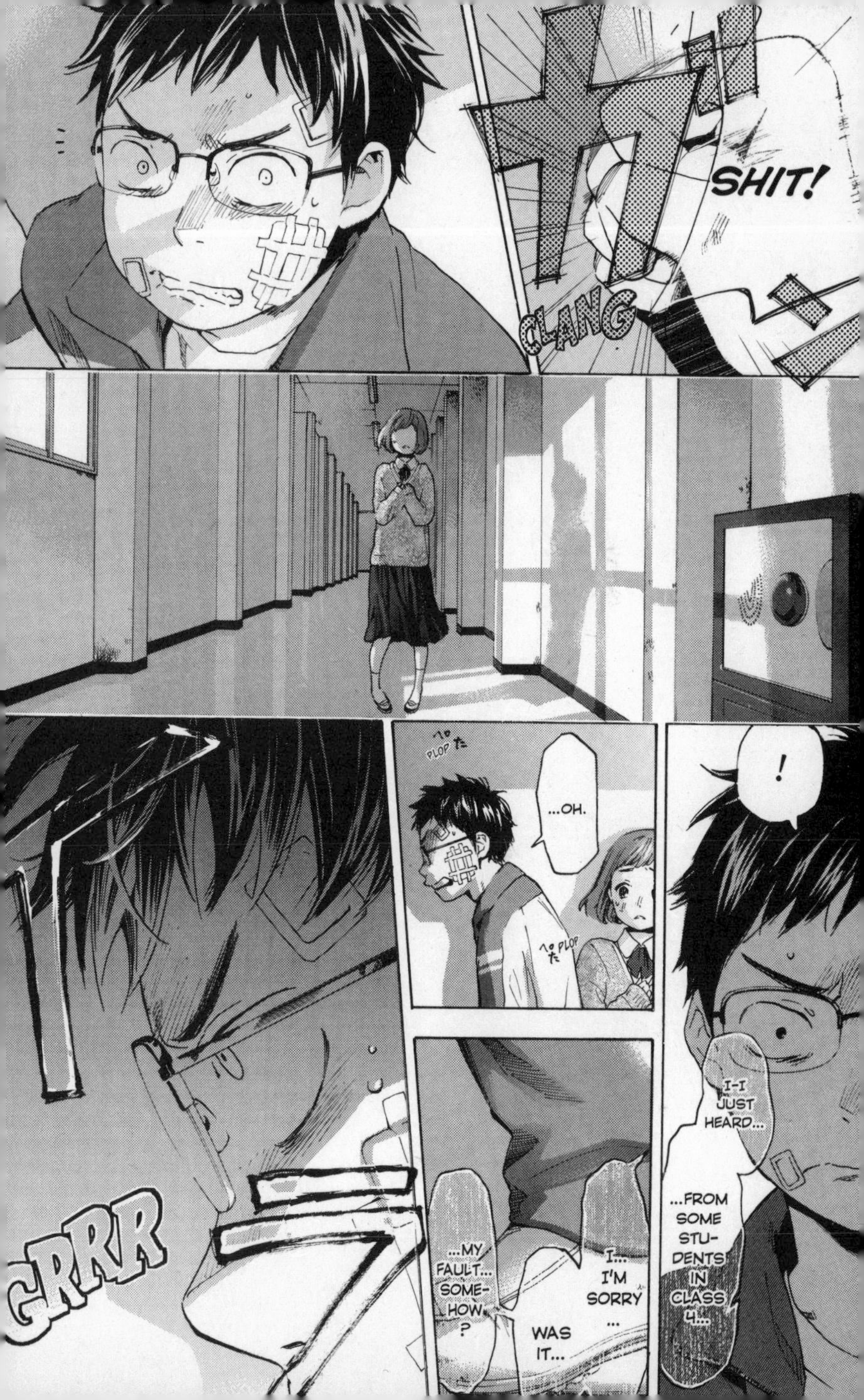
SHIT!
CLANG
!
I-I JUST HEARD...
...FROM SOME STU-DENTS IN CLASS 4...
PLOP
...OH.
PLOP
I... I'M SORRY ...
WAS IT...
...MY FAULT... SOME-HOW ?
GRRR

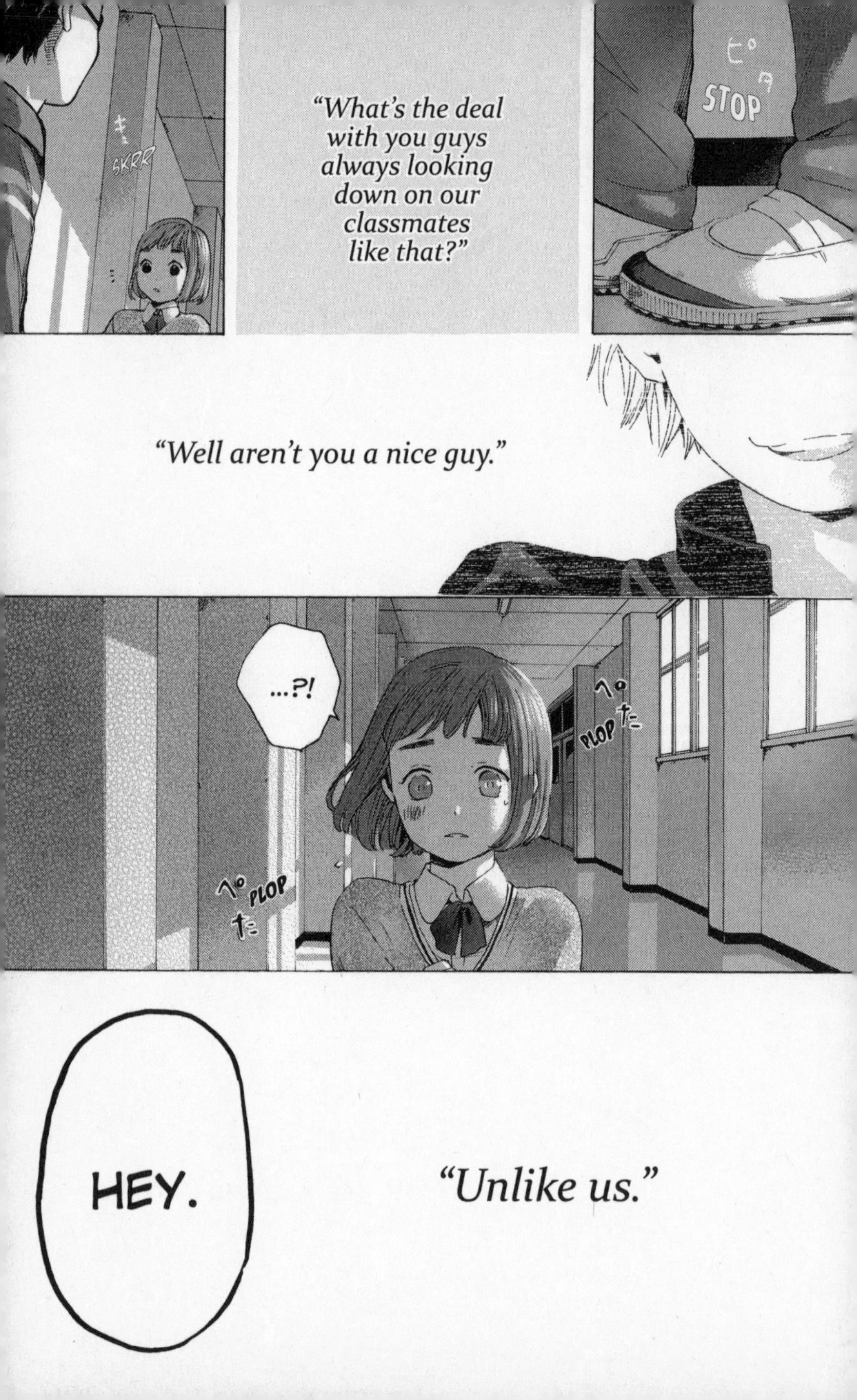

STOP
"What's the deal with you guys always looking down on our classmates like that?"
SKRR
"Well aren't you a nice guy."
...?!
PLOP
PLOP
"Unlike us."
HEY.

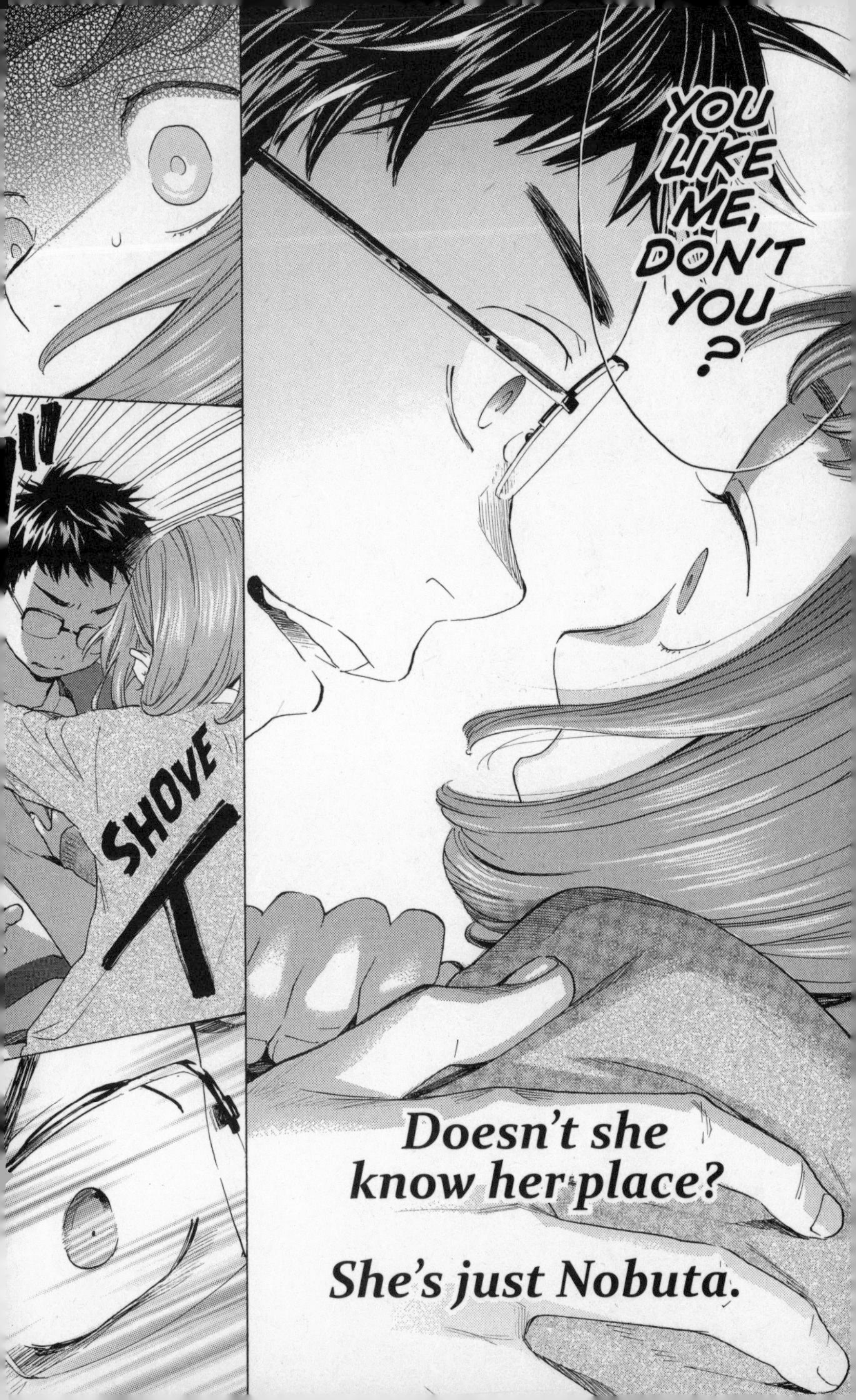
YOU LIKE ME, DON'T YOU?
Doesn't she know her place?
She's just Nobuta.
SHOVE

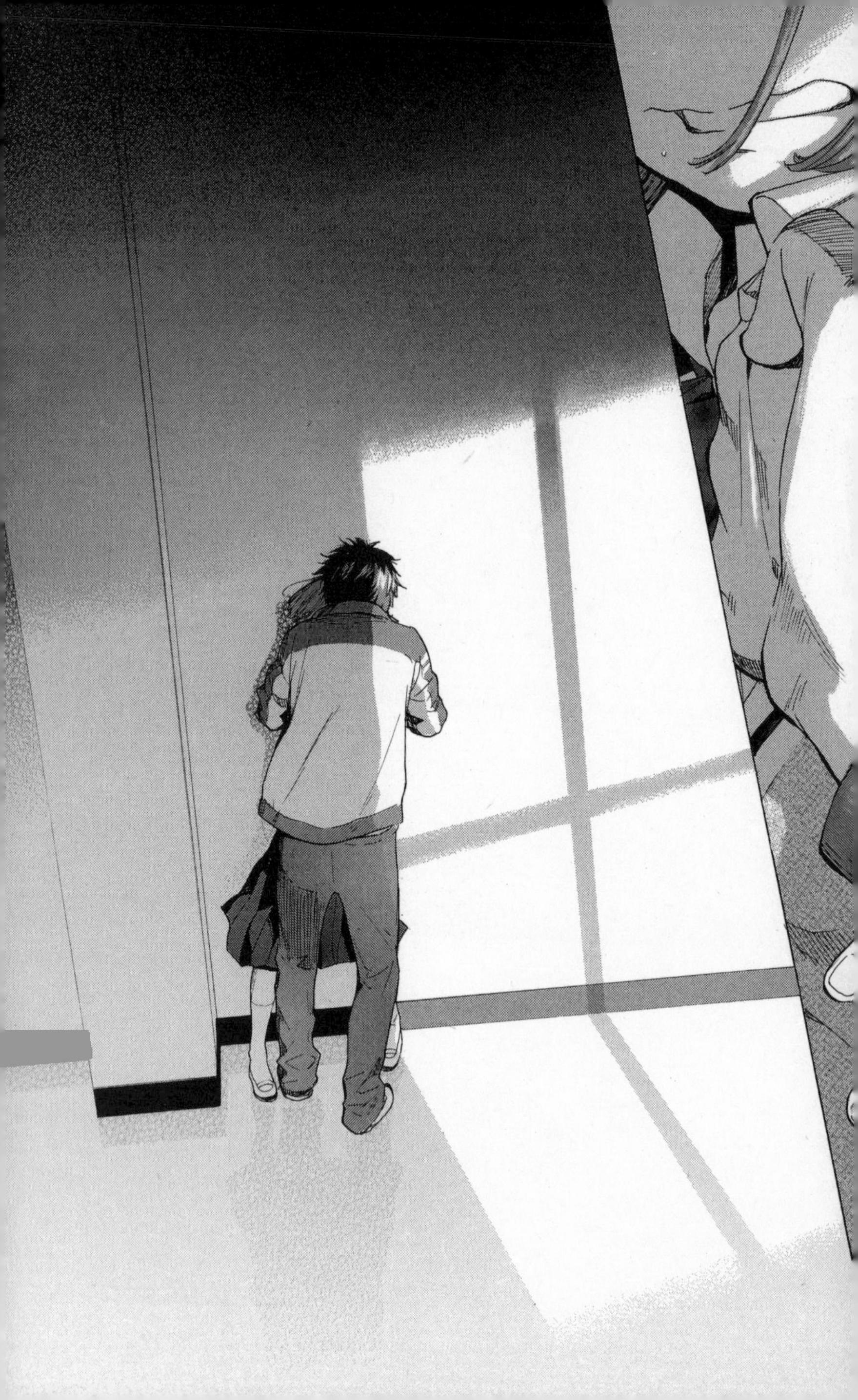

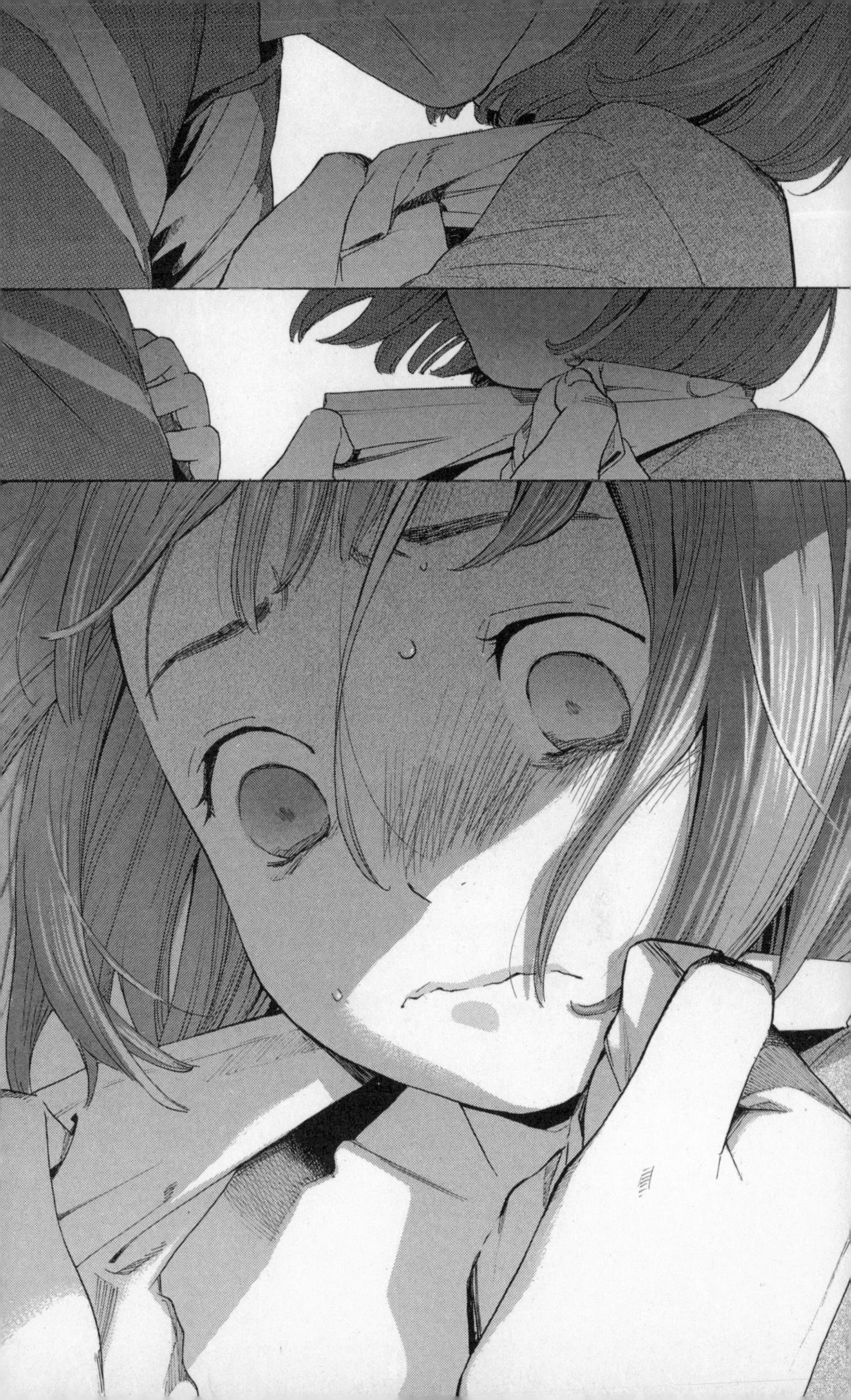

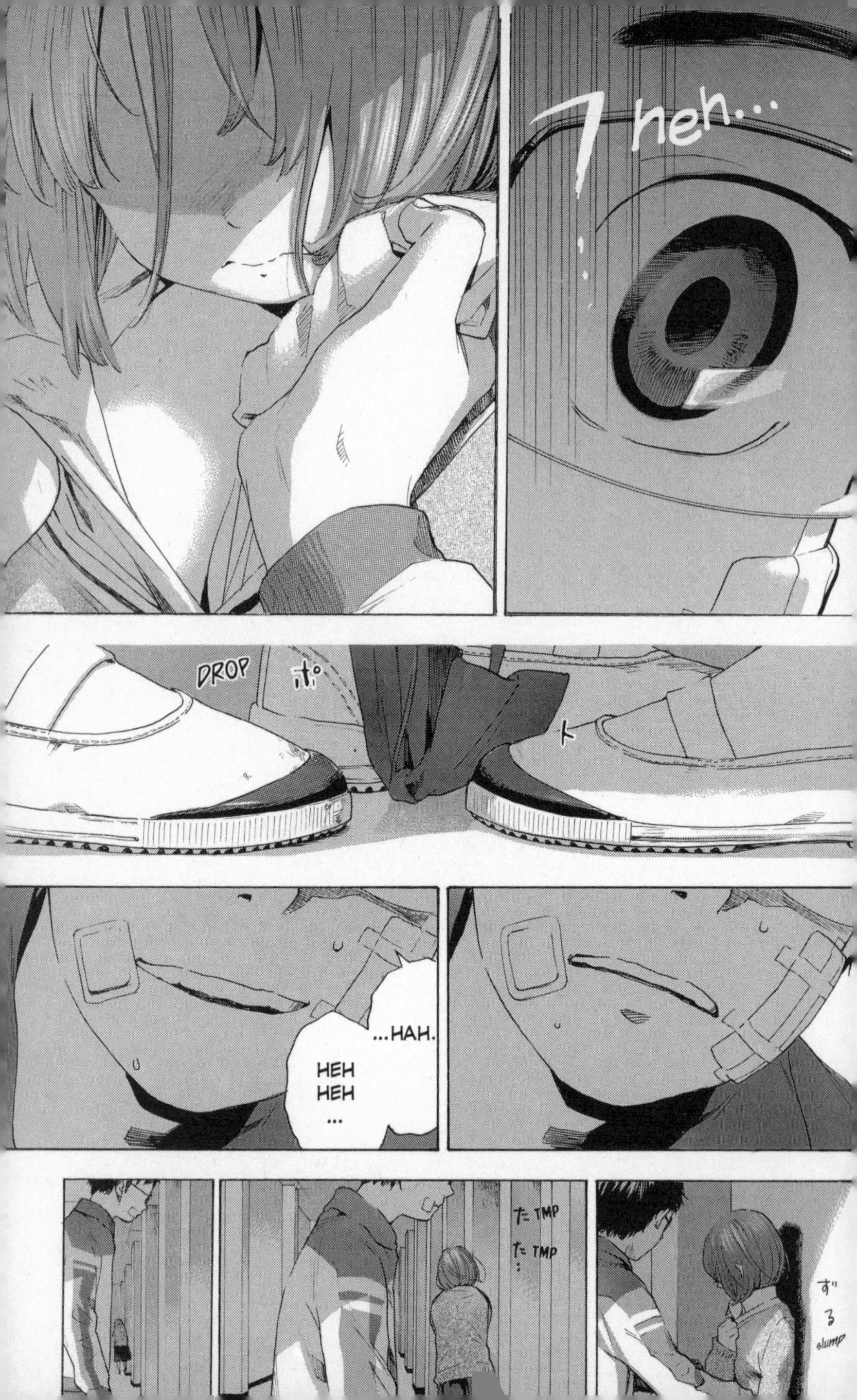

フ heh...
ト
ぽ
DROP
...HAH.
HEH HEH ...
ずる
slump
た TMP
た TMP

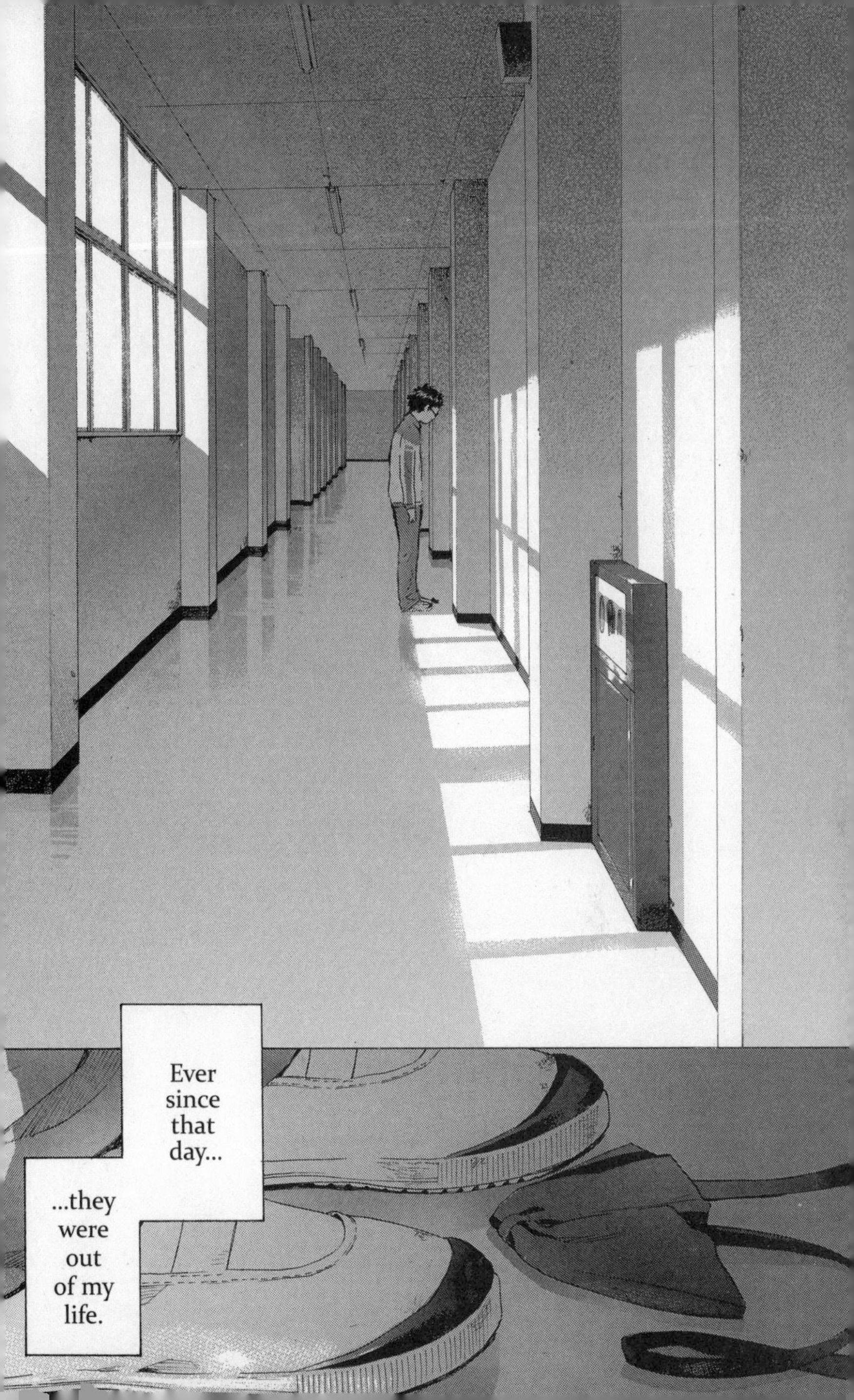
Ever since that day...
...they were out of my life.

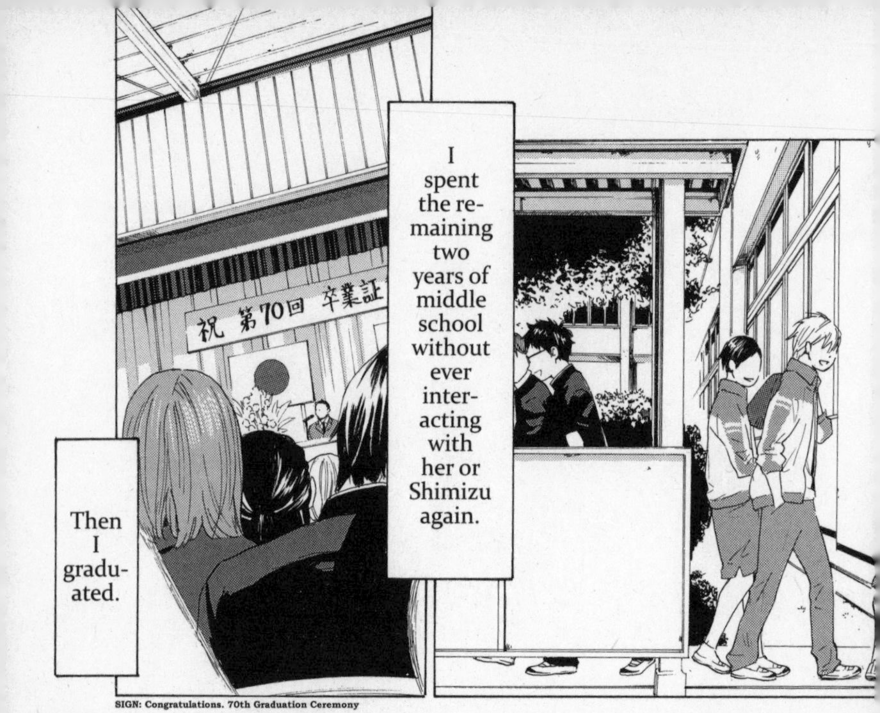
I spent the remaining two years of middle school without ever interacting with her or Shimizu again.
Then I graduated.
祝 第70回 卒業証
SIGN: Congratulations. 70th Graduation Ceremony

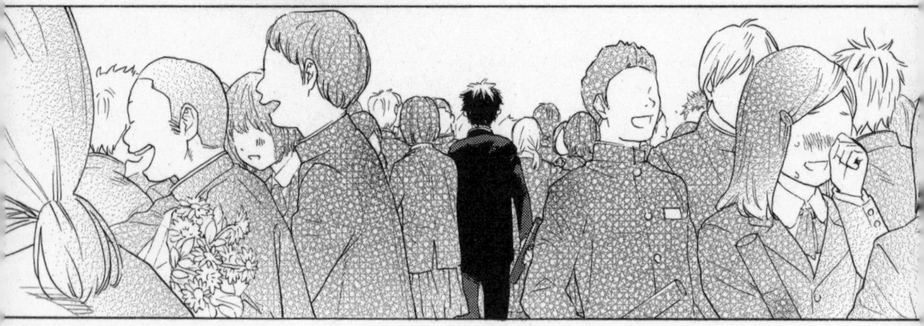

With that,
I thought I'd
be able to put
everything that
happened in
middle school
behind me,
like it'd never
happened.

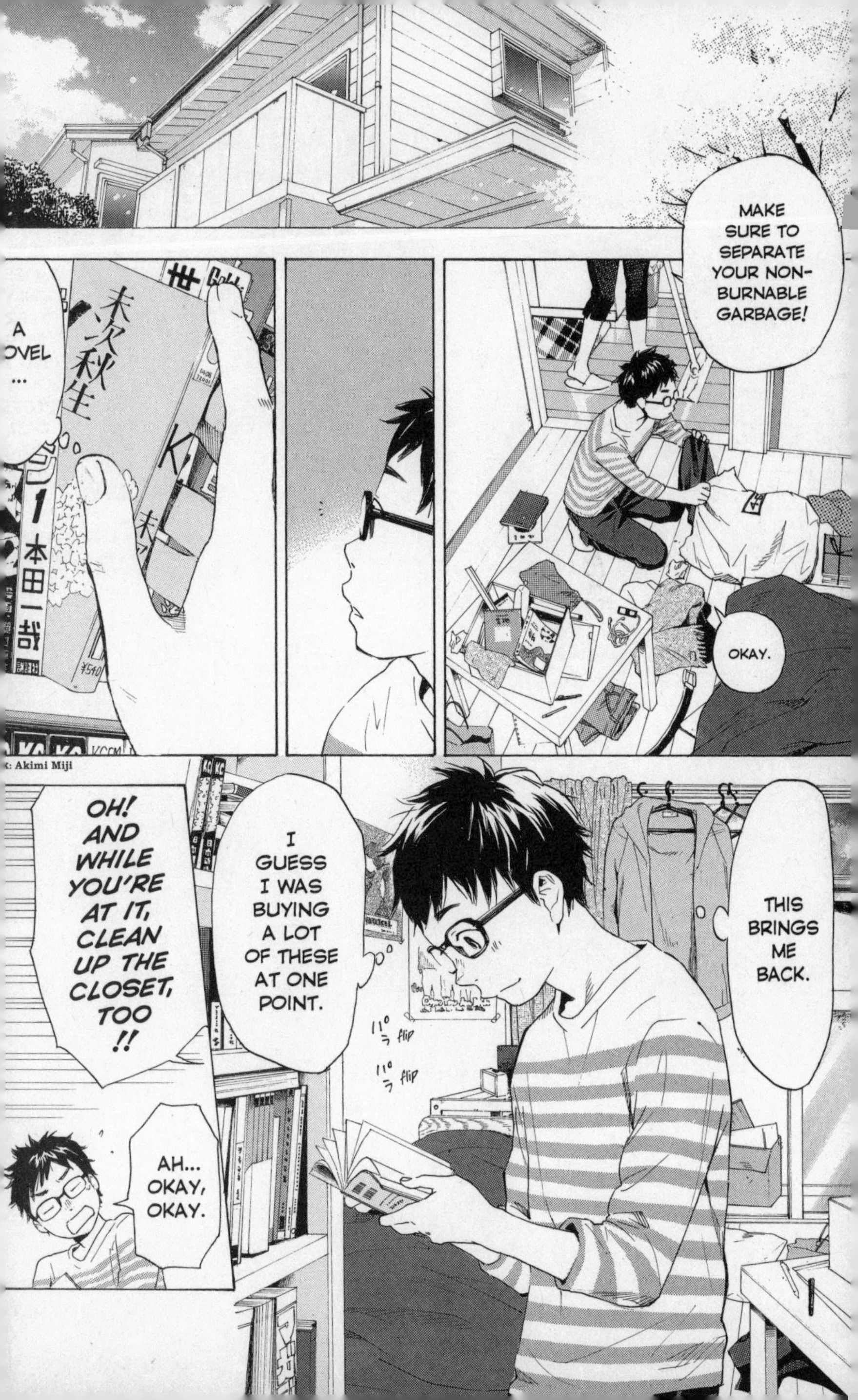
MAKE SURE TO SEPARATE YOUR NON-BURNABLE GARBAGE!
OKAY.
A OVEL ...
K: Akimi Miji
THIS BRINGS ME BACK.
flip
flip
I GUESS I WAS BUYING A LOT OF THESE AT ONE POINT.
OH! AND WHILE YOU'RE AT IT, CLEAN UP THE CLOSET, TOO!!
AH... OKAY, OKAY.

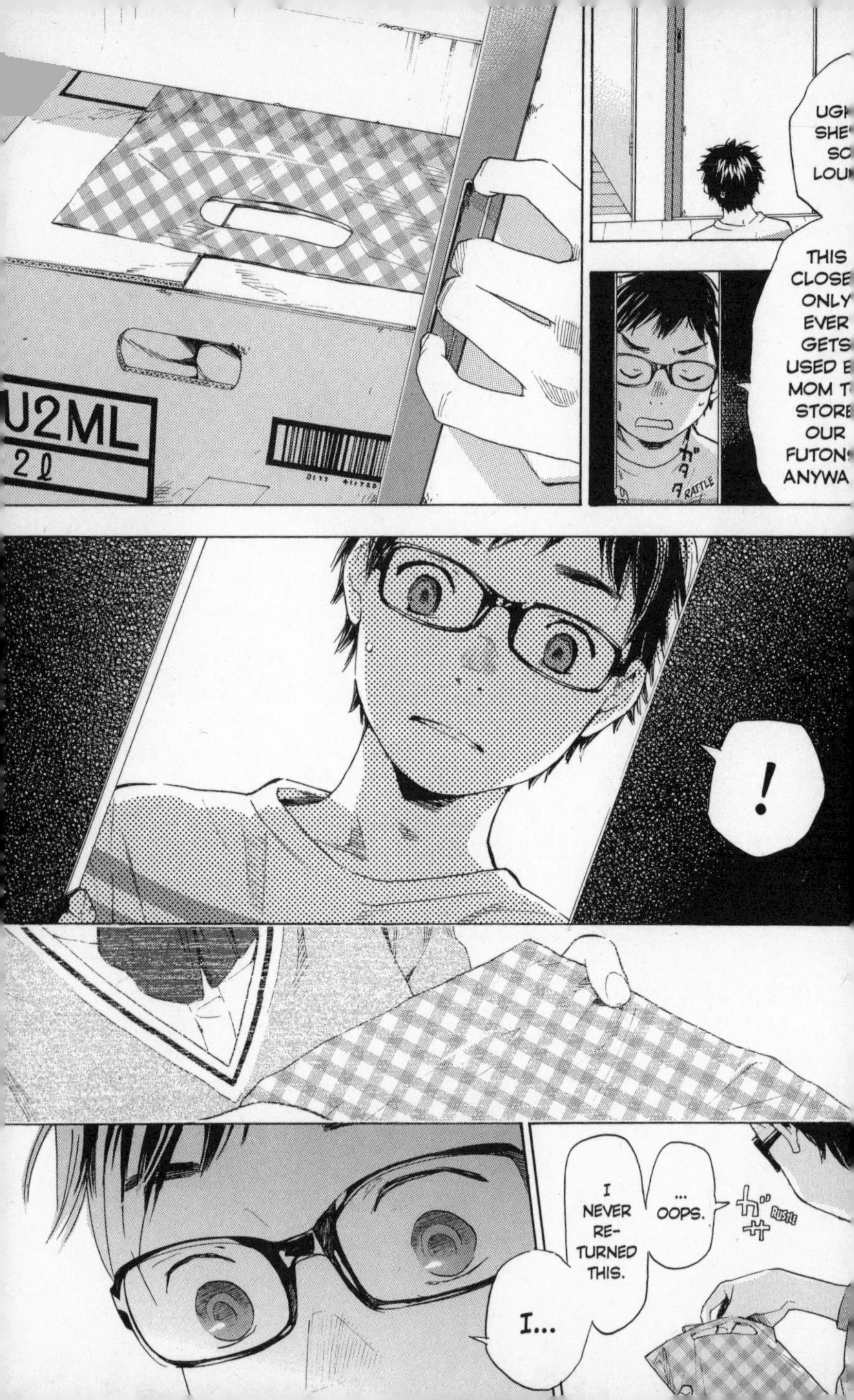

UG SHE SO LOU
THIS CLOSE ONLY EVER GETS USED B MOM T STORE OUR FUTON ANYWA
RATTLE
U2ML
2l
!
RUSTLE
... OOPS.
I NEVER RE-TURNED THIS.
I...

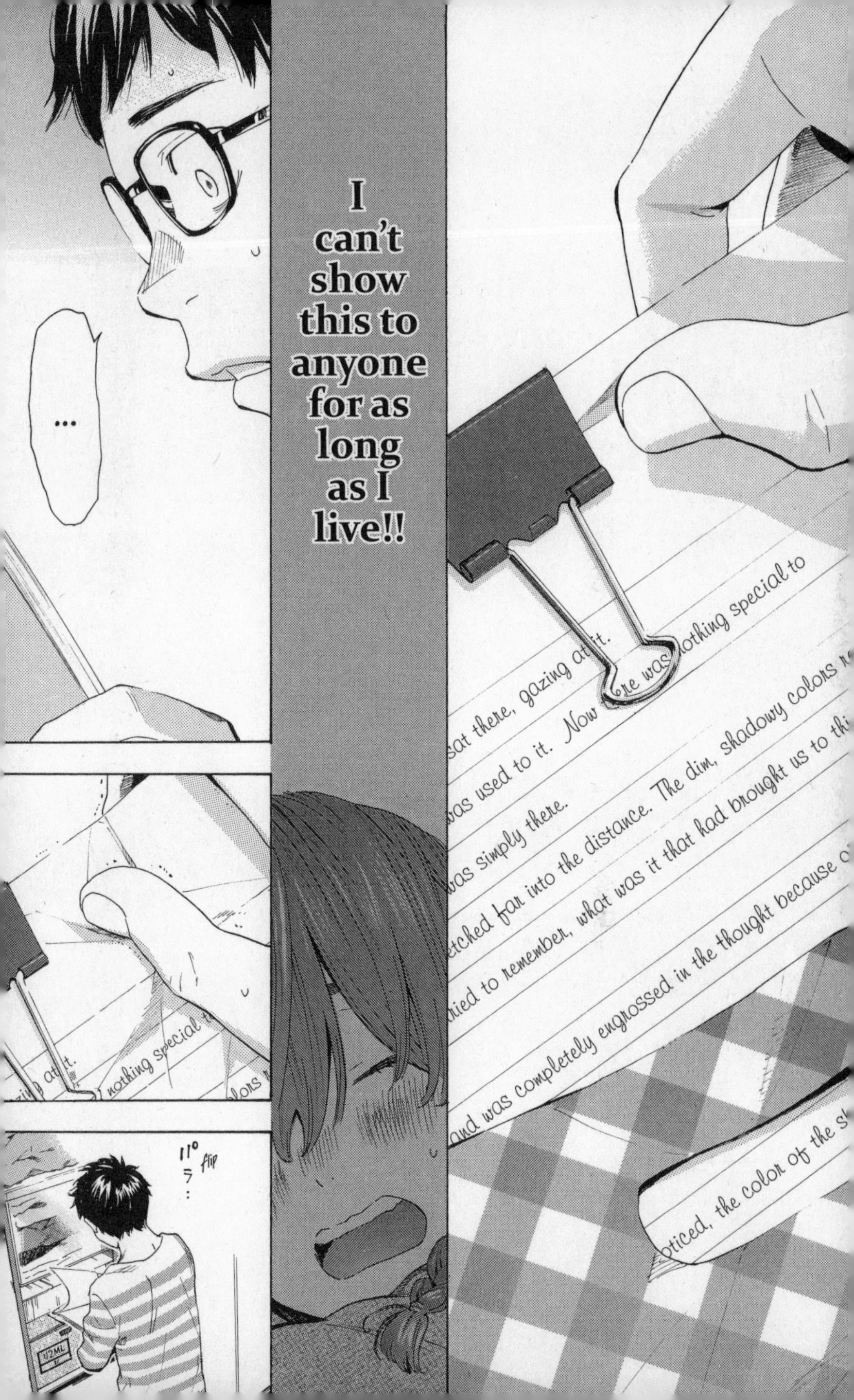
sat there, gazing at it.
was used to it. Now re was nothing special to
was simply there.
etched far into the distance. The dim, shadowy colors
ried to remember, what was it that had brought us to
and was completely engrossed in the thought because
oticed, the color of the
I can't show this to anyone for as long as I live!!
...
at it.
nothing special
flip

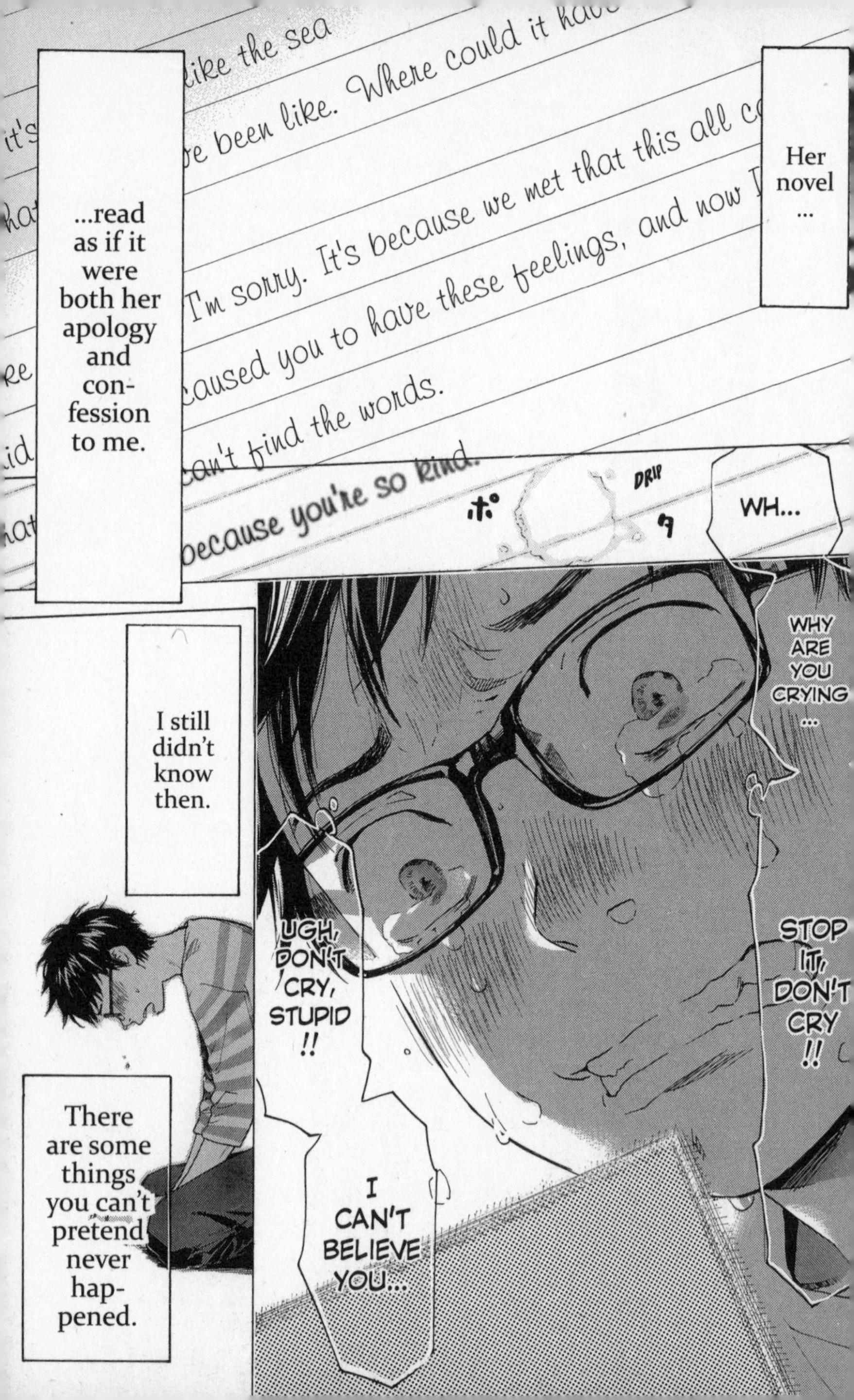
Her novel...
like the sea
been like. Where could it have
I'm sorry. It's because we met that this all c
caused you to have these feelings, and now I
can't find the words.
because you're so kind.
...read as if it were both her apology and confession to me.
DRIP
WH...
WHY ARE YOU CRYING...
STOP IT, DON'T CRY!!
UGH, DON'T CRY, STUPID!!
I CAN'T BELIEVE YOU...
I still didn't know then.
There are some things you can't pretend never happened.

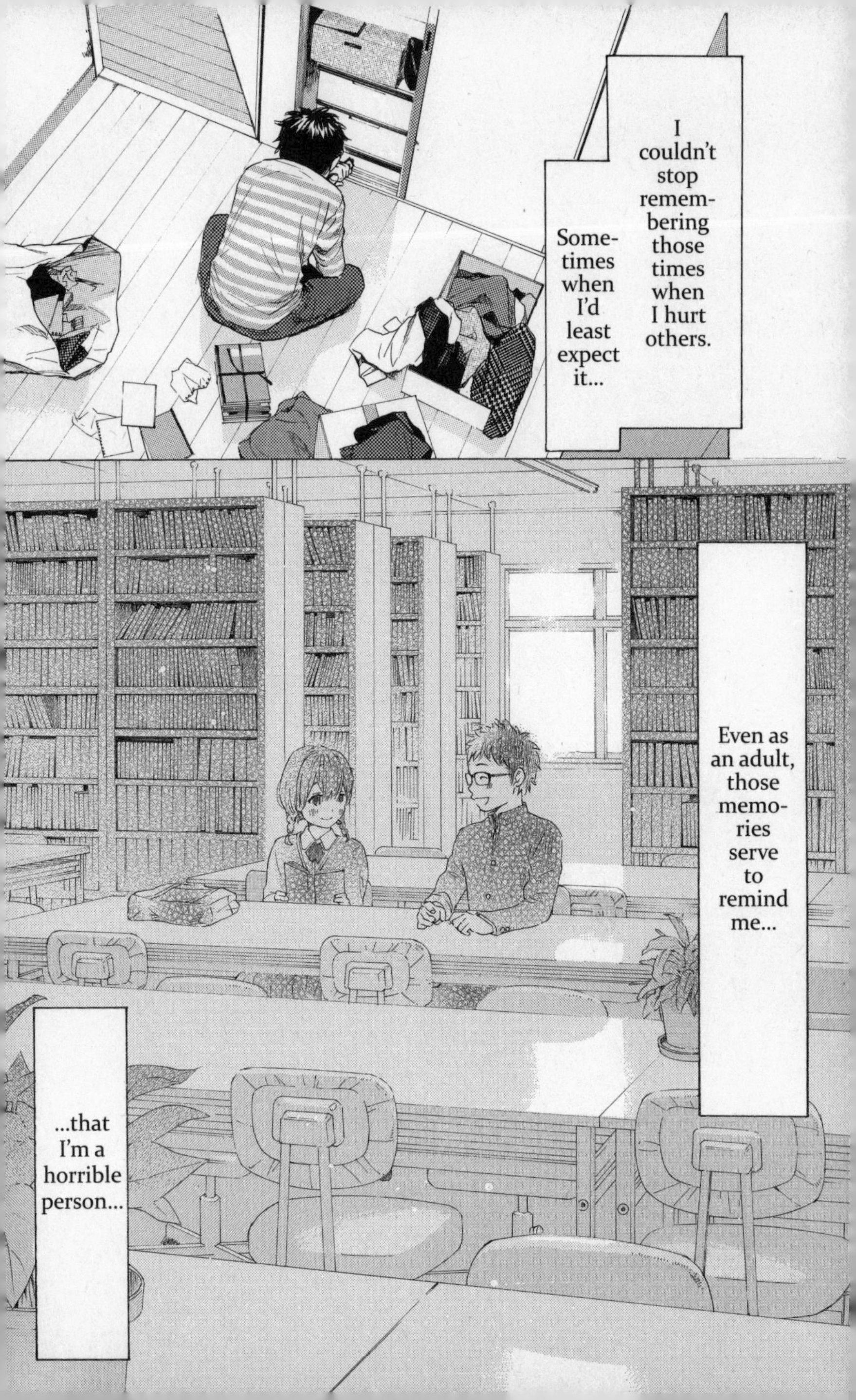
I couldn't stop remembering those times when I hurt others.
Sometimes when I'd least expect it...
Even as an adult, those memories serve to remind me...
...that I'm a horrible person...

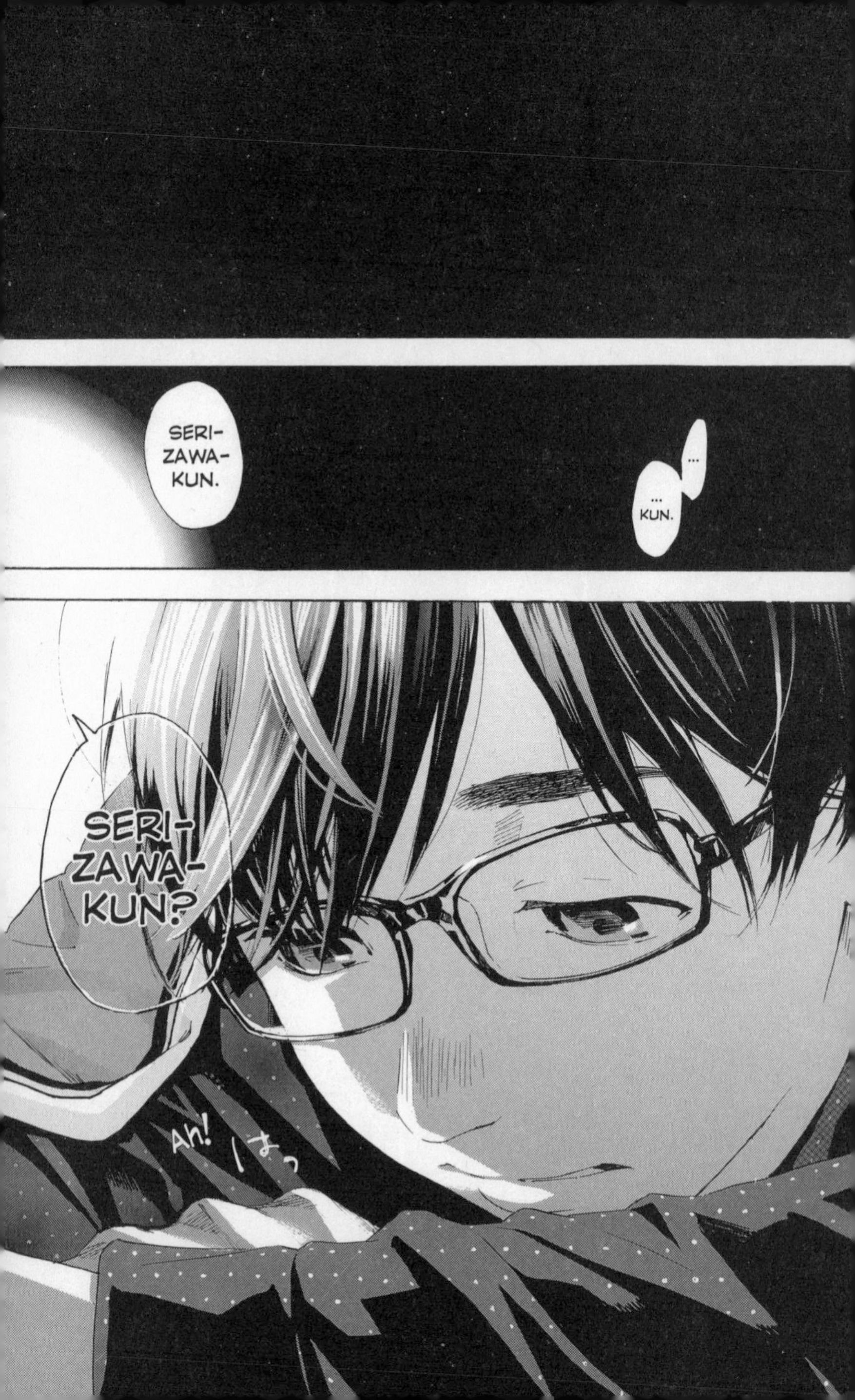
...
... KUN.
SERI-ZAWA-KUN.
SERI-ZAWA-KUN?
Ah! はっ

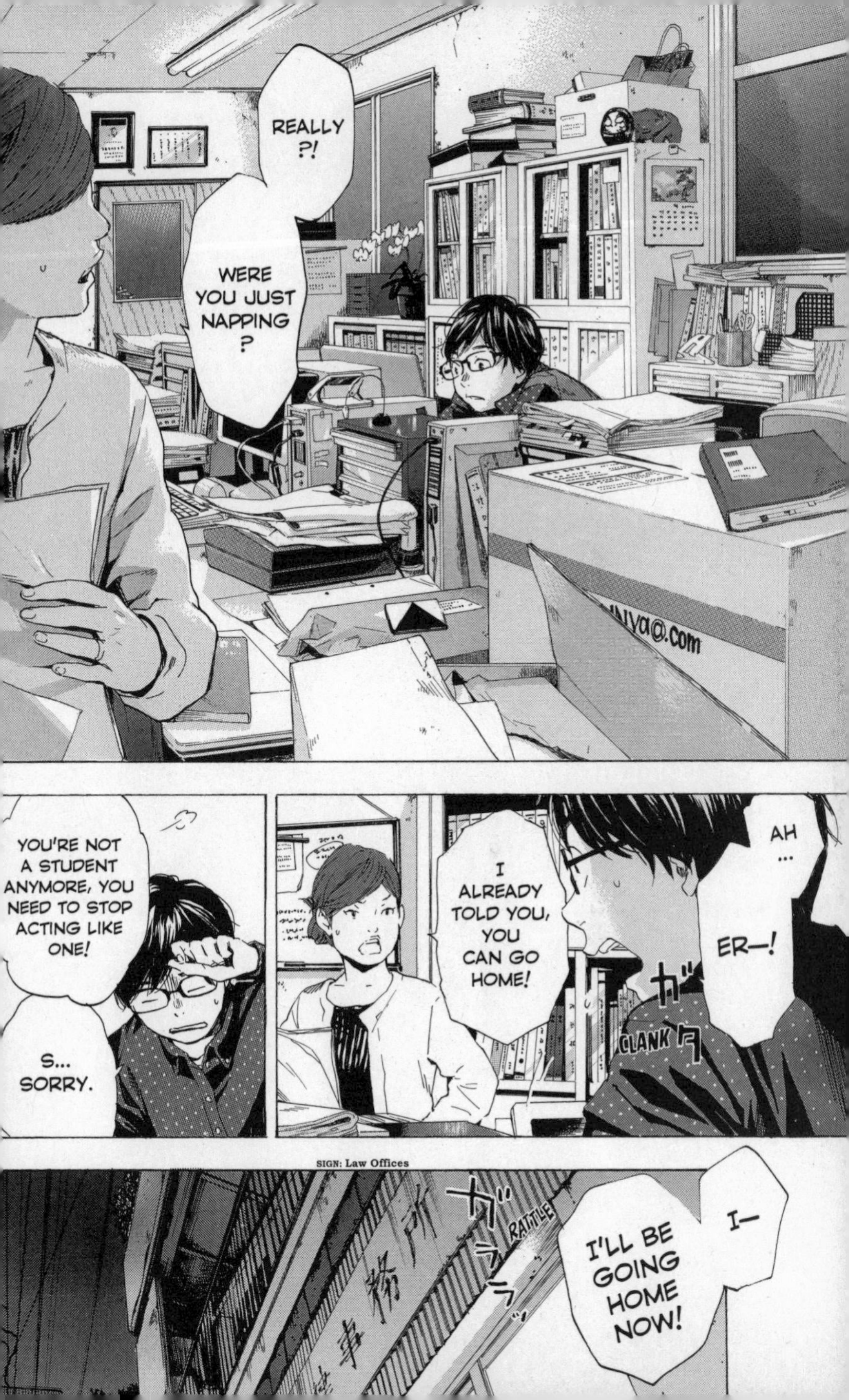
REALLY ?!
WERE YOU JUST NAPPING ?
AH ...
ER—!
CLANK
I ALREADY TOLD YOU, YOU CAN GO HOME!
YOU'RE NOT A STUDENT ANYMORE, YOU NEED TO STOP ACTING LIKE ONE!
S... SORRY.
SIGN: Law Offices
RATTLE
I—
I'LL BE GOING HOME NOW!

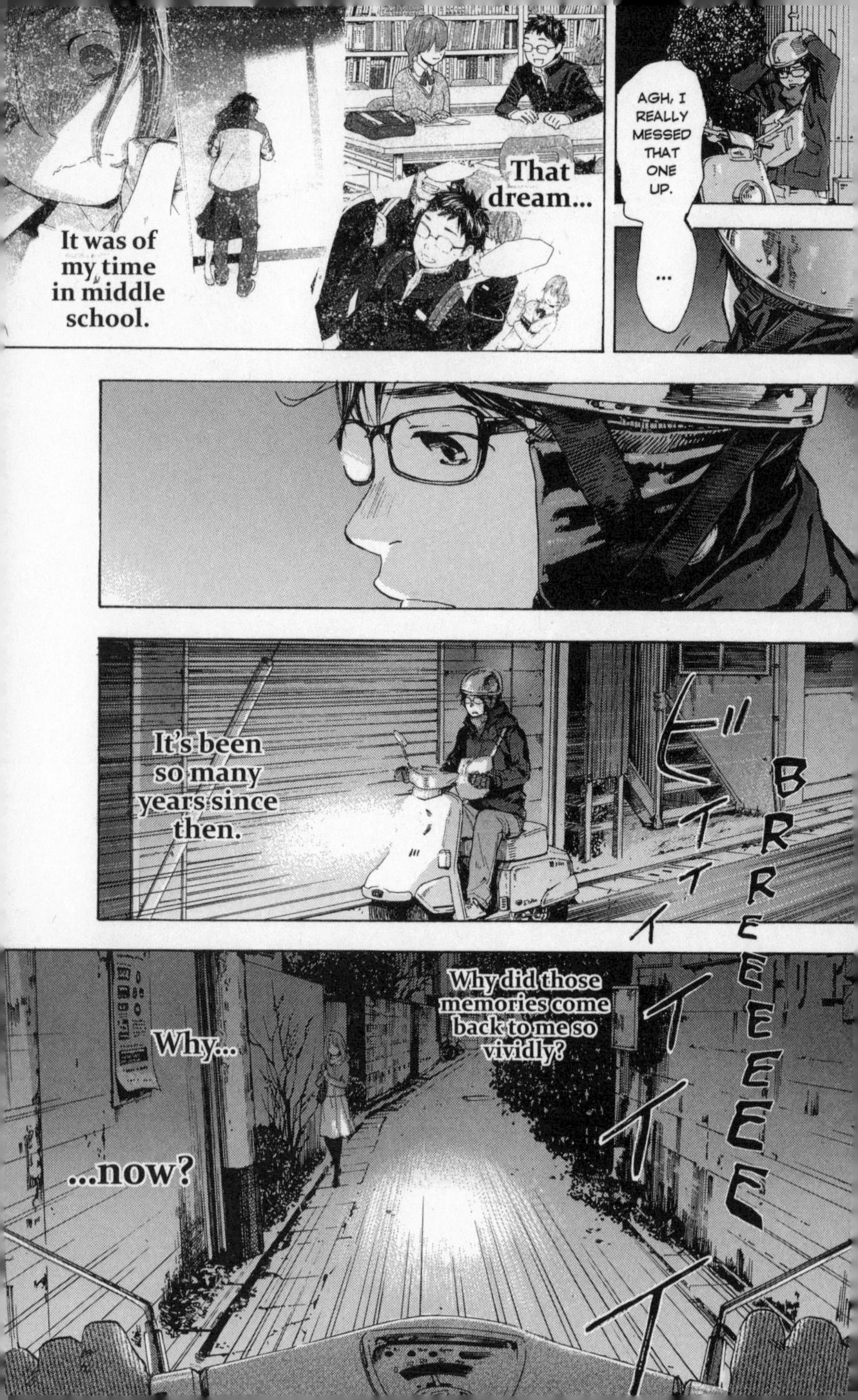
AGH, I REALLY MESSED THAT ONE UP.
...
That dream...
It was of my time in middle school.
It's been so many years since then.
ビイイイイイイ
BRREEEEEE
Why did those memories come back to me so vividly?
Why...
...now?

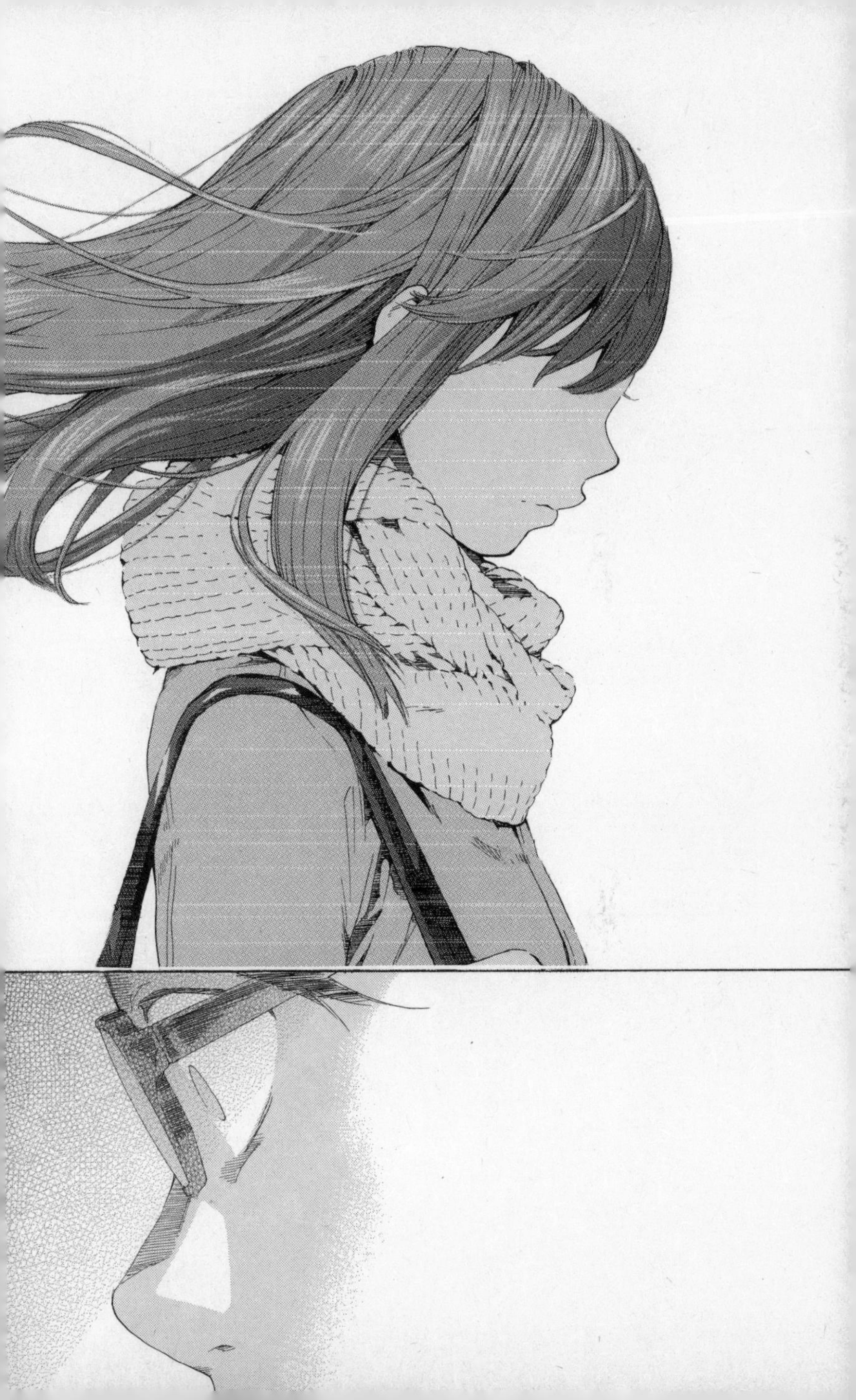

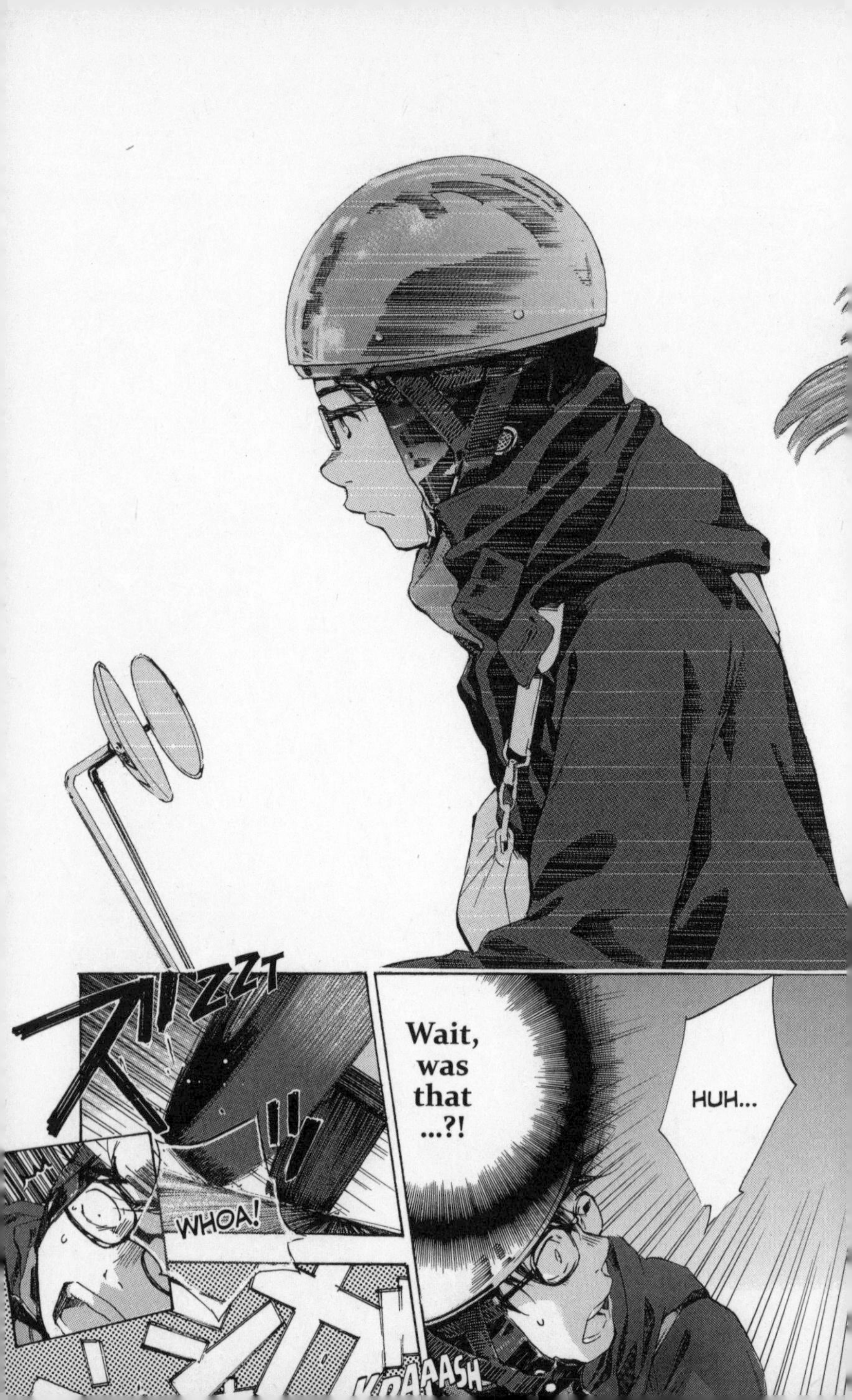
HUH...
Wait, was that ...?!
ZZZT
WHOA!
KRAAASH

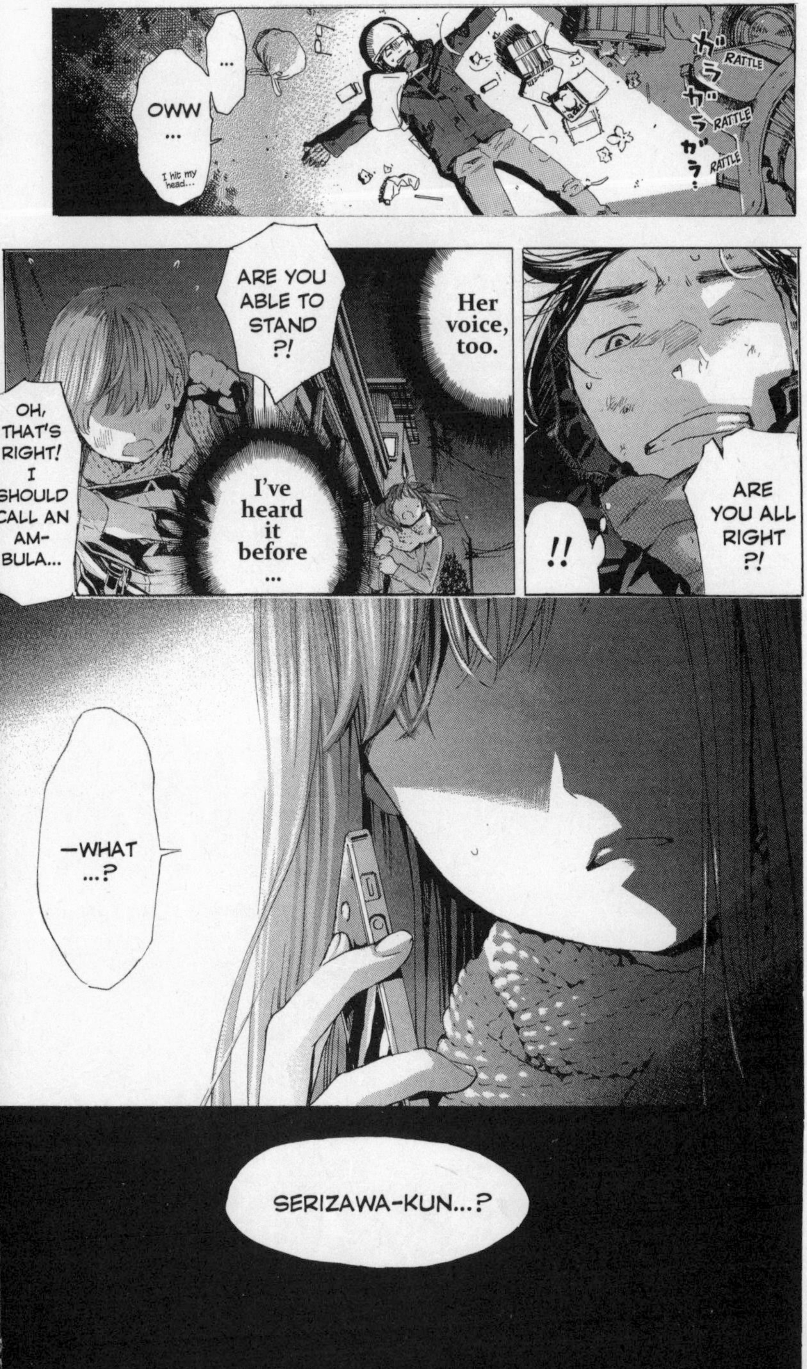
ガラ RATTLE
ガラ RATTLE
ガラ RATTLE
...
OWW ...
I hit my head...
ARE YOU ALL RIGHT ?!
!!
Her voice, too.
ARE YOU ABLE TO STAND ?!
I've heard it before ...
OH, THAT'S RIGHT! I SHOULD CALL AN AM-BULA...
—WHAT ...?
SERIZAWA-KUN...?

Forget Me Not

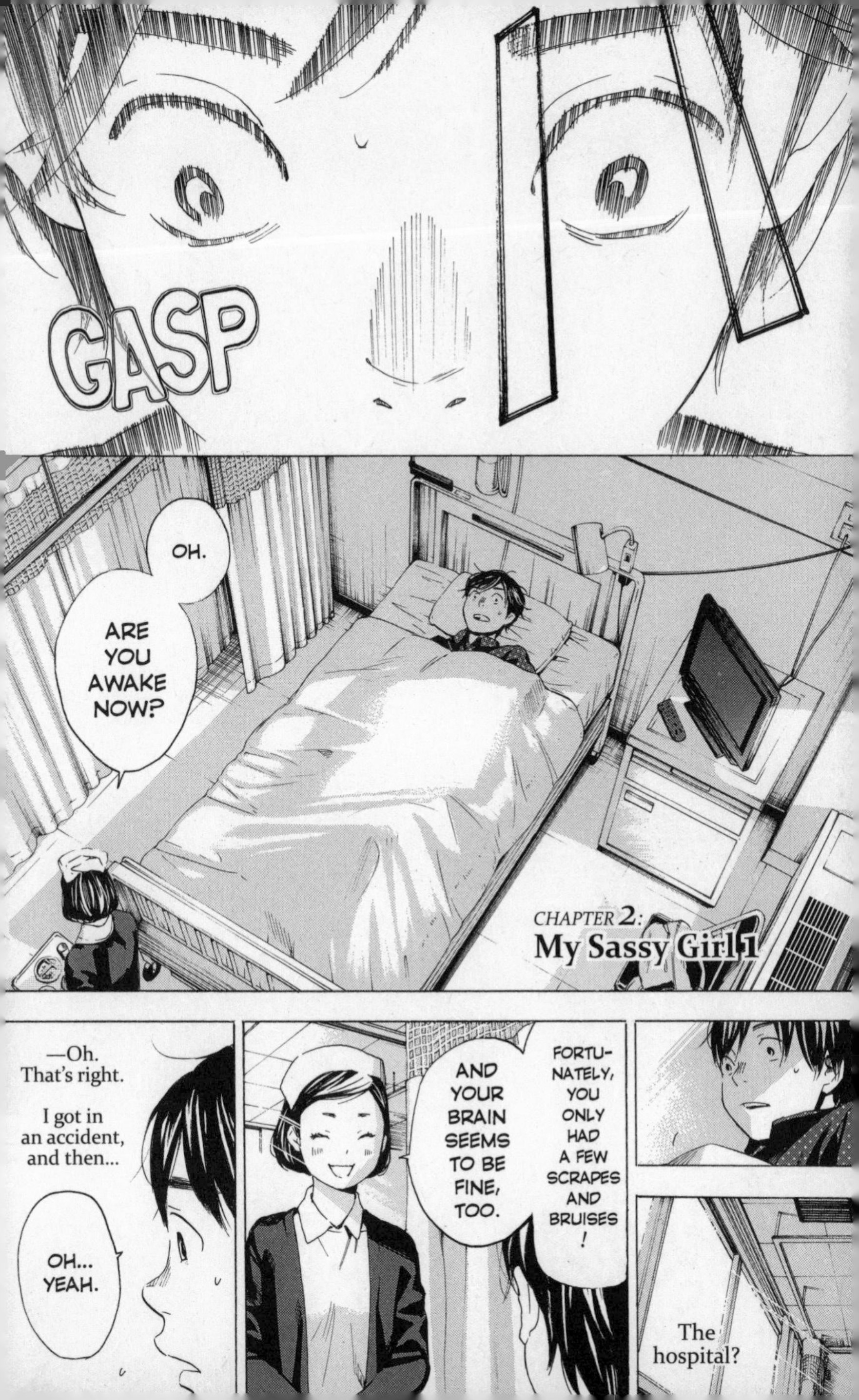
GASP
OH.
ARE YOU AWAKE NOW?
CHAPTER 2: My Sassy Girl 1
The hospital?
FORTU-NATELY, YOU ONLY HAD A FEW SCRAPES AND BRUISES!
AND YOUR BRAIN SEEMS TO BE FINE, TOO.
—Oh. That's right.
I got in an accident, and then...
OH... YEAH.

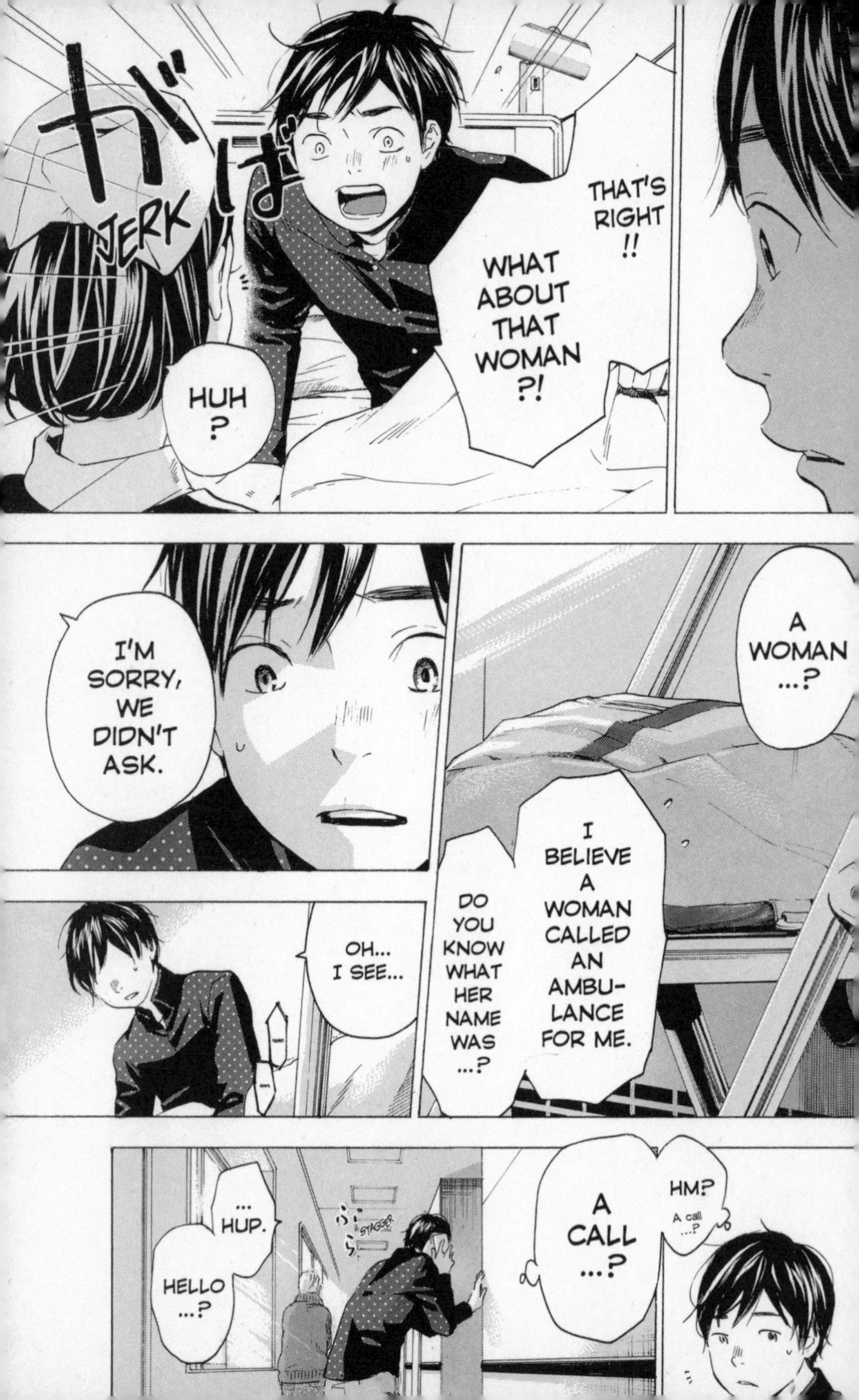

THAT'S RIGHT !!
WHAT ABOUT THAT WOMAN ?!
JERK
HUH ?
A WOMAN ...?
I BELIEVE A WOMAN CALLED AN AMBULANCE FOR ME.
DO YOU KNOW WHAT HER NAME WAS ...?
I'M SORRY, WE DIDN'T ASK.
OH... I SEE...
HM?
A call ...?
A CALL ...?
... HUP.
STAGGER
HELLO ...?

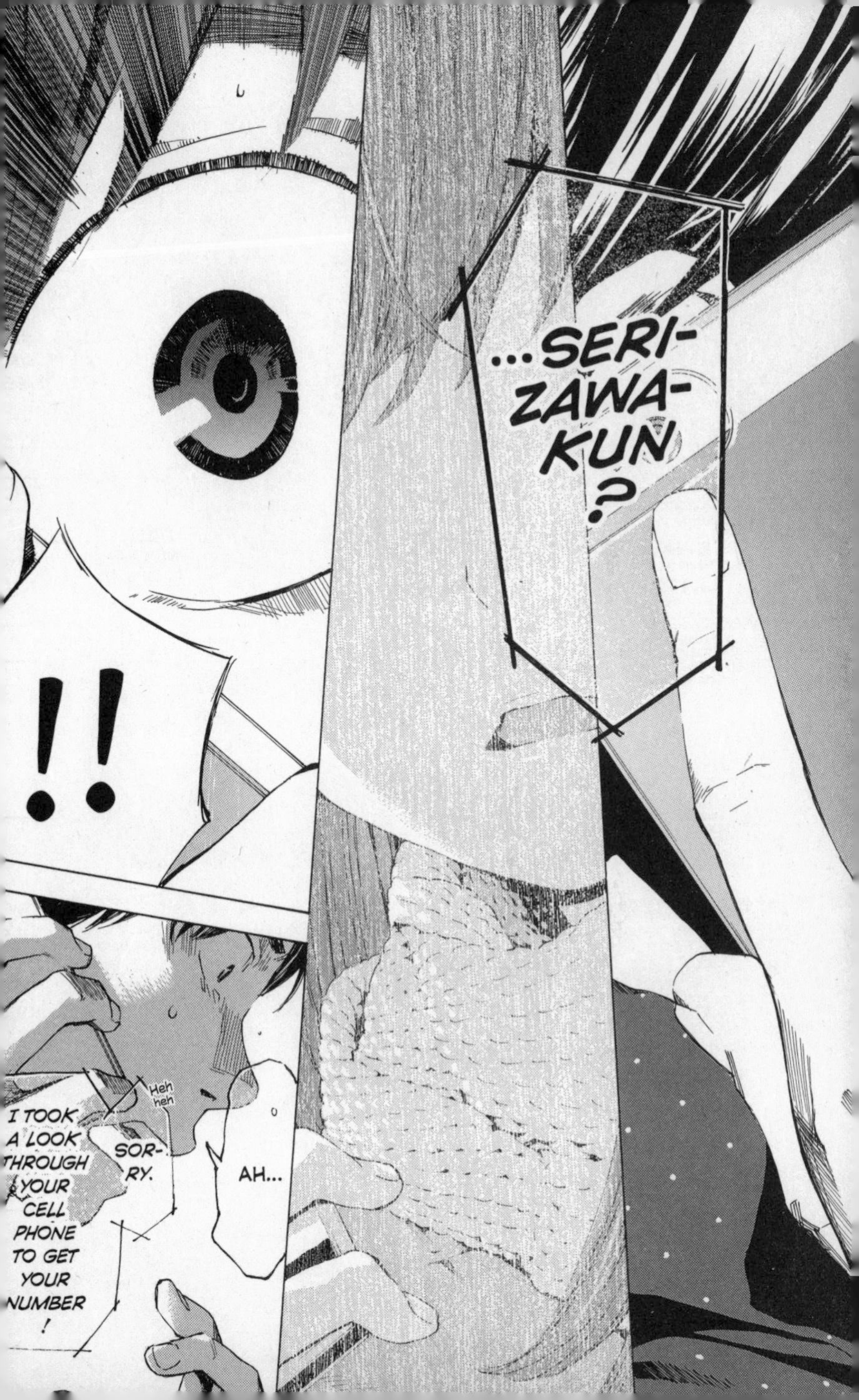
...SERI-ZAWA-KUN?
!!
AH...
Heh heh
SOR-RY.
I TOOK A LOOK THROUGH YOUR CELL PHONE TO GET YOUR NUMBER!

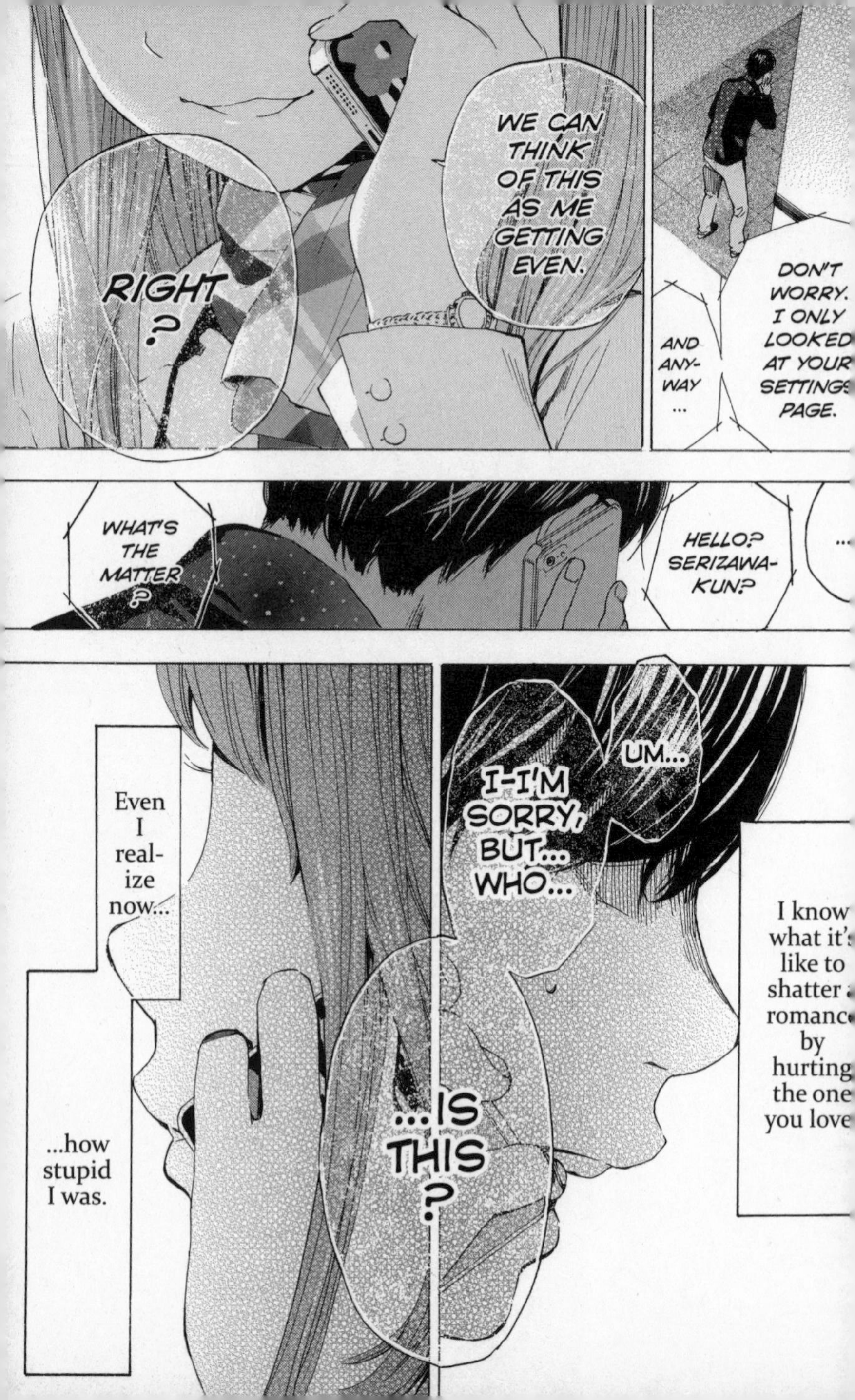
DON'T WORRY. I ONLY LOOKED AT YOUR SETTINGS PAGE.
AND ANYWAY ...
WE CAN THINK OF THIS AS ME GETTING EVEN.
RIGHT?
...
HELLO? SERIZAWA-KUN?
WHAT'S THE MATTER?
I know what it's like to shatter a romance by hurting the one you love
UM...
I-I'M SORRY, BUT... WHO...
...IS THIS?
Even I realize now...
...how stupid I was.

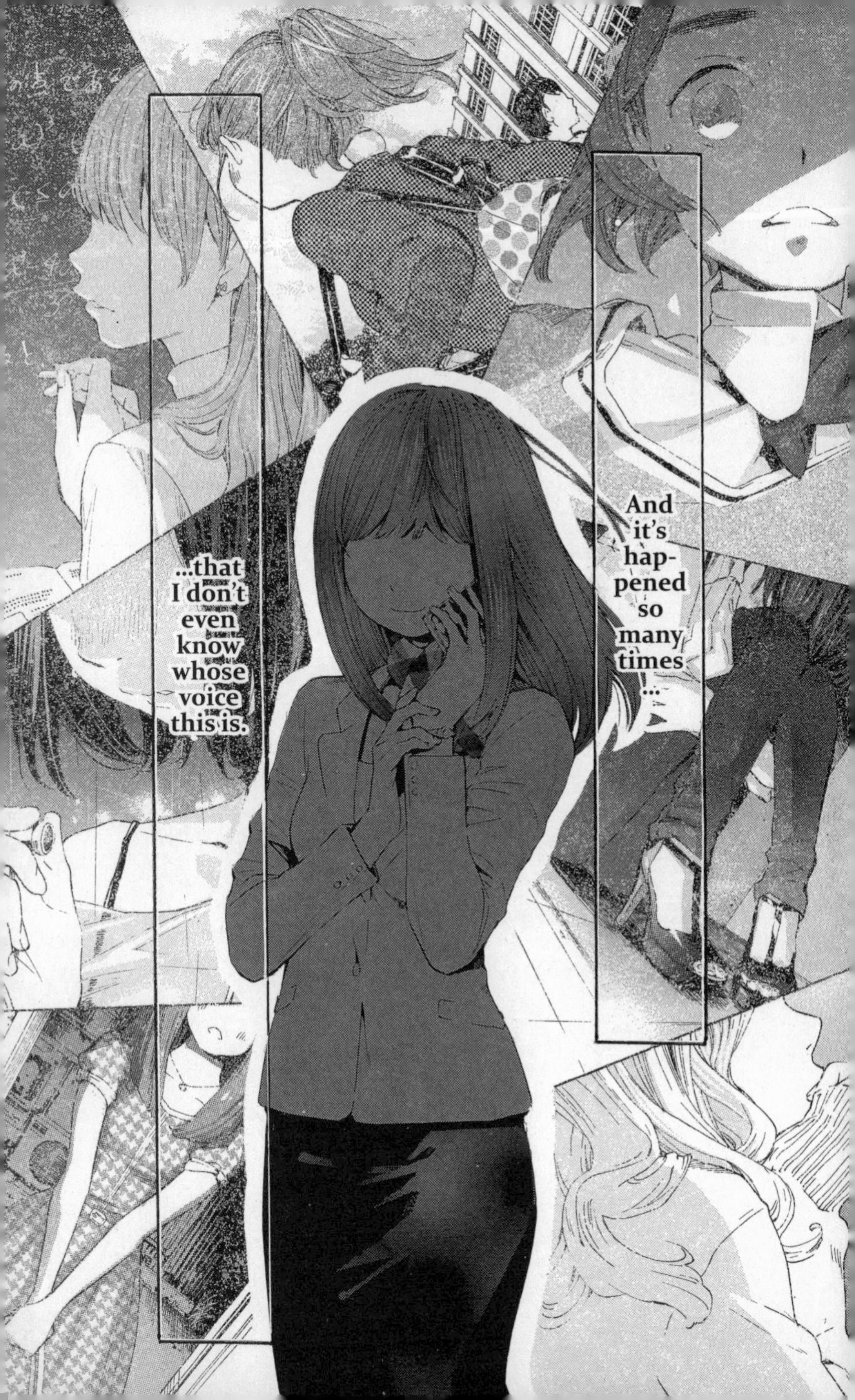
And it's hap-pened so many times...
...that I don't even know whose voice this is.

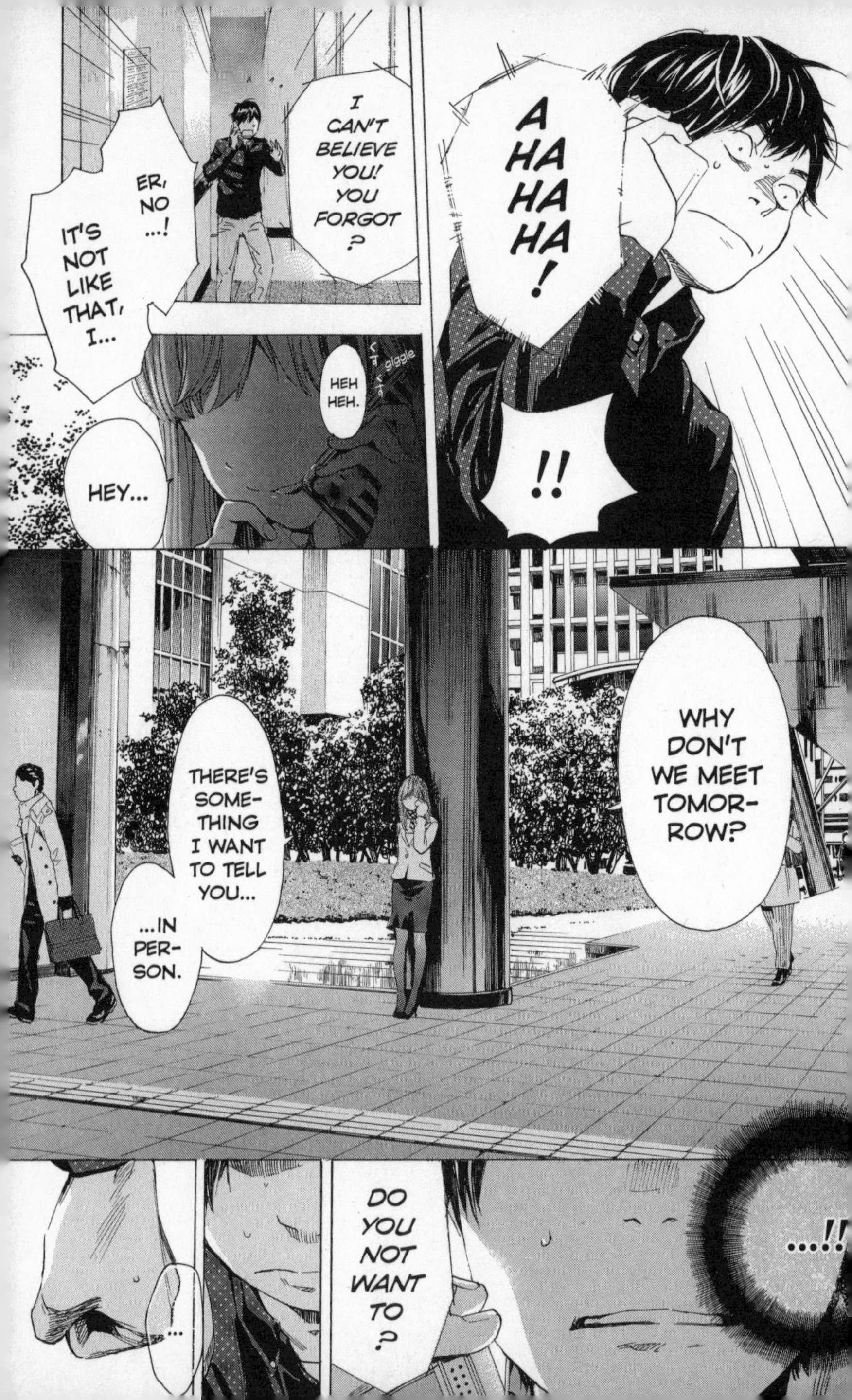
AHAHAHA!
!!
I CAN'T BELIEVE YOU! YOU FORGOT?
ER, NO ...!
IT'S NOT LIKE THAT, I...
HEH HEH.
giggle
HEY...
WHY DON'T WE MEET TOMORROW?
THERE'S SOMETHING I WANT TO TELL YOU...
...IN PERSON.
...!!
DO YOU NOT WANT TO?
...

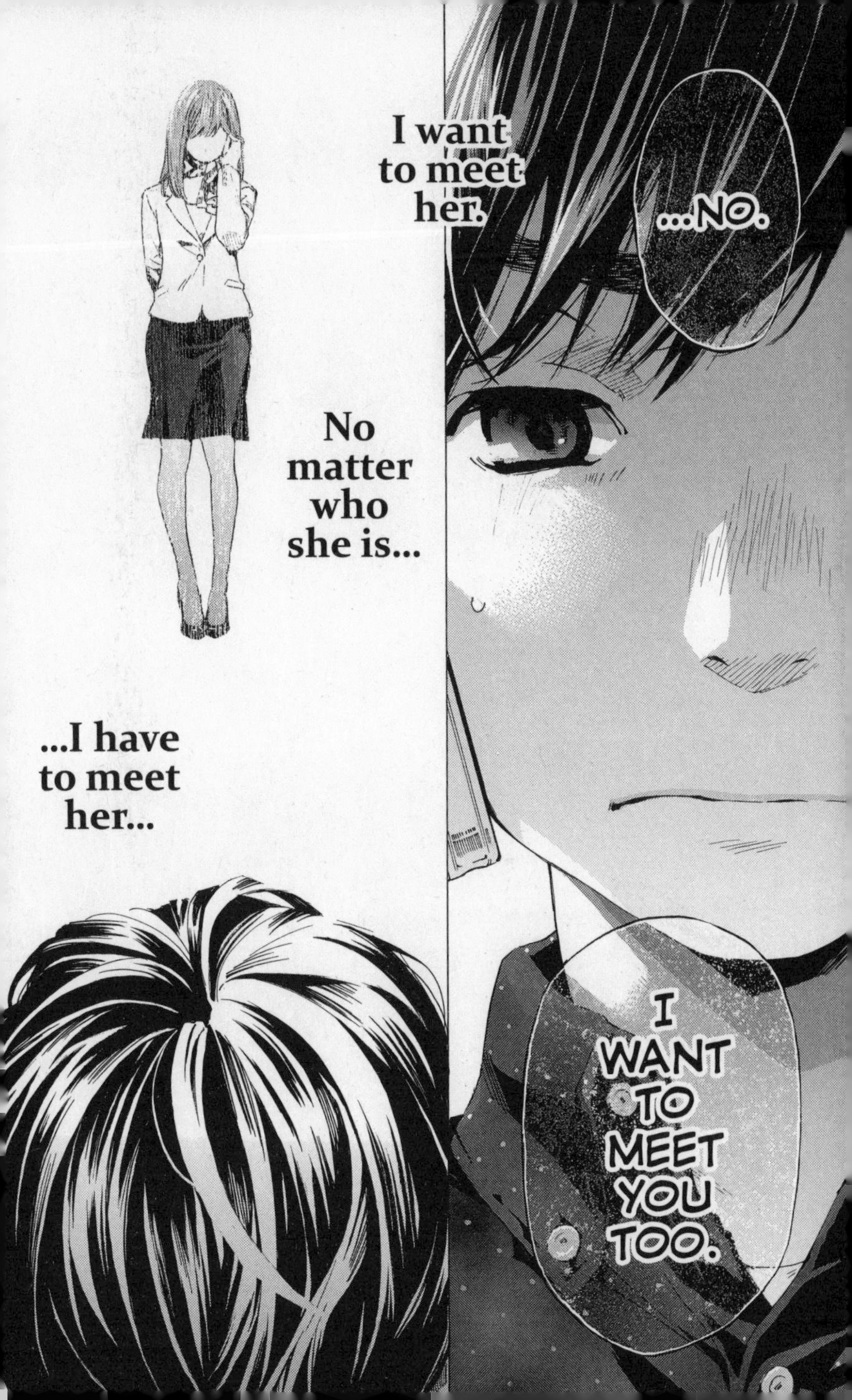
I want to meet her.
...NO.
I WANT TO MEET YOU TOO.
No matter who she is...
...I have to meet her...

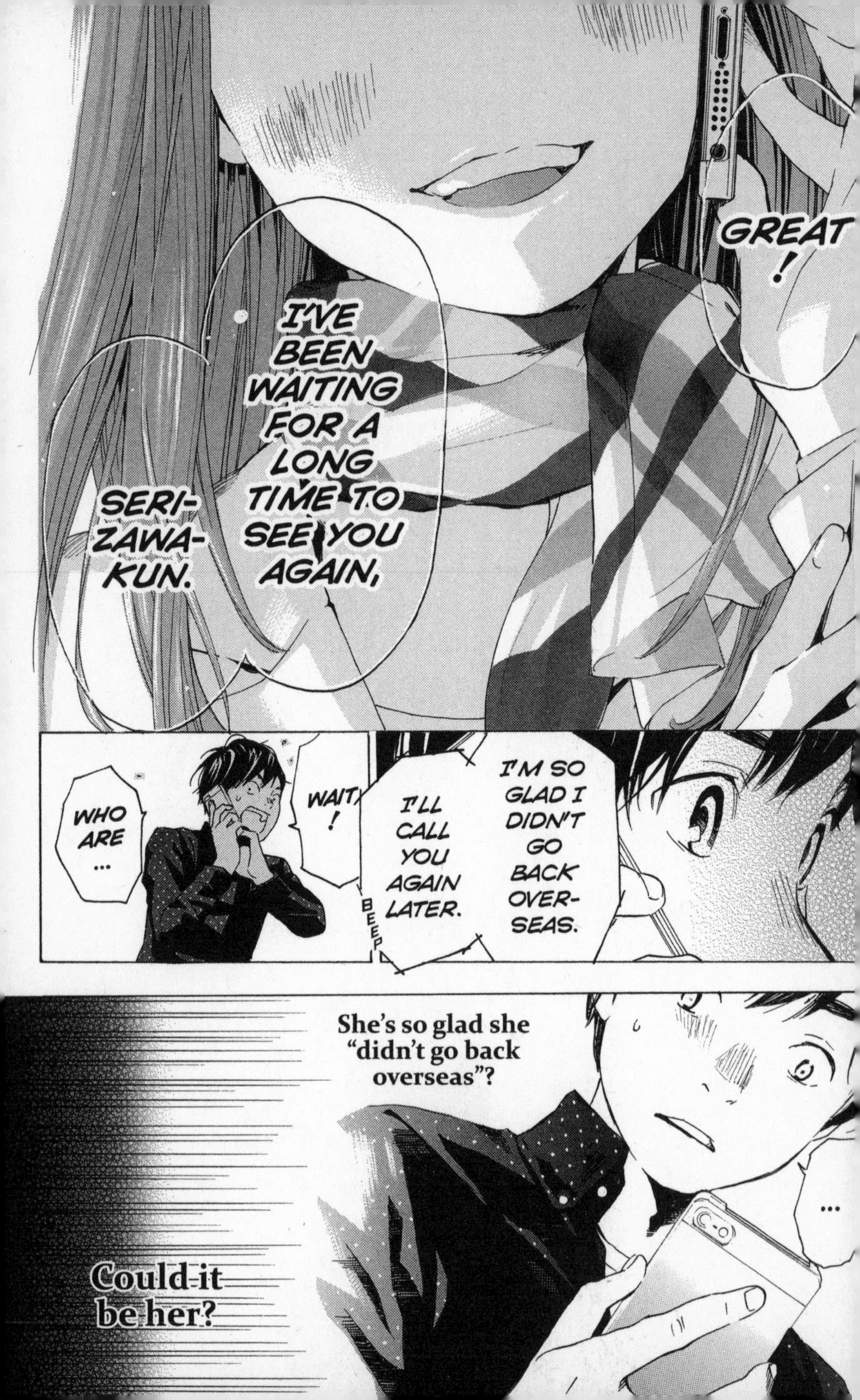
GREAT!
I'VE BEEN WAITING FOR A LONG TIME TO SEE YOU AGAIN,
SERI-ZAWA-KUN.
I'M SO GLAD I DIDN'T GO BACK OVER-SEAS.
I'LL CALL YOU AGAIN LATER.
BEEP
WAIT!
WHO ARE ...
She's so glad she "didn't go back overseas"?
...
Could it be her?

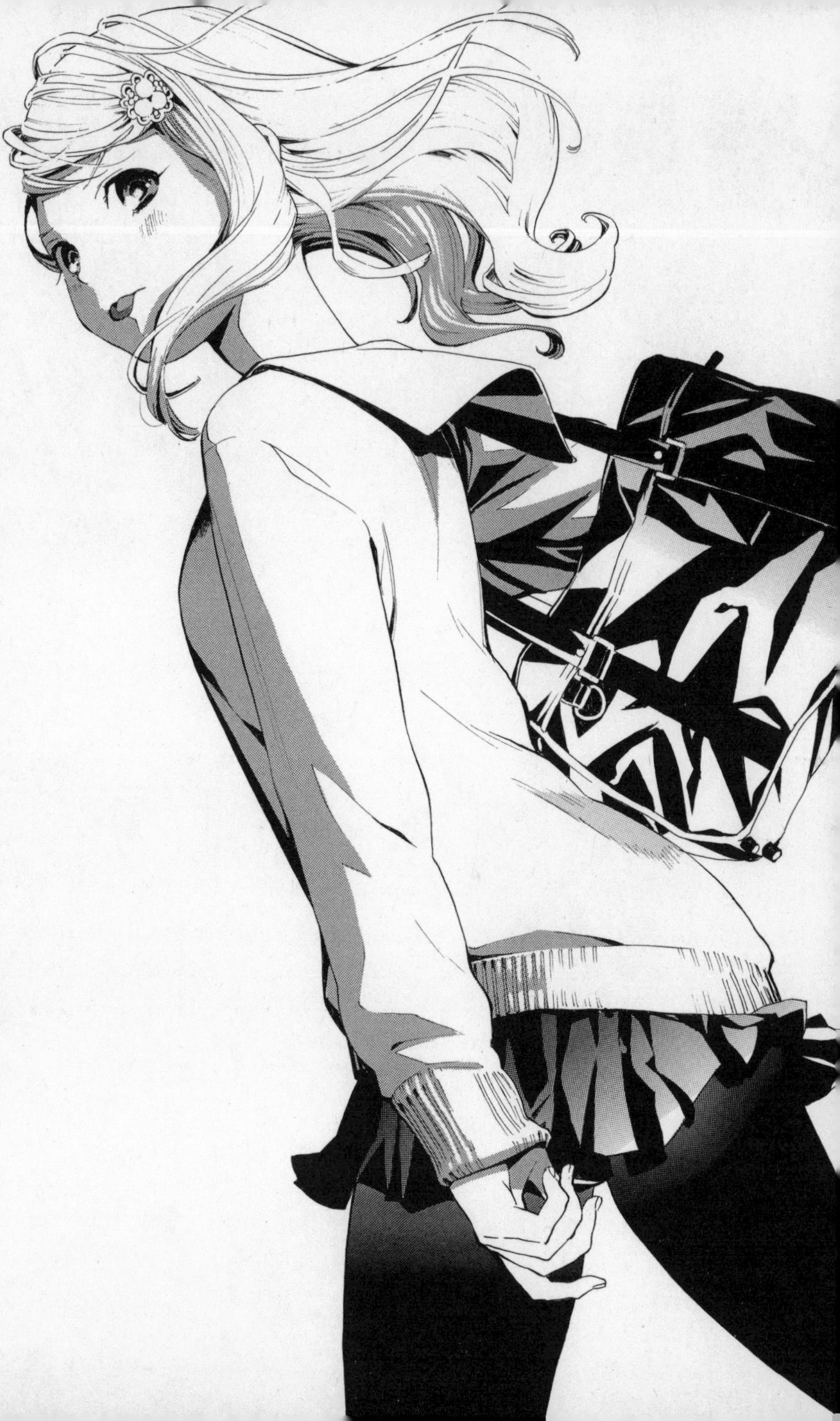

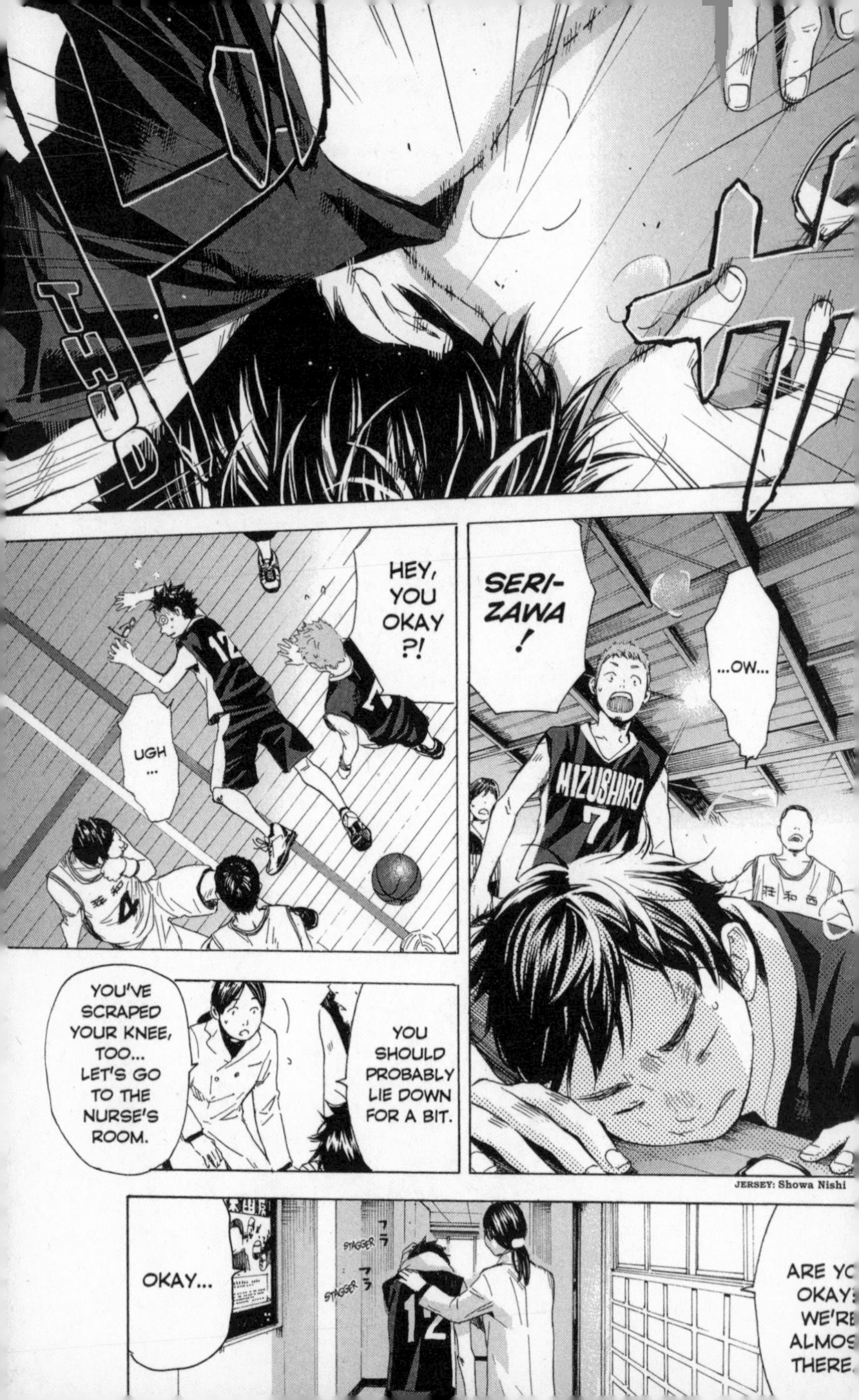
THUD
SERI-ZAWA!
...OW...
HEY, YOU OKAY?!
UGH...
YOU SHOULD PROBABLY LIE DOWN FOR A BIT.
YOU'VE SCRAPED YOUR KNEE, TOO... LET'S GO TO THE NURSE'S ROOM.
JERSEY: Showa Nishi
ARE YO OKAY WE'RE ALMOS THERE
STAGGER
STAGGER
OKAY...

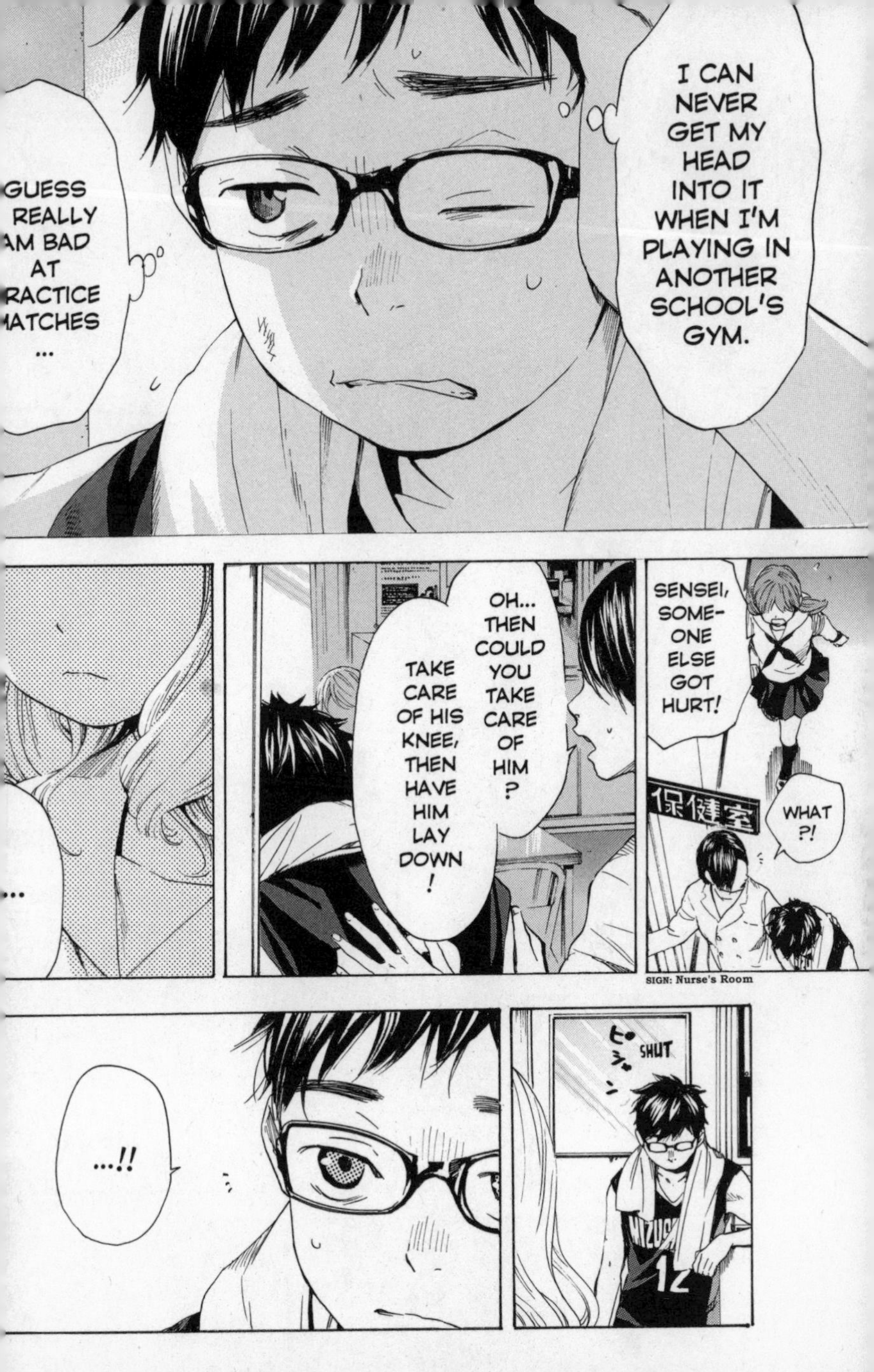
I CAN NEVER GET MY HEAD INTO IT WHEN I'M PLAYING IN ANOTHER SCHOOL'S GYM.
GUESS REALLY AM BAD AT RACTICE ATCHES ...
SENSEI, SOME-ONE ELSE GOT HURT!
WHAT?!
保健室
OH... THEN COULD YOU TAKE CARE OF HIM?
TAKE CARE OF HIS KNEE, THEN HAVE HIM LAY DOWN!
...
ピシャン
SHUT
...!!
HIZUO
12
SIGN: Nurse's Room

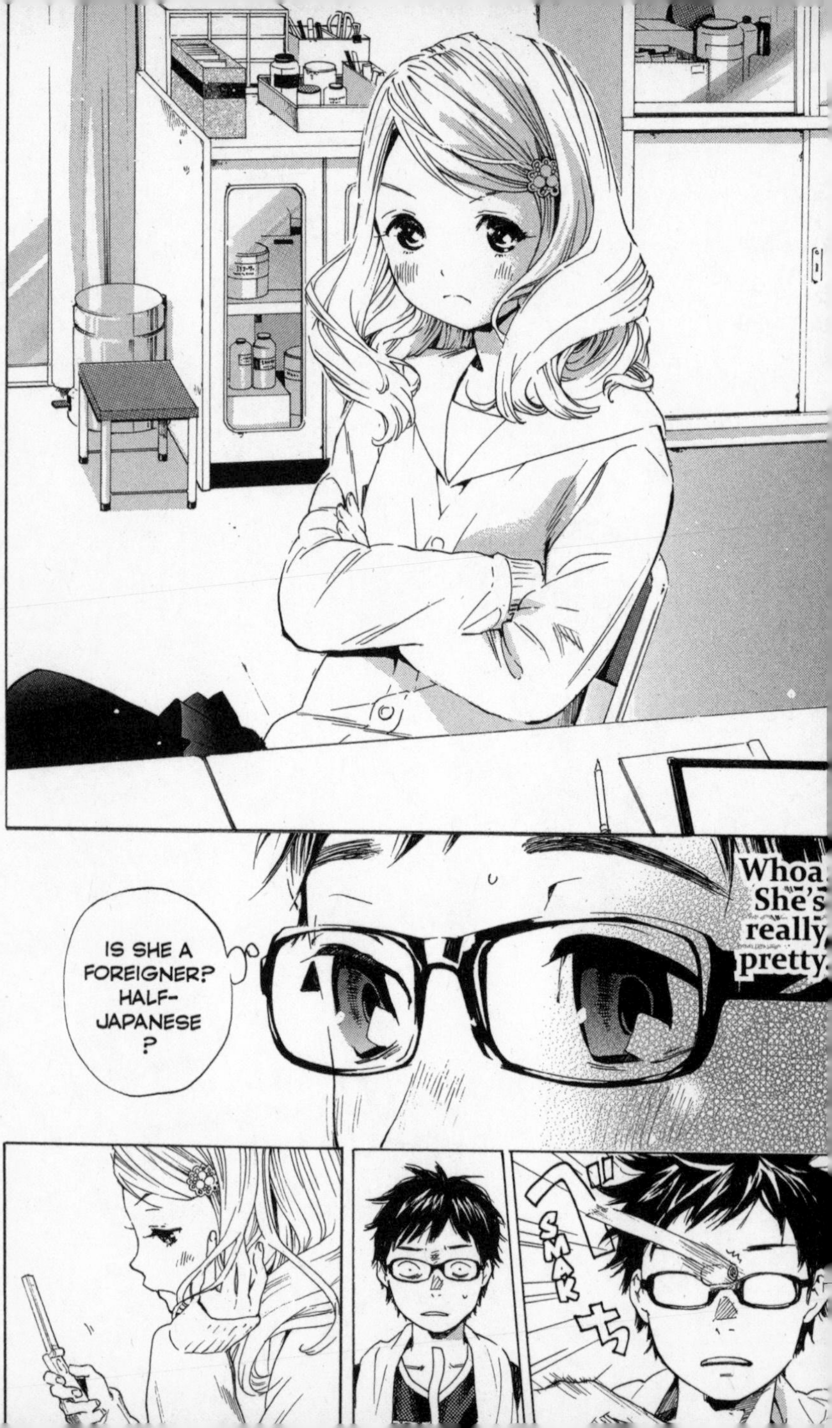
Whoa. She's really pretty.
IS SHE A FOREIGNER? HALF-JAPANESE?
SMAK
ち

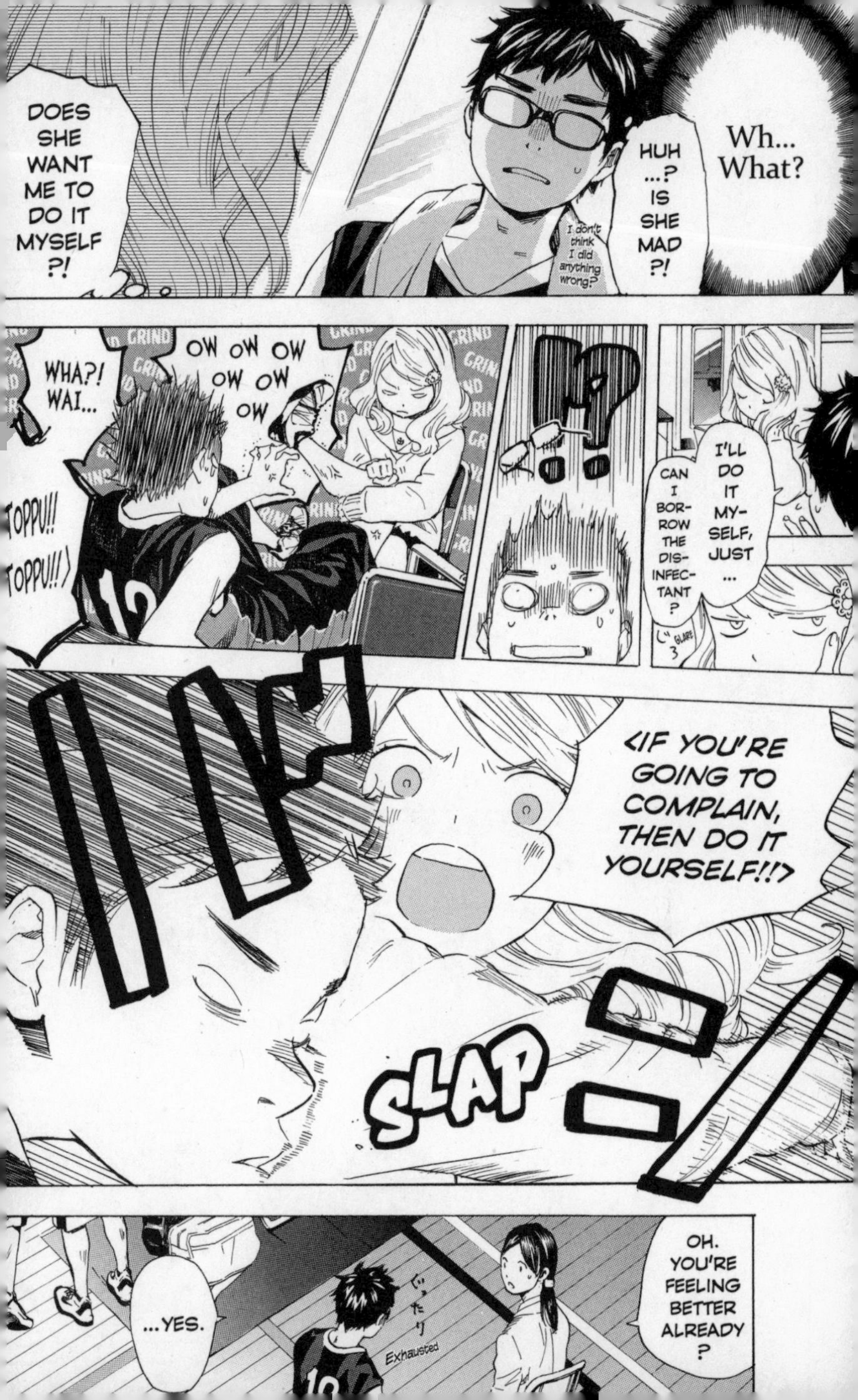
Wh... What?
HUH...? IS SHE MAD?!
I don't think I did anything wrong?
DOES SHE WANT ME TO DO IT MYSELF?!
I'LL DO IT MYSELF, JUST...
CAN I BORROW THE DISINFECTANT?
GLARE
!?
OW OW OW OW OW OW
WHA?! WAI...
TOPPU!! TOPPU!!>
<IF YOU'RE GOING TO COMPLAIN, THEN DO IT YOURSELF!!>
SLAP
OH. YOU'RE FEELING BETTER ALREADY?
...YES.
Exhausted

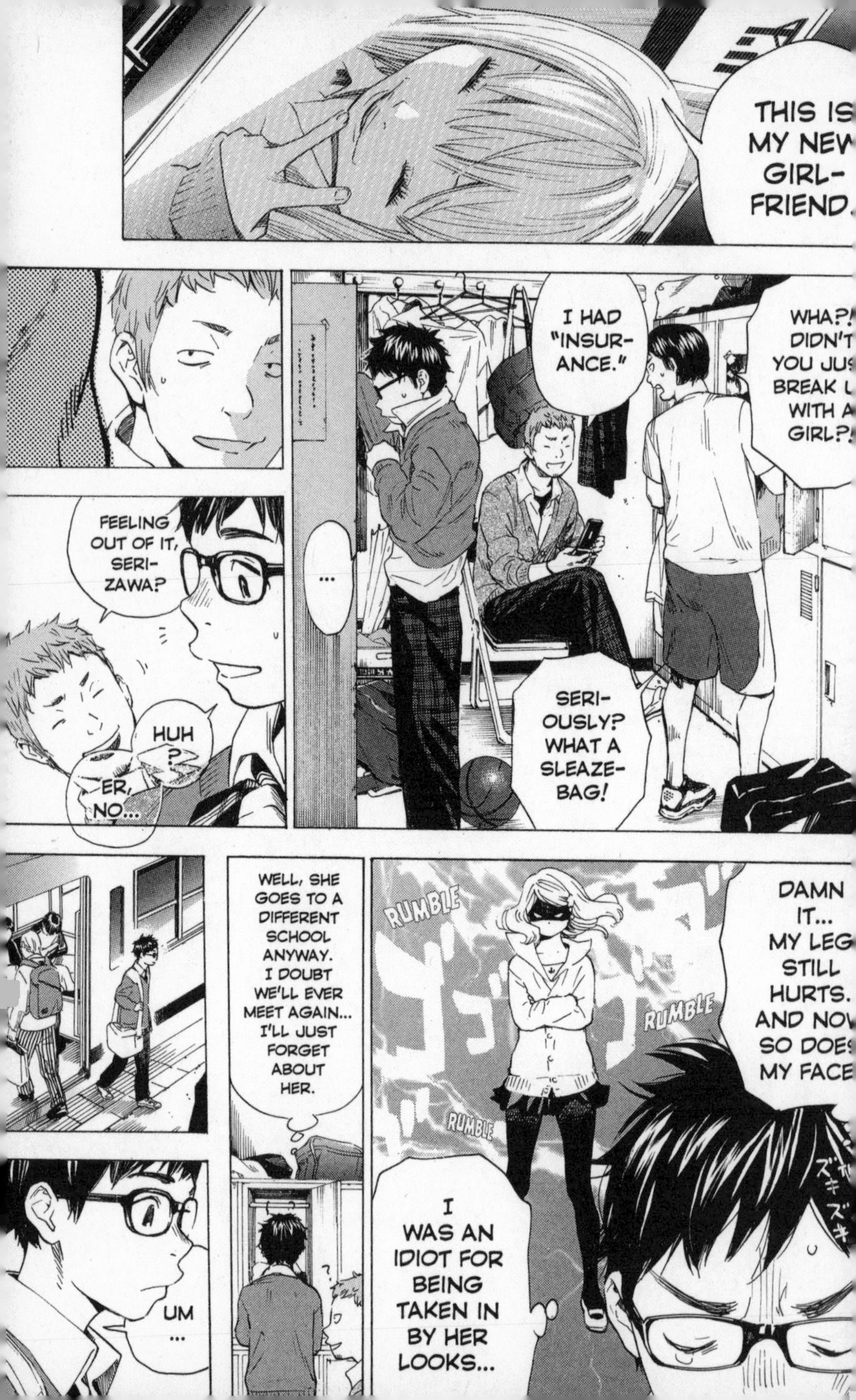

THIS IS MY NEW GIRL-FRIEND.
WHA?! DIDN'T YOU JUST BREAK UP WITH A GIRL?!
I HAD "INSURANCE."
SERI-OUSLY? WHAT A SLEAZE-BAG!
...
FEELING OUT OF IT, SERI-ZAWA?
HUH?
ER, NO...
DAMN IT... MY LEG STILL HURTS. AND NOW SO DOES MY FACE.
RUMBLE
RUMBLE
RUMBLE
I WAS AN IDIOT FOR BEING TAKEN IN BY HER LOOKS...
WELL, SHE GOES TO A DIFFERENT SCHOOL ANYWAY. I DOUBT WE'LL EVER MEET AGAIN... I'LL JUST FORGET ABOUT HER.
UM ...

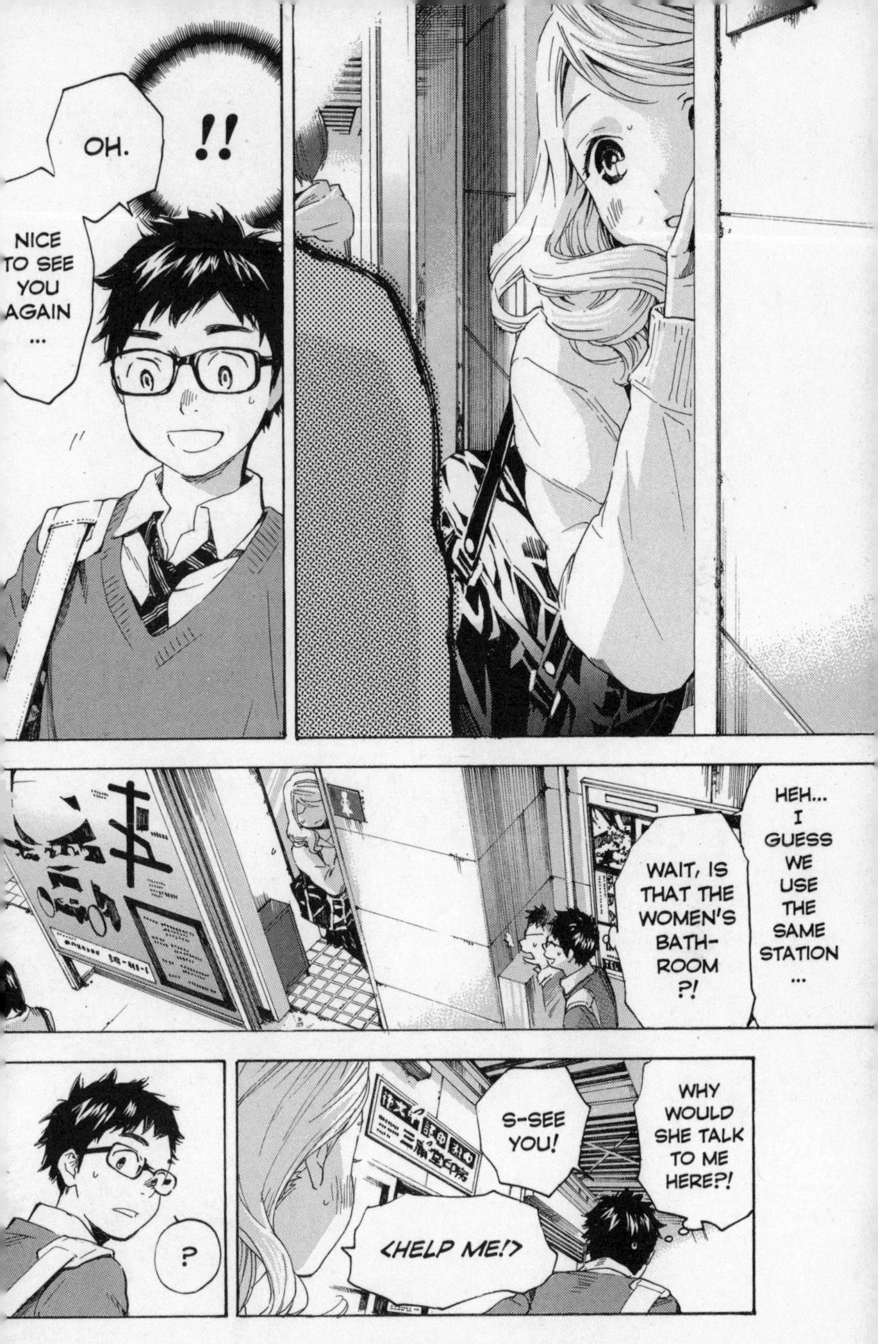
!!
OH.
NICE TO SEE YOU AGAIN ...
HEH... I GUESS WE USE THE SAME STATION ...
WAIT, IS THAT THE WOMEN'S BATH-ROOM ?!
WHY WOULD SHE TALK TO ME HERE?!
S-SEE YOU!
<HELP ME!>
?

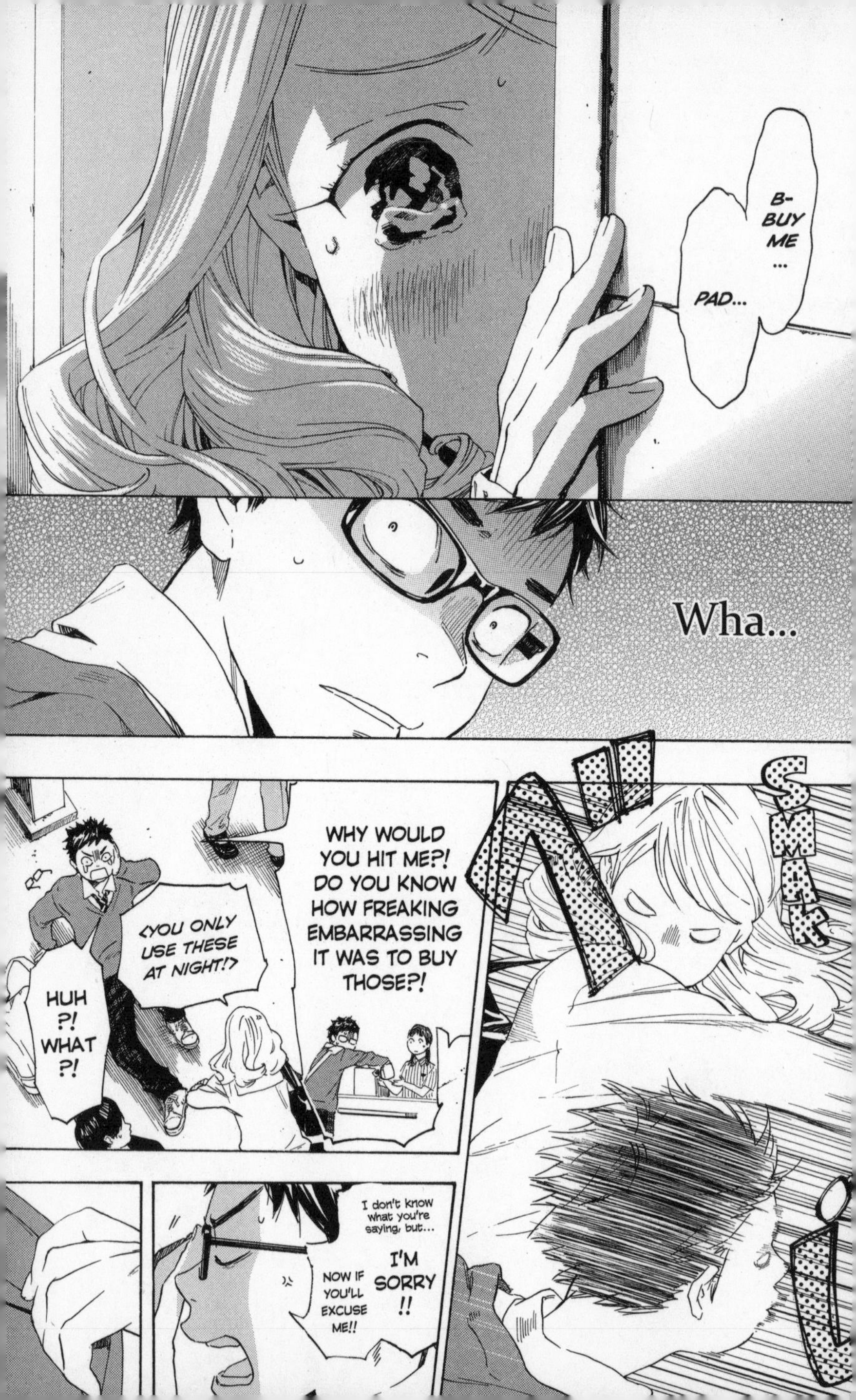
B-BUY ME ... PAD...
Wha...
WHY WOULD YOU HIT ME?! DO YOU KNOW HOW FREAKING EMBARRASSING IT WAS TO BUY THOSE?!
<YOU ONLY USE THESE AT NIGHT!>
HUH ?! WHAT ?!
I don't know what you're saying, but...
I'M SORRY !!
NOW IF YOU'LL EXCUSE ME!!

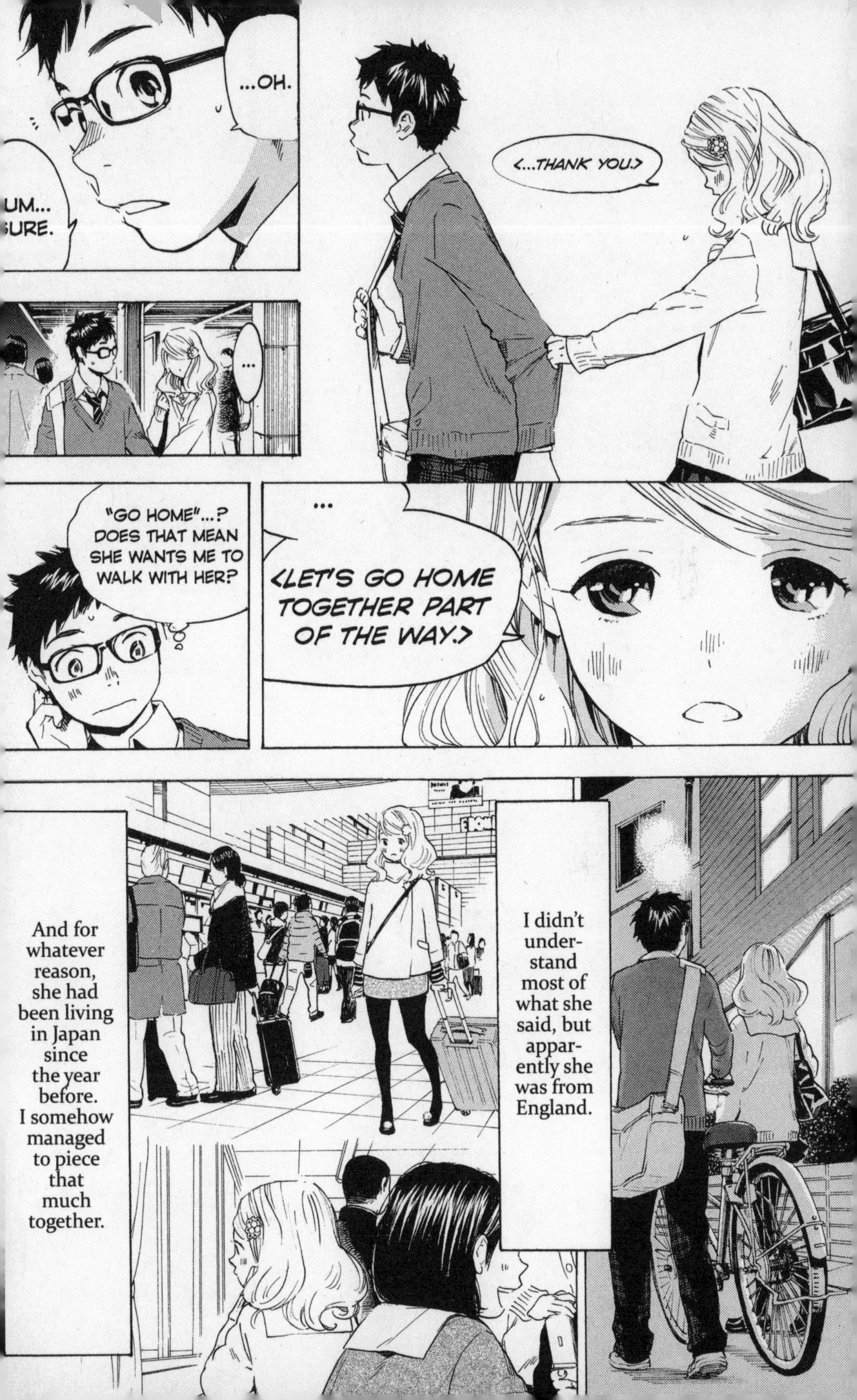
<...THANK YOU.>
...OH.
UM... SURE.
...
...
<LET'S GO HOME TOGETHER PART OF THE WAY.>
"GO HOME"...? DOES THAT MEAN SHE WANTS ME TO WALK WITH HER?
I didn't understand most of what she said, but apparently she was from England.
And for whatever reason, she had been living in Japan since the year before. I somehow managed to piece that much together.

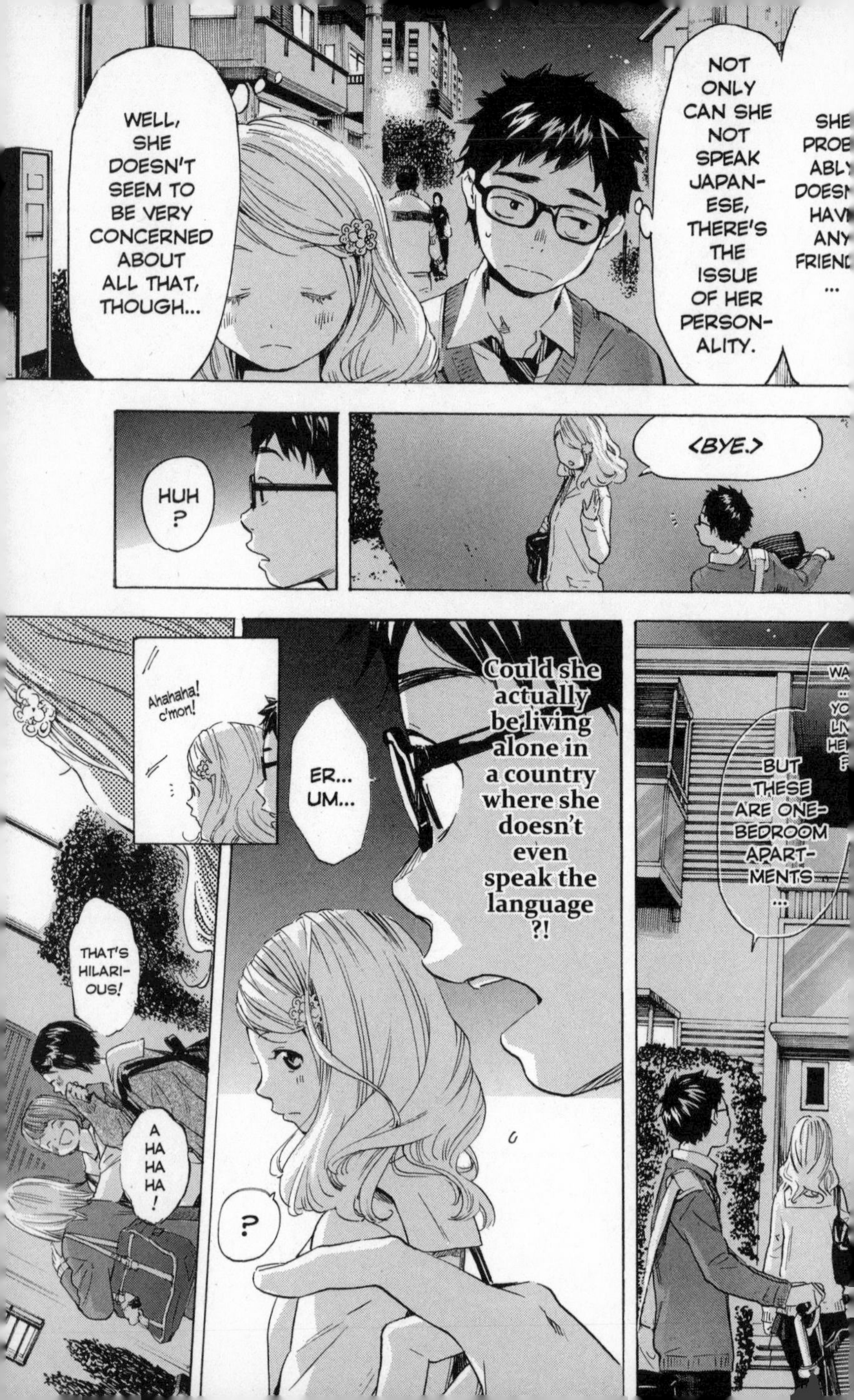
NOT ONLY CAN SHE NOT SPEAK JAPANESE, THERE'S THE ISSUE OF HER PERSONALITY.
WELL, SHE DOESN'T SEEM TO BE VERY CONCERNED ABOUT ALL THAT, THOUGH...
<BYE.>
HUH?
BUT THESE ARE ONE-BEDROOM APARTMENTS...
Could she actually be living alone in a country where she doesn't even speak the language?!
ER... UM...
?
Ahahaha! c'mon!
THAT'S HILARIOUS!
A HA HA HA!

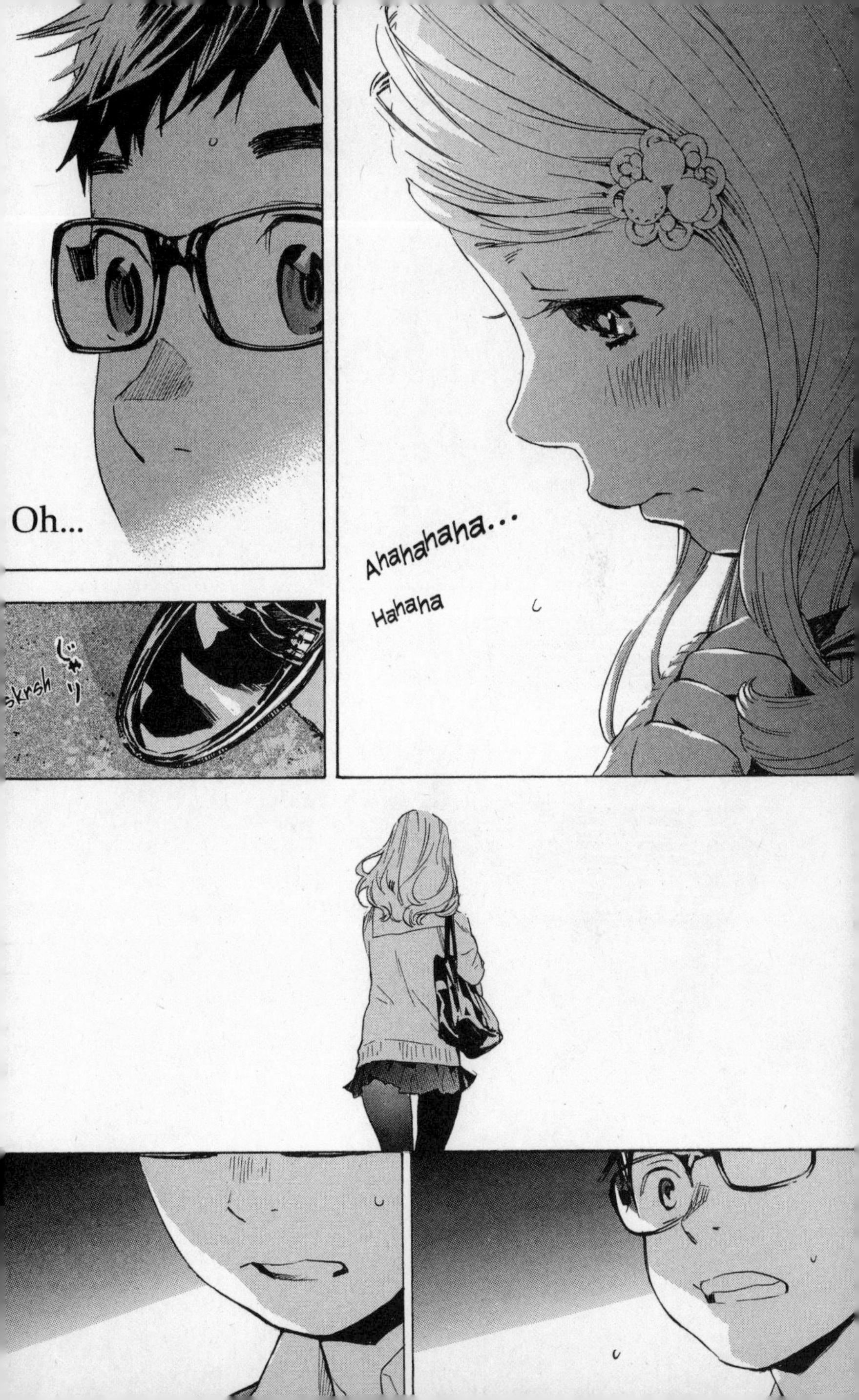
Ahahahaha...
Hahaha
Oh...
じゃり
skrsh

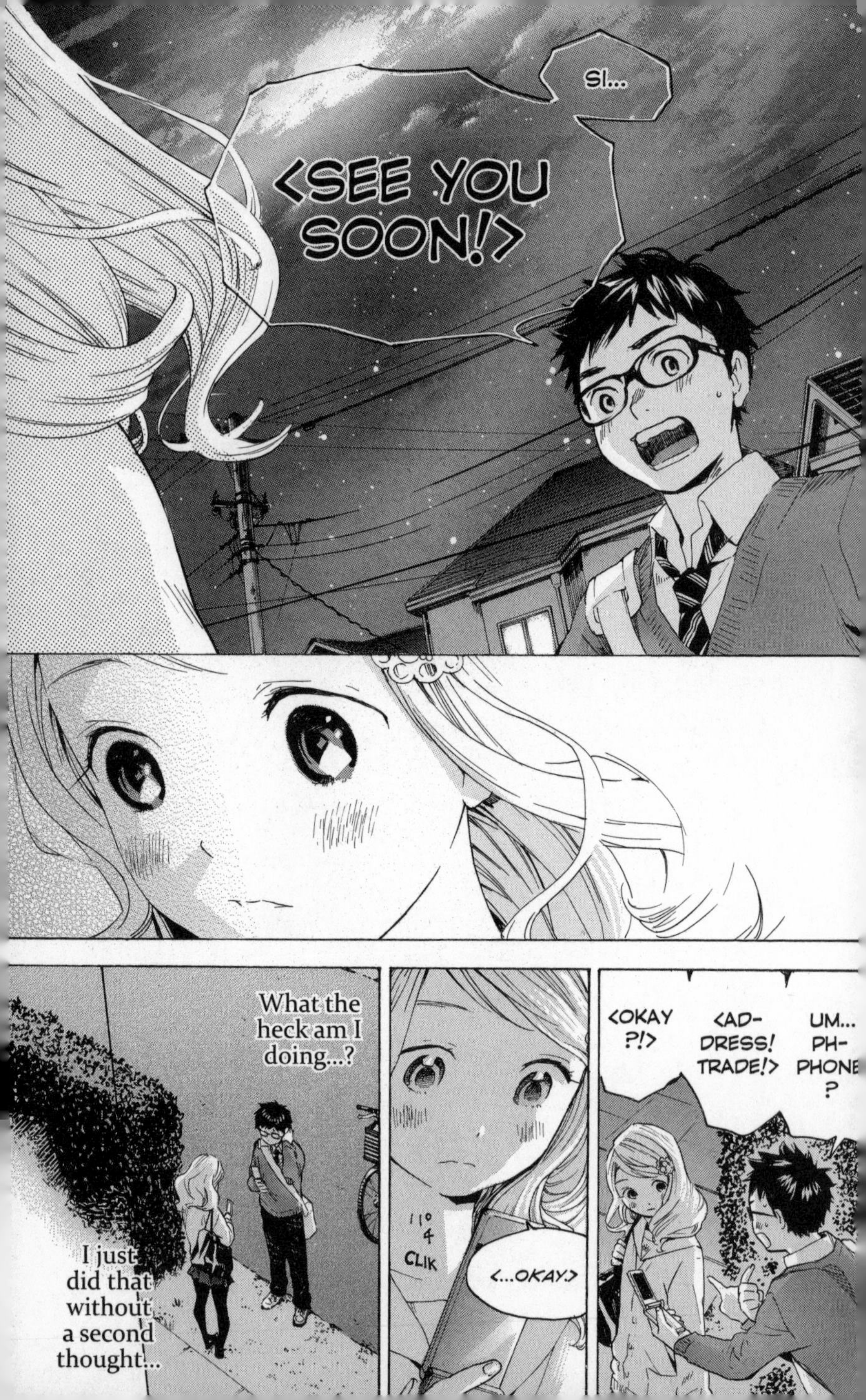
SI...
<SEE YOU SOON!>
UM... PH-PHONE ?
<AD-DRESS! TRADE!>
<OKAY ?!>
CLIK
<...OKAY.>
What the heck am I doing...?
I just did that without a second thought...

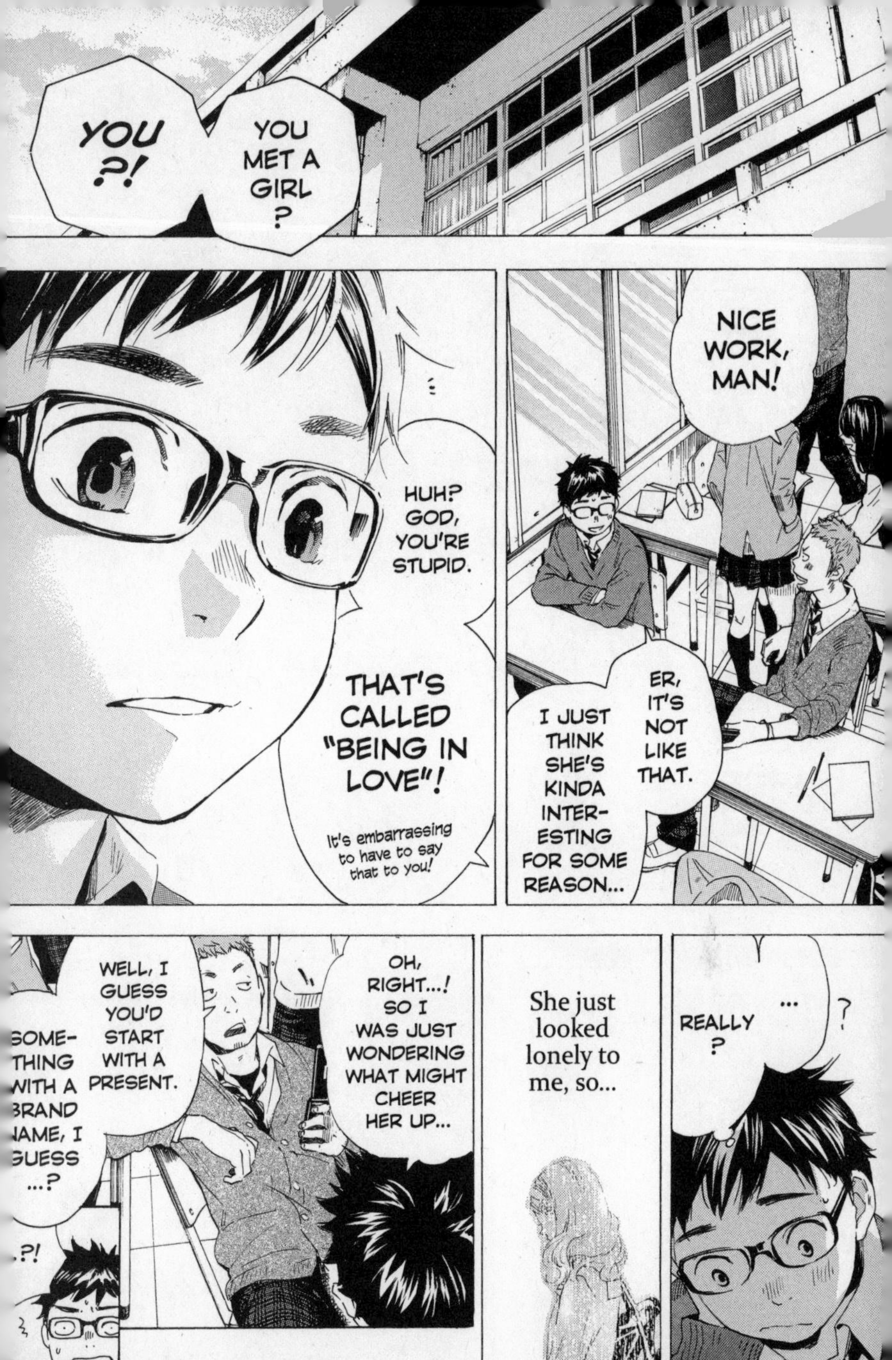
YOU MET A GIRL?
YOU ?!
NICE WORK, MAN!
ER, IT'S NOT LIKE THAT.
I JUST THINK SHE'S KINDA INTER-ESTING FOR SOME REASON...
HUH? GOD, YOU'RE STUPID.
THAT'S CALLED "BEING IN LOVE"!
It's embarrassing to have to say that to you!
...?
REALLY?
She just looked lonely to me, so...
OH, RIGHT...! SO I WAS JUST WONDERING WHAT MIGHT CHEER HER UP...
WELL, I GUESS YOU'D START WITH A PRESENT.
SOME-THING WITH A BRAND NAME, I GUESS ...?
.?!

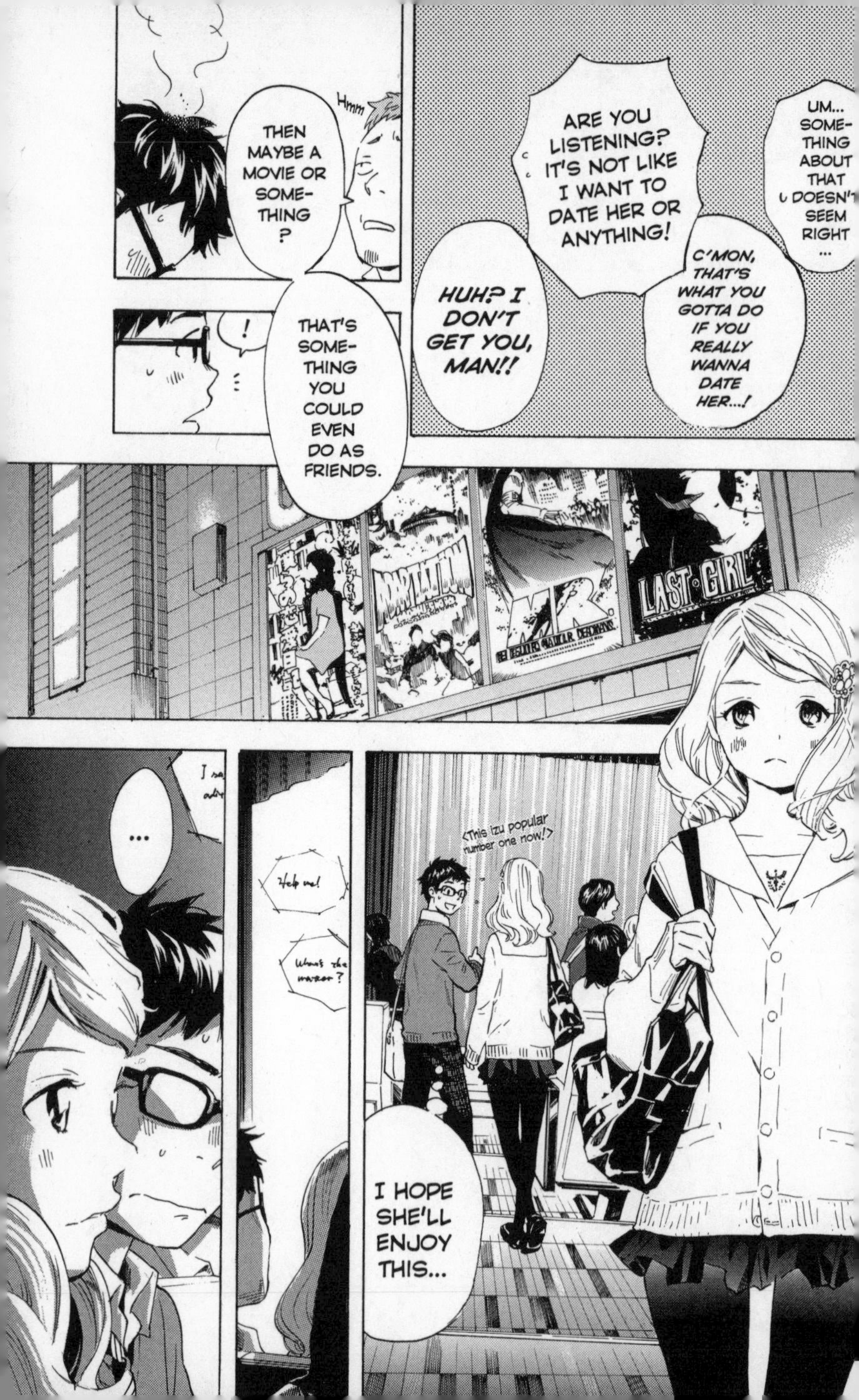
UM... SOMETHING ABOUT THAT DOESN'T SEEM RIGHT...
ARE YOU LISTENING? IT'S NOT LIKE I WANT TO DATE HER OR ANYTHING!
C'MON, THAT'S WHAT YOU GOTTA DO IF YOU REALLY WANNA DATE HER...!
HUH? I DON'T GET YOU, MAN!!
Hmm
THEN MAYBE A MOVIE OR SOMETHING?
!
THAT'S SOMETHING YOU COULD EVEN DO AS FRIENDS.
LAST GIRL
<This izu popular number one now!>
I HOPE SHE'LL ENJOY THIS...
Help me!
What's the matter?
...

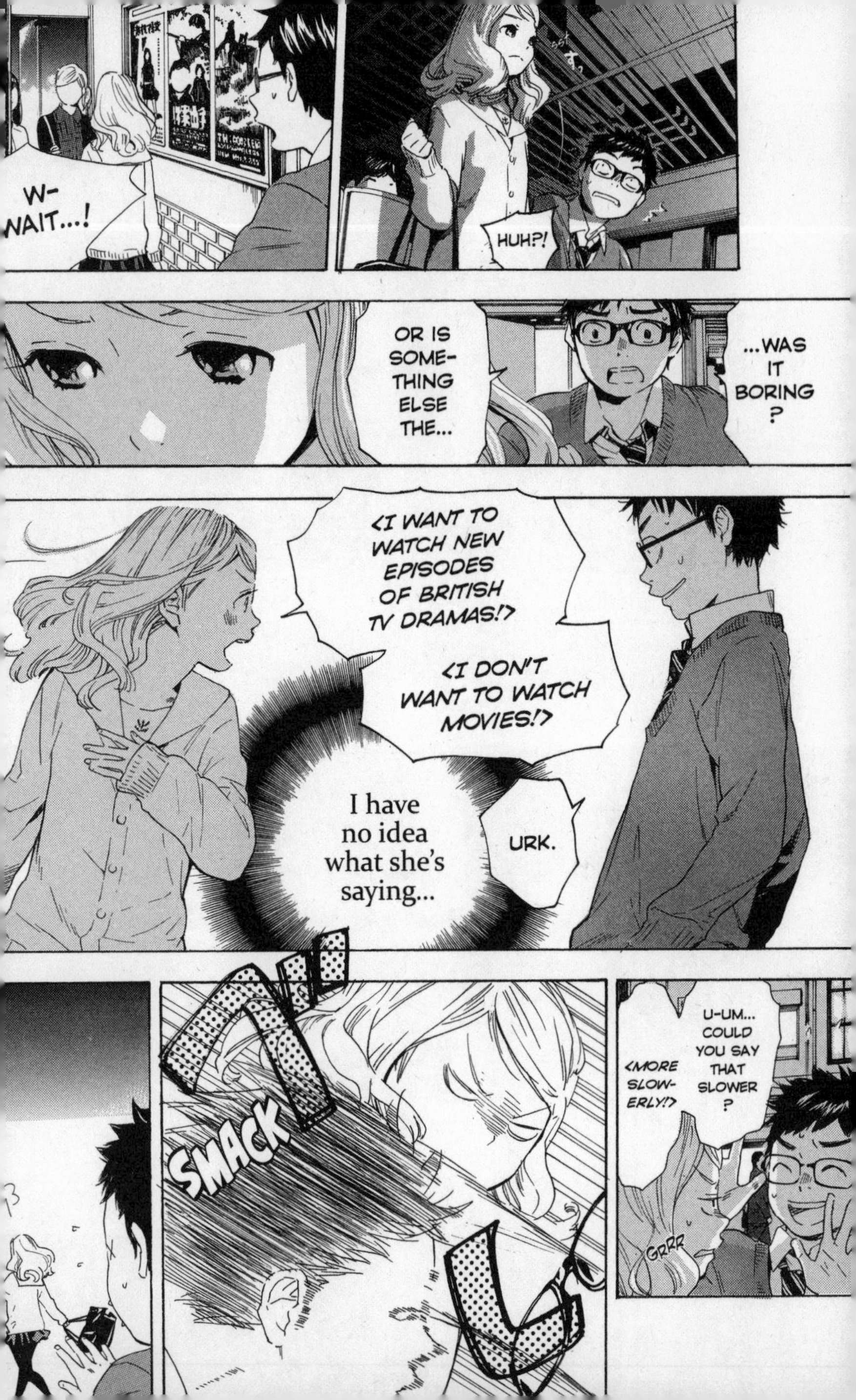
HUH?!
W- WAIT...!
...WAS IT BORING?
OR IS SOMETHING ELSE THE...
<I WANT TO WATCH NEW EPISODES OF BRITISH TV DRAMAS!>
<I DON'T WANT TO WATCH MOVIES!>
URK.
I have no idea what she's saying...
U-UM... COULD YOU SAY THAT SLOWER?
<MORE SLOW-ERLY!>
GRRR
SMACK

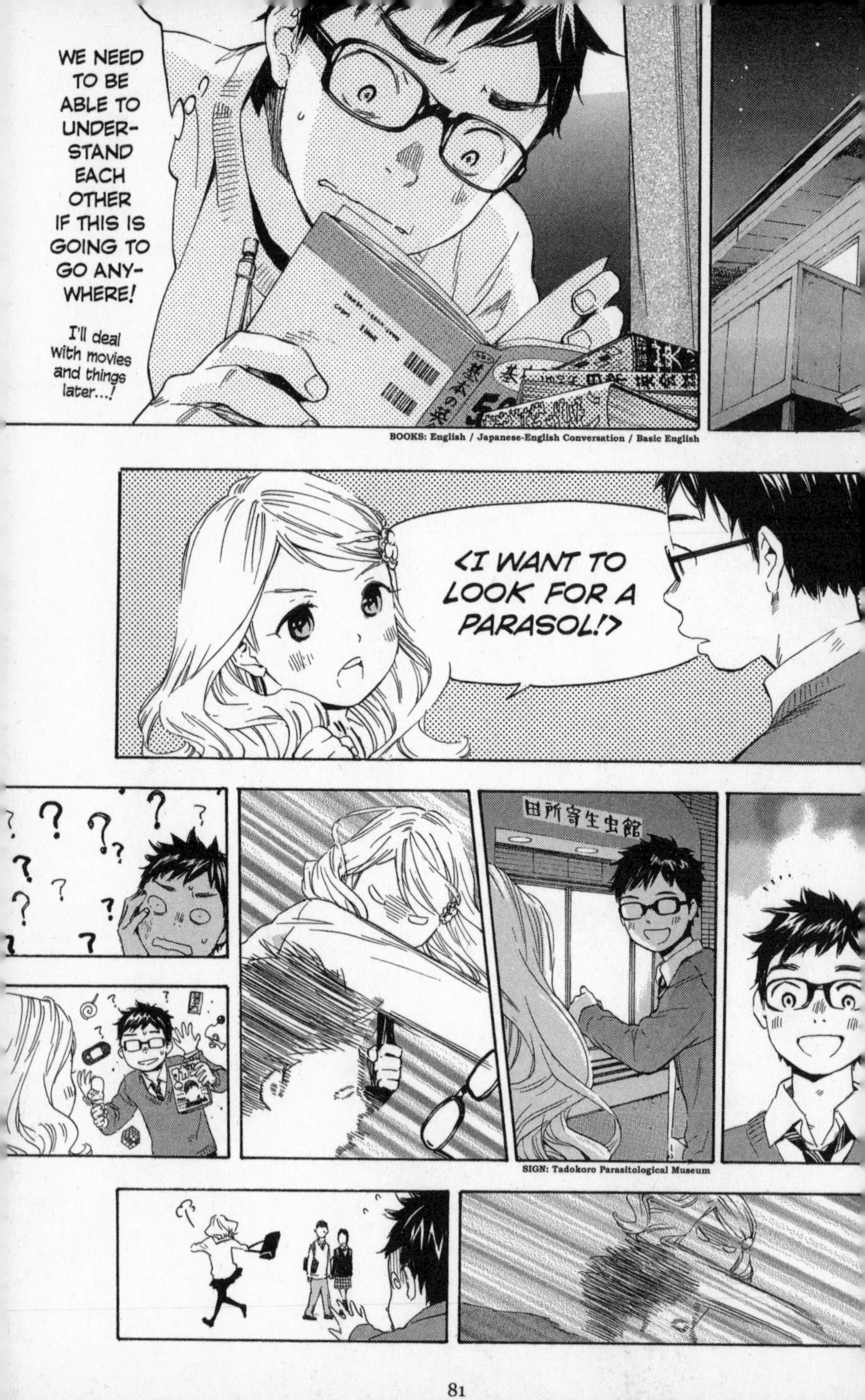
WE NEED TO BE ABLE TO UNDERSTAND EACH OTHER IF THIS IS GOING TO GO ANYWHERE!
I'll deal with movies and things later...!
BOOKS: English / Japanese-English Conversation / Basic English
<I WANT TO LOOK FOR A PARASOL!>
SIGN: Tadokoro Parasitological Museum

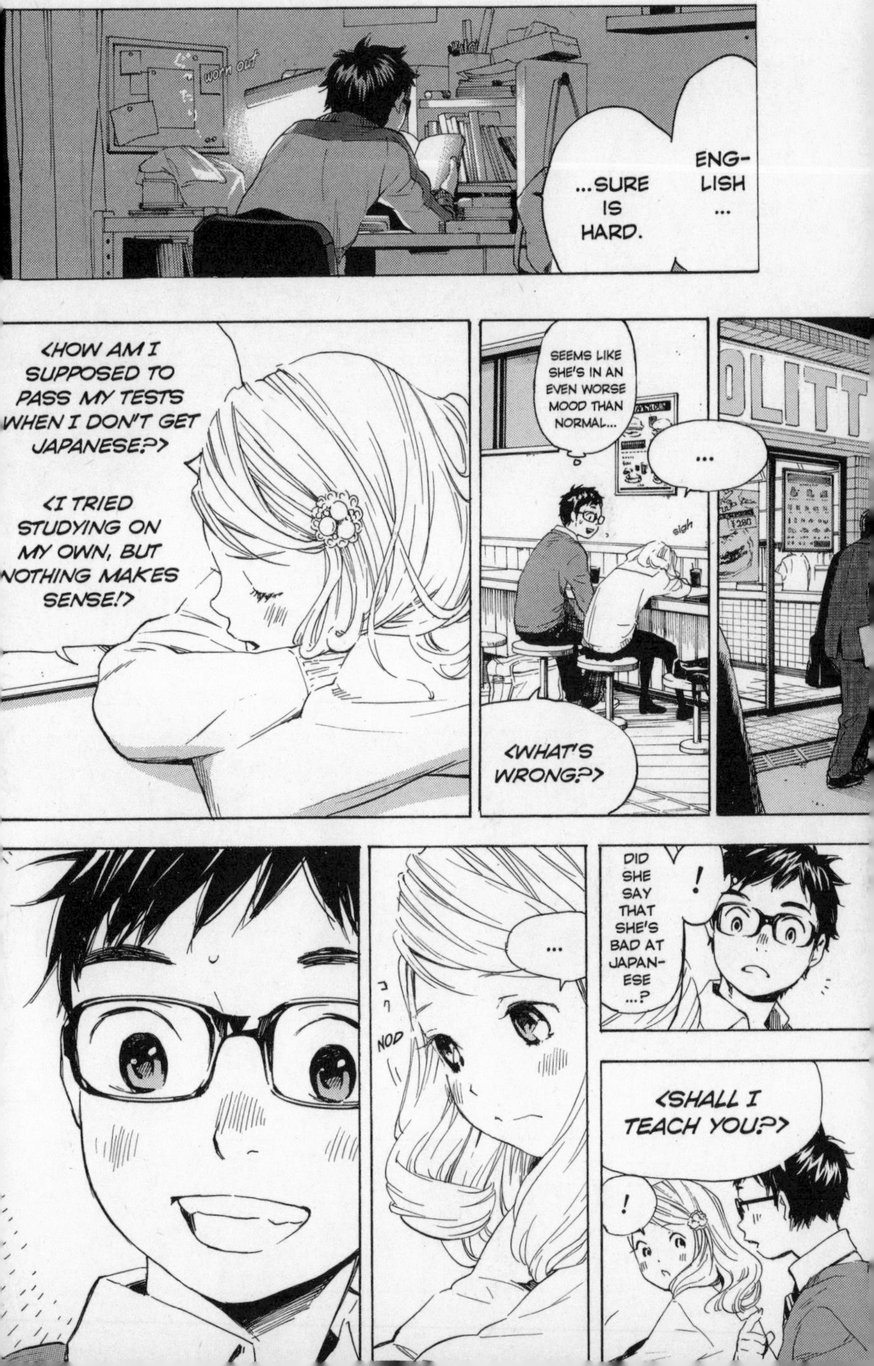
worn out
ENG-LISH...
...SURE IS HARD.
SEEMS LIKE SHE'S IN AN EVEN WORSE MOOD THAN NORMAL...
...
sigh
<WHAT'S WRONG?>
<HOW AM I SUPPOSED TO PASS MY TESTS WHEN I DON'T GET JAPANESE?>
<I TRIED STUDYING ON MY OWN, BUT NOTHING MAKES SENSE!>
!
DID SHE SAY THAT SHE'S BAD AT JAPANESE...?
<SHALL I TEACH YOU?>
!
...
NOD

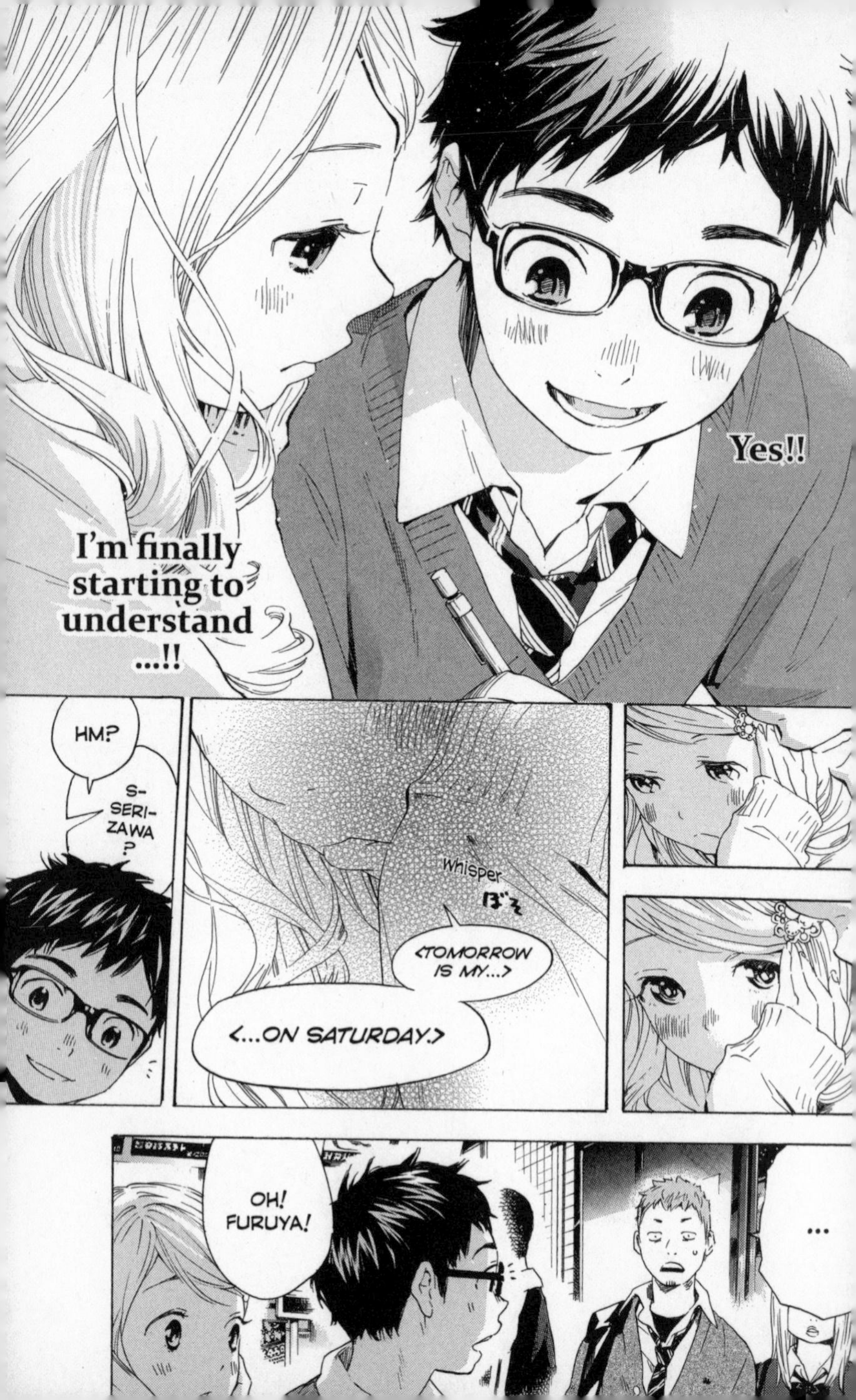
Yes!!
I'm finally starting to understand ...!!
whisper
ぼそ
<TOMORROW IS MY...>
<...ON SATURDAY.>
HM?
S-SERIZAWA?
...
OH! FURUYA!

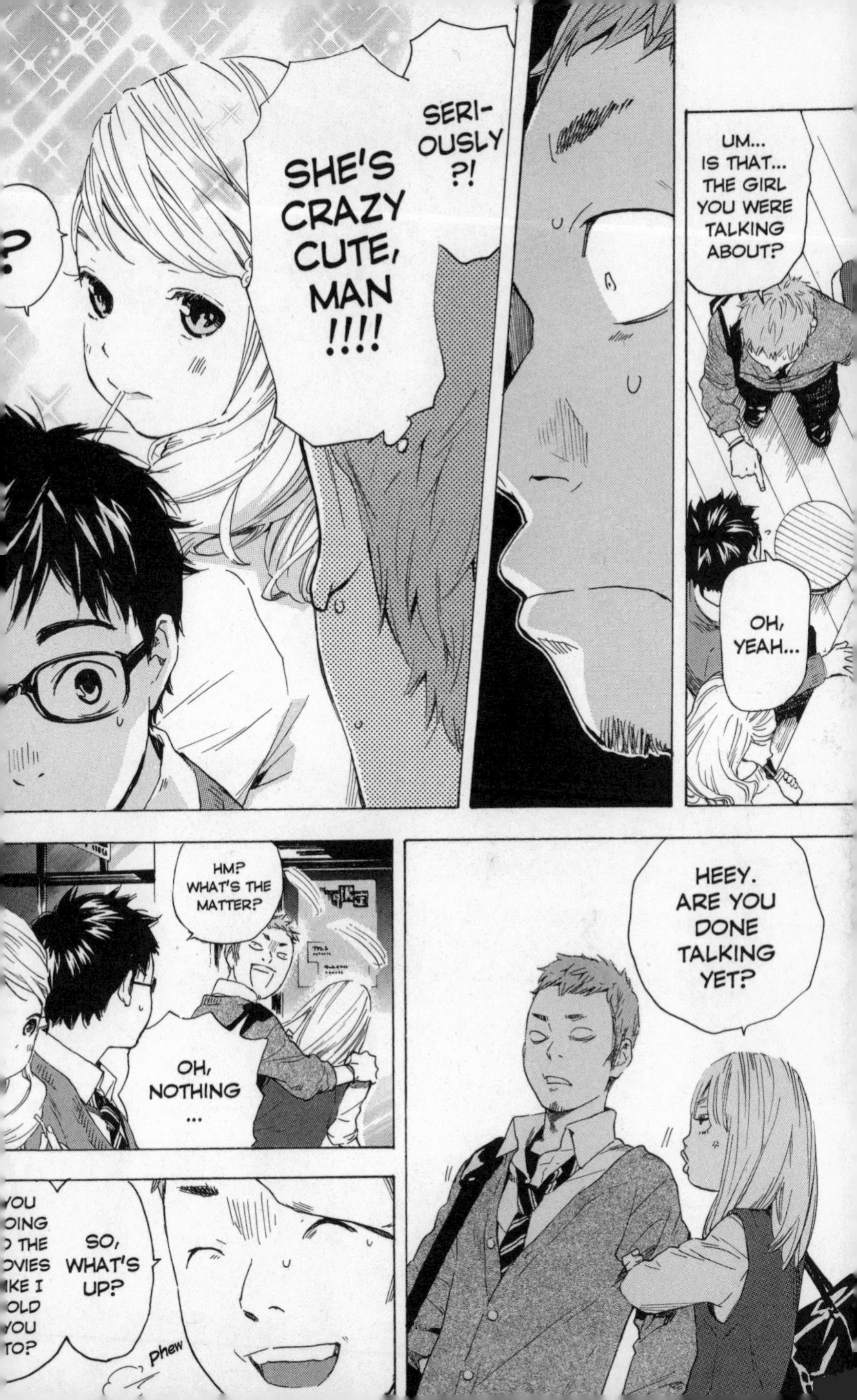
UM... IS THAT... THE GIRL YOU WERE TALKING ABOUT?
OH, YEAH...
SERI-OUSLY?!
SHE'S CRAZY CUTE, MAN!!!!
?
HEEY. ARE YOU DONE TALKING YET?
HM? WHAT'S THE MATTER?
OH, NOTHING...
SO, WHAT'S UP?
YOU OING THE OVIES IKE I OLD YOU TO?
phew

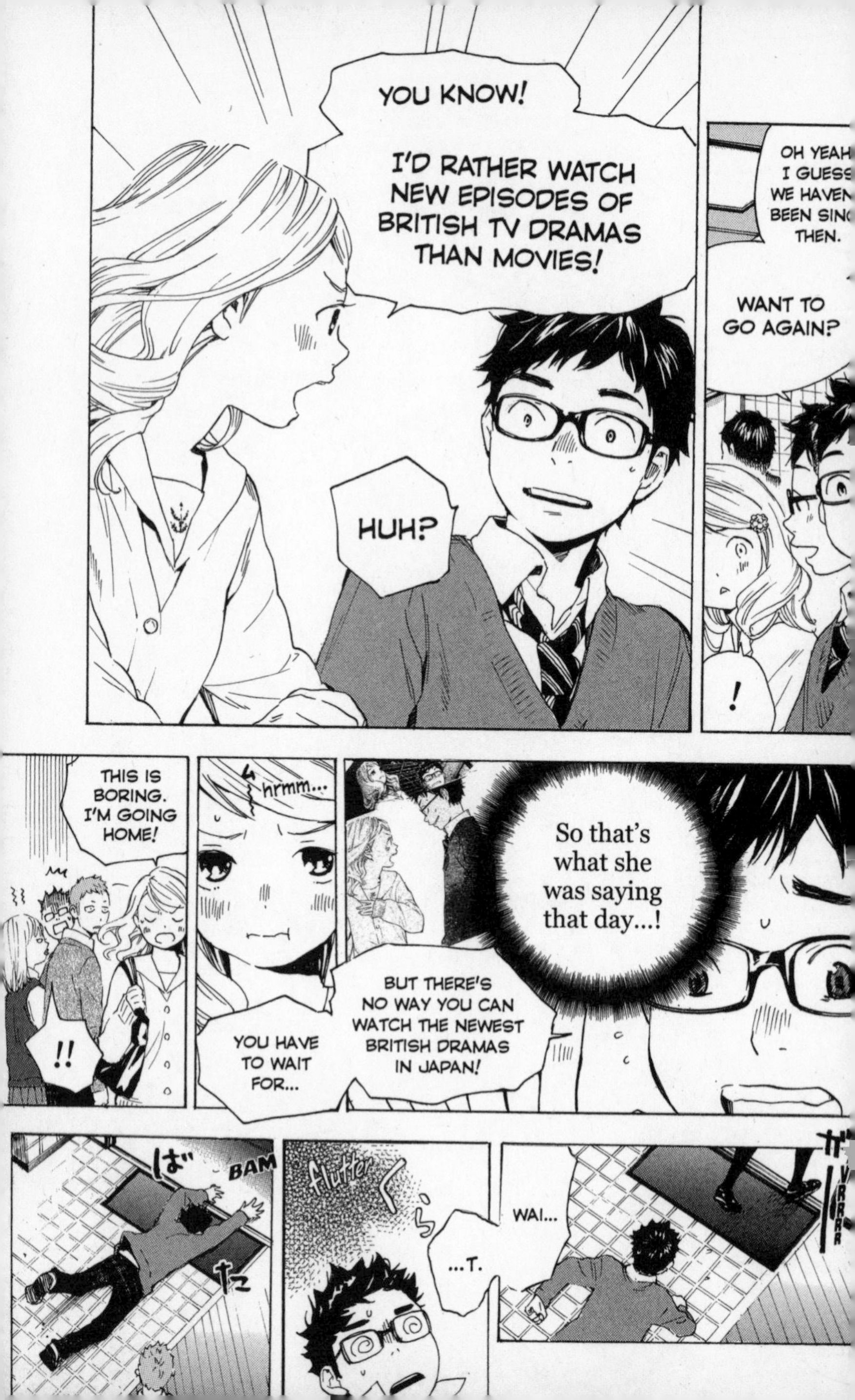
OH YEAH I GUESS WE HAVEN BEEN SINC THEN.
WANT TO GO AGAIN?
!
YOU KNOW!
I'D RATHER WATCH NEW EPISODES OF BRITISH TV DRAMAS THAN MOVIES!
HUH?
So that's what she was saying that day...!
BUT THERE'S NO WAY YOU CAN WATCH THE NEWEST BRITISH DRAMAS IN JAPAN!
YOU HAVE TO WAIT FOR...
hrmm...
THIS IS BORING. I'M GOING HOME!
!!
VRRRR
WAI...
flutter
...T.
BAM

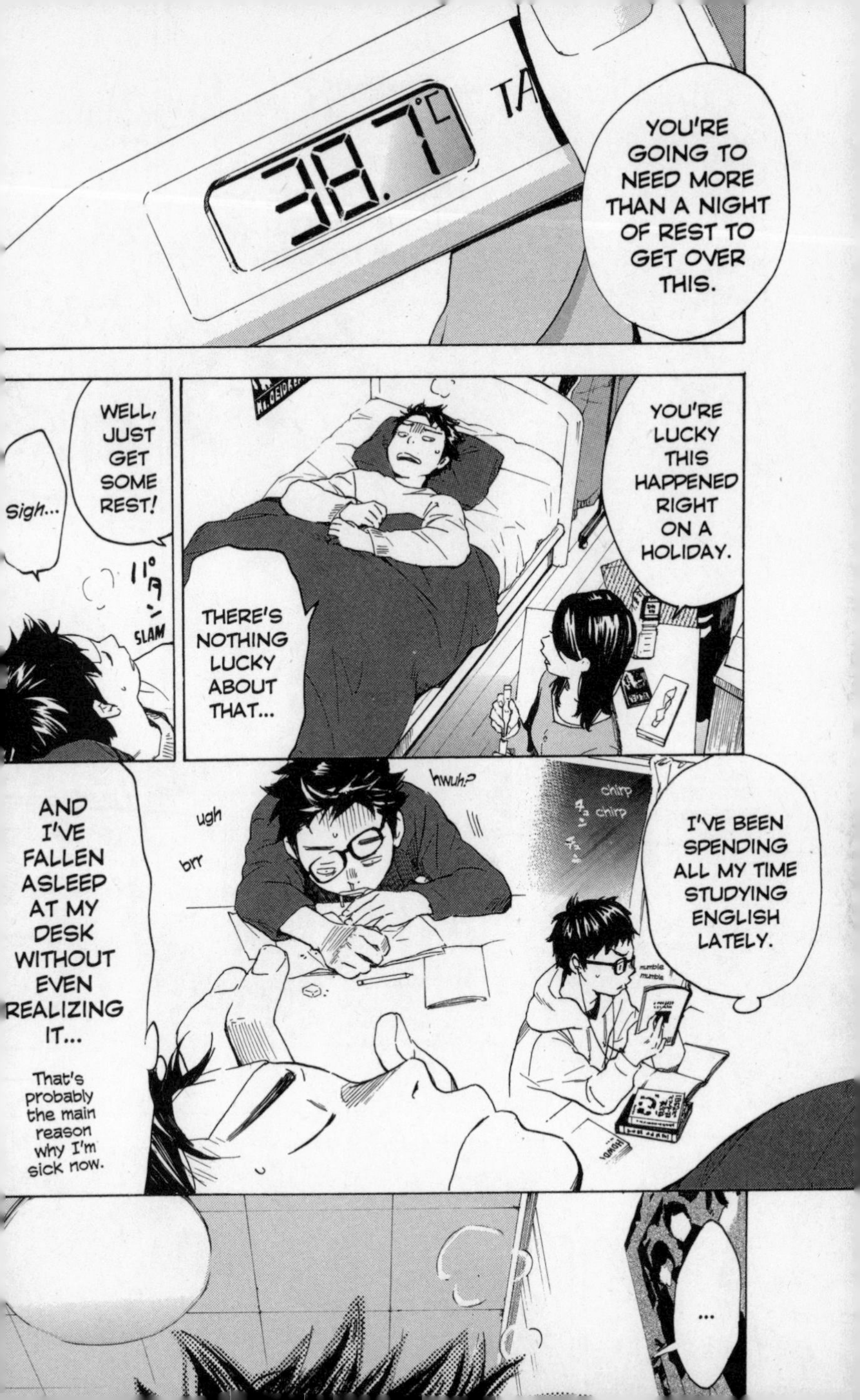
38.7°C
TA
YOU'RE GOING TO NEED MORE THAN A NIGHT OF REST TO GET OVER THIS.
YOU'RE LUCKY THIS HAPPENED RIGHT ON A HOLIDAY.
THERE'S NOTHING LUCKY ABOUT THAT...
WELL, JUST GET SOME REST!
Sigh...
SLAM
I'VE BEEN SPENDING ALL MY TIME STUDYING ENGLISH LATELY.
mumble mumble
chirp chirp
hwuh?
ugh
brr
AND I'VE FALLEN ASLEEP AT MY DESK WITHOUT EVEN REALIZING IT...
That's probably the main reason why I'm sick now.
...

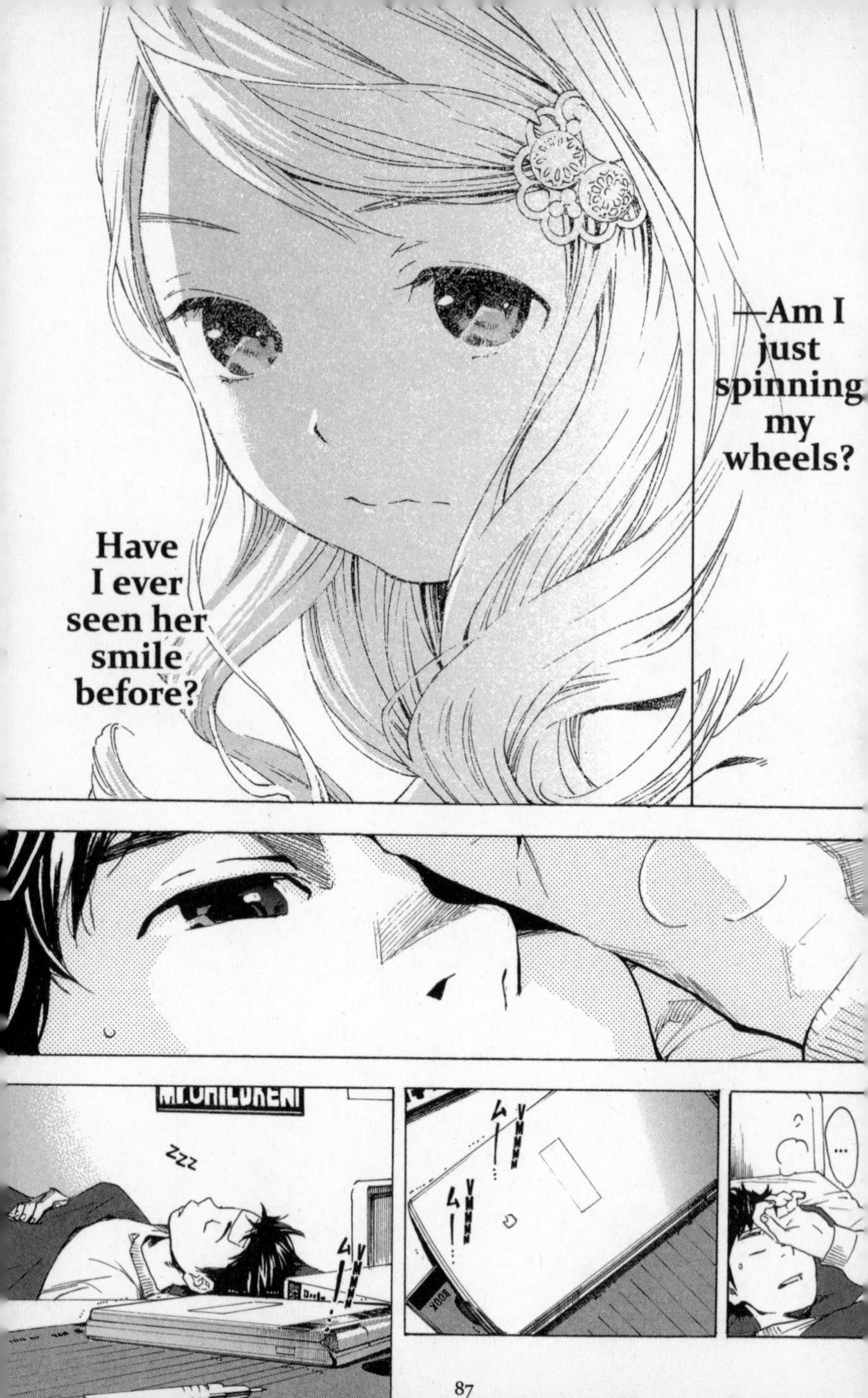
—Am I just spinning my wheels?
Have I ever seen her smile before?
...
ZZZ

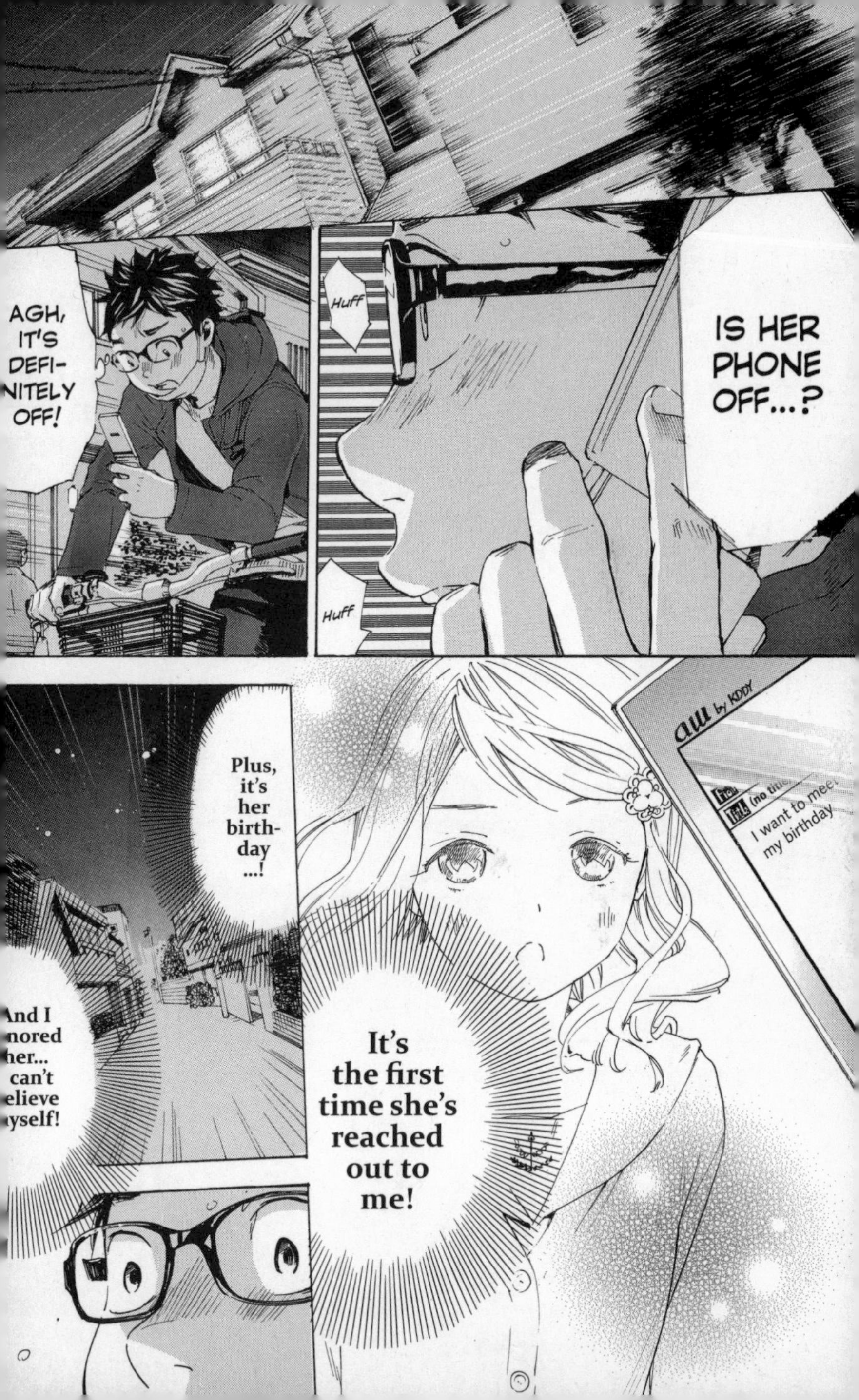

IS HER PHONE OFF...?
Huff
Huff
AGH, IT'S DEFINITELY OFF!
au by KDDY
(no title
I want to mee
my birthday
It's the first time she's reached out to me!
Plus, it's her birthday...!
And I
nored
her...
can't
elieve
yself!

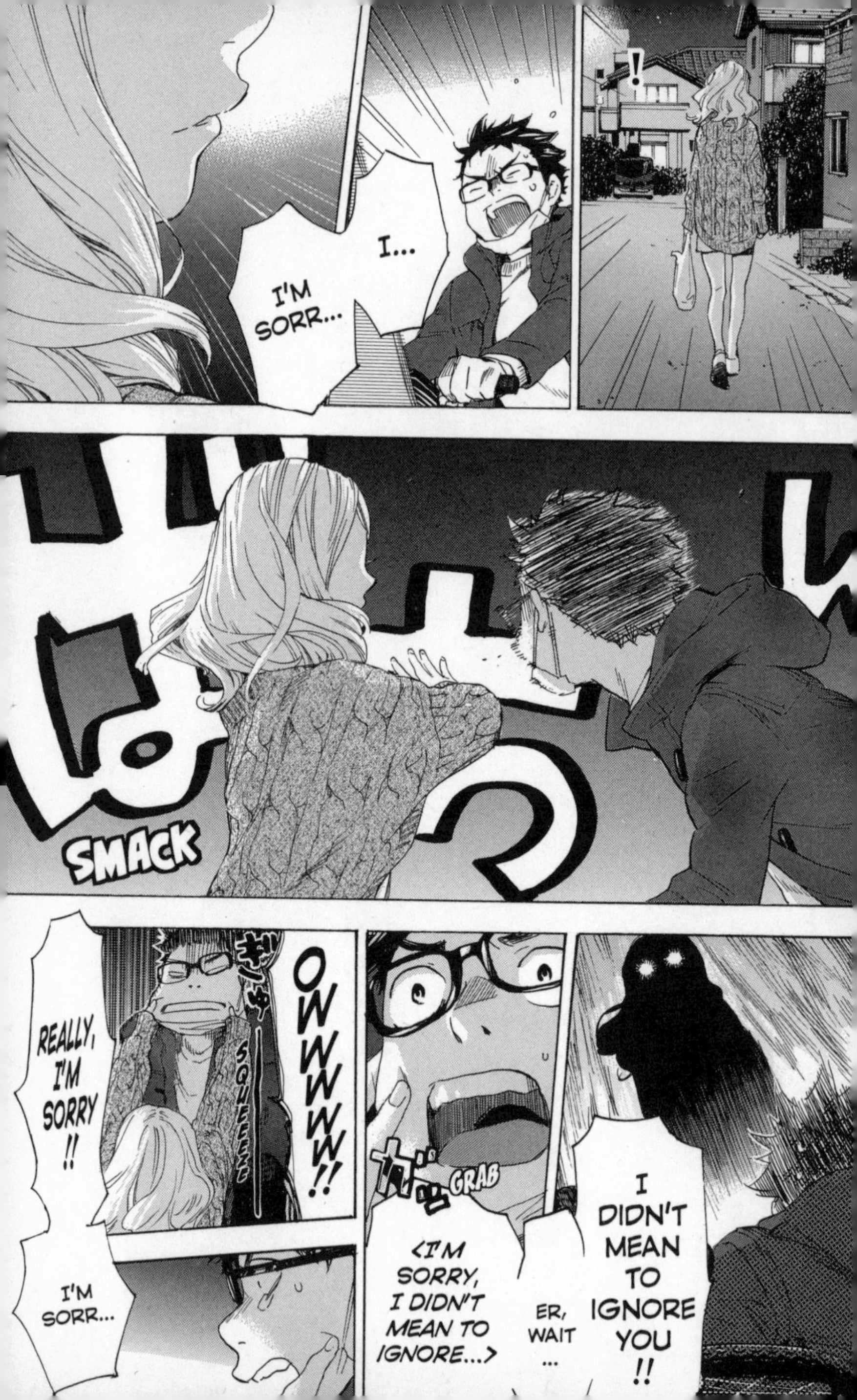
!
I...
I'M SORR...
SMACK
I DIDN'T MEAN TO IGNORE YOU !!
ER, WAIT ...
GRAB
<I'M SORRY, I DIDN'T MEAN TO IGNORE...>
OWWWWWW!!
SQUEEEZE
REALLY, I'M SORRY !!
I'M SORR...

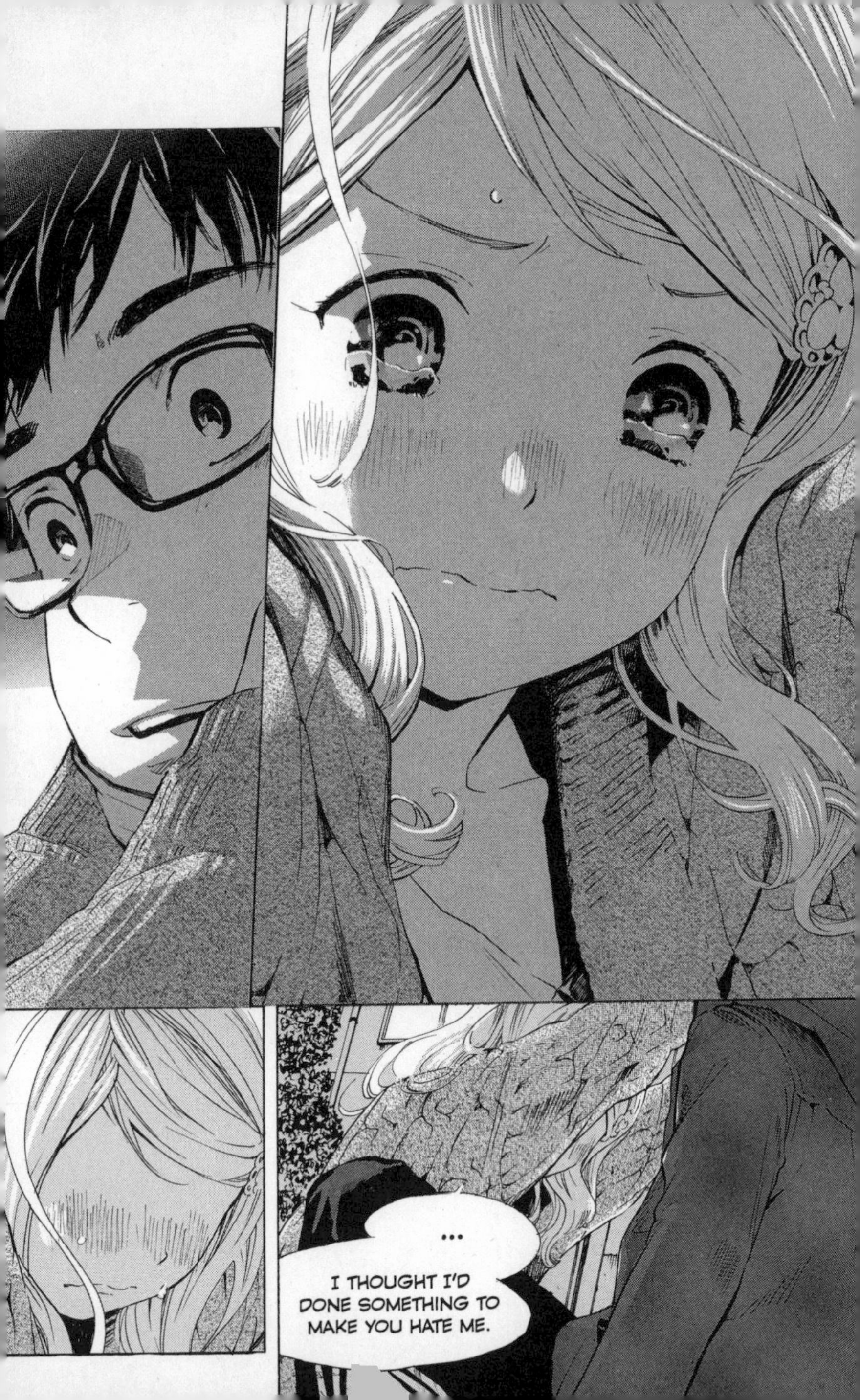
...
I THOUGHT I'D DONE SOMETHING TO MAKE YOU HATE ME.

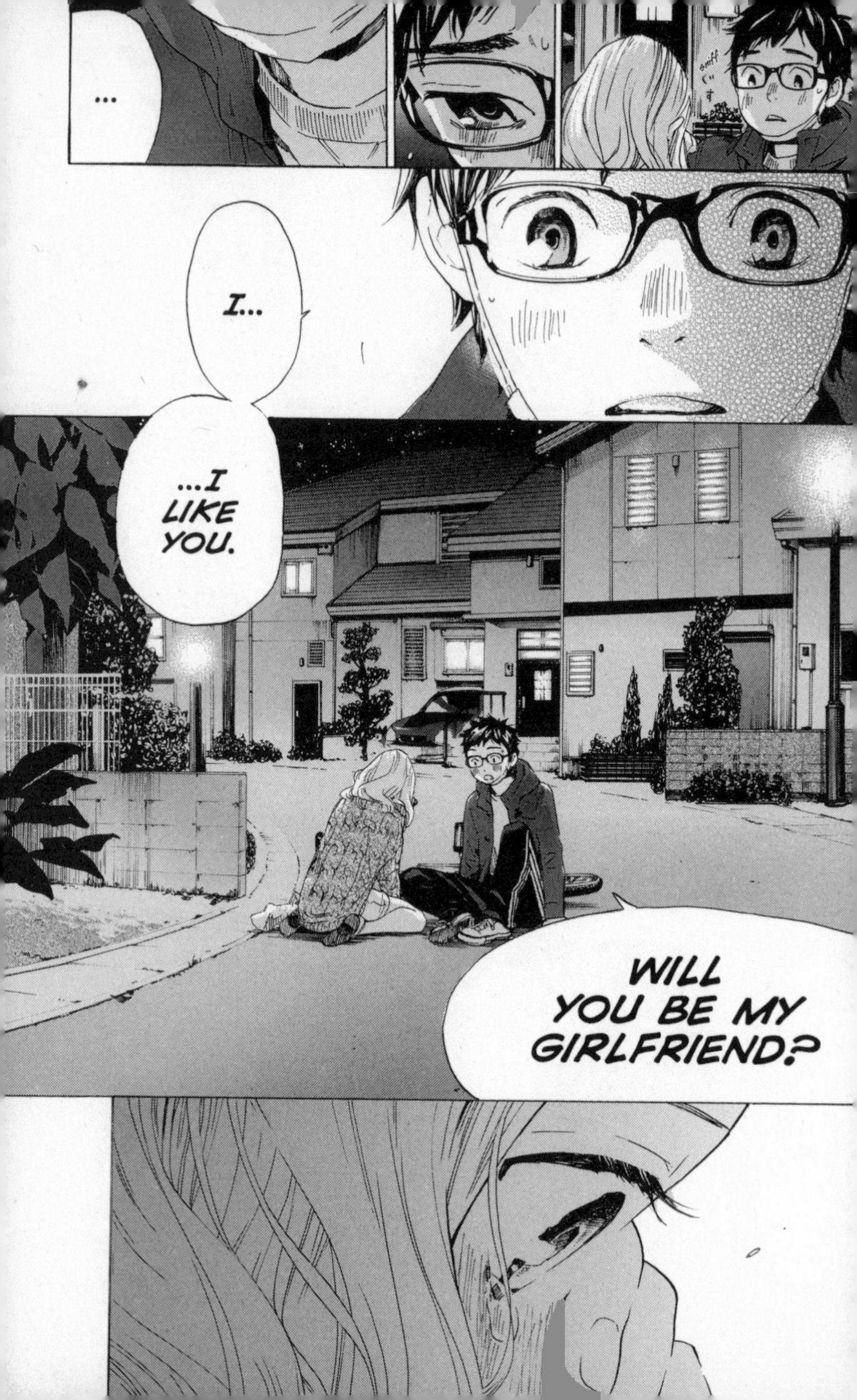
sniff
...
I...
...I LIKE YOU.
WILL YOU BE MY GIRLFRIEND?

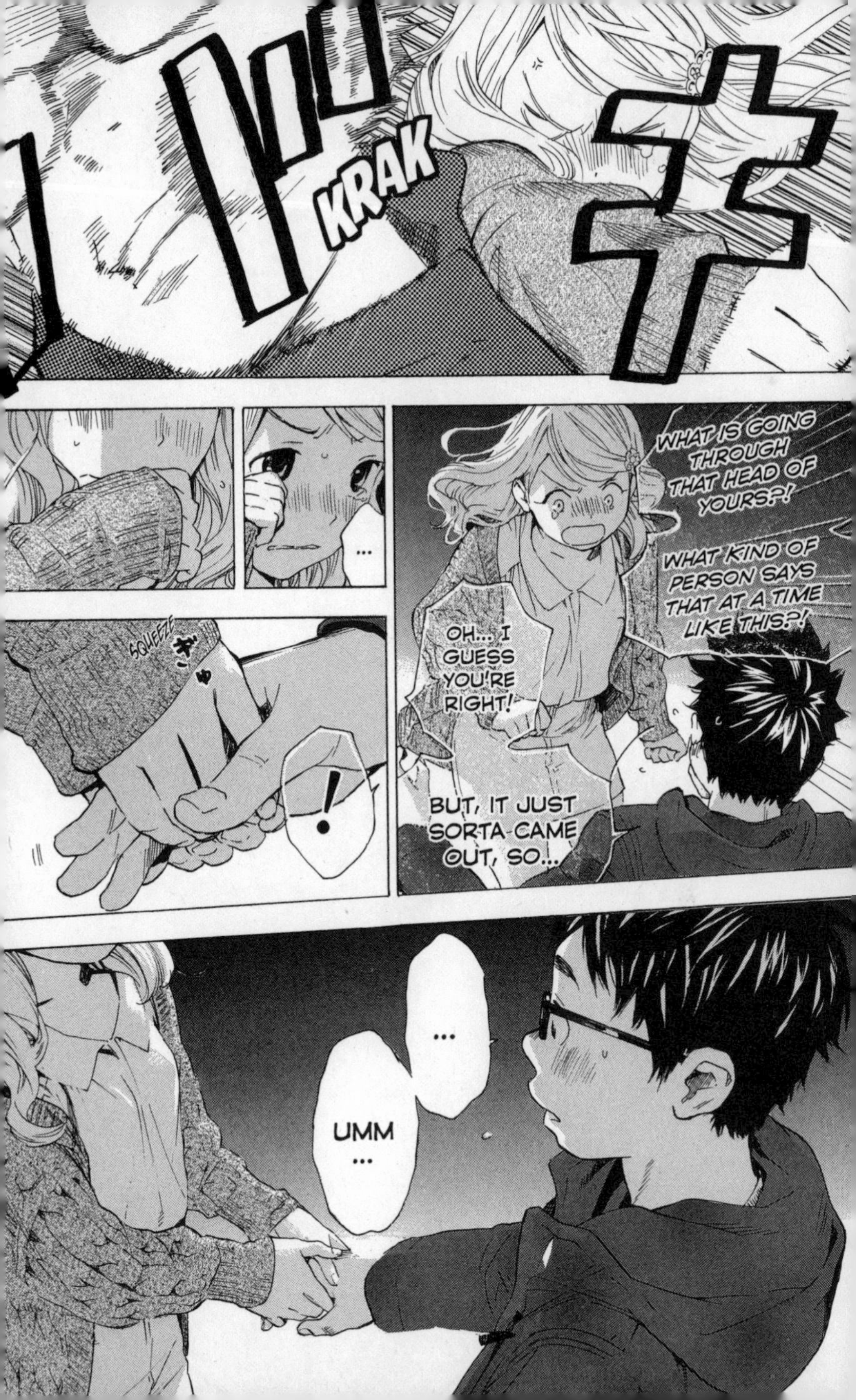
KRAK
WHAT IS GOING THROUGH THAT HEAD OF YOURS?!
WHAT KIND OF PERSON SAYS THAT AT A TIME LIKE THIS?!
OH... I GUESS YOU'RE RIGHT!
BUT, IT JUST SORTA CAME OUT, SO...
...
SQUEEZE
!
...
UMM ...

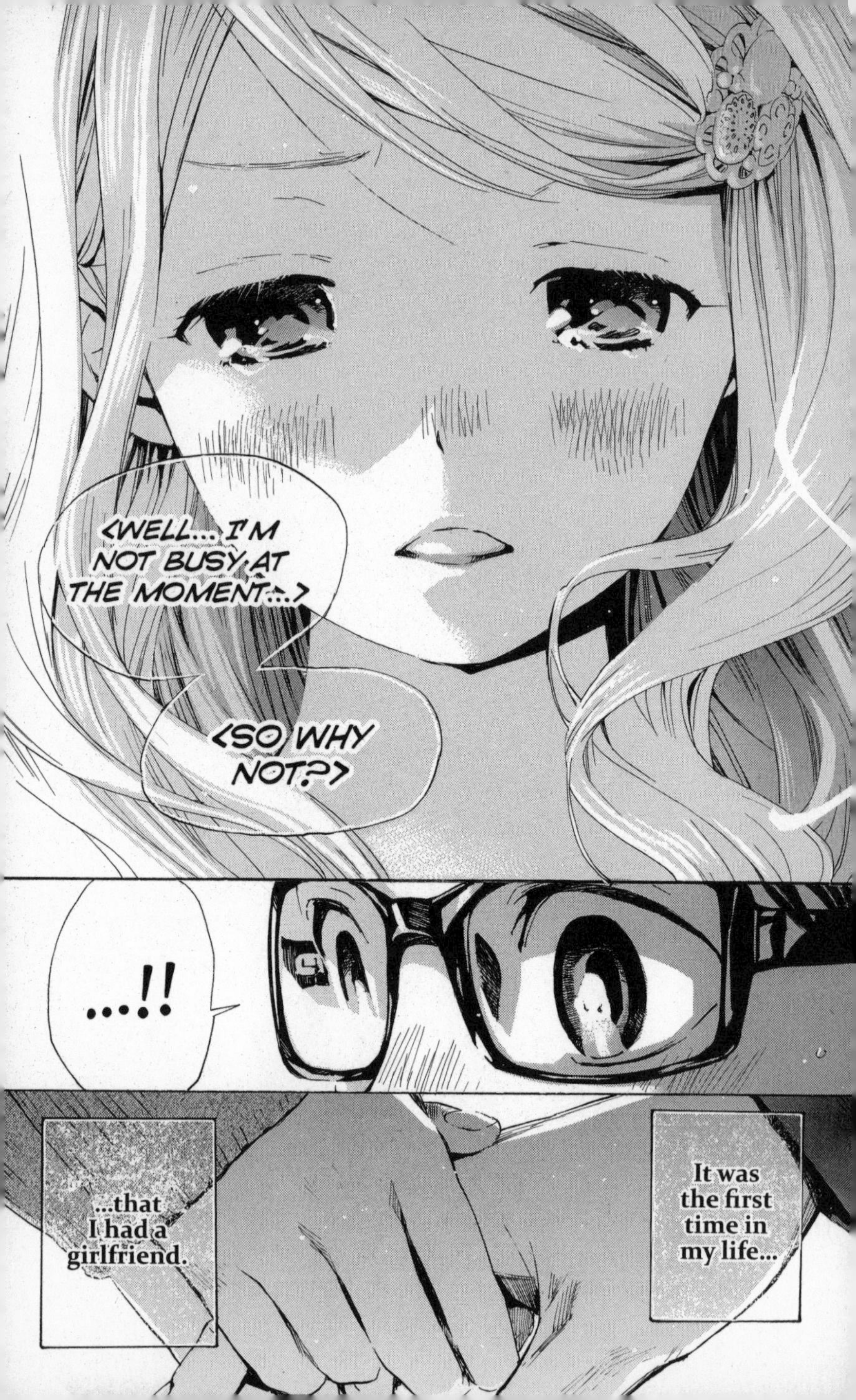
<WELL... I'M NOT BUSY AT THE MOMENT...>
<SO WHY NOT?>
...!!
It was the first time in my life...
...that I had a girlfriend.

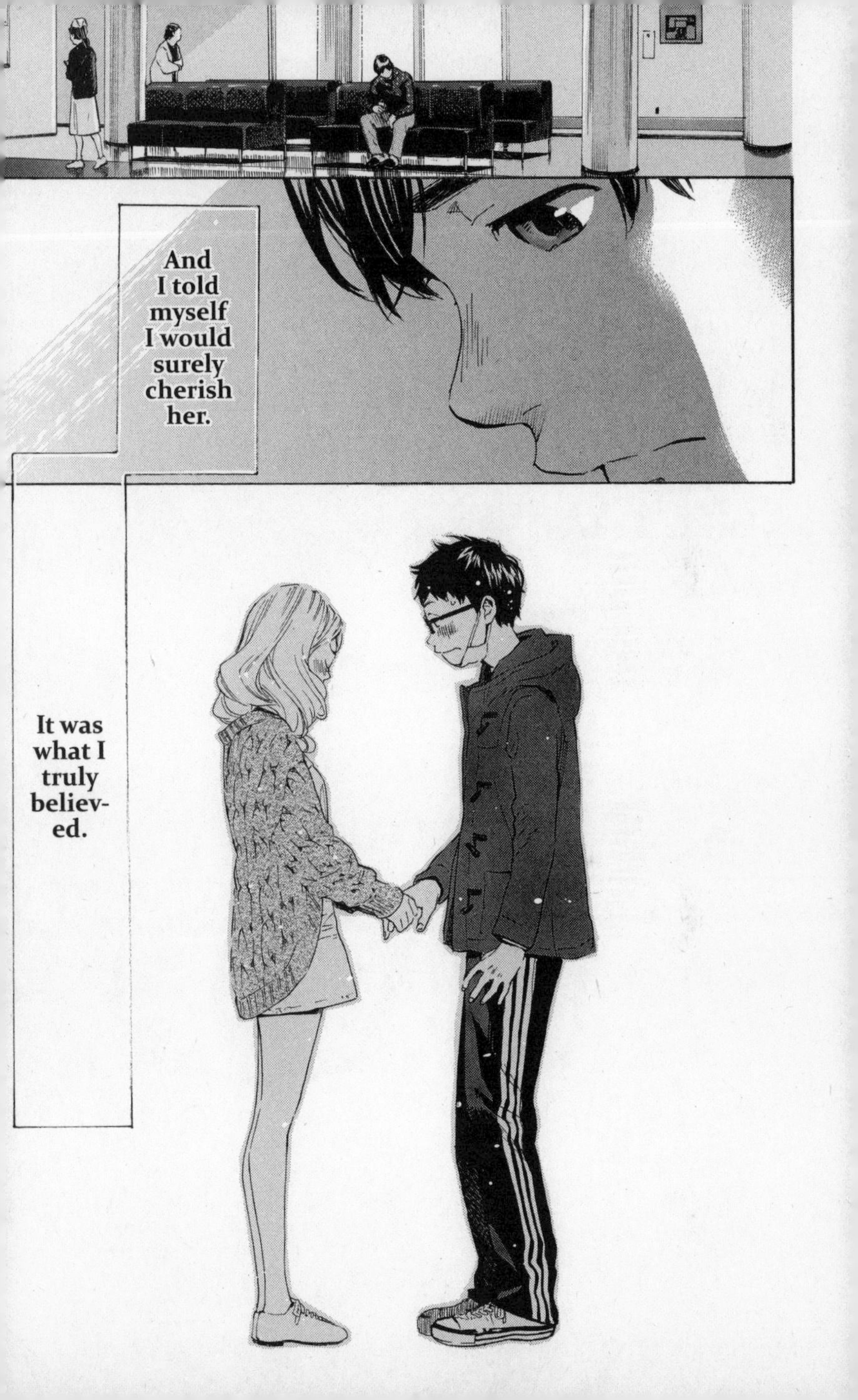
And I told myself I would surely cherish her.
It was what I truly believev-ed.

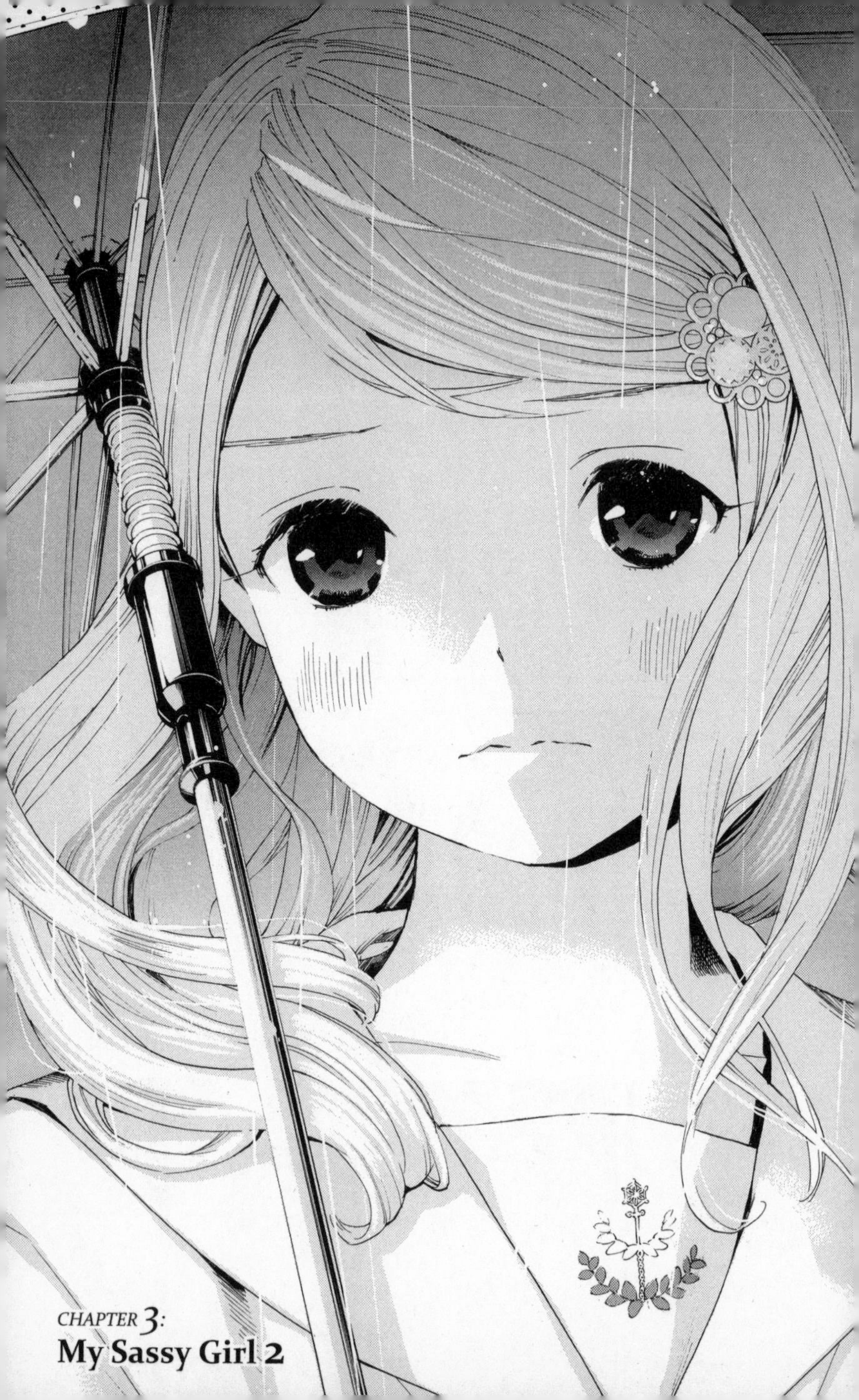

CHAPTER 3:

My Sassy Girl 2

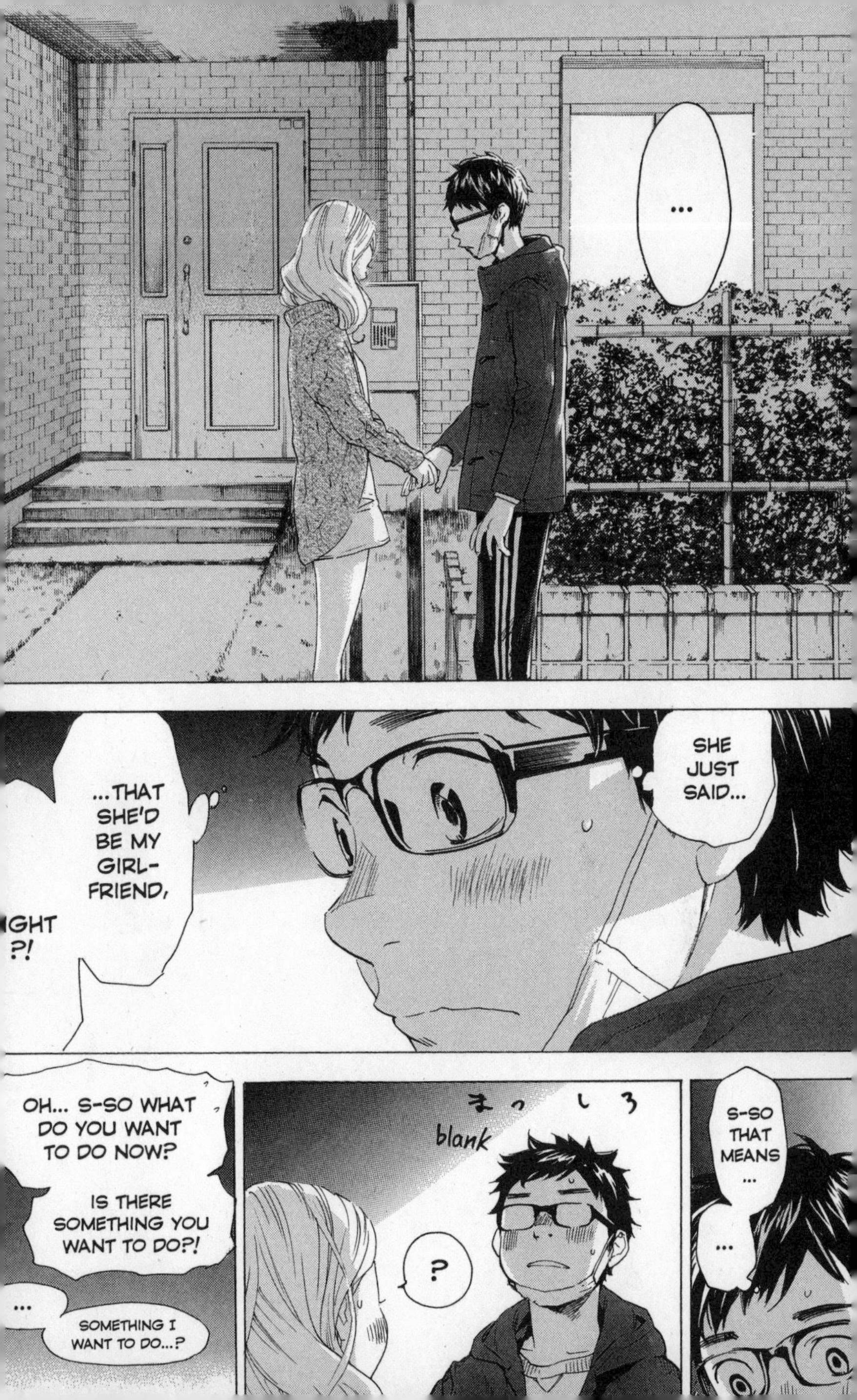
...
SHE JUST SAID...
...THAT SHE'D BE MY GIRL-FRIEND,
GHT ?!
S-SO THAT MEANS ...
...
まっしろ
blank
?
OH... S-SO WHAT DO YOU WANT TO DO NOW?
IS THERE SOMETHING YOU WANT TO DO?!
...
SOMETHING I WANT TO DO...?

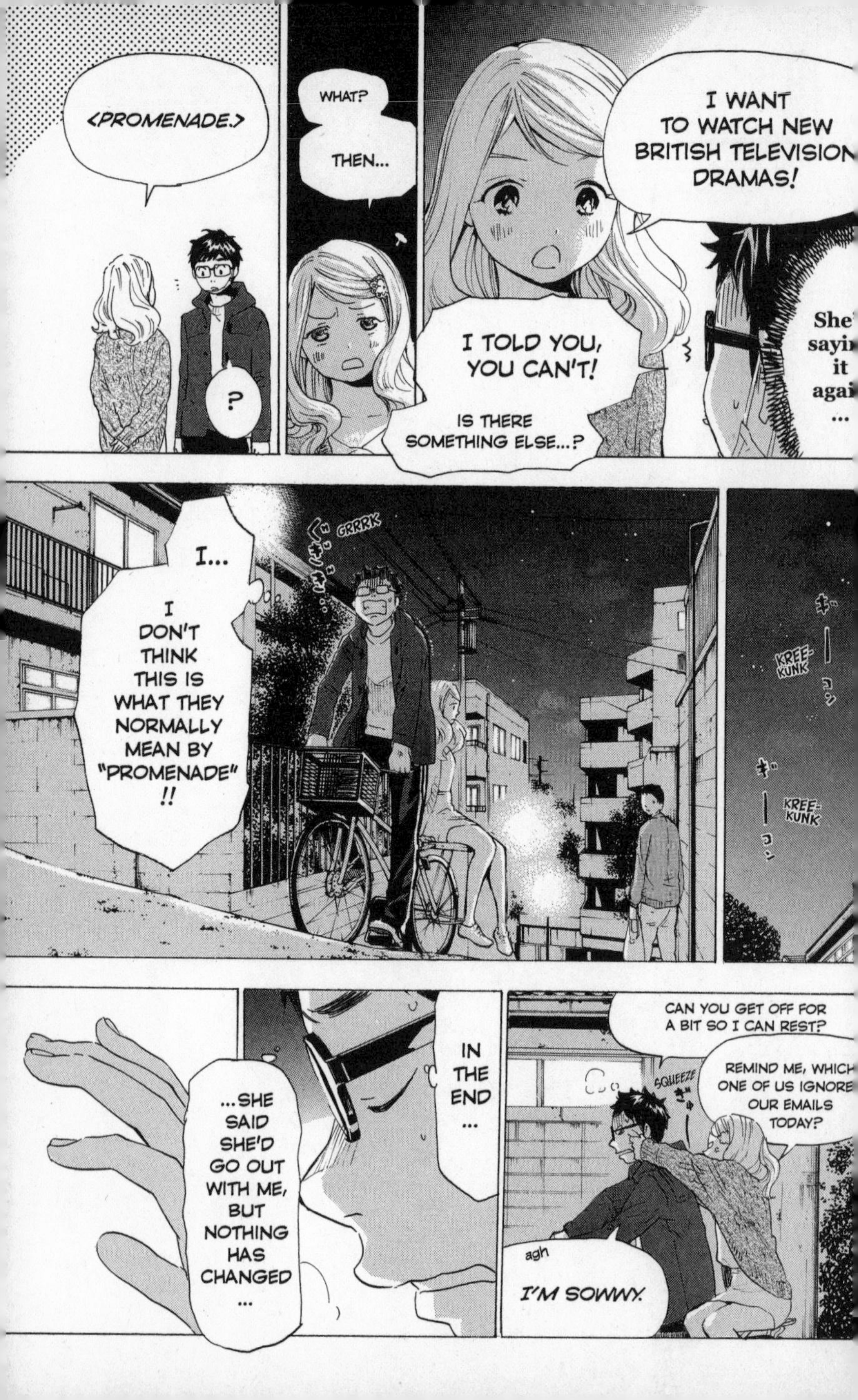
I WANT TO WATCH NEW BRITISH TELEVISION DRAMAS!
She' sayi it agai ...
I TOLD YOU, YOU CAN'T!
IS THERE SOMETHING ELSE...?
WHAT?
THEN...
<PROMENADE.>
?
KREE-KUNK
KREE-KUNK
GRRRK
I...
I DON'T THINK THIS IS WHAT THEY NORMALLY MEAN BY "PROMENADE"!!
CAN YOU GET OFF FOR A BIT SO I CAN REST?
REMIND ME, WHICH ONE OF US IGNORE OUR EMAILS TODAY?
SQUEEZE
agh
I'M SOWWY.
IN THE END...
...SHE SAID SHE'D GO OUT WITH ME, BUT NOTHING HAS CHANGED...

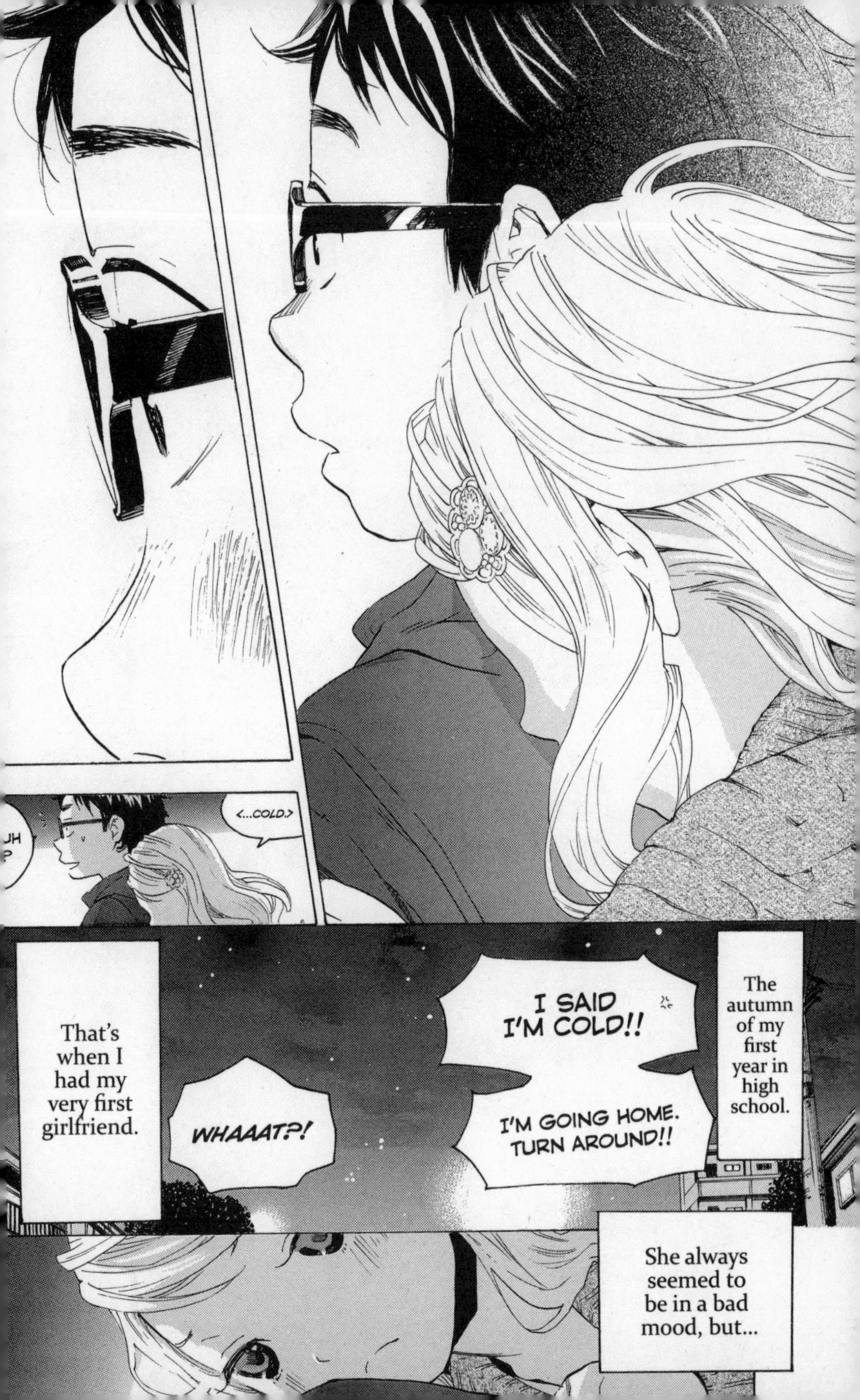

<...COLD.>
The autumn of my first year in high school.
I SAID I'M COLD!!
I'M GOING HOME. TURN AROUND!!
WHAAAT?!
That's when I had my very first girlfriend.
She always seemed to be in a bad mood, but...

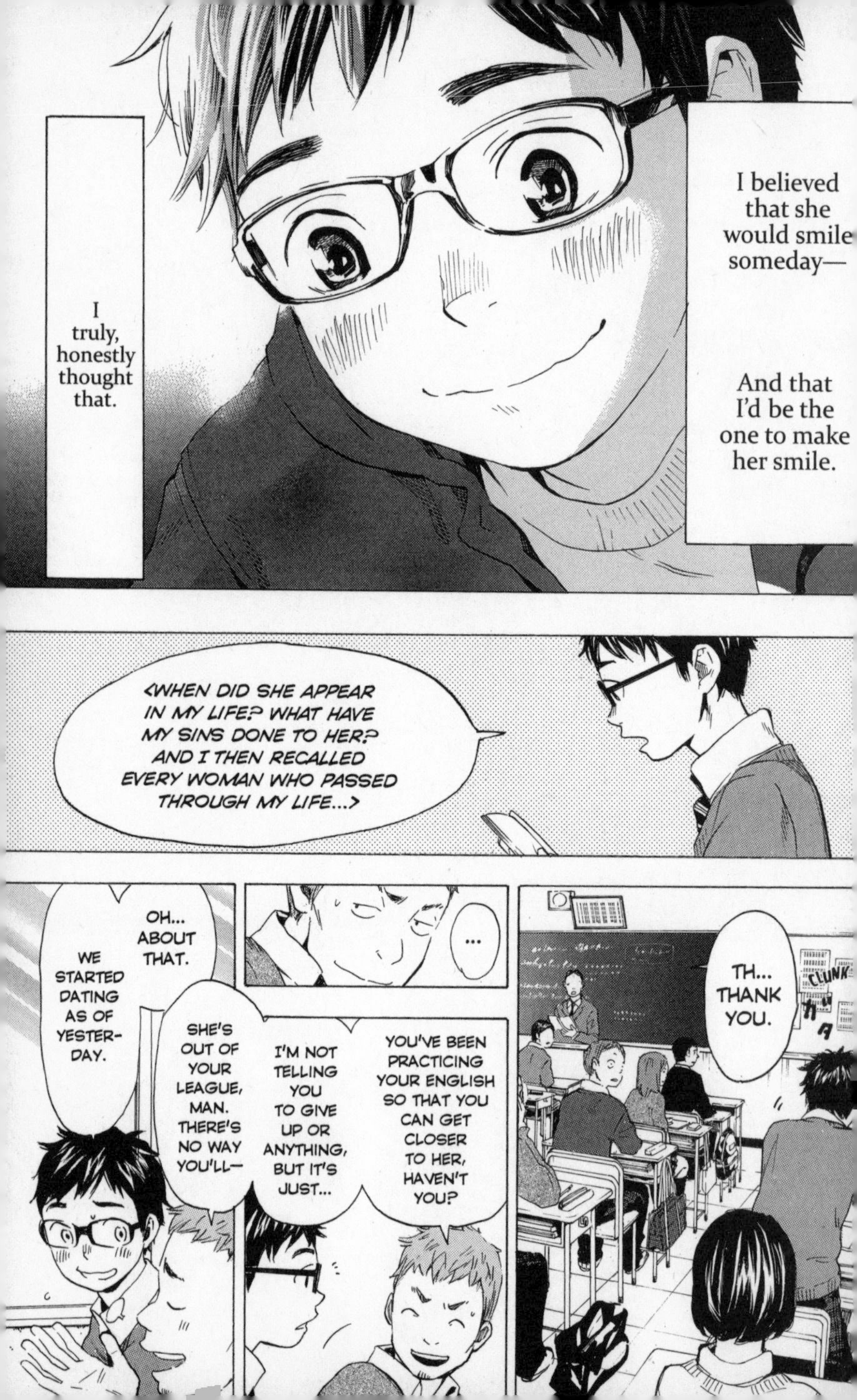
I believed that she would smile someday—
And that I'd be the one to make her smile.
I truly, honestly thought that.
<WHEN DID SHE APPEAR IN MY LIFE? WHAT HAVE MY SINS DONE TO HER? AND I THEN RECALLED EVERY WOMAN WHO PASSED THROUGH MY LIFE...>
CLUNK
TH... THANK YOU.
...
YOU'VE BEEN PRACTICING YOUR ENGLISH SO THAT YOU CAN GET CLOSER TO HER, HAVEN'T YOU?
I'M NOT TELLING YOU TO GIVE UP OR ANYTHING, BUT IT'S JUST...
SHE'S OUT OF YOUR LEAGUE, MAN. THERE'S NO WAY YOU'LL—
OH... ABOUT THAT.
WE STARTED DATING AS OF YESTERDAY.

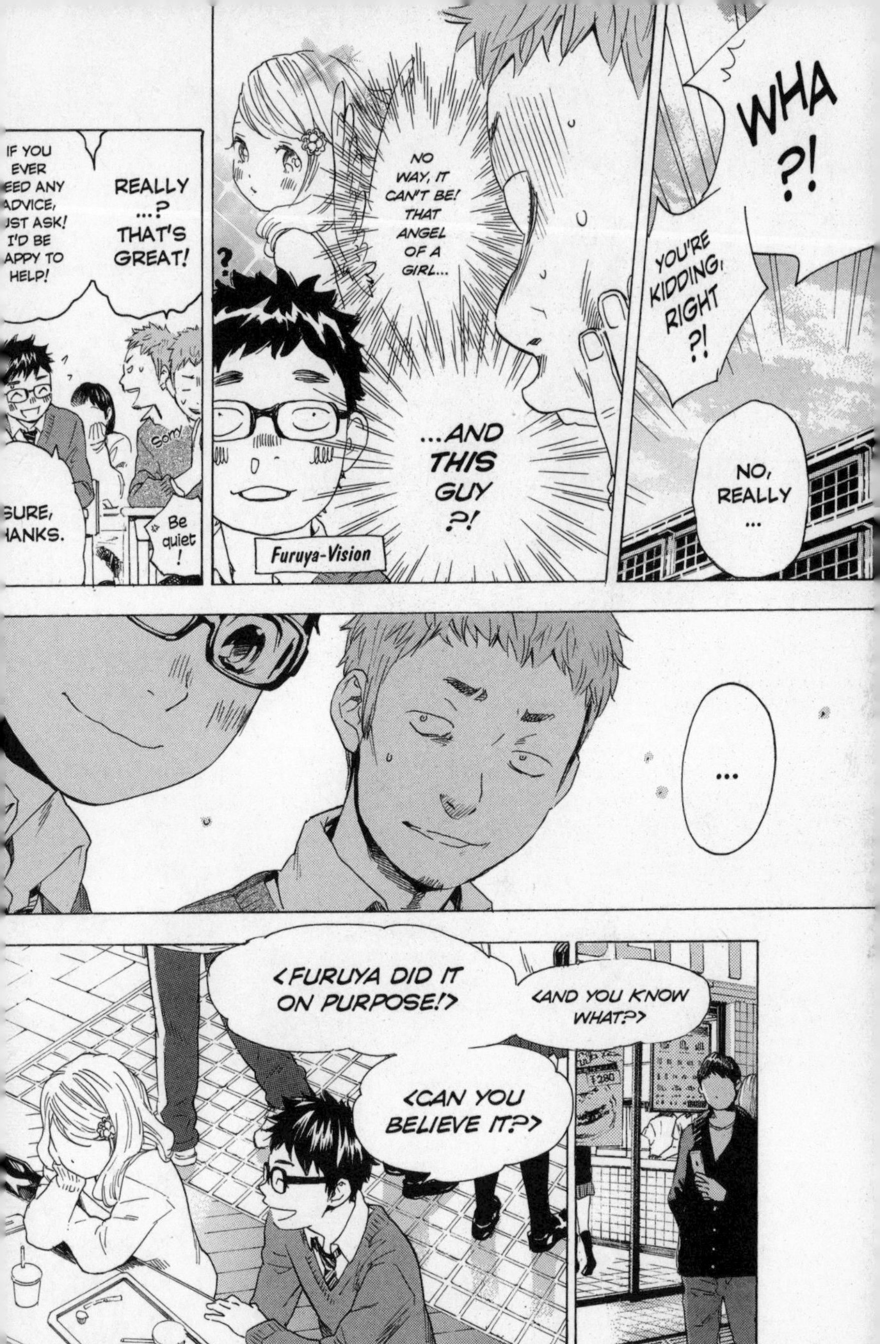
WHA ?!
YOU'RE KIDDING, RIGHT ?!
NO, REALLY ...
NO WAY, IT CAN'T BE! THAT ANGEL OF A GIRL...
...AND THIS GUY ?!
Furuya-Vision
REALLY ...? THAT'S GREAT!
IF YOU EVER EED ANY ADVICE, UST ASK! I'D BE APPY TO HELP!
Sorry
Be quiet !
SURE, HANKS.
...
<FURUYA DID IT ON PURPOSE!>
<AND YOU KNOW WHAT?>
<CAN YOU BELIEVE IT?>

<UM...>

<NOTHING.>

<OH, WHAT?>

<SORRY, CAN YOU REPEAT THAT?>

Oh God. I'm the worst.

ACK...

ER...

I need to keep working on my English...

This isn't nearly good enough!

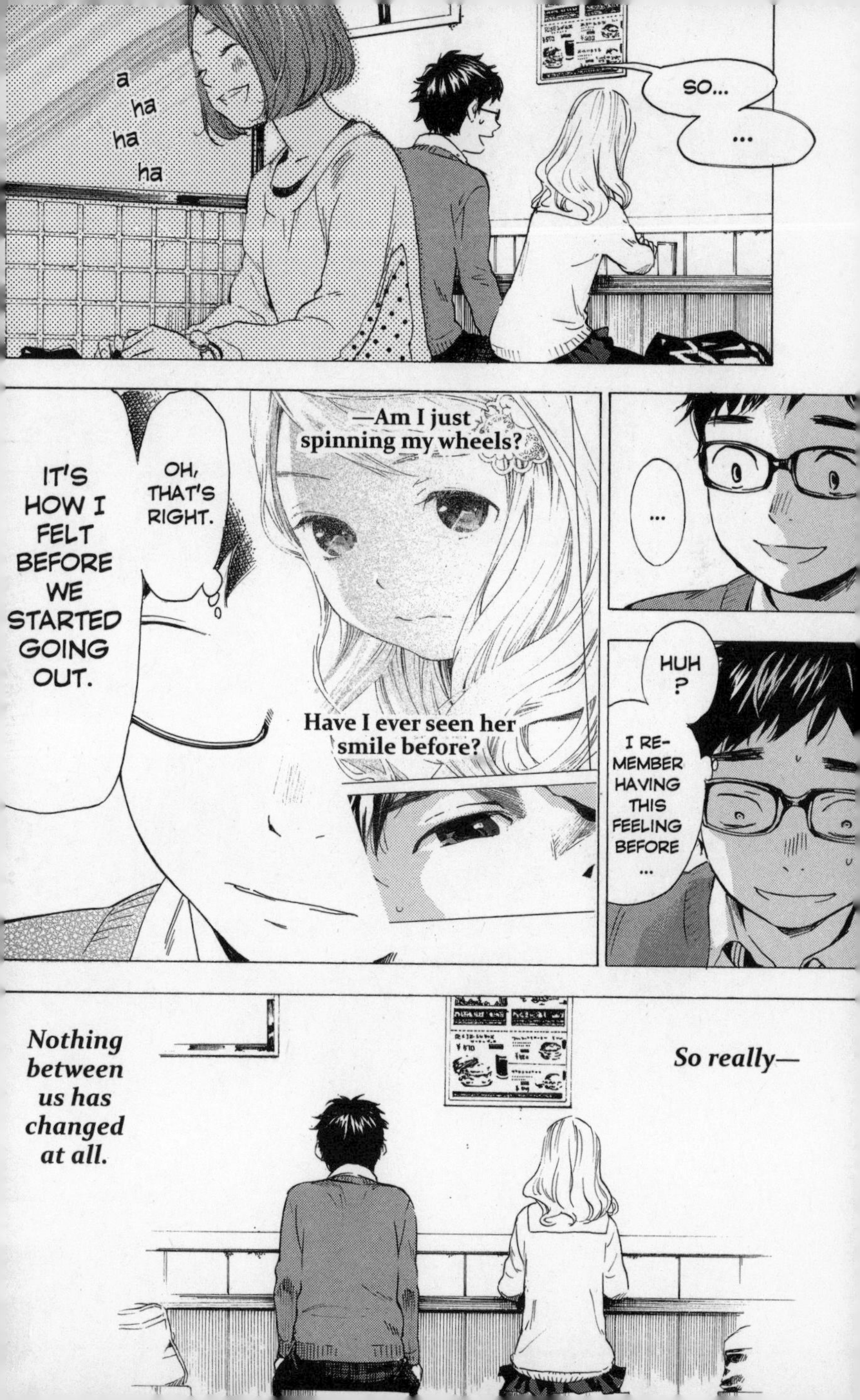
SO...
...
a ha ha ha
...
HUH?
I RE-MEMBER HAVING THIS FEELING BEFORE...
—Am I just spinning my wheels?
OH, THAT'S RIGHT.
IT'S HOW I FELT BEFORE WE STARTED GOING OUT.
Have I ever seen her smile before?
So really—
Nothing between us has changed at all.

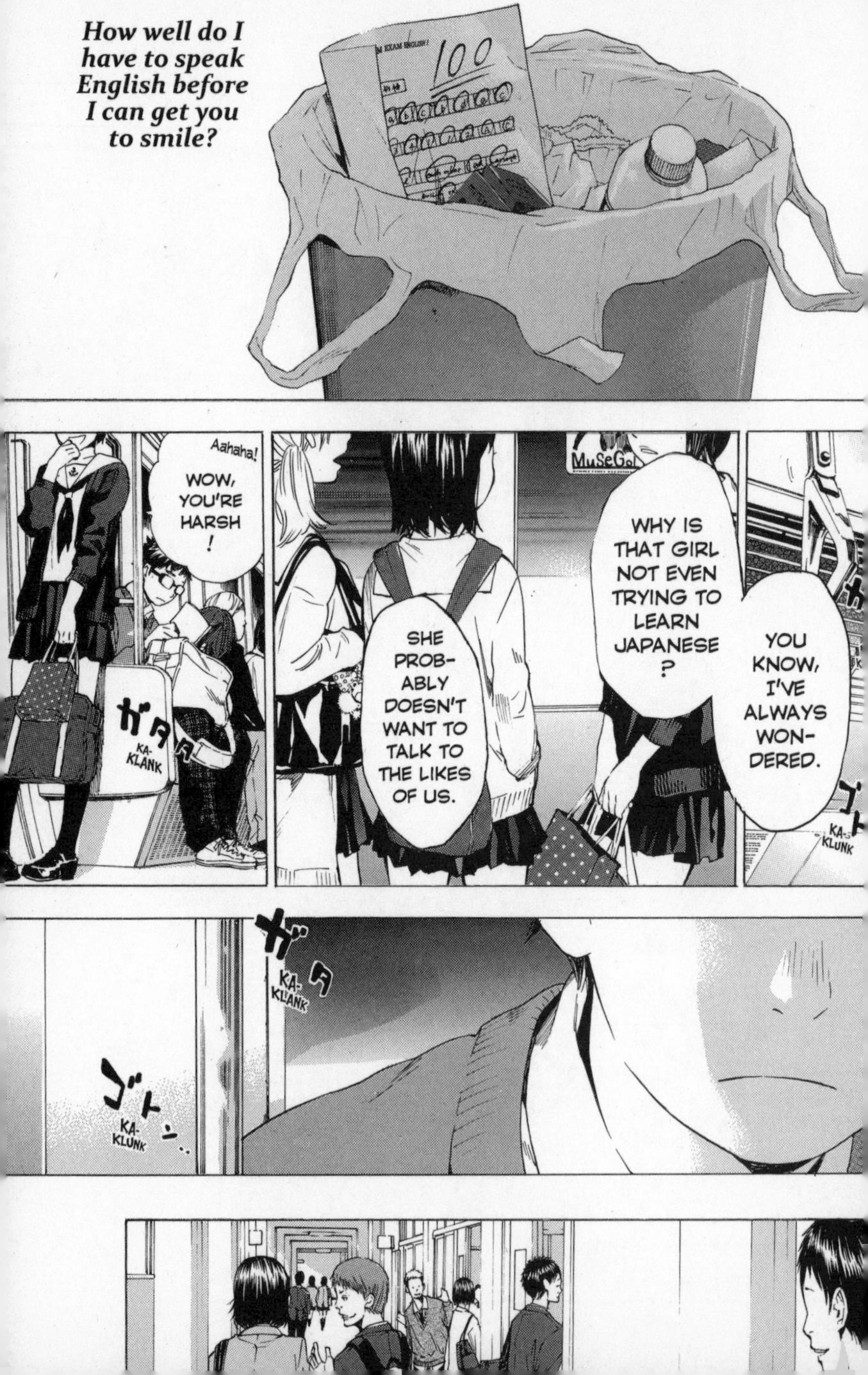
How well do I have to speak English before I can get you to smile?
100
YOU KNOW, I'VE ALWAYS WONDERED.
KA-KLUNK
WHY IS THAT GIRL NOT EVEN TRYING TO LEARN JAPANESE?
SHE PROBABLY DOESN'T WANT TO TALK TO THE LIKES OF US.
Aahaha!
WOW, YOU'RE HARSH!
KA-KLANK
KA-KLANK
KA-KLUNK

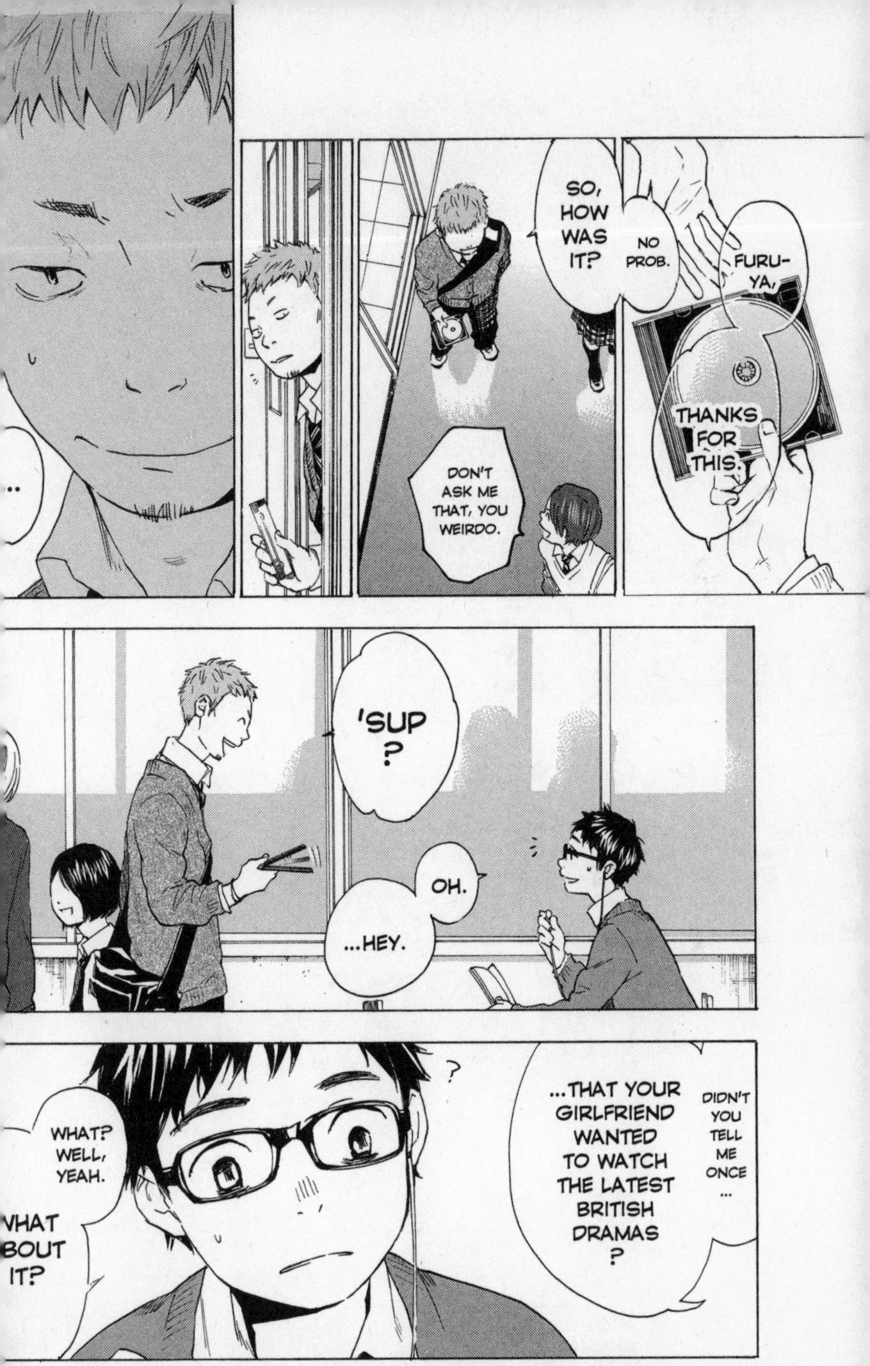
FURU-YA,
THANKS FOR THIS.
NO PROB.
SO, HOW WAS IT?
DON'T ASK ME THAT, YOU WEIRDO.
...
'SUP?
OH.
...HEY.
DIDN'T YOU TELL ME ONCE...
...THAT YOUR GIRLFRIEND WANTED TO WATCH THE LATEST BRITISH DRAMAS?
WHAT? WELL, YEAH.
VHAT BOUT IT?

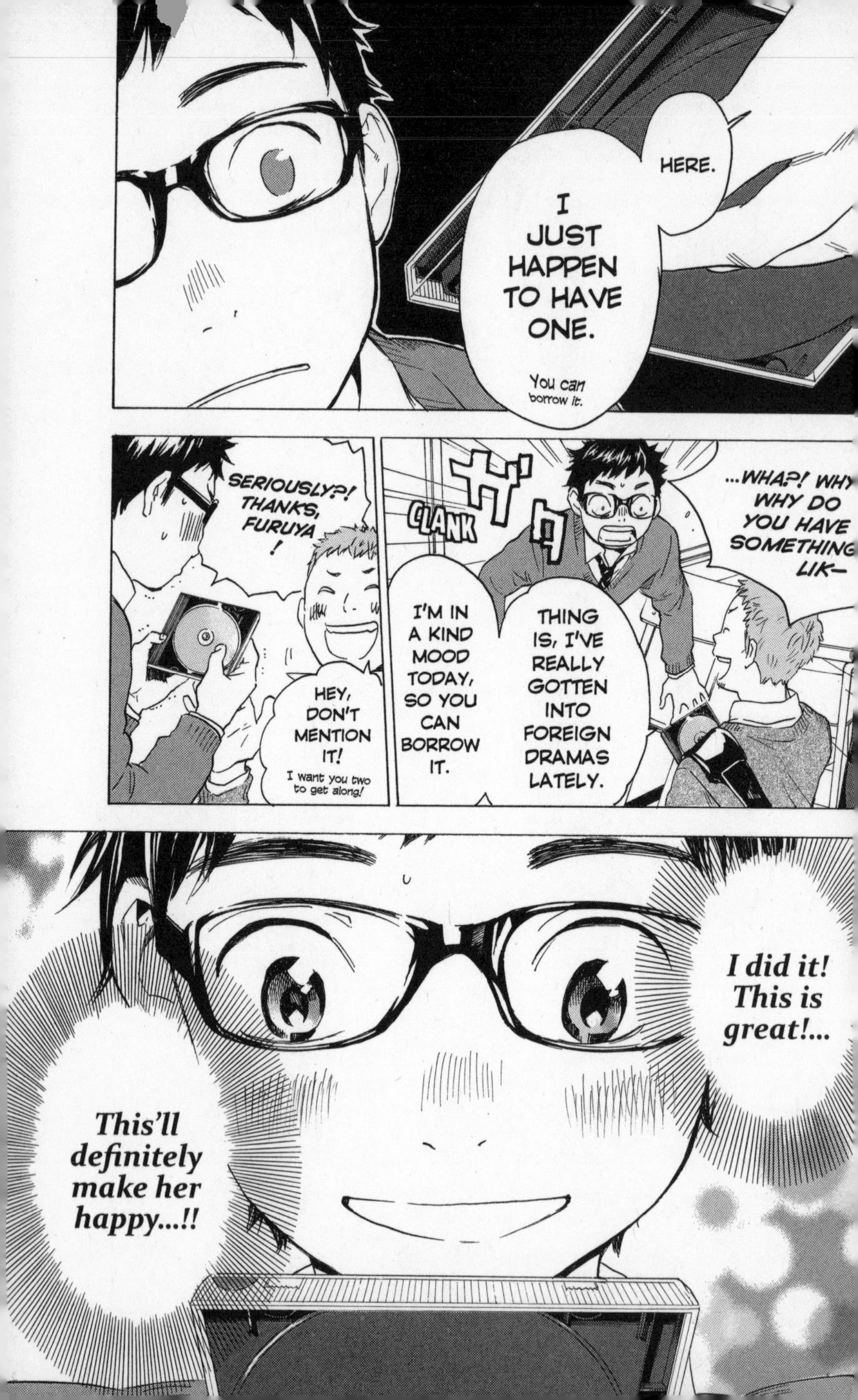
HERE.
I JUST HAPPEN TO HAVE ONE.
You can borrow it.
...WHA?! WHY WHY DO YOU HAVE SOMETHING LIK—
CLANK
THING IS, I'VE REALLY GOTTEN INTO FOREIGN DRAMAS LATELY.
I'M IN A KIND MOOD TODAY, SO YOU CAN BORROW IT.
SERIOUSLY?! THANKS, FURUYA!
HEY, DON'T MENTION IT!
I want you two to get along!
I did it! This is great!...
This'll definitely make her happy...!!

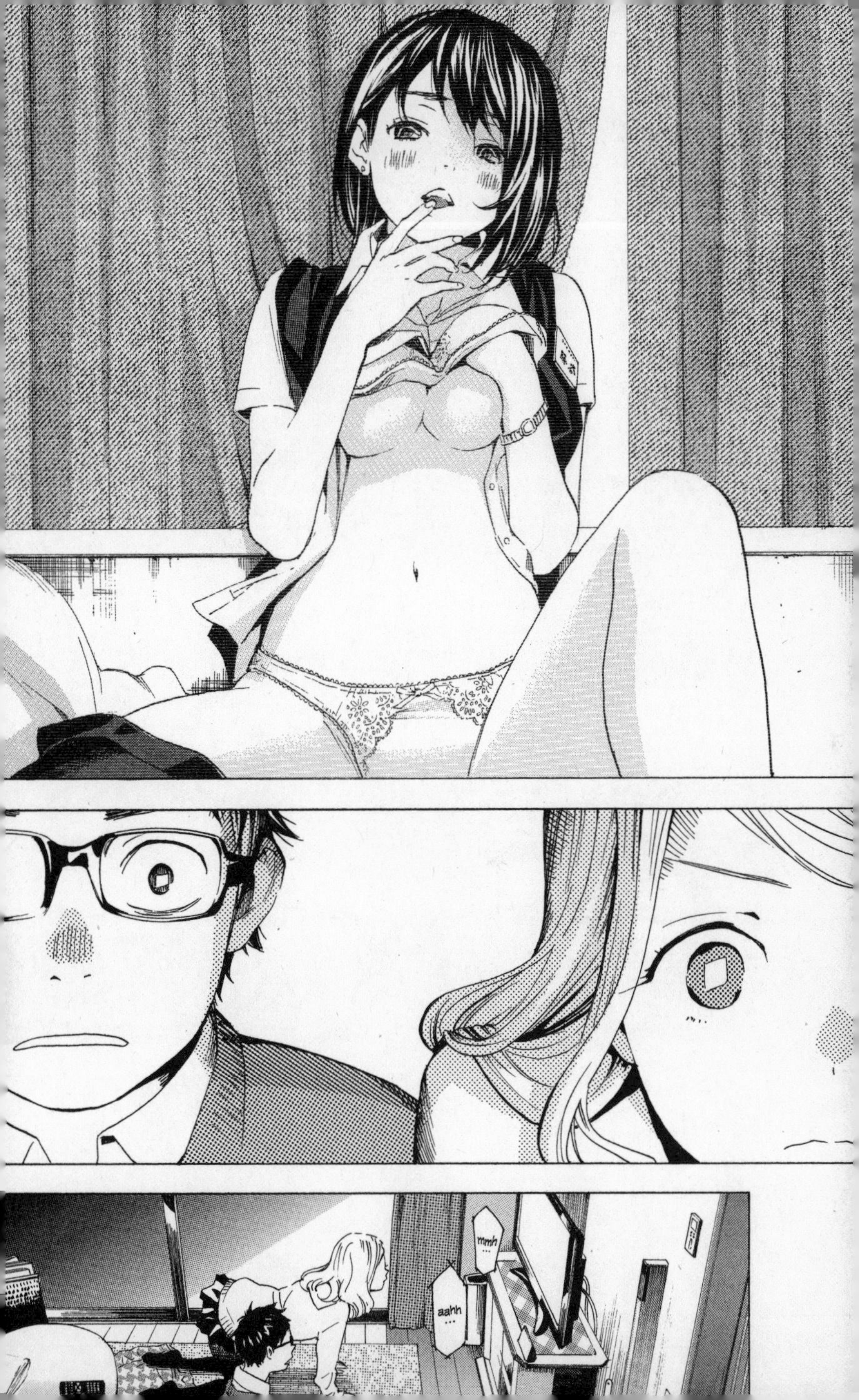
mmh
...
aahh
...

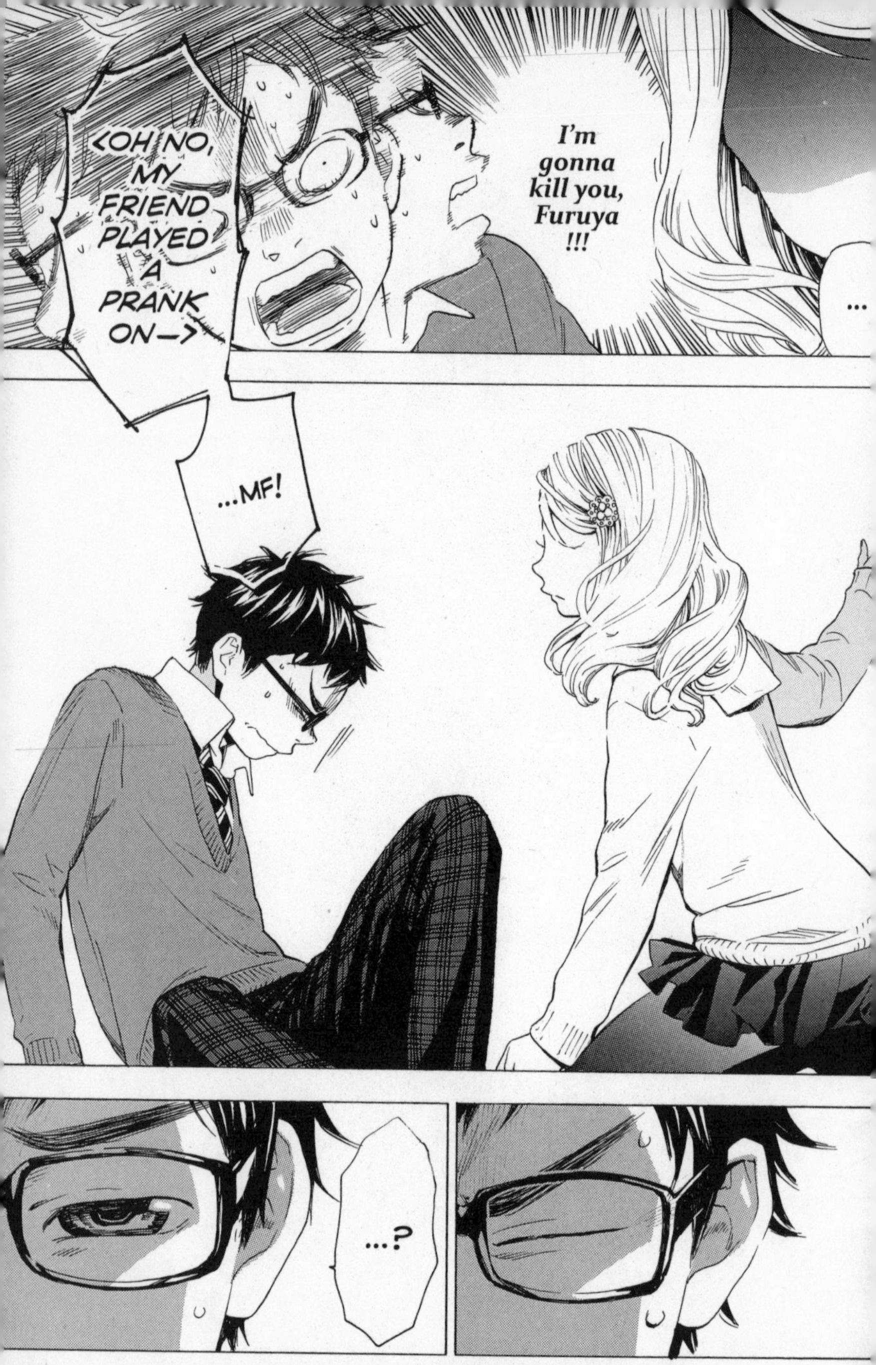
...
I'm gonna kill you, Furuya!!!
<OH NO, MY FRIEND PLAYED A PRANK ON—>
...MF!
...?

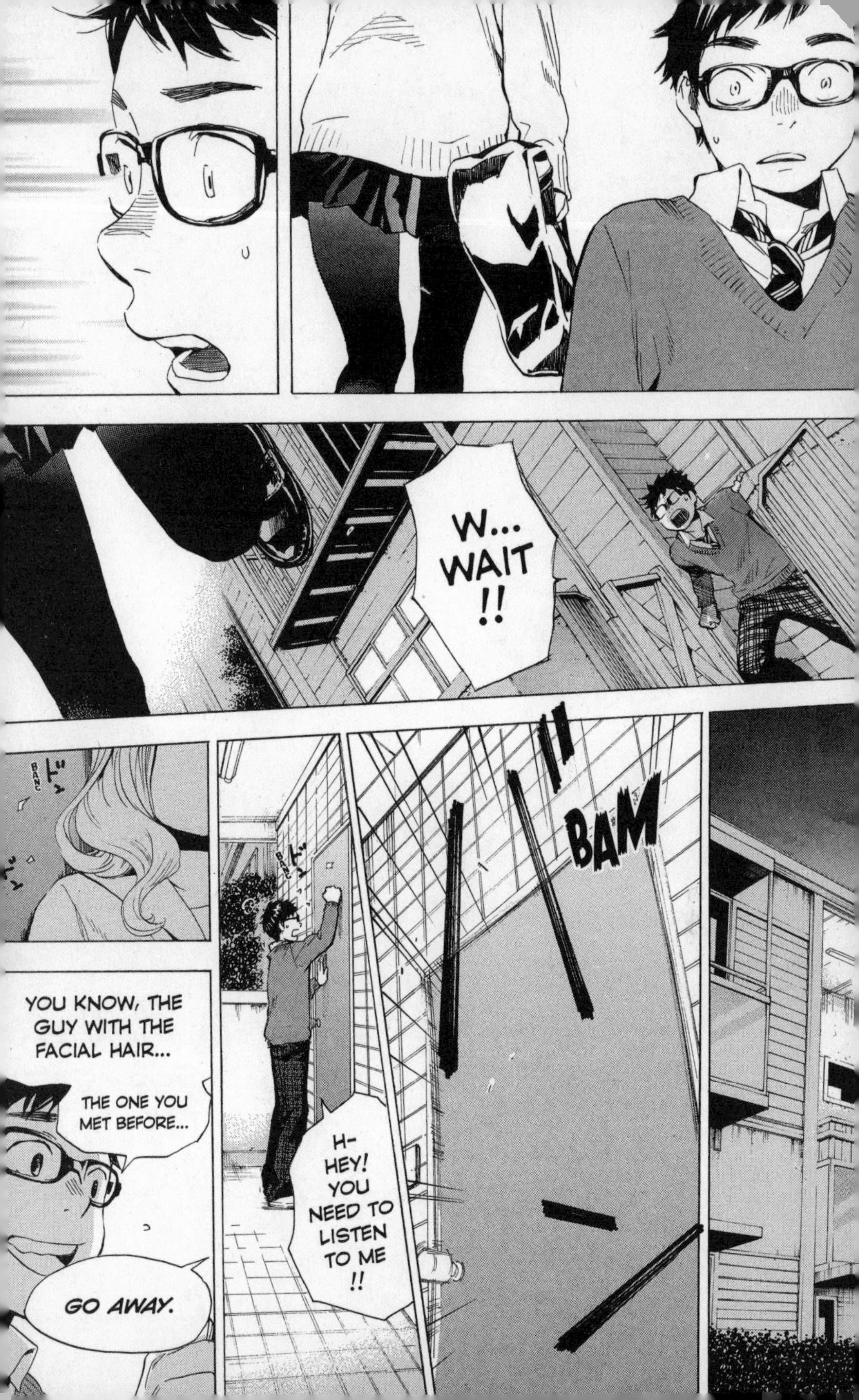
W... WAIT !!
BAM
BANG
H- HEY! YOU NEED TO LISTEN TO ME !!
BANG
YOU KNOW, THE GUY WITH THE FACIAL HAIR...
THE ONE YOU MET BEFORE...
GO AWAY.

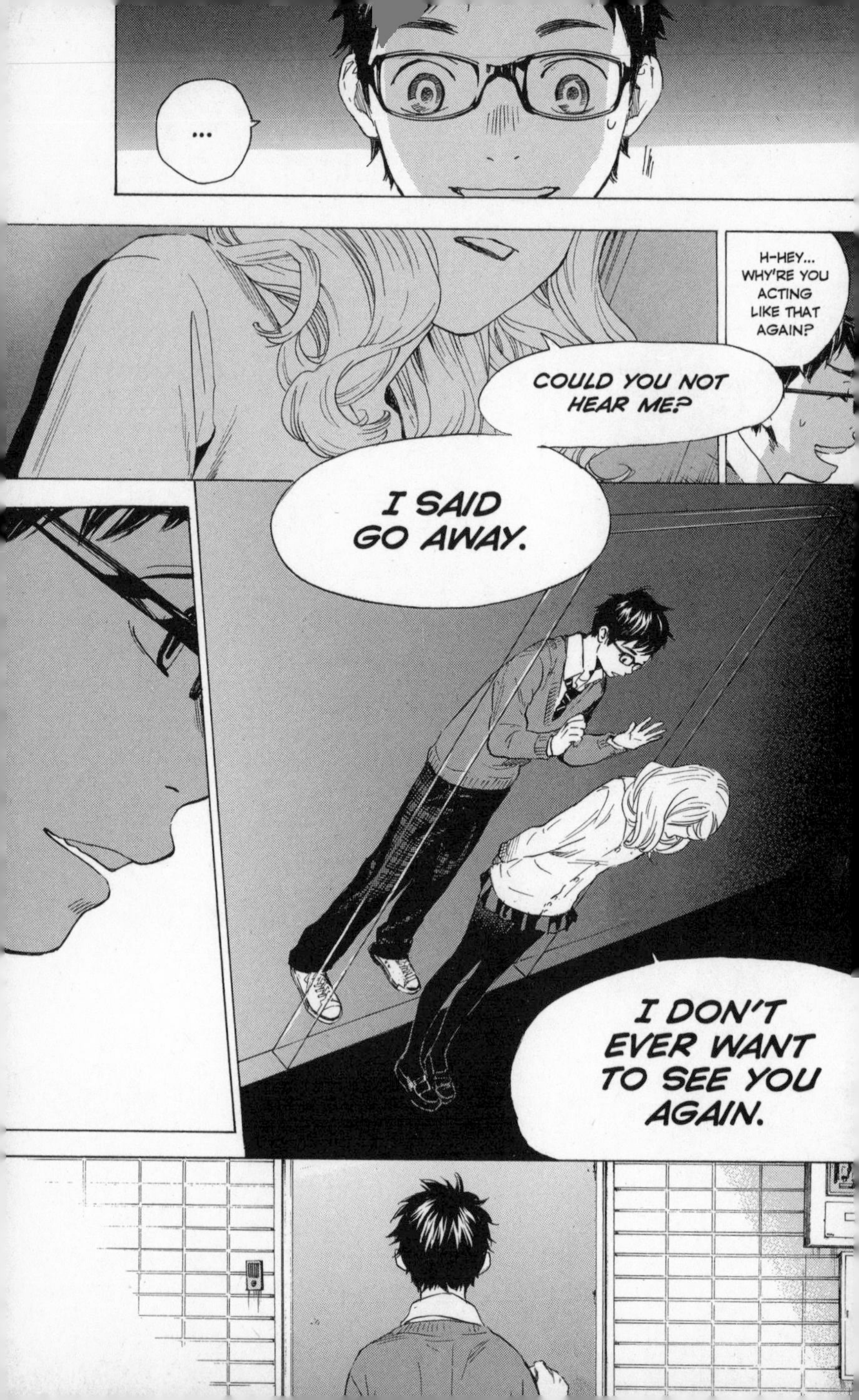
...
H-HEY... WHY'RE YOU ACTING LIKE THAT AGAIN?
COULD YOU NOT HEAR ME?
I SAID GO AWAY.
I DON'T EVER WANT TO SEE YOU AGAIN.

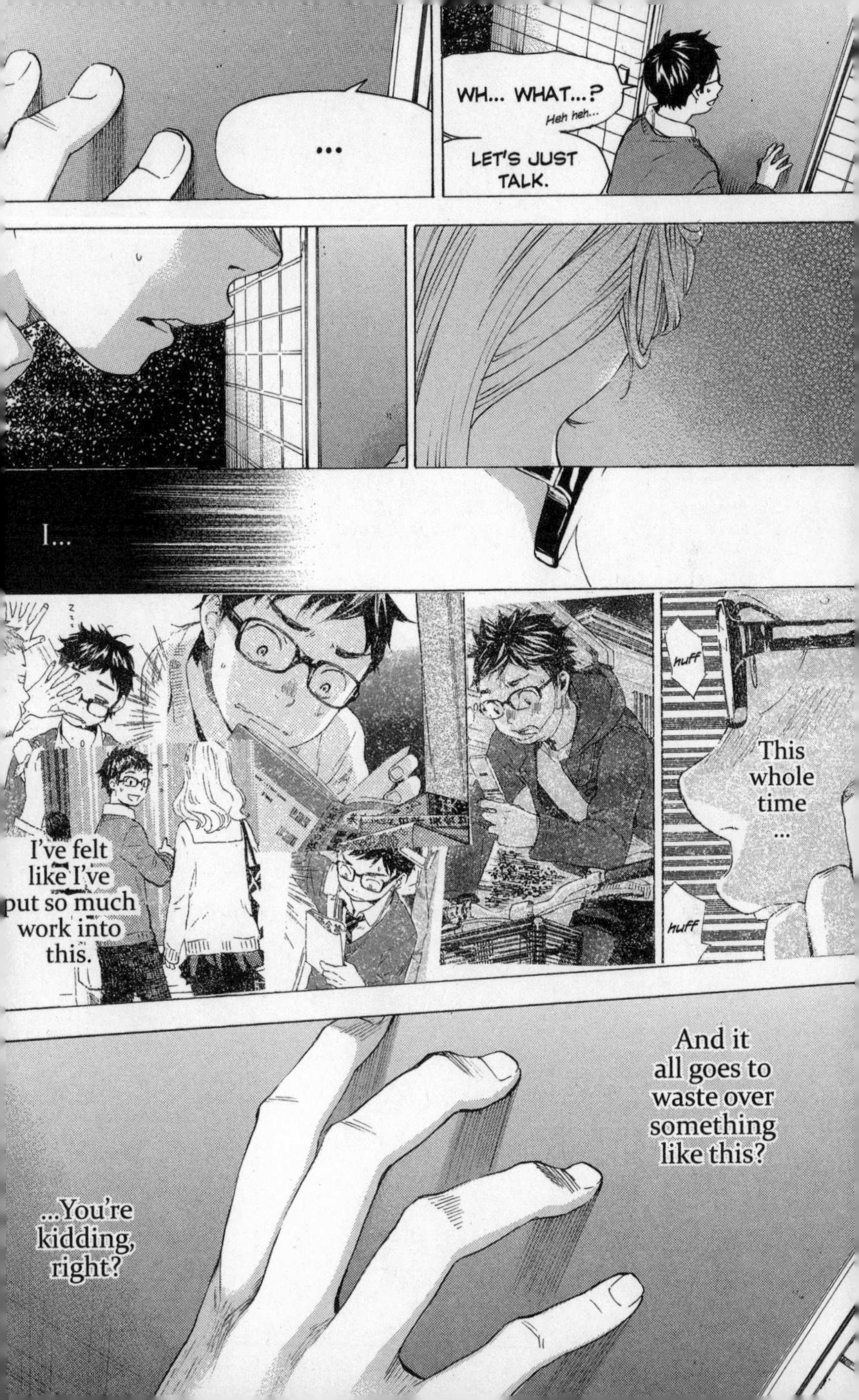
WH... WHAT...?
Heh heh...
LET'S JUST TALK.
...
I...
huff
This whole time ...
huff
I've felt like I've put so much work into this.
And it all goes to waste over something like this?
...You're kidding, right?

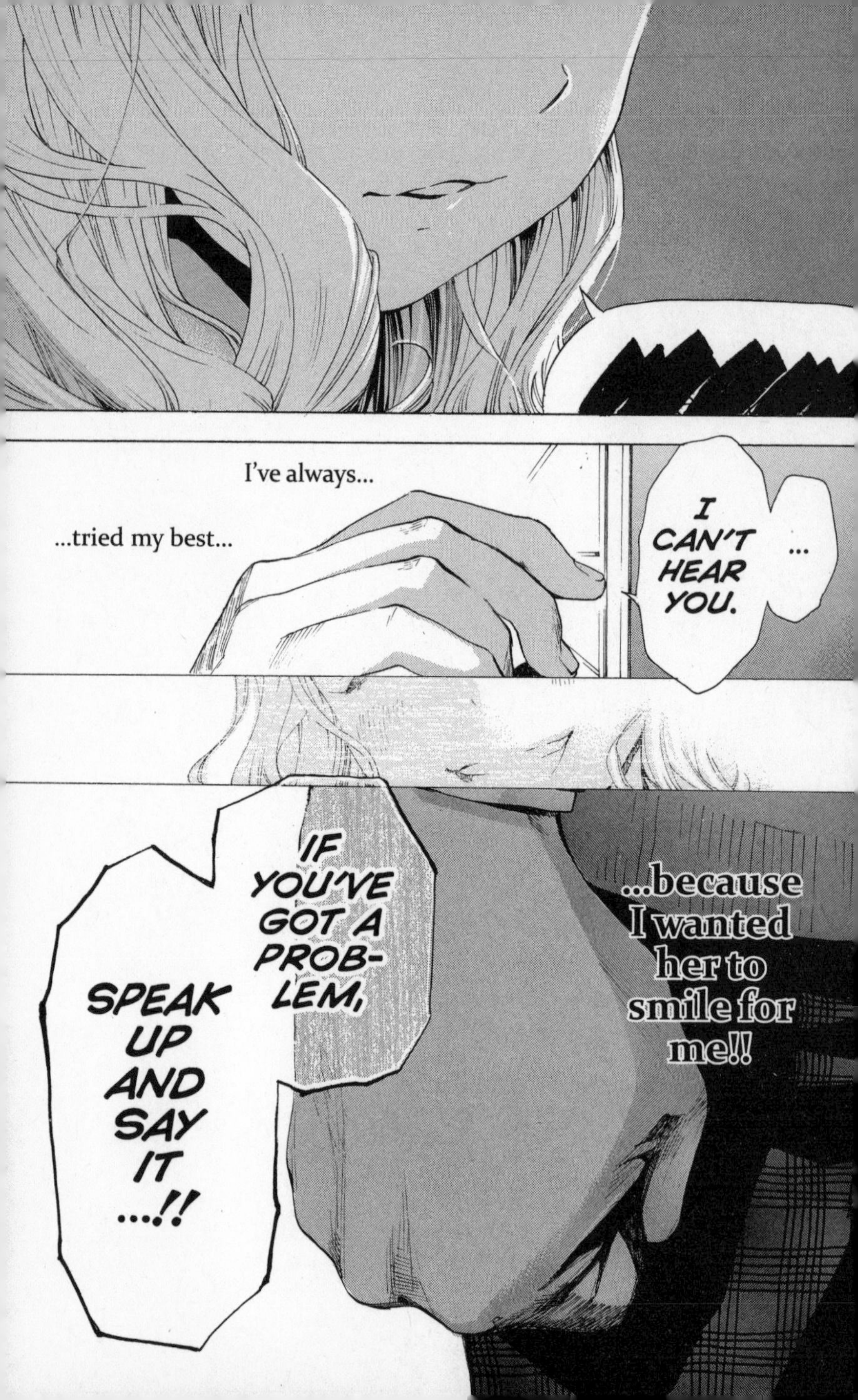
I CAN'T HEAR YOU. ...
I've always...
...tried my best...
...because I wanted her to smile for me!!
IF YOU'VE GOT A PROB-LEM, SPEAK UP AND SAY IT ...!!

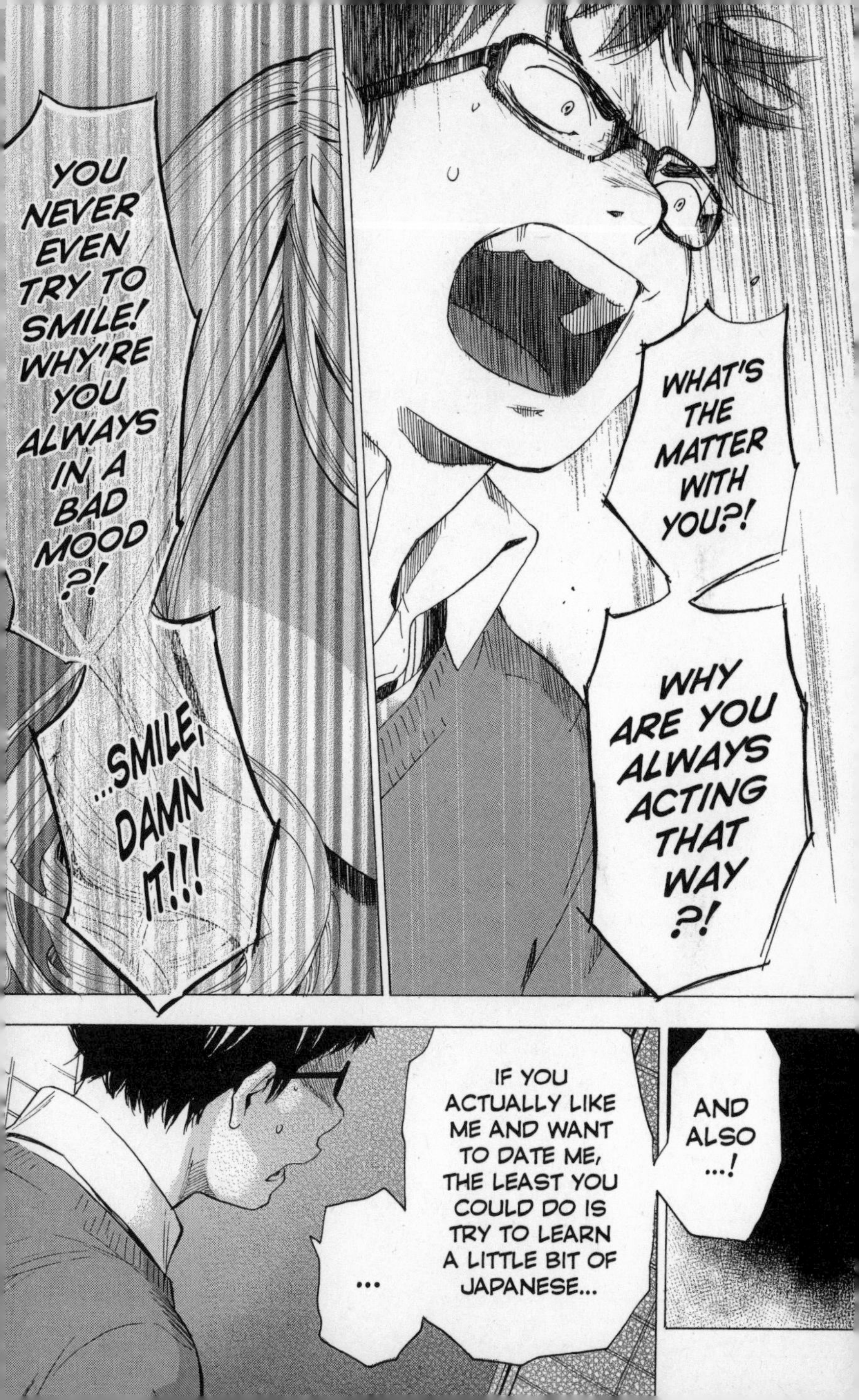
WHAT'S THE MATTER WITH YOU?!
WHY ARE YOU ALWAYS ACTING THAT WAY?!
YOU NEVER EVEN TRY TO SMILE! WHY'RE YOU ALWAYS IN A BAD MOOD?!
...SMILE, DAMN IT!!!
AND ALSO ...!
IF YOU ACTUALLY LIKE ME AND WANT TO DATE ME, THE LEAST YOU COULD DO IS TRY TO LEARN A LITTLE BIT OF JAPANESE...
...

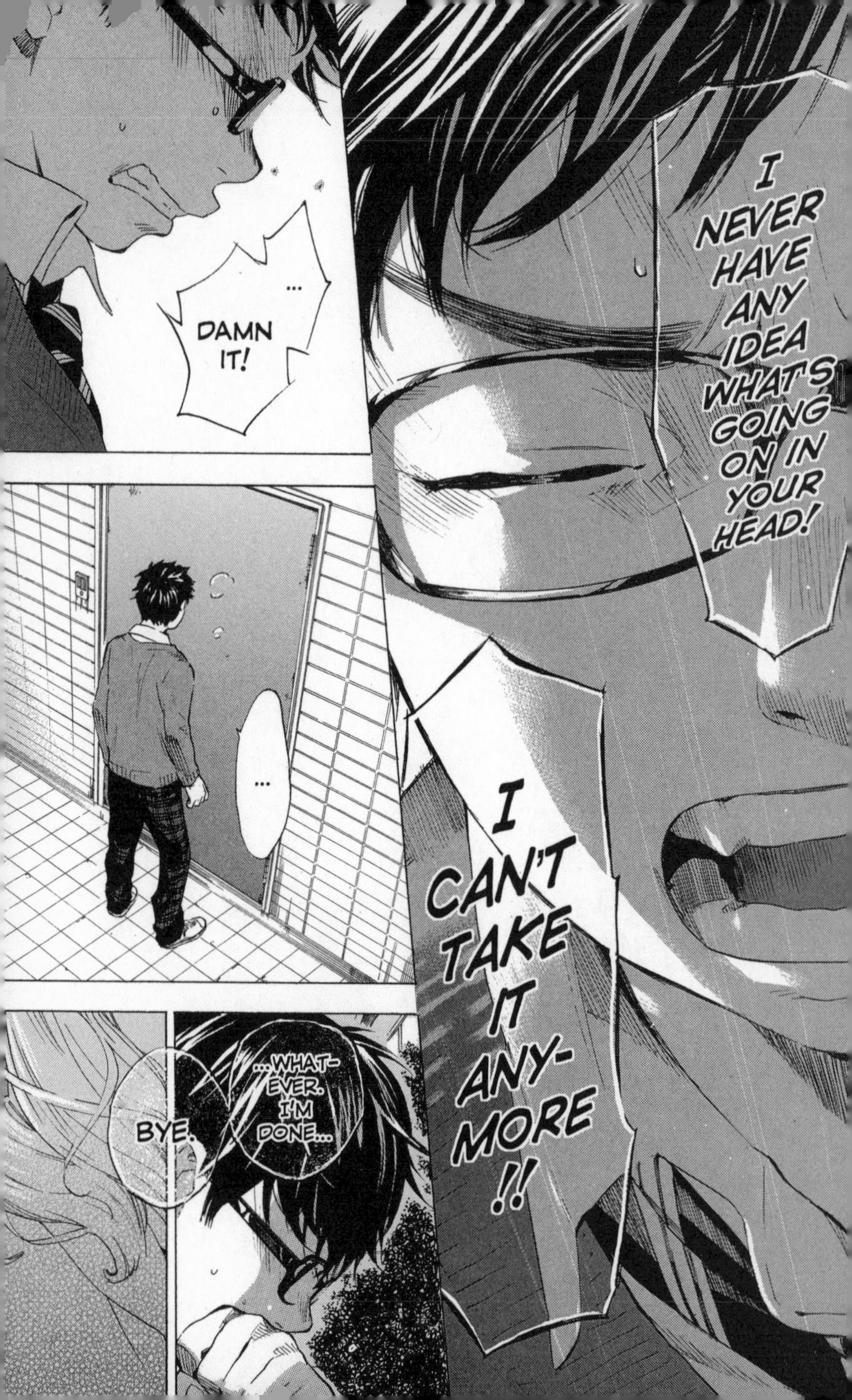
I NEVER HAVE ANY IDEA WHAT'S GOING ON IN YOUR HEAD!
I CAN'T TAKE IT ANY-MORE!!
... DAMN IT!
...
...WHAT-EVER. I'M DONE...
BYE.

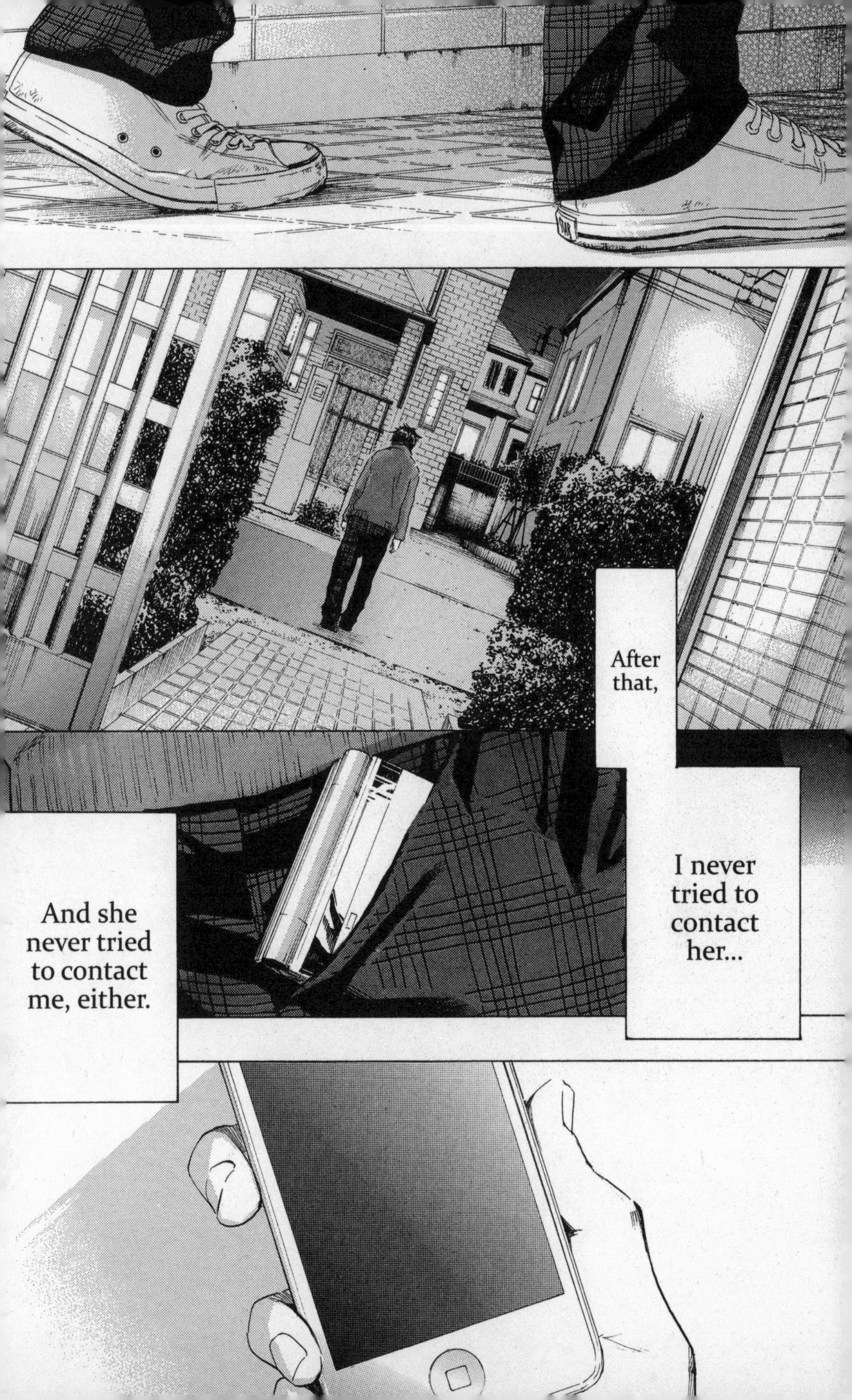
After that,
I never tried to contact her...
And she never tried to contact me, either.

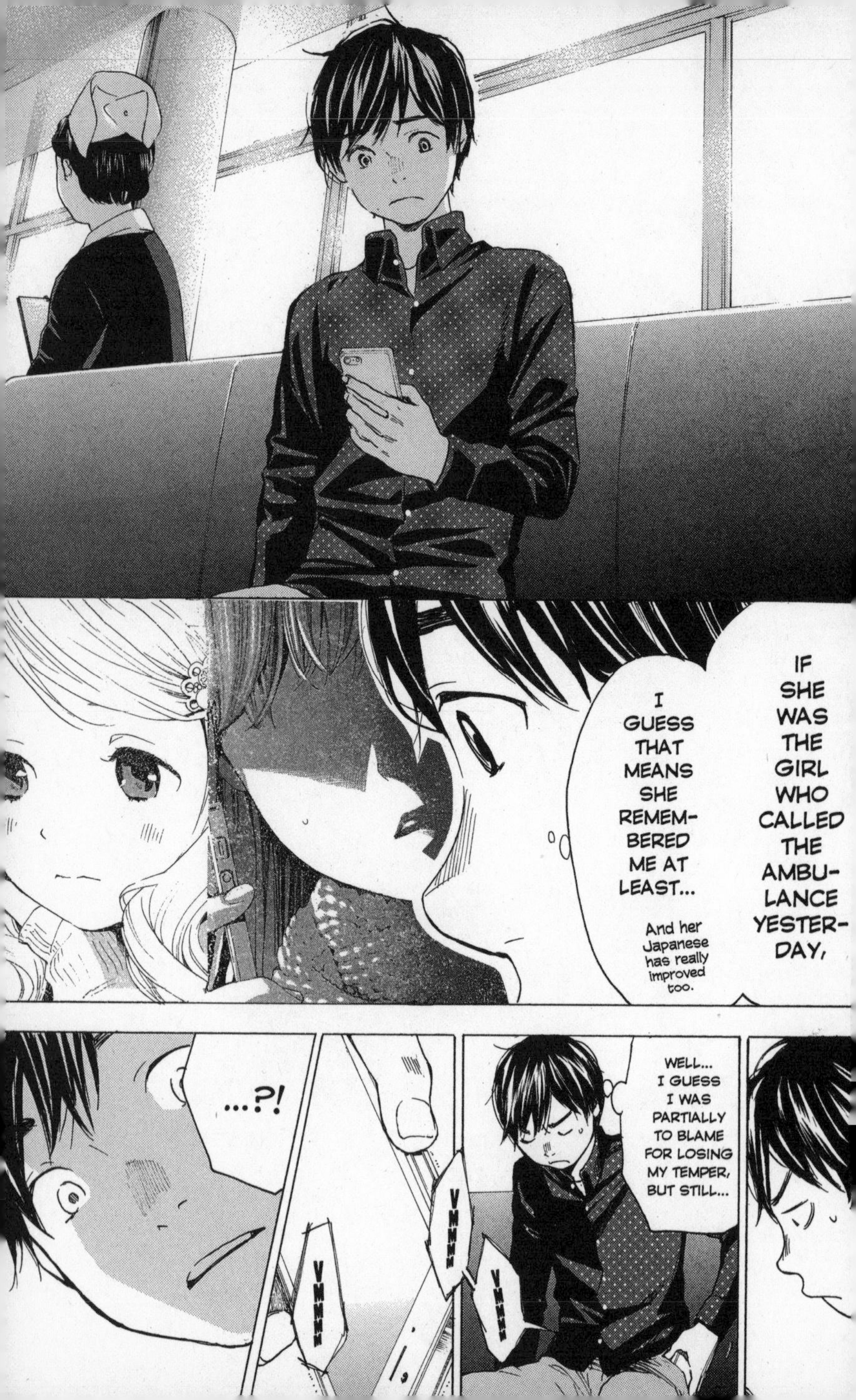
IF SHE WAS THE GIRL WHO CALLED THE AMBULANCE YESTERDAY,
I GUESS THAT MEANS SHE REMEMBERED ME AT LEAST...
And her Japanese has really improved too.
WELL... I GUESS I WAS PARTIALLY TO BLAME FOR LOSING MY TEMPER, BUT STILL...
VMMMMM
VMMMMM
VMMMMM
...?!

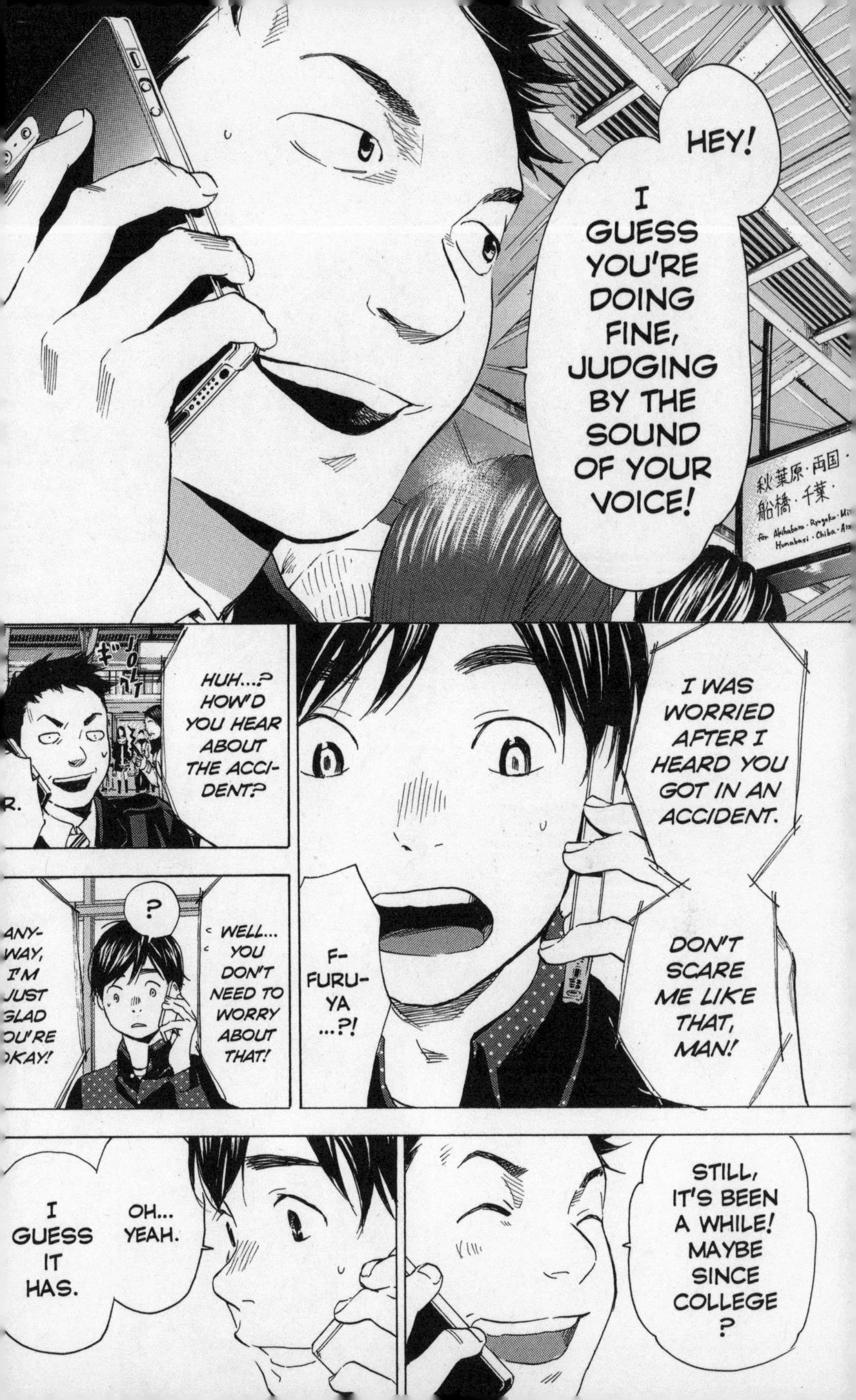
HEY!
I GUESS YOU'RE DOING FINE, JUDGING BY THE SOUND OF YOUR VOICE!
秋葉原・両国・
船橋・千葉・
I WAS WORRIED AFTER I HEARD YOU GOT IN AN ACCIDENT.
DON'T SCARE ME LIKE THAT, MAN!
F-FURUYA...?!
HUH...? HOW'D YOU HEAR ABOUT THE ACCIDENT?
?
WELL... YOU DON'T NEED TO WORRY ABOUT THAT!
ANYWAY, I'M JUST GLAD OU'RE KAY!
STILL, IT'S BEEN A WHILE! MAYBE SINCE COLLEGE?
OH... YEAH.
I GUESS IT HAS.

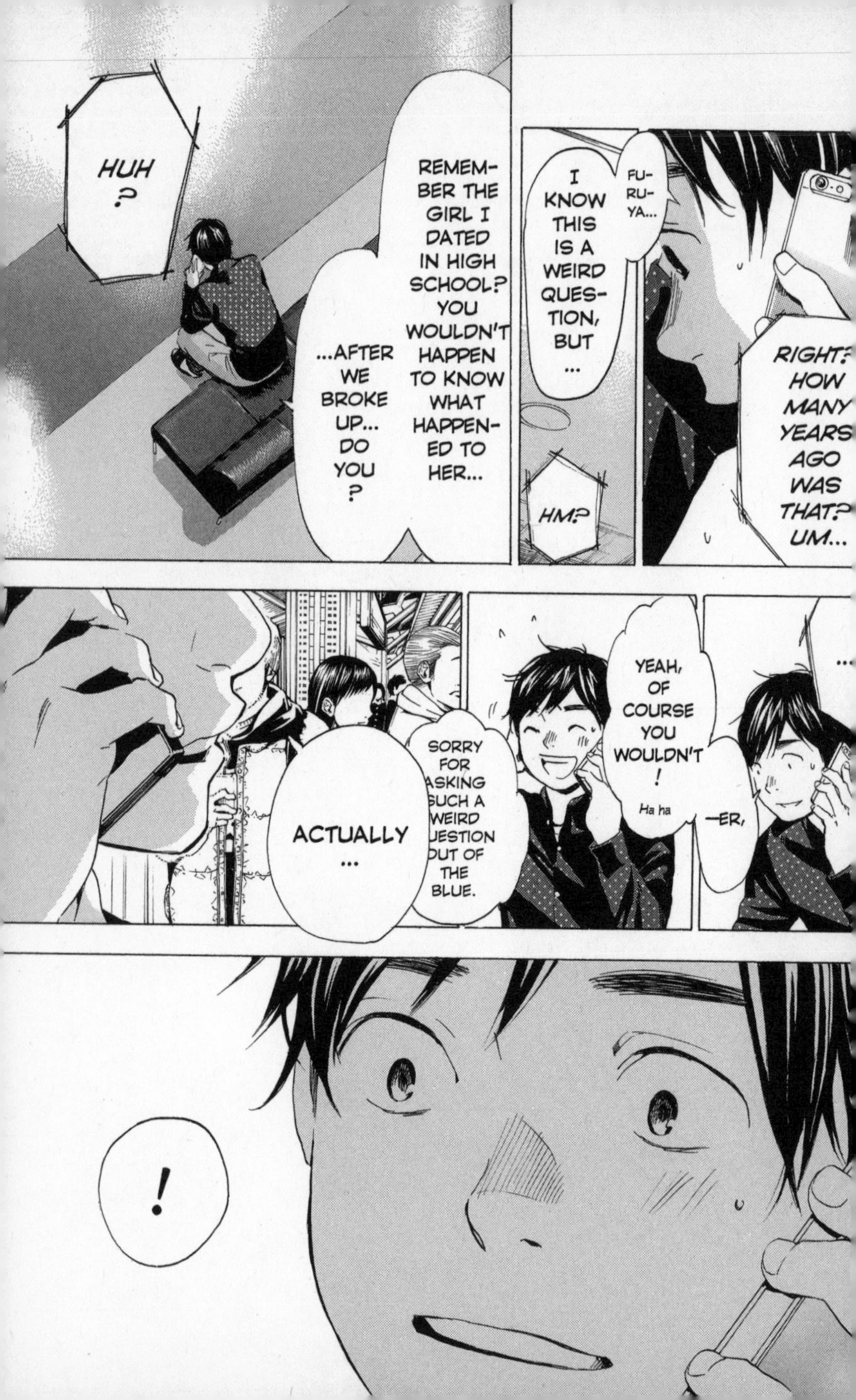
RIGHT? HOW MANY YEARS AGO WAS THAT? UM...
FU-RU-YA...
I KNOW THIS IS A WEIRD QUES-TION, BUT...
HM?
REMEM-BER THE GIRL I DATED IN HIGH SCHOOL? YOU WOULDN'T HAPPEN TO KNOW WHAT HAPPEN-ED TO HER...
...AFTER WE BROKE UP... DO YOU?
HUH?
...
—ER,
YEAH, OF COURSE YOU WOULDN'T!
Ha ha
SORRY FOR ASKING SUCH A WEIRD UESTION UT OF THE BLUE.
ACTUALLY...
!

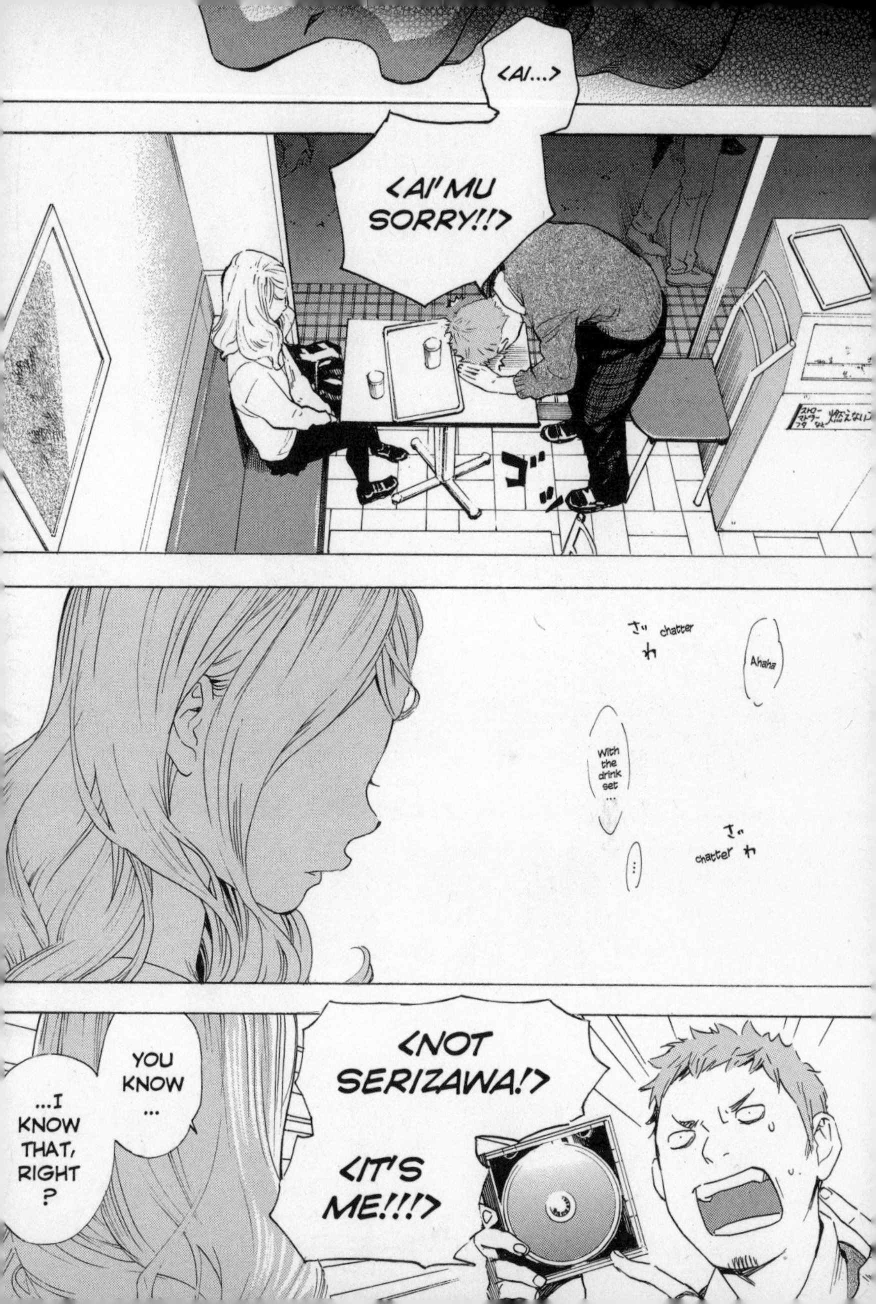
<AI...>
<AI'MU SORRY!!>
ゴッ
ざわ chatter
Ahaha
With the drink set...
...
ざわ chatter
<NOT SERIZAWA!>
<IT'S ME!!!>
YOU KNOW...
...I KNOW THAT, RIGHT?

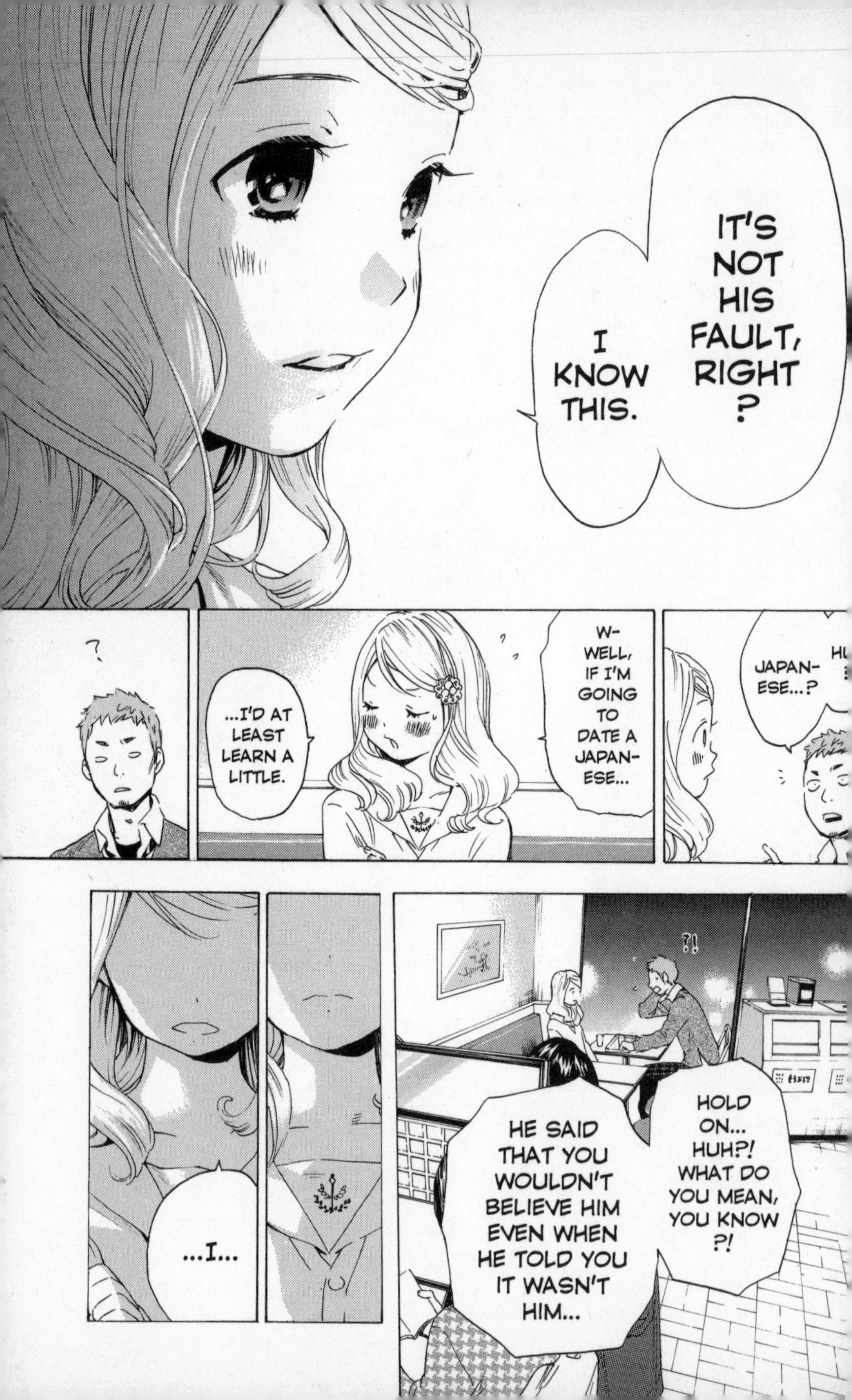
IT'S NOT HIS FAULT, RIGHT?
I KNOW THIS.
HU
JAPAN-ESE...?
W-WELL, IF I'M GOING TO DATE A JAPAN-ESE...
...I'D AT LEAST LEARN A LITTLE.
?
?!
HOLD ON... HUH?! WHAT DO YOU MEAN, YOU KNOW?!
HE SAID THAT YOU WOULDN'T BELIEVE HIM EVEN WHEN HE TOLD YOU IT WASN'T HIM...
...I...

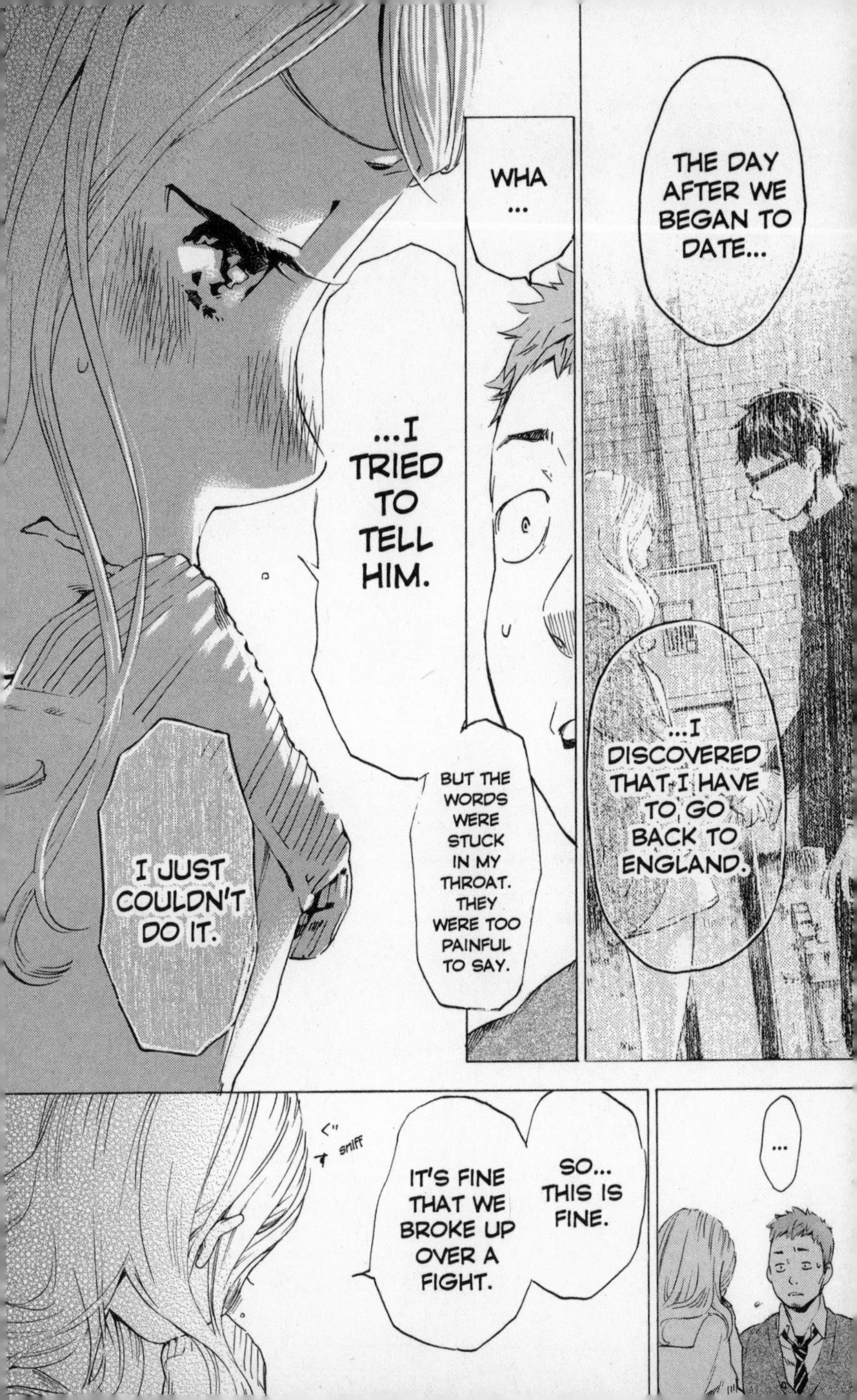
THE DAY AFTER WE BEGAN TO DATE...
...I DISCOVERED THAT I HAVE TO GO BACK TO ENGLAND.
WHA ...
...I TRIED TO TELL HIM.
BUT THE WORDS WERE STUCK IN MY THROAT. THEY WERE TOO PAINFUL TO SAY.
I JUST COULDN'T DO IT.
...
SO... THIS IS FINE.
IT'S FINE THAT WE BROKE UP OVER A FIGHT.
sniff

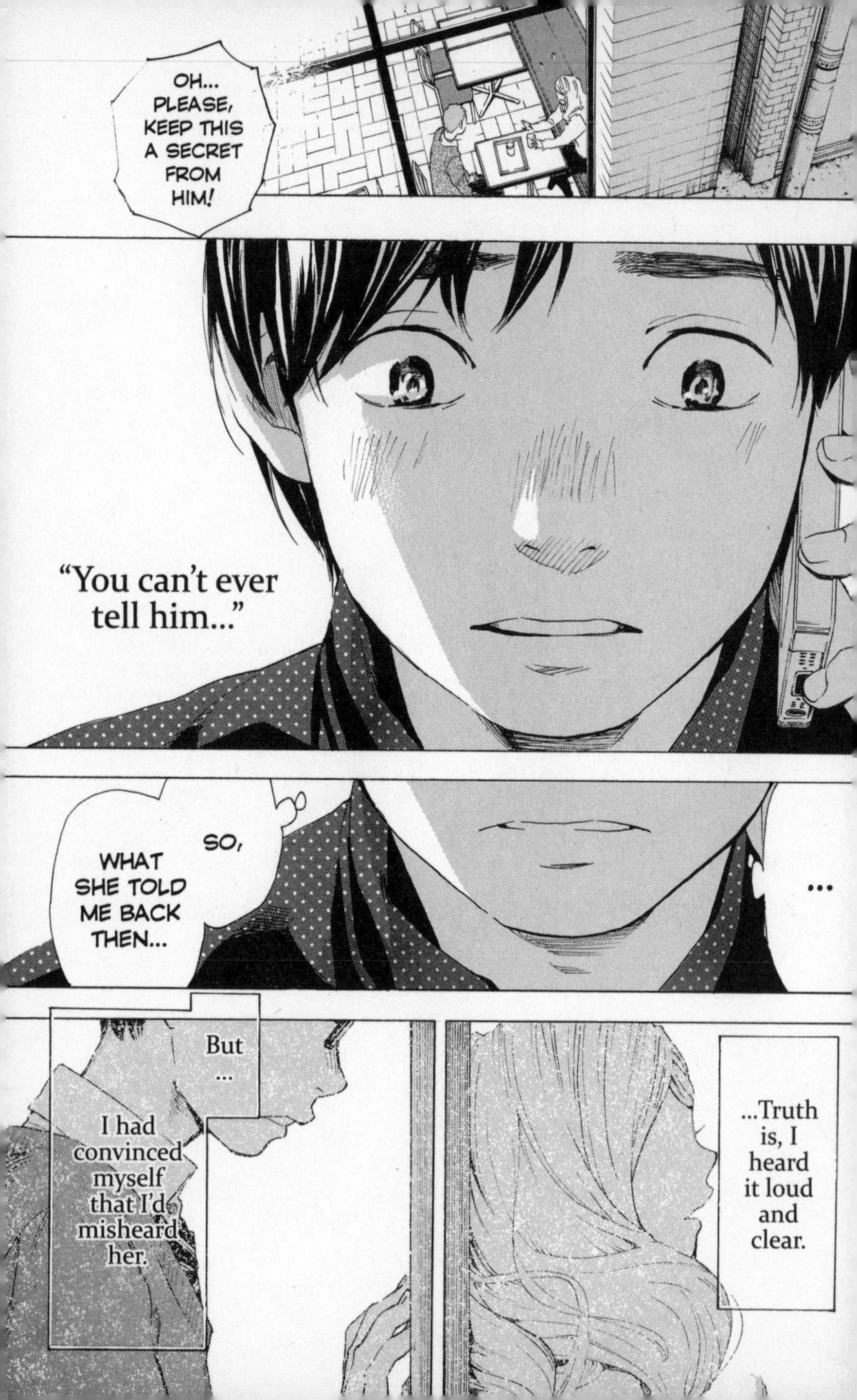
OH... PLEASE, KEEP THIS A SECRET FROM HIM!
"You can't ever tell him..."
...
SO, WHAT SHE TOLD ME BACK THEN...
...Truth is, I heard it loud and clear.
But...
I had convinced myself that I'd misheard her.

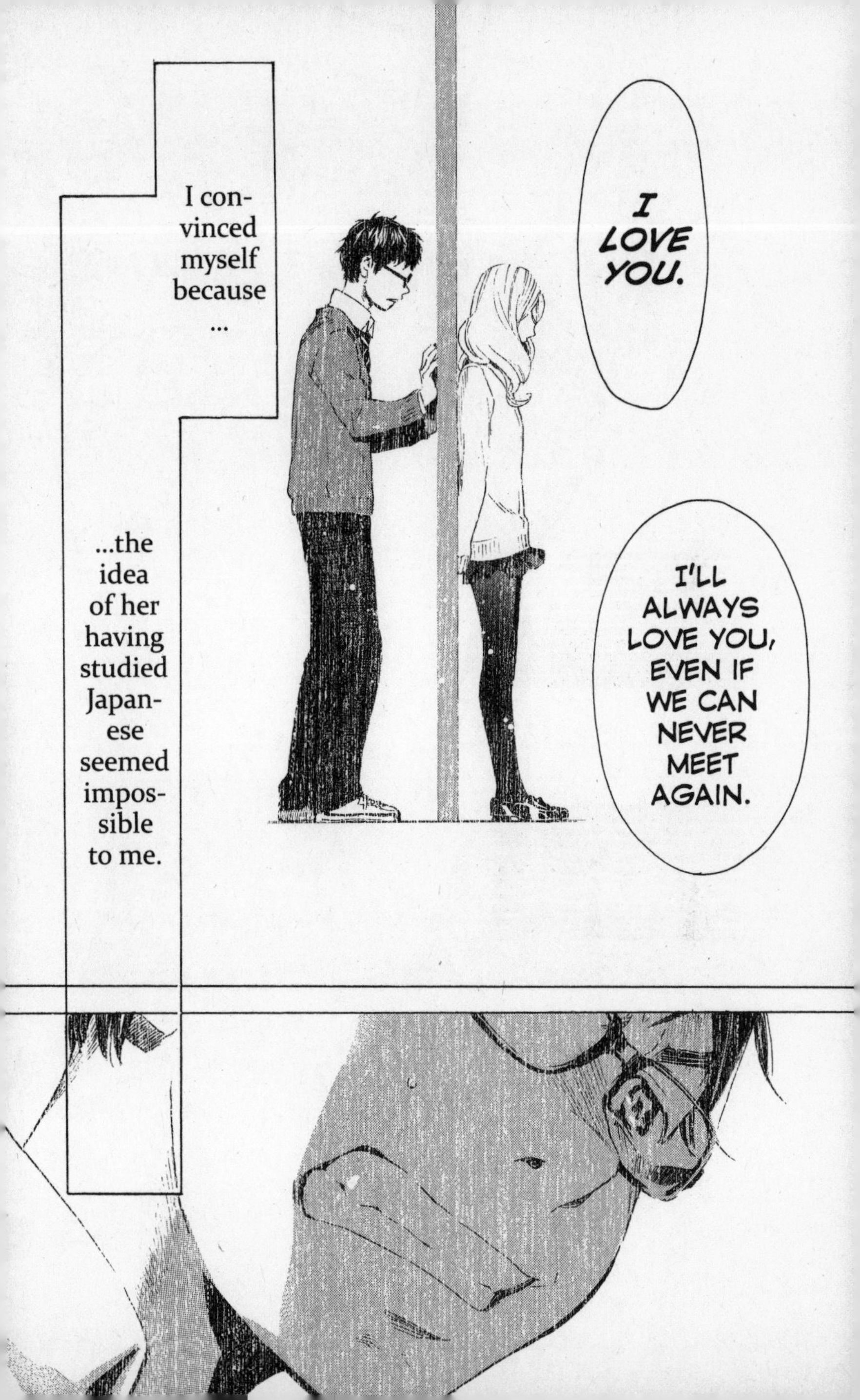
I LOVE YOU.
I'LL ALWAYS LOVE YOU, EVEN IF WE CAN NEVER MEET AGAIN.
I convinced myself because ...
...the idea of her having studied Japanese seemed impossible to me.

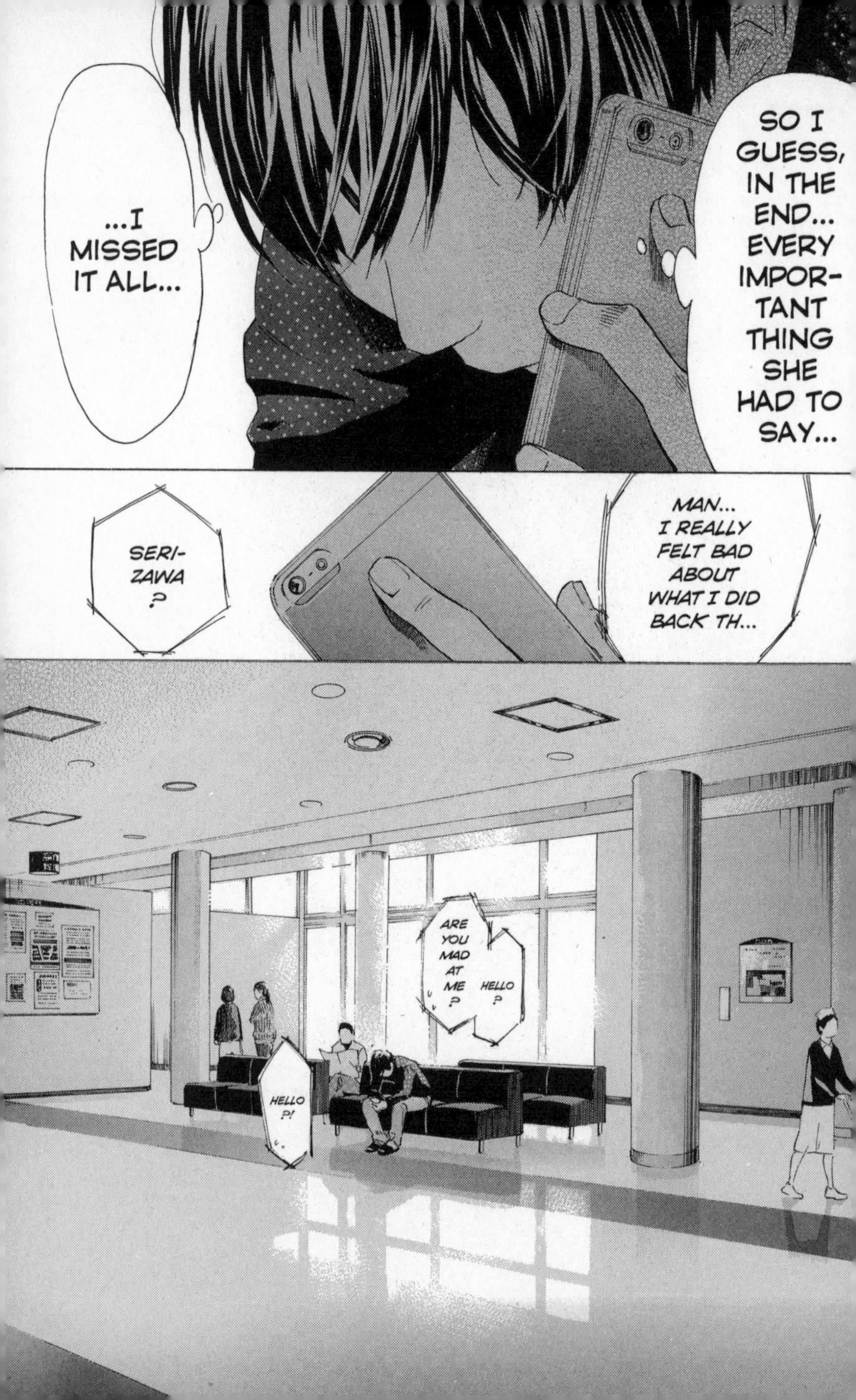
SO I GUESS, IN THE END... EVERY IMPOR-TANT THING SHE HAD TO SAY...
...I MISSED IT ALL...
MAN... I REALLY FELT BAD ABOUT WHAT I DID BACK TH...
SERI-ZAWA?
HELLO?
ARE YOU MAD AT ME?
HELLO?!

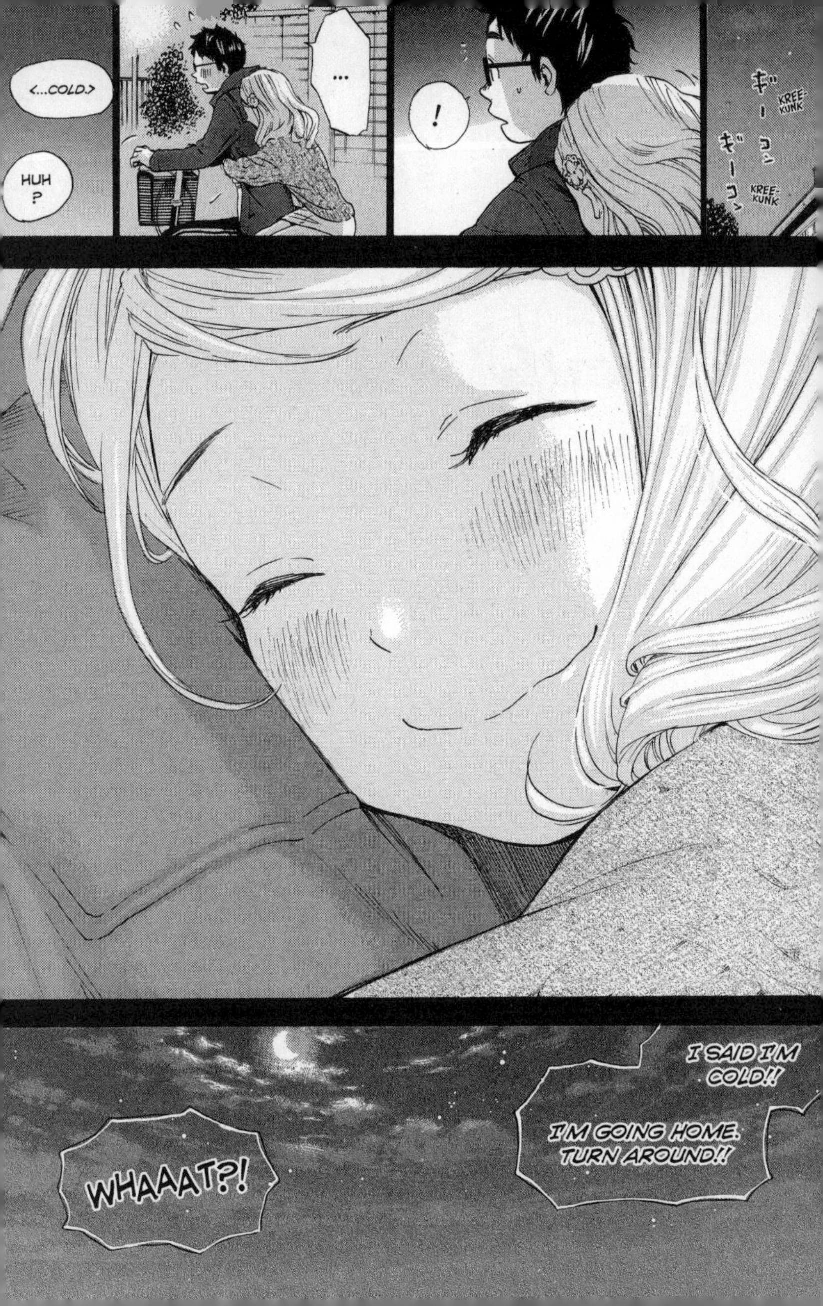
ギーコ
KREE-KUNK
ギーコ
KREE-KUNK
!
...
<...COLD.>
HUH ?
I SAID I'M COLD!!
I'M GOING HOME. TURN AROUND!!
WHAAAT?!

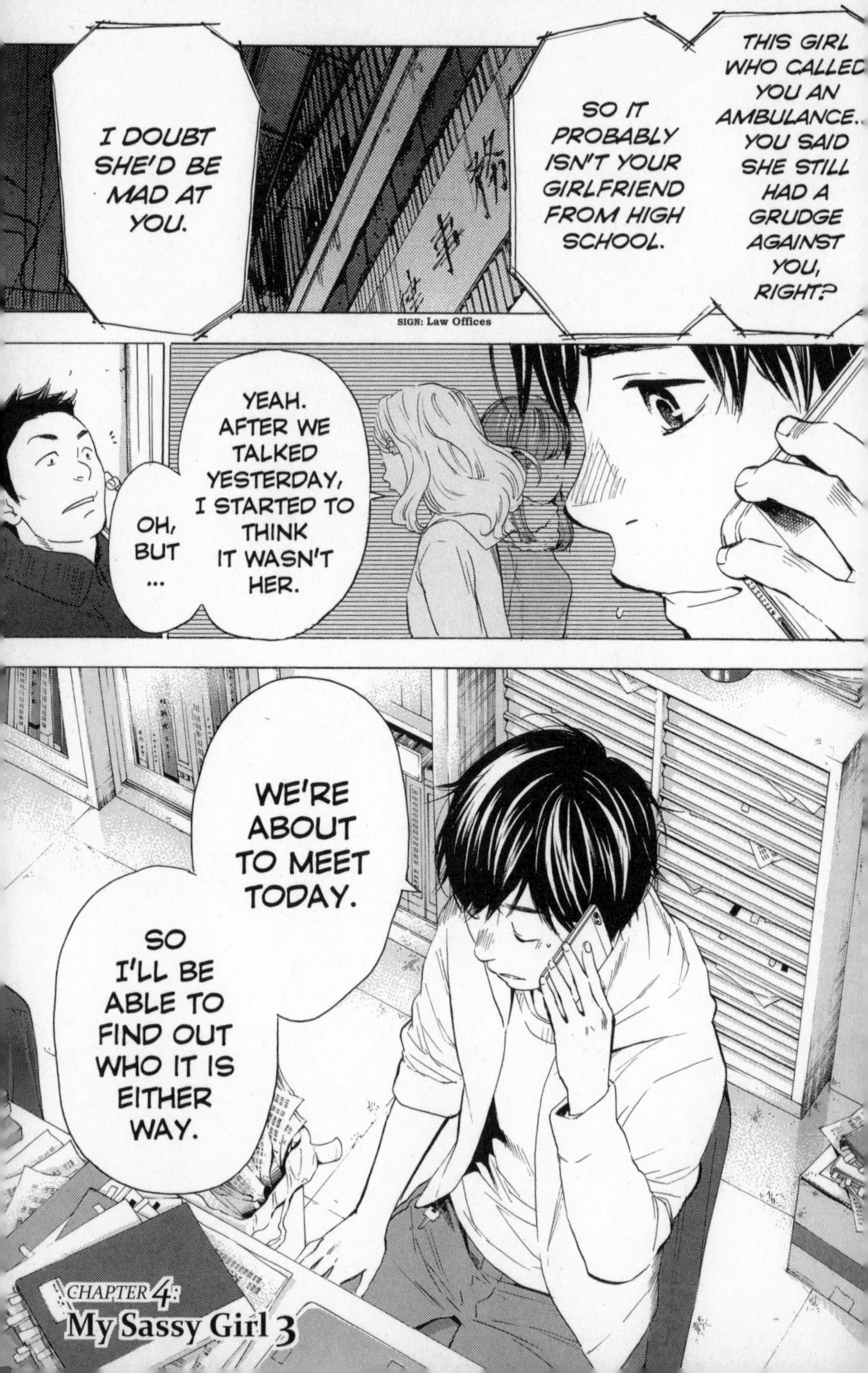
THIS GIRL WHO CALLED YOU AN AMBULANCE... YOU SAID SHE STILL HAD A GRUDGE AGAINST YOU, RIGHT?
SO IT PROBABLY ISN'T YOUR GIRLFRIEND FROM HIGH SCHOOL.
I DOUBT SHE'D BE MAD AT YOU.
SIGN: Law Offices
YEAH. AFTER WE TALKED YESTERDAY, I STARTED TO THINK IT WASN'T HER.
OH, BUT ...
WE'RE ABOUT TO MEET TODAY.
SO I'LL BE ABLE TO FIND OUT WHO IT IS EITHER WAY.
CHAPTER 4:
My Sassy Girl 3

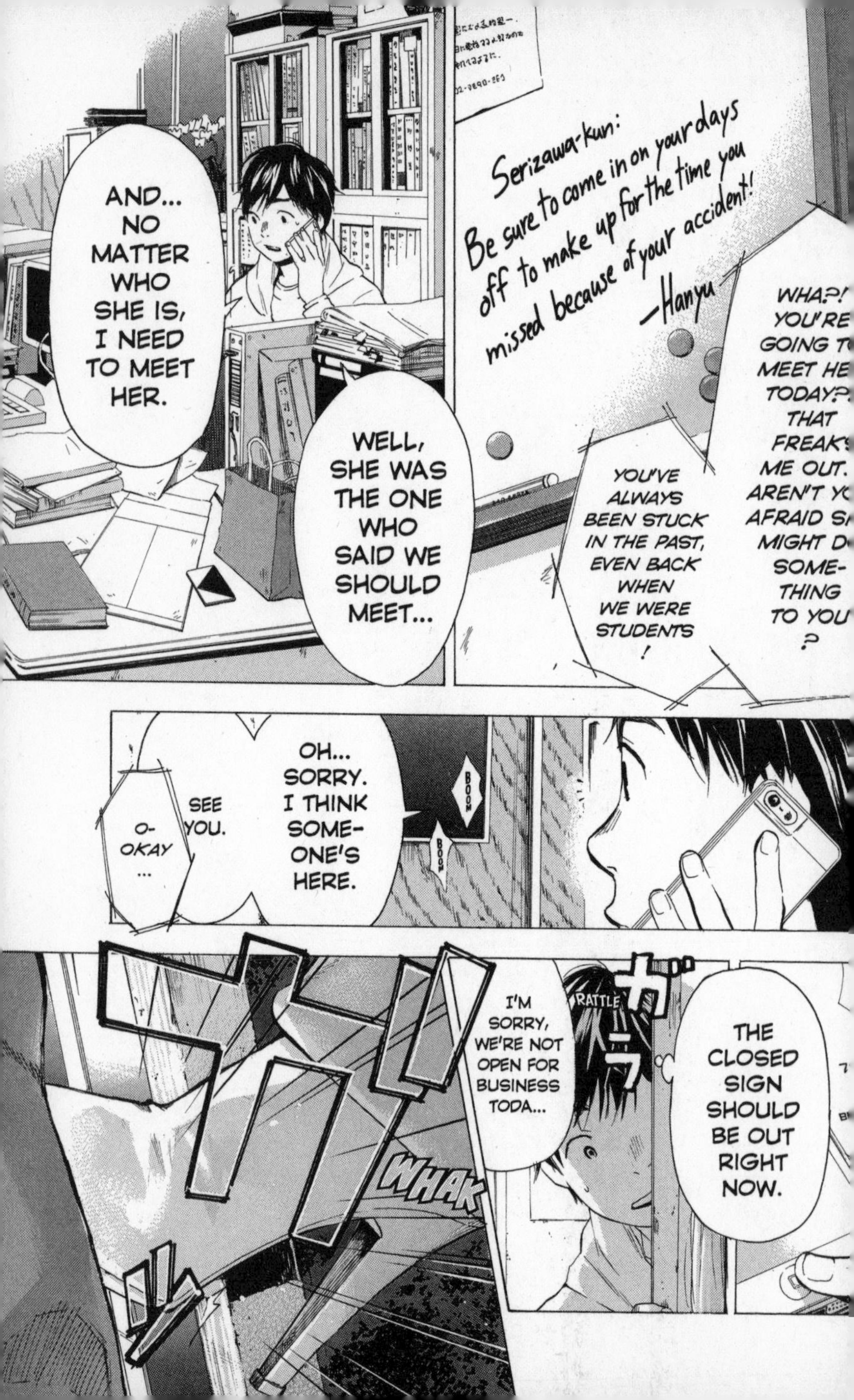
Serizawa-kun: Be sure to come in on your days off to make up for the time you missed because of your accident! —Hanyu
WHA?! YOU'RE GOING T MEET HE TODAY?! THAT FREAKS ME OUT. AREN'T YO AFRAID S MIGHT D SOME-THING TO YOU ?
YOU'VE ALWAYS BEEN STUCK IN THE PAST, EVEN BACK WHEN WE WERE STUDENTS !
WELL, SHE WAS THE ONE WHO SAID WE SHOULD MEET...
AND... NO MATTER WHO SHE IS, I NEED TO MEET HER.
BOOM
BOOM
OH... SORRY. I THINK SOME-ONE'S HERE.
SEE YOU.
O-OKAY ...
THE CLOSED SIGN SHOULD BE OUT RIGHT NOW.
RATTLE
I'M SORRY, WE'RE NOT OPEN FOR BUSINESS TODA...
WHAK

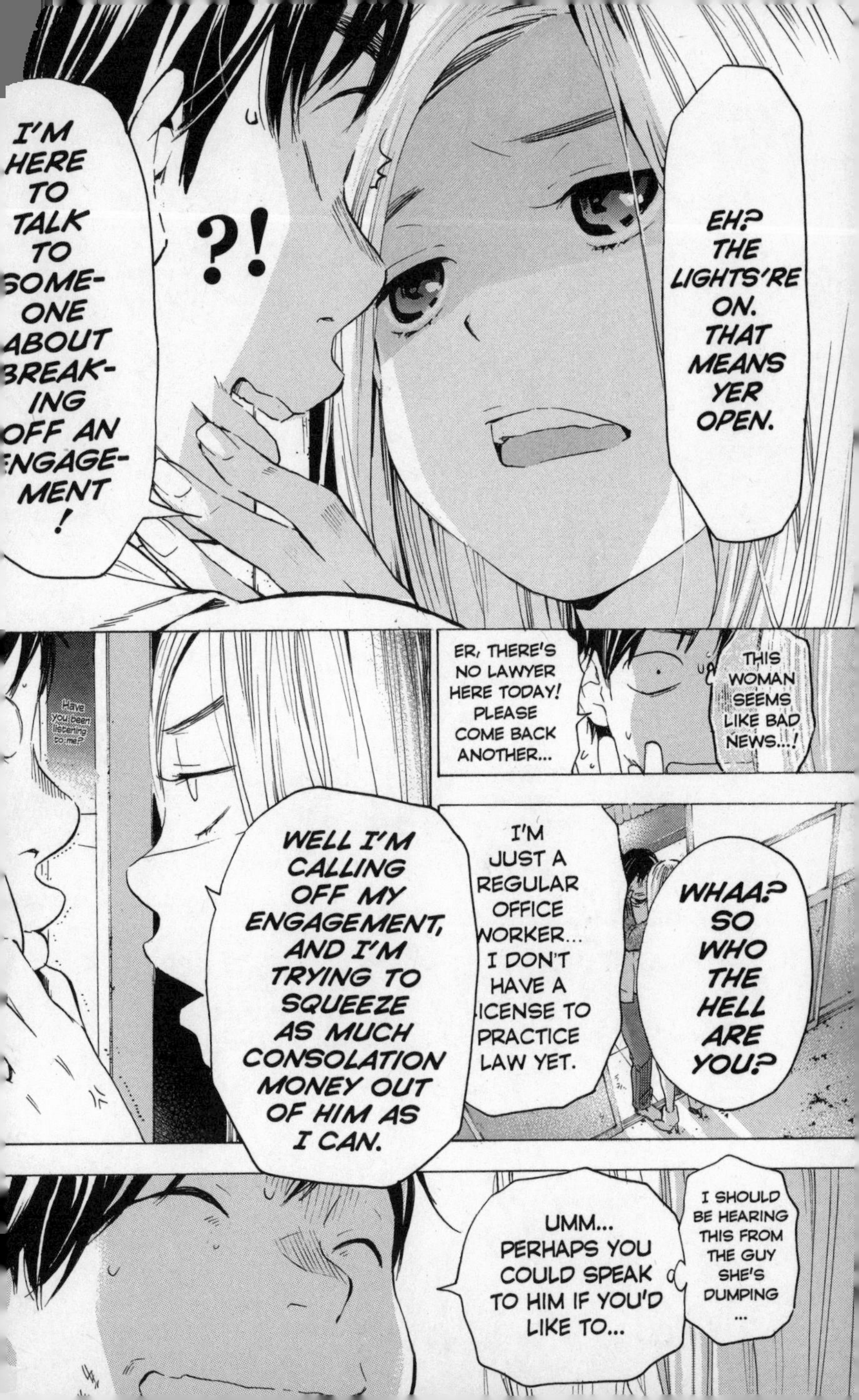
EH? THE LIGHTS'RE ON. THAT MEANS YER OPEN.
?!
I'M HERE TO TALK TO SOMEONE ABOUT BREAKING OFF AN ENGAGEMENT!
THIS WOMAN SEEMS LIKE BAD NEWS...!
ER, THERE'S NO LAWYER HERE TODAY! PLEASE COME BACK ANOTHER...
WHAA? SO WHO THE HELL ARE YOU?
I'M JUST A REGULAR OFFICE WORKER... I DON'T HAVE A LICENSE TO PRACTICE LAW YET.
Have you been listening to me?
WELL I'M CALLING OFF MY ENGAGEMENT, AND I'M TRYING TO SQUEEZE AS MUCH CONSOLATION MONEY OUT OF HIM AS I CAN.
I SHOULD BE HEARING THIS FROM THE GUY SHE'S DUMPING...
UMM... PERHAPS YOU COULD SPEAK TO HIM IF YOU'D LIKE TO...

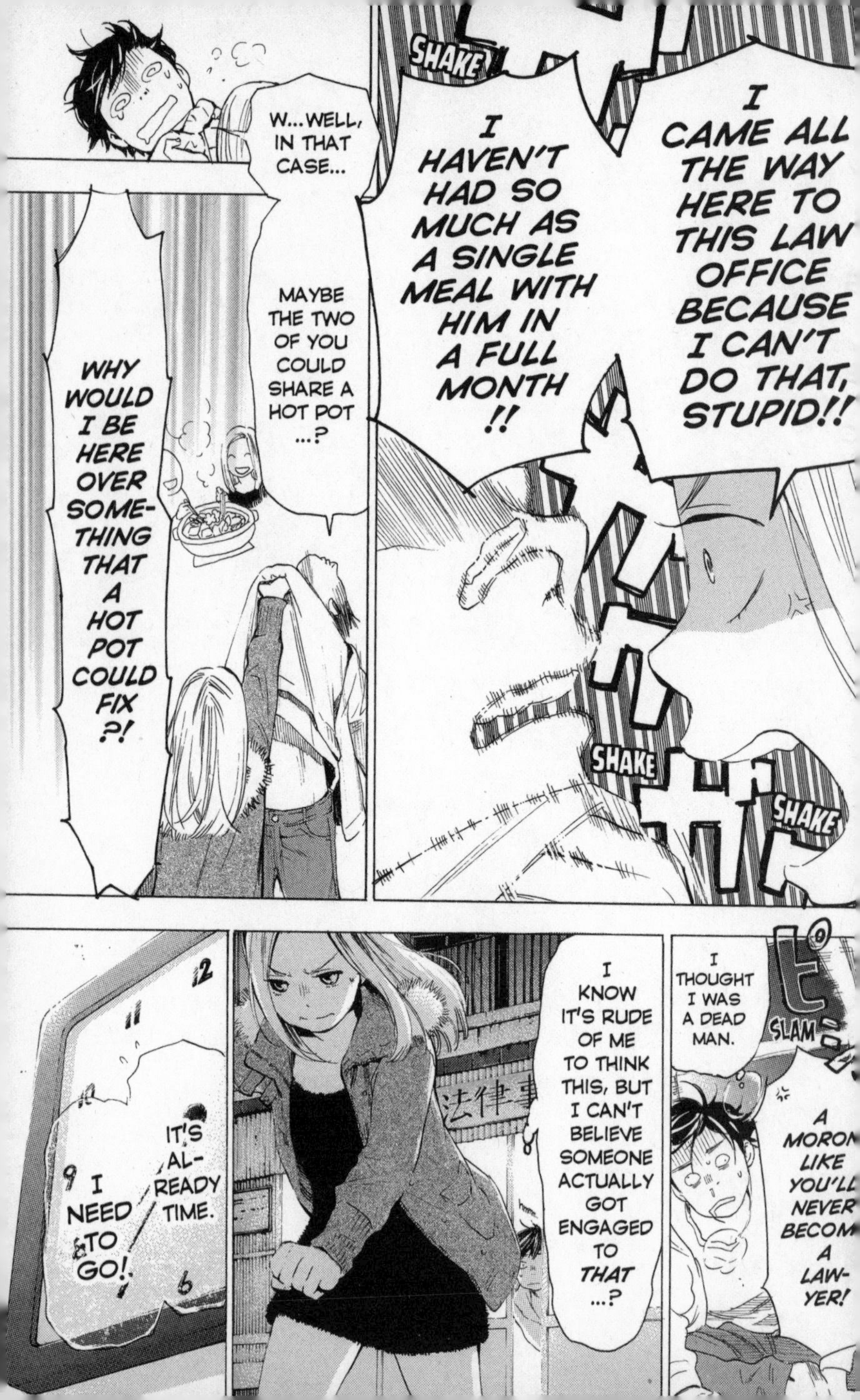
SHAKE
I CAME ALL THE WAY HERE TO THIS LAW OFFICE BECAUSE I CAN'T DO THAT, STUPID!!
I HAVEN'T HAD SO MUCH AS A SINGLE MEAL WITH HIM IN A FULL MONTH !!
SHAKE
SHAKE
W...WELL, IN THAT CASE...
MAYBE THE TWO OF YOU COULD SHARE A HOT POT ...?
WHY WOULD I BE HERE OVER SOME-THING THAT A HOT POT COULD FIX ?!
SLAM
A MORON LIKE YOU'LL NEVER BECOME A LAWYER!
I THOUGHT I WAS A DEAD MAN.
I KNOW IT'S RUDE OF ME TO THINK THIS, BUT I CAN'T BELIEVE SOMEONE ACTUALLY GOT ENGAGED TO THAT ...?
法律事
IT'S AL-READY TIME.
I NEED TO GO!

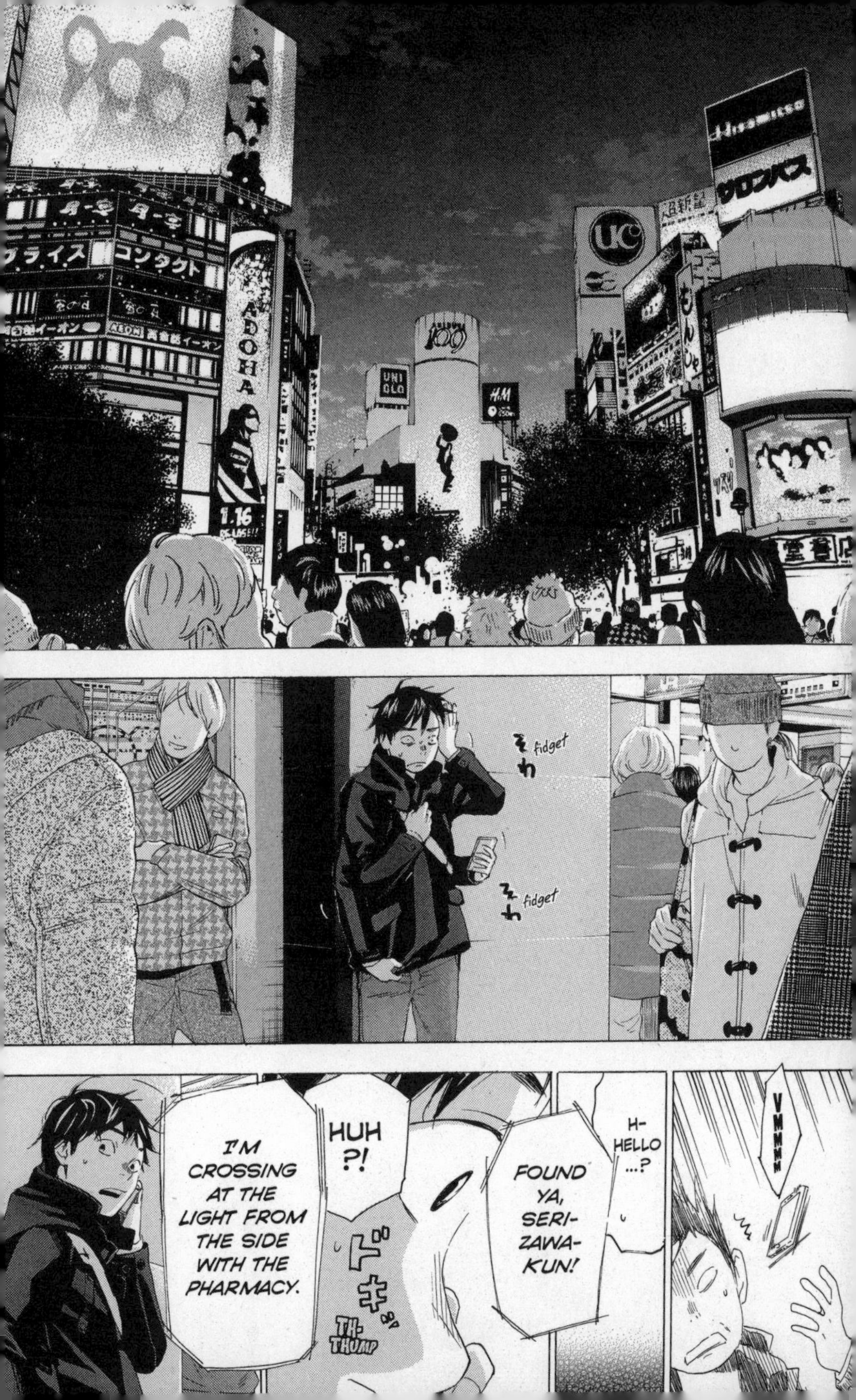

コンタクト
サロンパス
UNI QLO
109
H&M
1.16
fidget
fidget
VMMMM
H- HELLO ...?
FOUND YA, SERI-ZAWA-KUN!
HUH ?!
TH-THUMP
I'M CROSSING AT THE LIGHT FROM THE SIDE WITH THE PHARMACY.

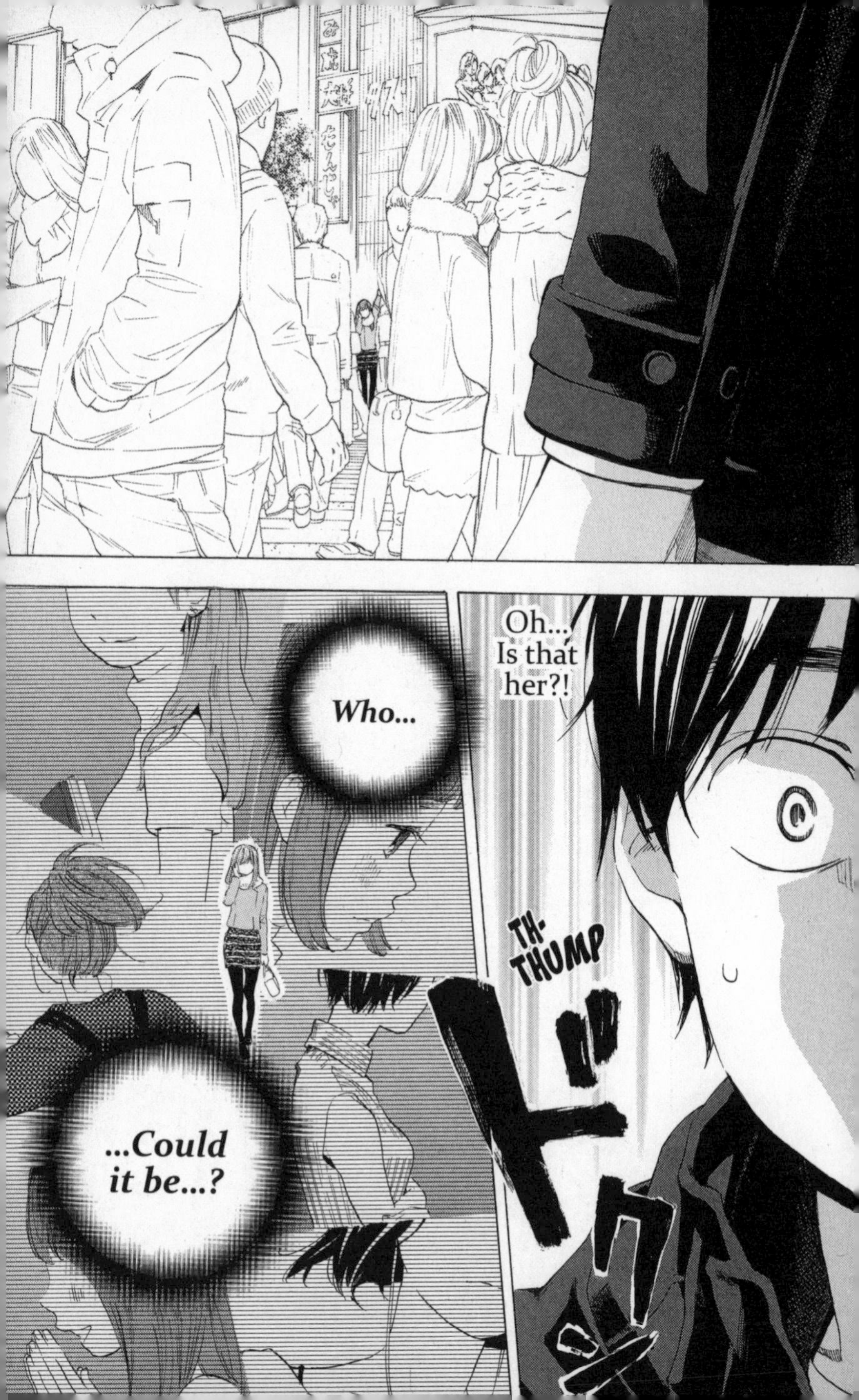
Oh... Is that her?!
TH-THUMP
Who...
...Could it be...?

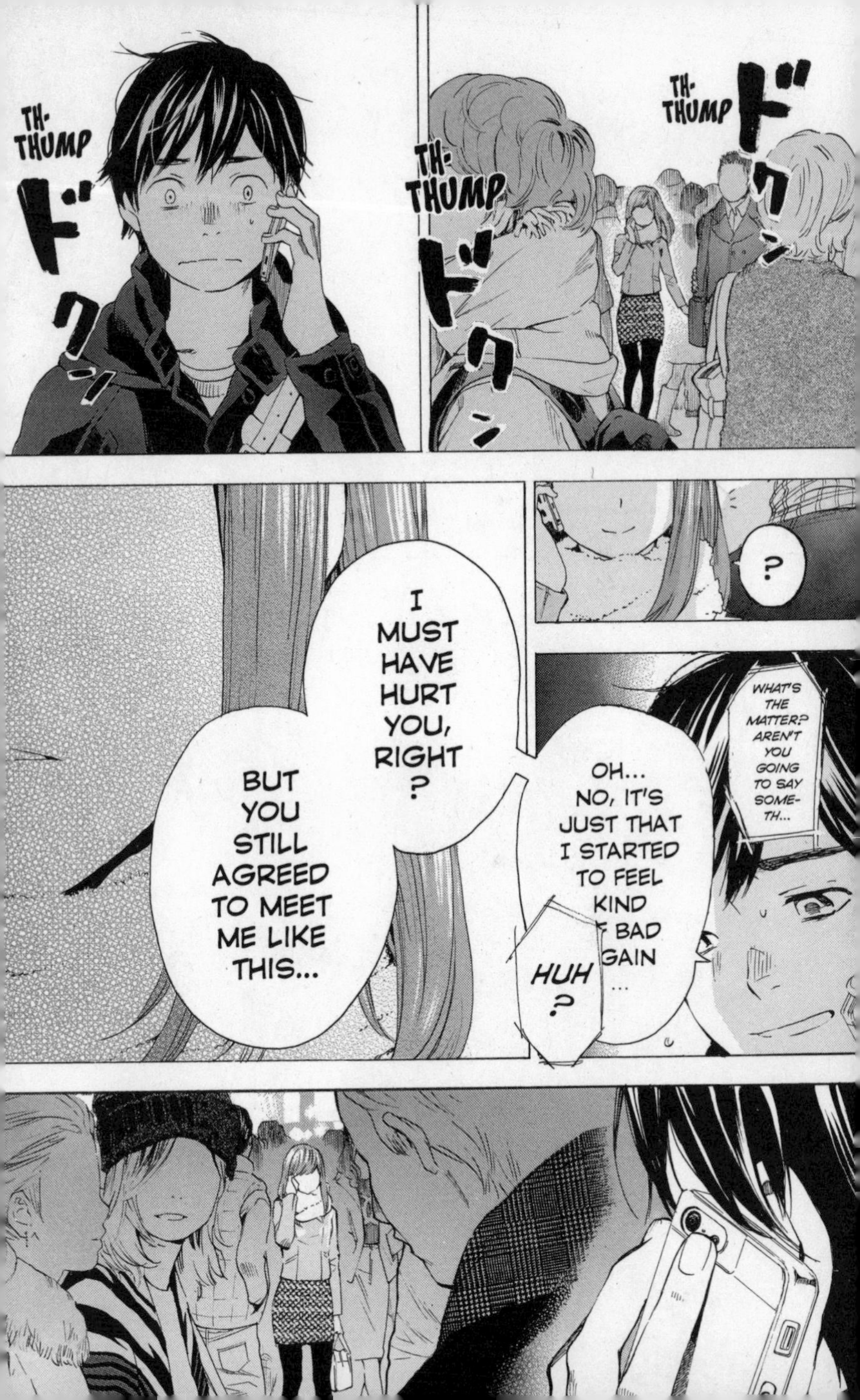
TH-THUMP
TH-THUMP
TH-THUMP
?
WHAT'S THE MATTER? AREN'T YOU GOING TO SAY SOMETH...
OH... NO, IT'S JUST THAT I STARTED TO FEEL KIND F BAD GAIN...
HUH?
I MUST HAVE HURT YOU, RIGHT?
BUT YOU STILL AGREED TO MEET ME LIKE THIS...

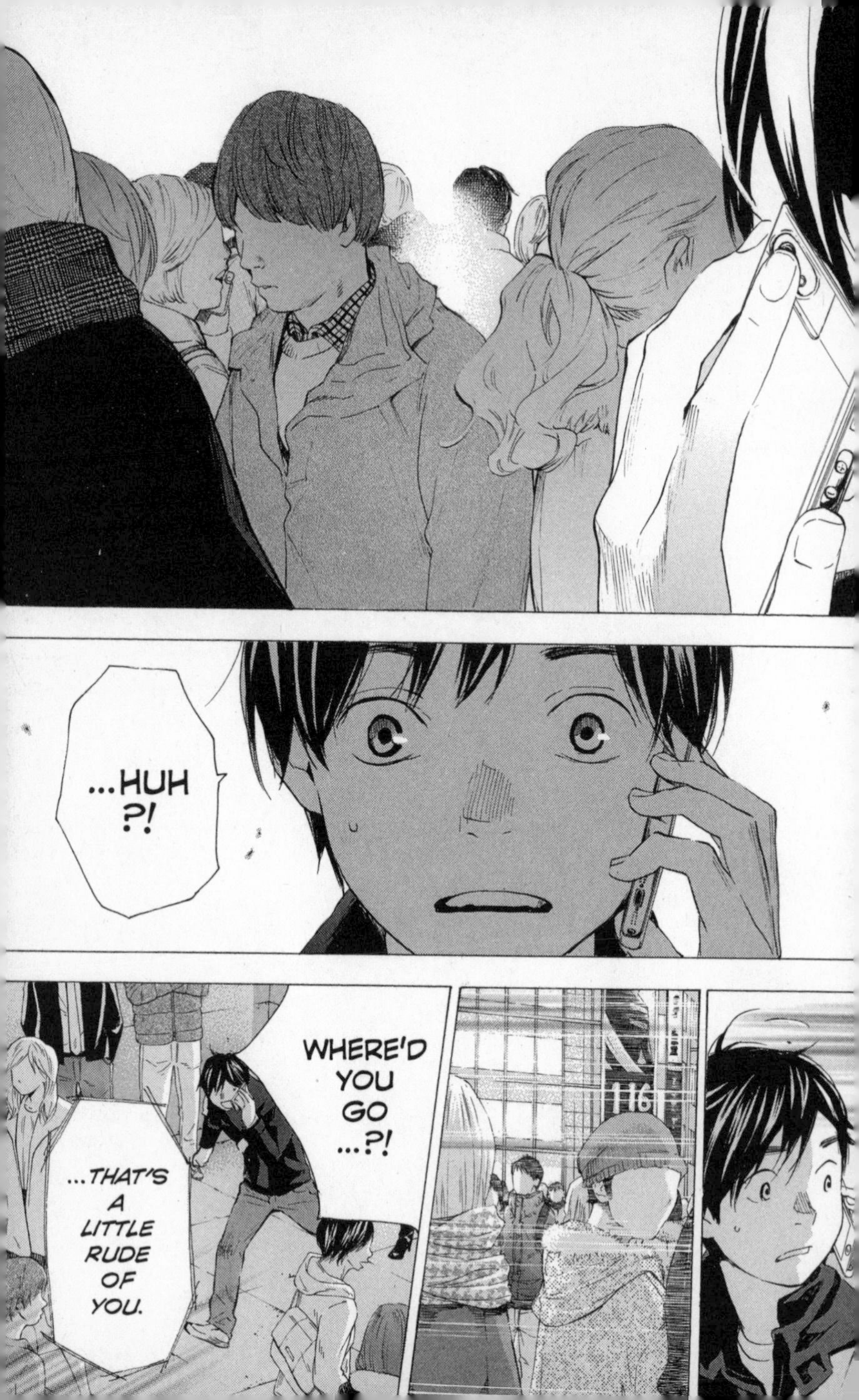
...HUH ?!
WHERE'D YOU GO ...?!
...THAT'S A LITTLE RUDE OF YOU.

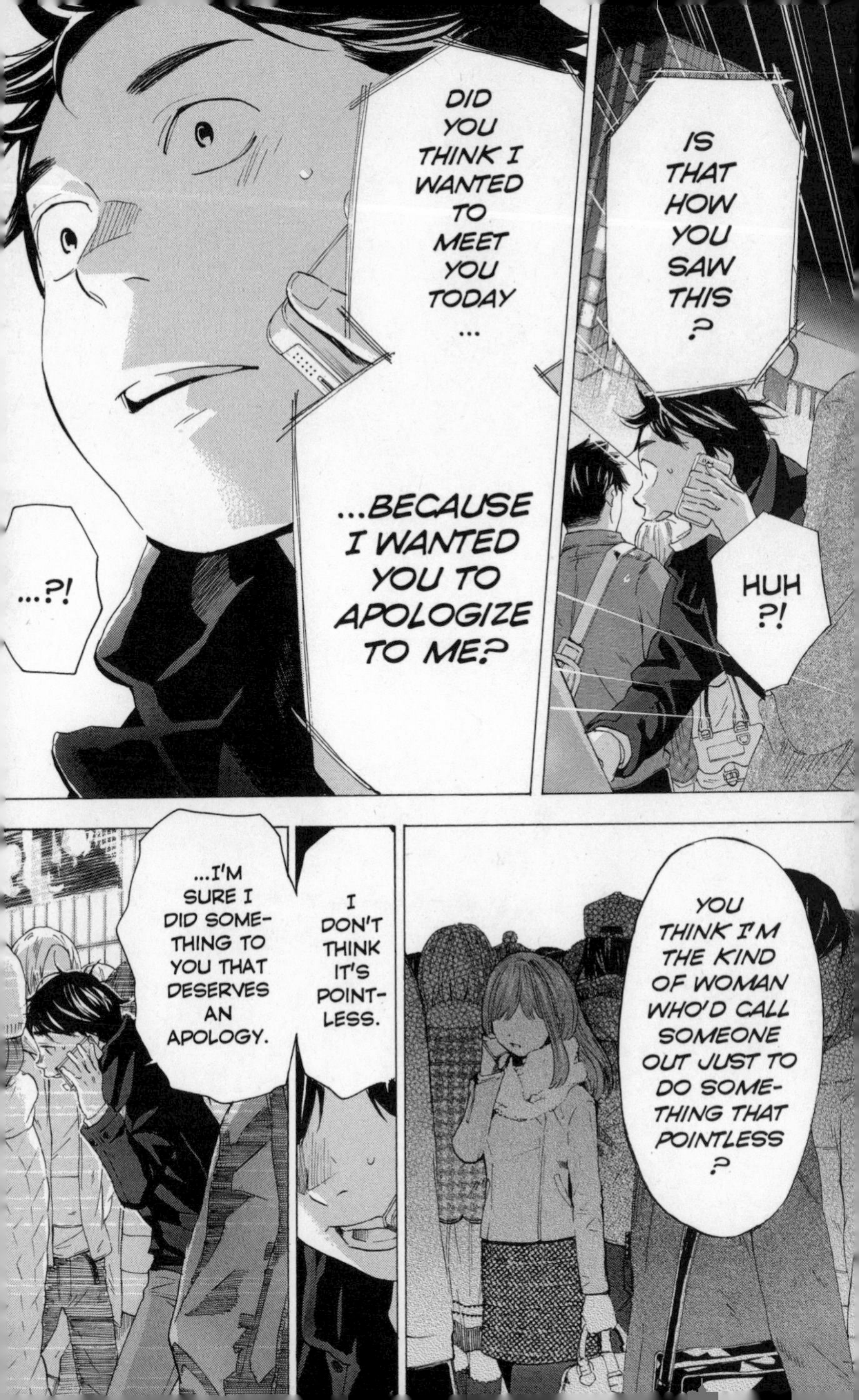
IS THAT HOW YOU SAW THIS?
HUH?!
DID YOU THINK I WANTED TO MEET YOU TODAY...
...BECAUSE I WANTED YOU TO APOLOGIZE TO ME?
...?!
YOU THINK I'M THE KIND OF WOMAN WHO'D CALL SOMEONE OUT JUST TO DO SOME-THING THAT POINTLESS?
I DON'T THINK IT'S POINT-LESS.
...I'M SURE I DID SOME-THING TO YOU THAT DESERVES AN APOLOGY.

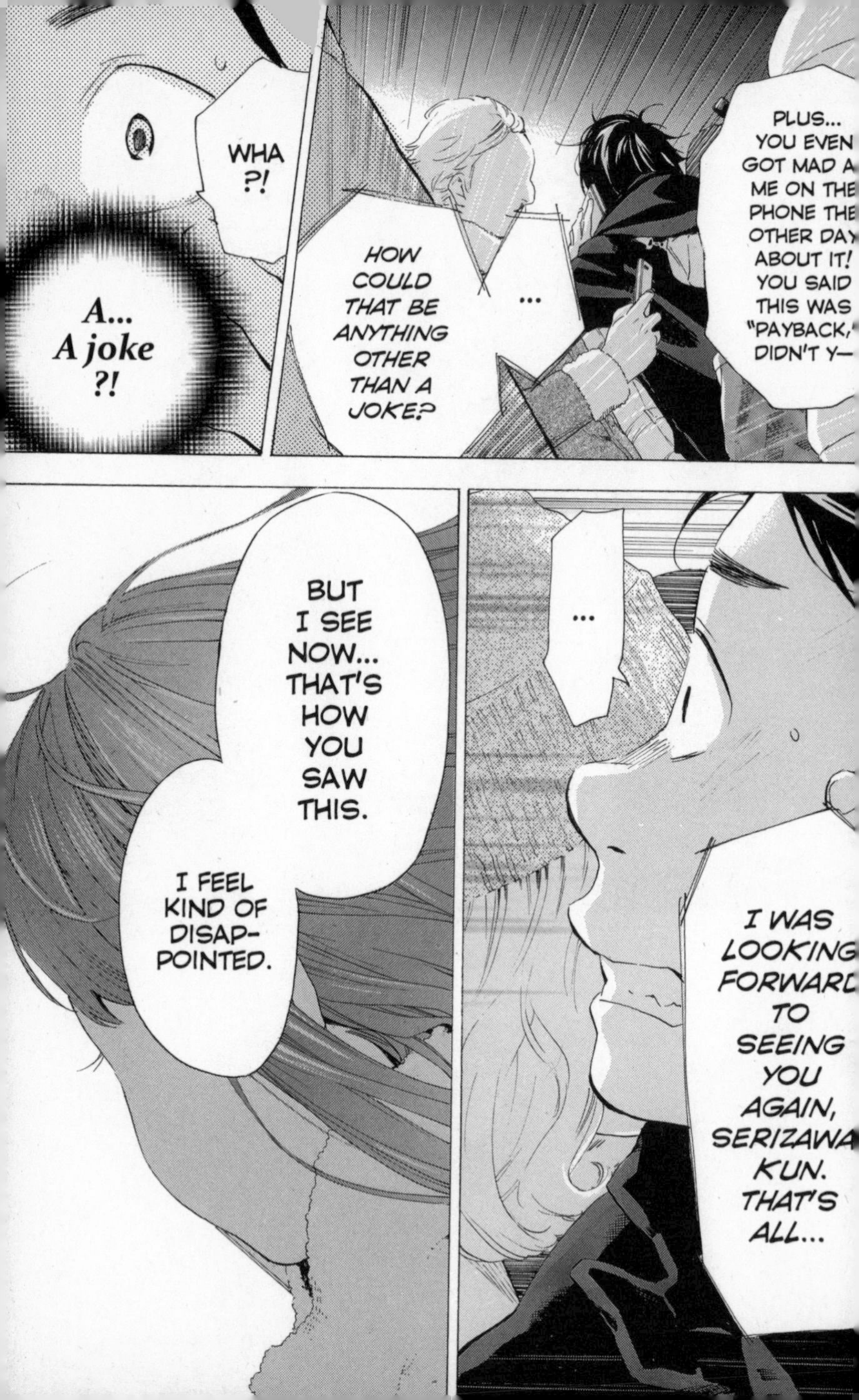
PLUS... YOU EVEN GOT MAD A ME ON THE PHONE THE OTHER DAY ABOUT IT! YOU SAID THIS WAS "PAYBACK," DIDN'T Y—
...
HOW COULD THAT BE ANYTHING OTHER THAN A JOKE?
WHA ?!
A... A joke ?!
...
I WAS LOOKING FORWARD TO SEEING YOU AGAIN, SERIZAWA KUN. THAT'S ALL...
BUT I SEE NOW... THAT'S HOW YOU SAW THIS.
I FEEL KIND OF DISAPPOINTED.

MAYBE WE SHOULDN'T MEET AFTER ALL.

BEEP

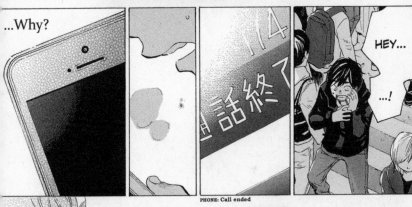

...Why?

HEY...

...!

PHONE: Call ended

Why would she do that?

I was just trying to apologize.

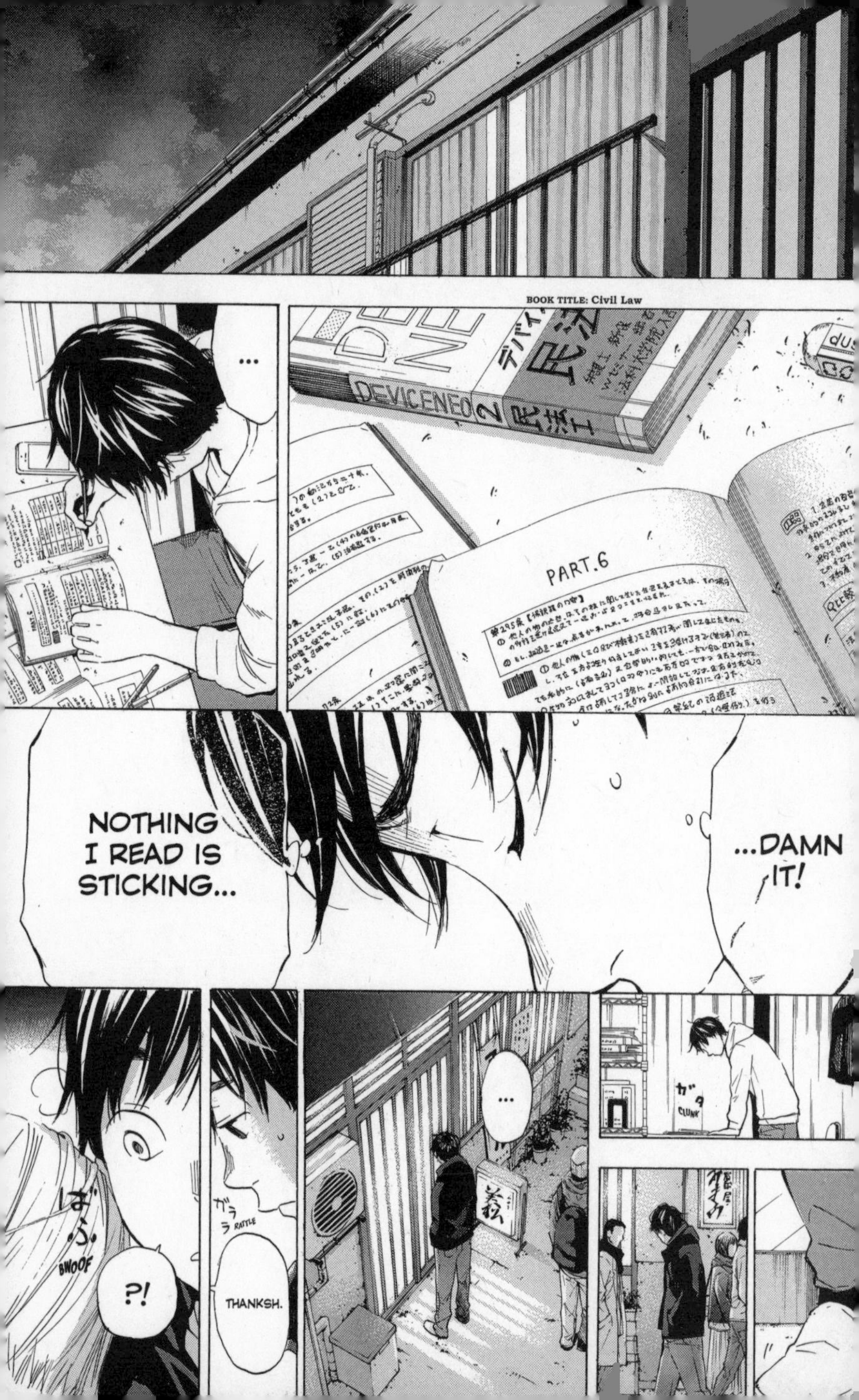
BOOK TITLE: Civil Law
DEVICENEO 2
PART.6
...
NOTHING I READ IS STICKING...
...DAMN IT!
ガタ
CLUNK
...
ガラ
RATTLE
THANKSH.
ばふ
BWOOF
?!

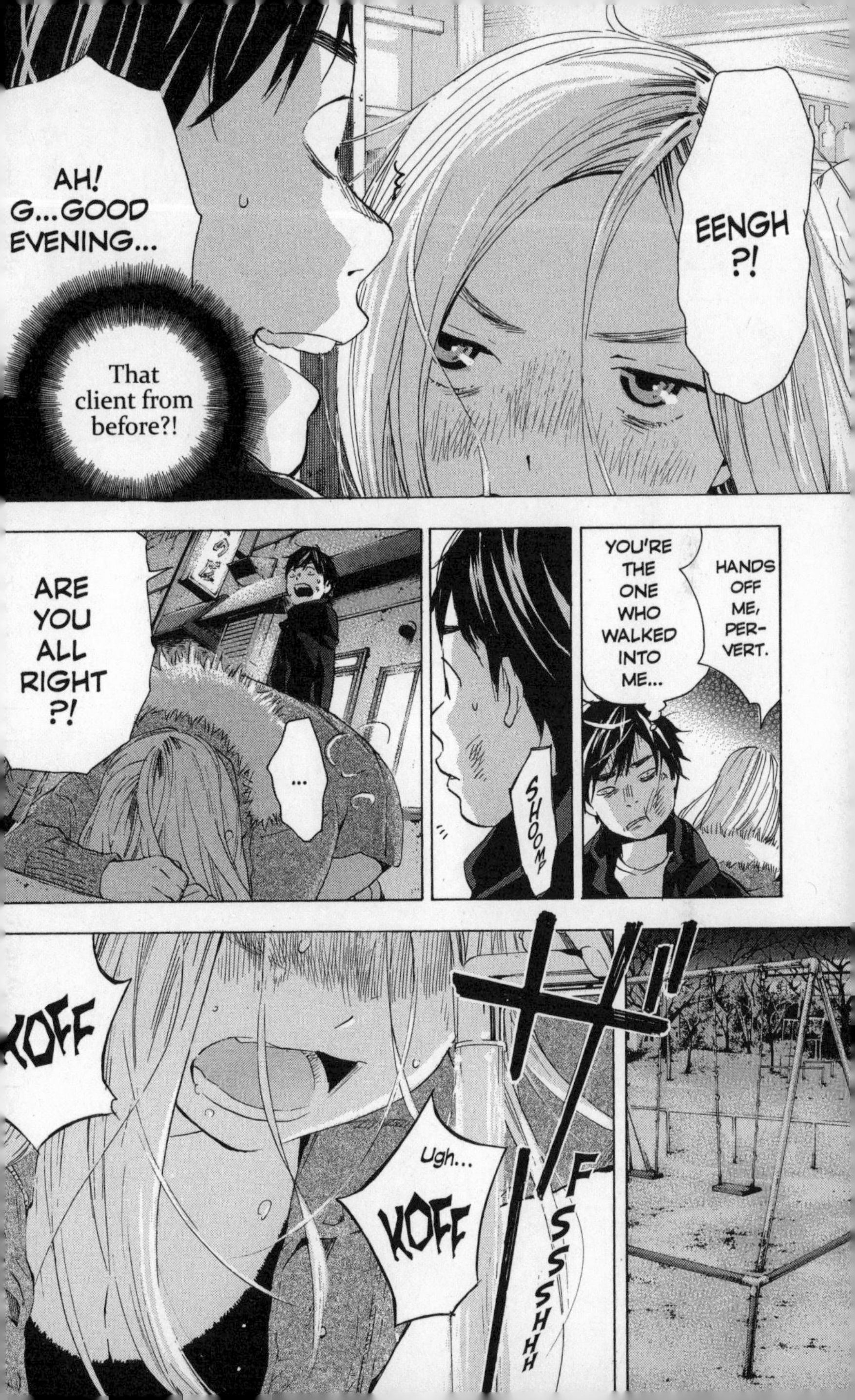
EENGH ?!
AH! G...GOOD EVENING...
That client from before?!
HANDS OFF ME, PER-VERT.
YOU'RE THE ONE WHO WALKED INTO ME...
SHOOMP
ARE YOU ALL RIGHT ?!
...
FSSSHHH
Ugh...
KOFF
KOFF

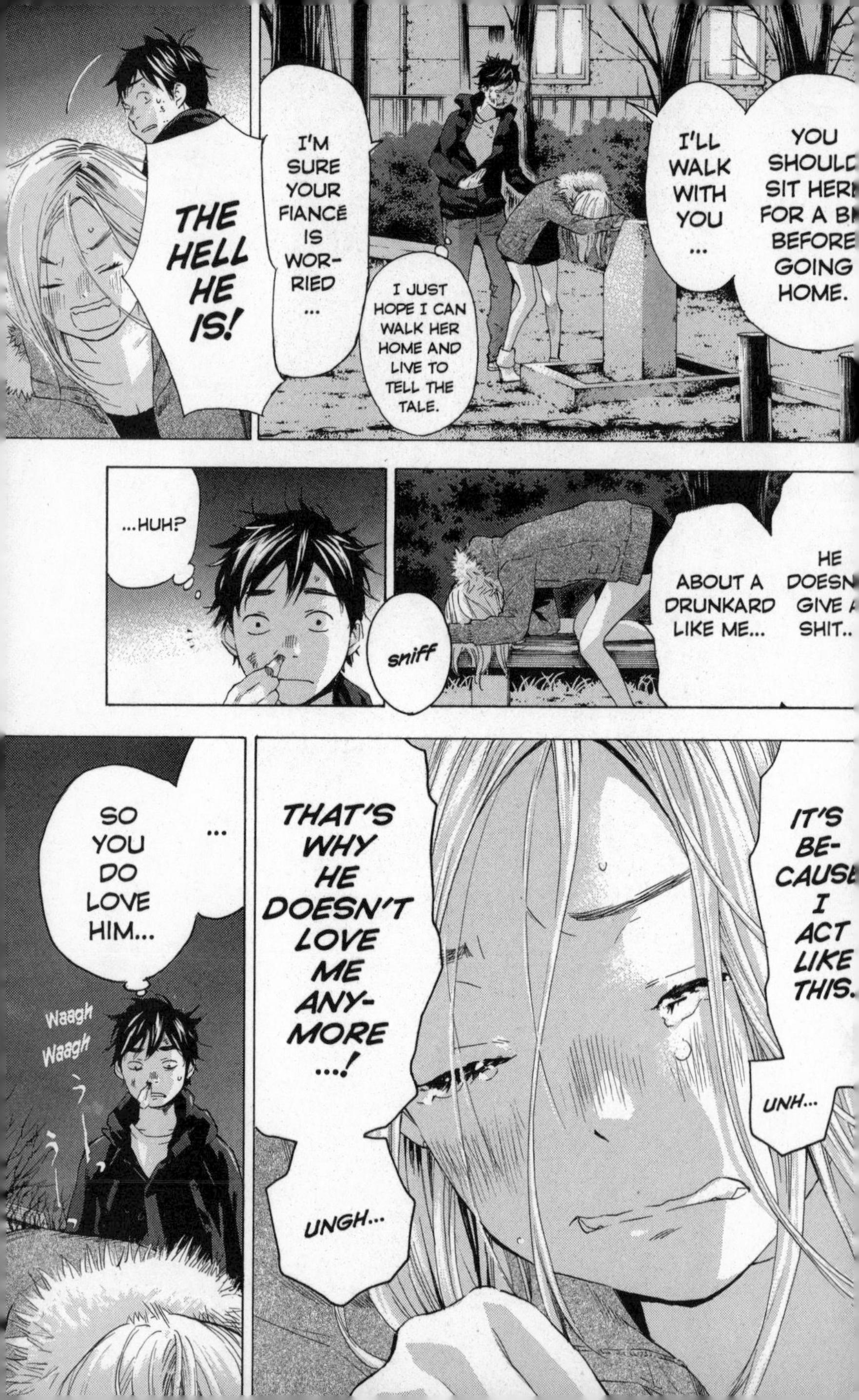

YOU SHOULD SIT HER FOR A B BEFORE GOING HOME.
I'LL WALK WITH YOU ...
I'M SURE YOUR FIANCÉ IS WOR- RIED ...
I JUST HOPE I CAN WALK HER HOME AND LIVE TO TELL THE TALE.
THE HELL HE IS!
HE DOESN GIVE A SHIT..
ABOUT A DRUNKARD LIKE ME...
sniff
...HUH?
IT'S BE- CAUSE I ACT LIKE THIS.
UNH...
THAT'S WHY HE DOESN'T LOVE ME ANY- MORE ...!
UNGH...
...
SO YOU DO LOVE HIM...
Waagh
Waagh

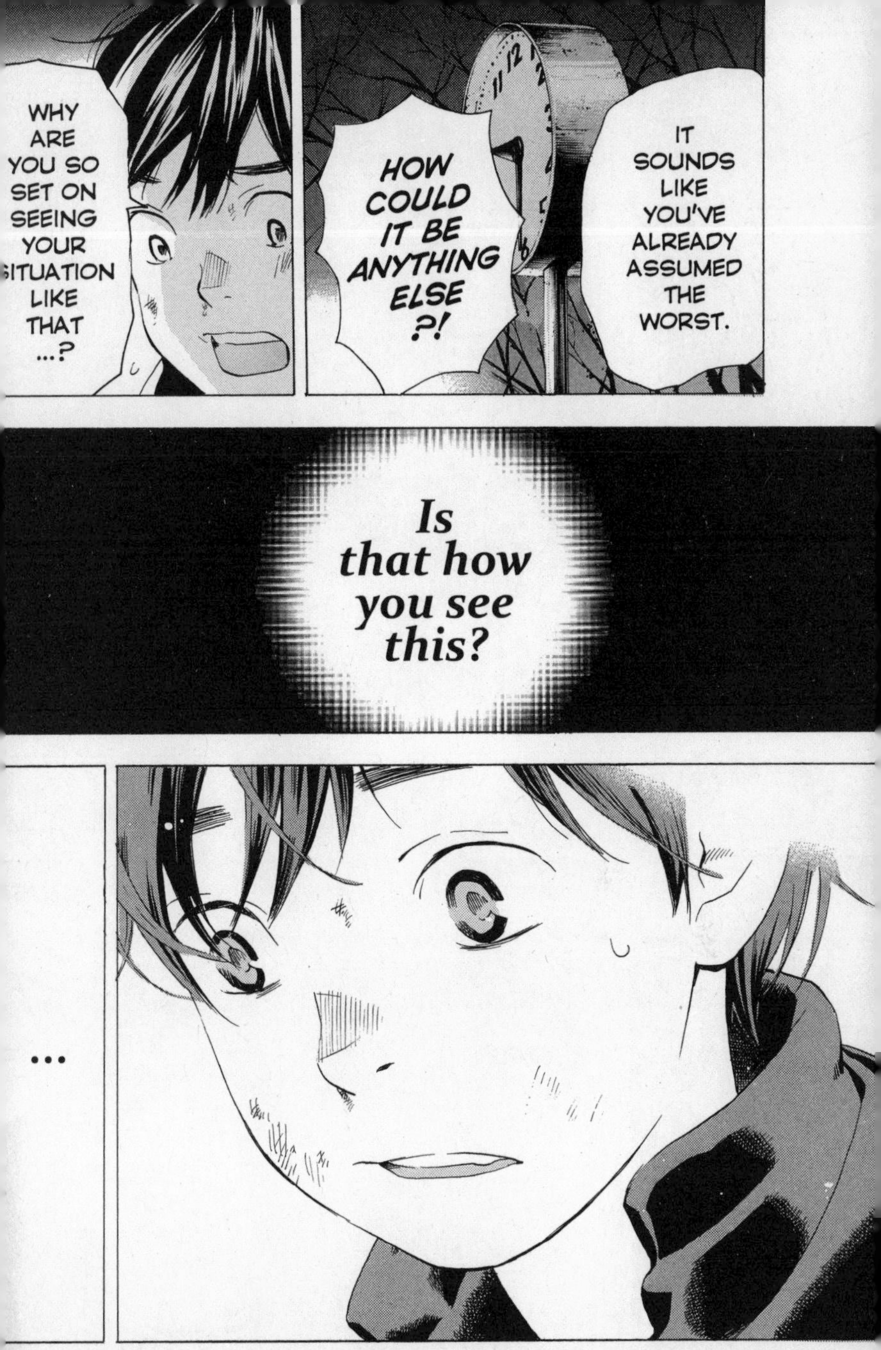
IT SOUNDS LIKE YOU'VE ALREADY ASSUMED THE WORST.
HOW COULD IT BE ANYTHING ELSE?!
WHY ARE YOU SO SET ON SEEING YOUR SITUATION LIKE THAT ...?
Is that how you see this?
...

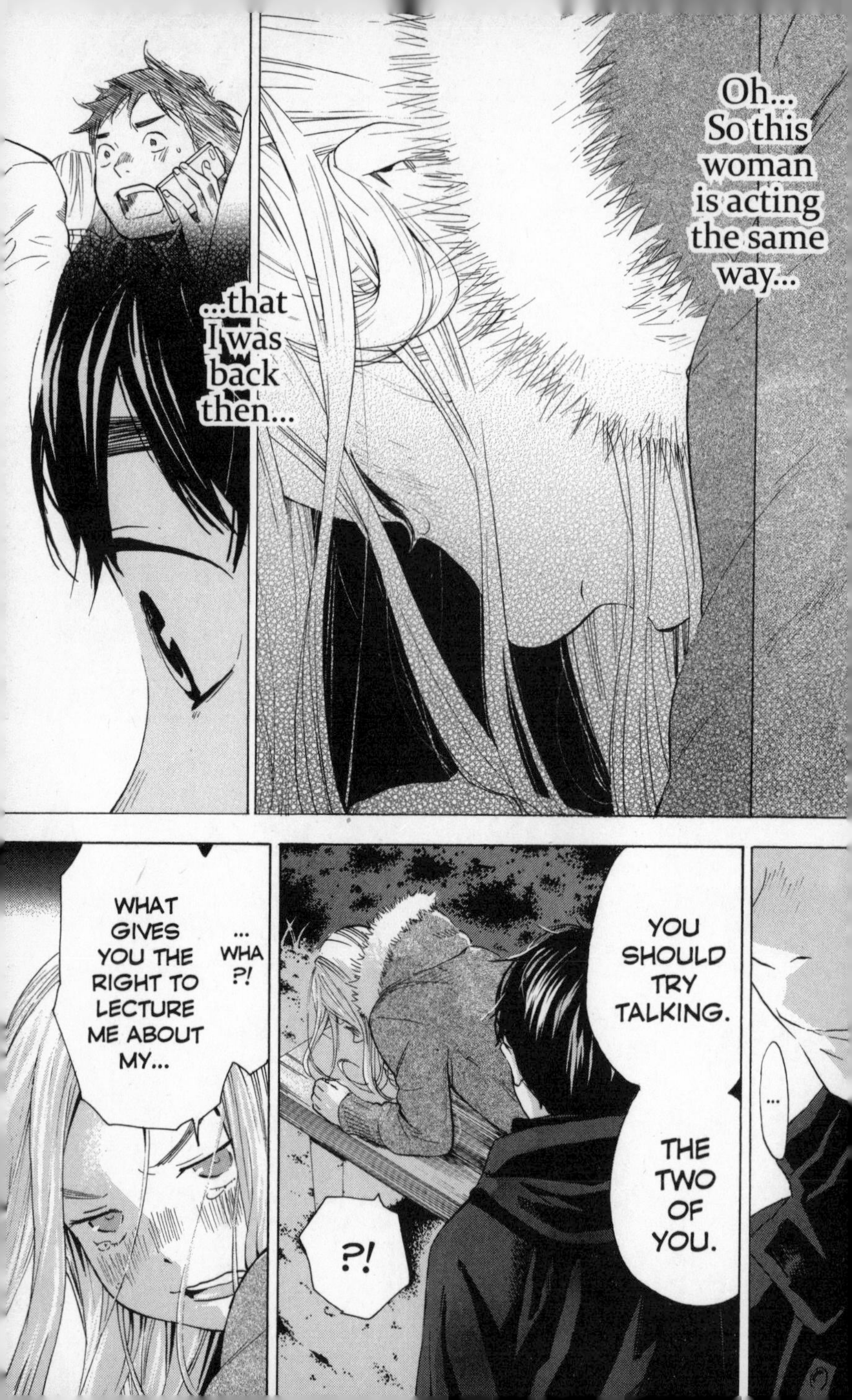
Oh... So this woman is acting the same way...
...that I was back then...
...
YOU SHOULD TRY TALKING.
THE TWO OF YOU.
?!
...WHA?!
WHAT GIVES YOU THE RIGHT TO LECTURE ME ABOUT MY...

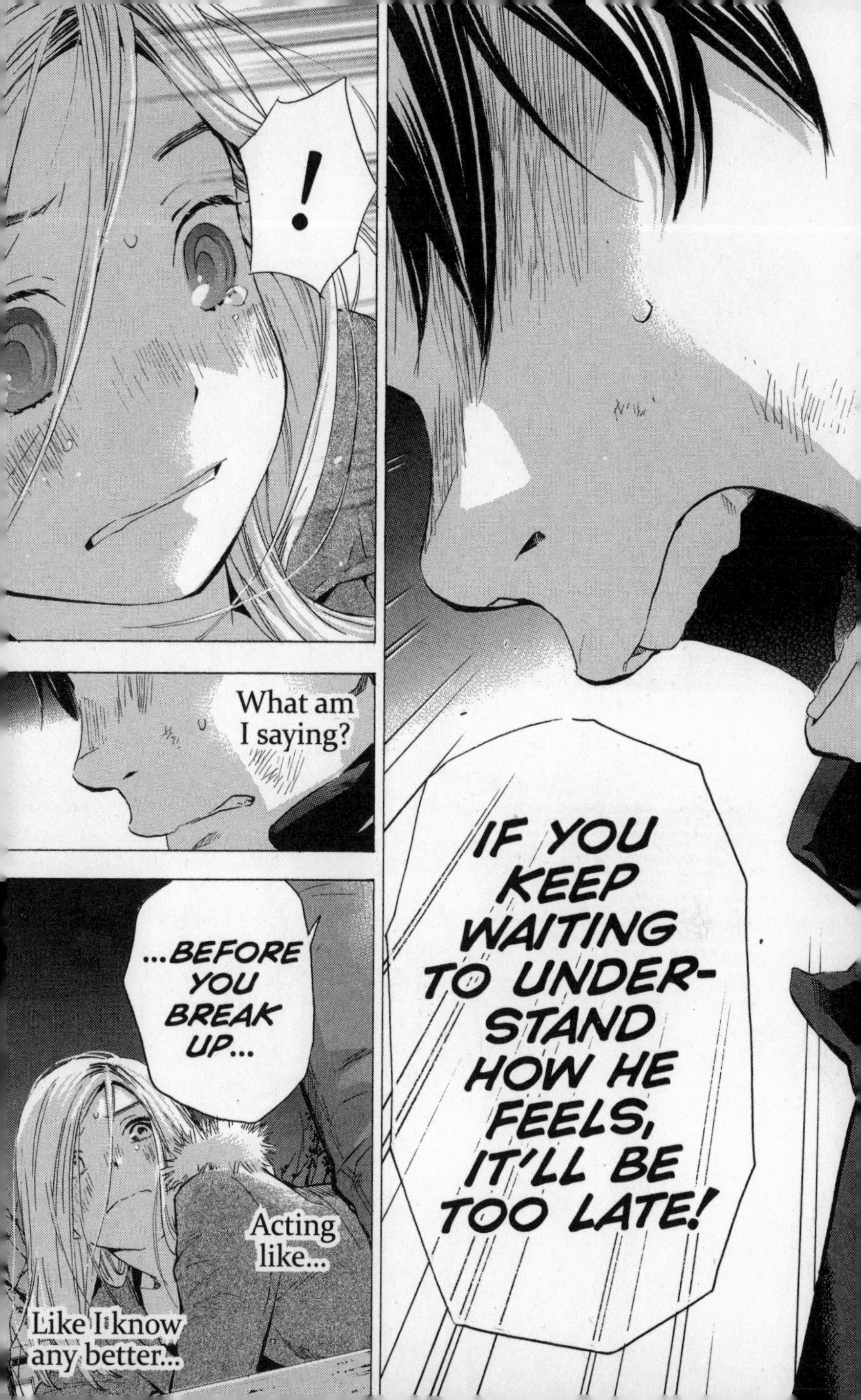
IF YOU KEEP WAITING TO UNDER-STAND HOW HE FEELS, IT'LL BE TOO LATE!
!
What am I saying?
...BEFORE YOU BREAK UP...
Acting like...
Like I know any better...

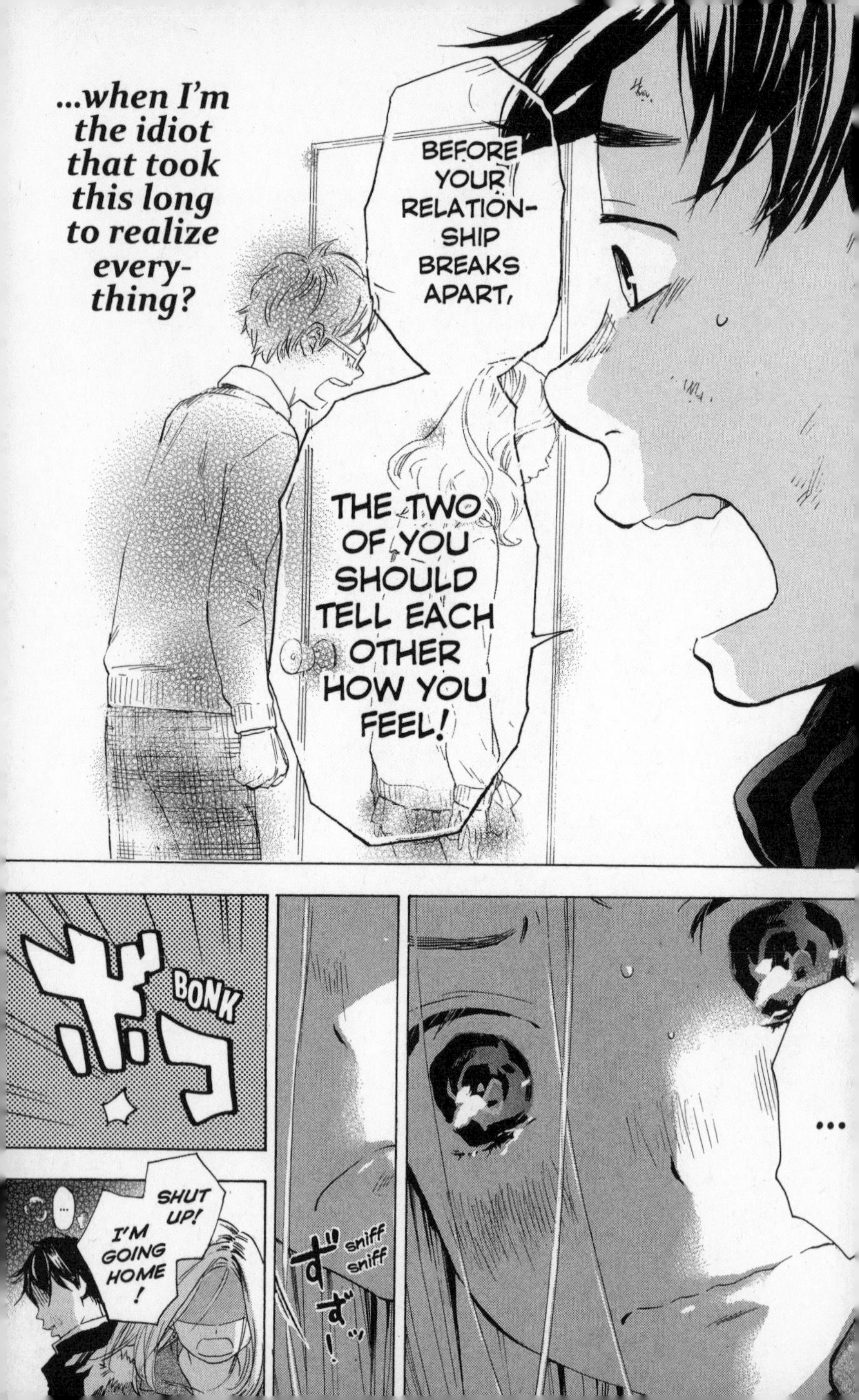
BEFORE YOUR RELATIONSHIP BREAKS APART,
THE TWO OF YOU SHOULD TELL EACH OTHER HOW YOU FEEL!
...when I'm the idiot that took this long to realize everything?
...
sniff sniff
BONK
...
SHUT UP! I'M GOING HOME!

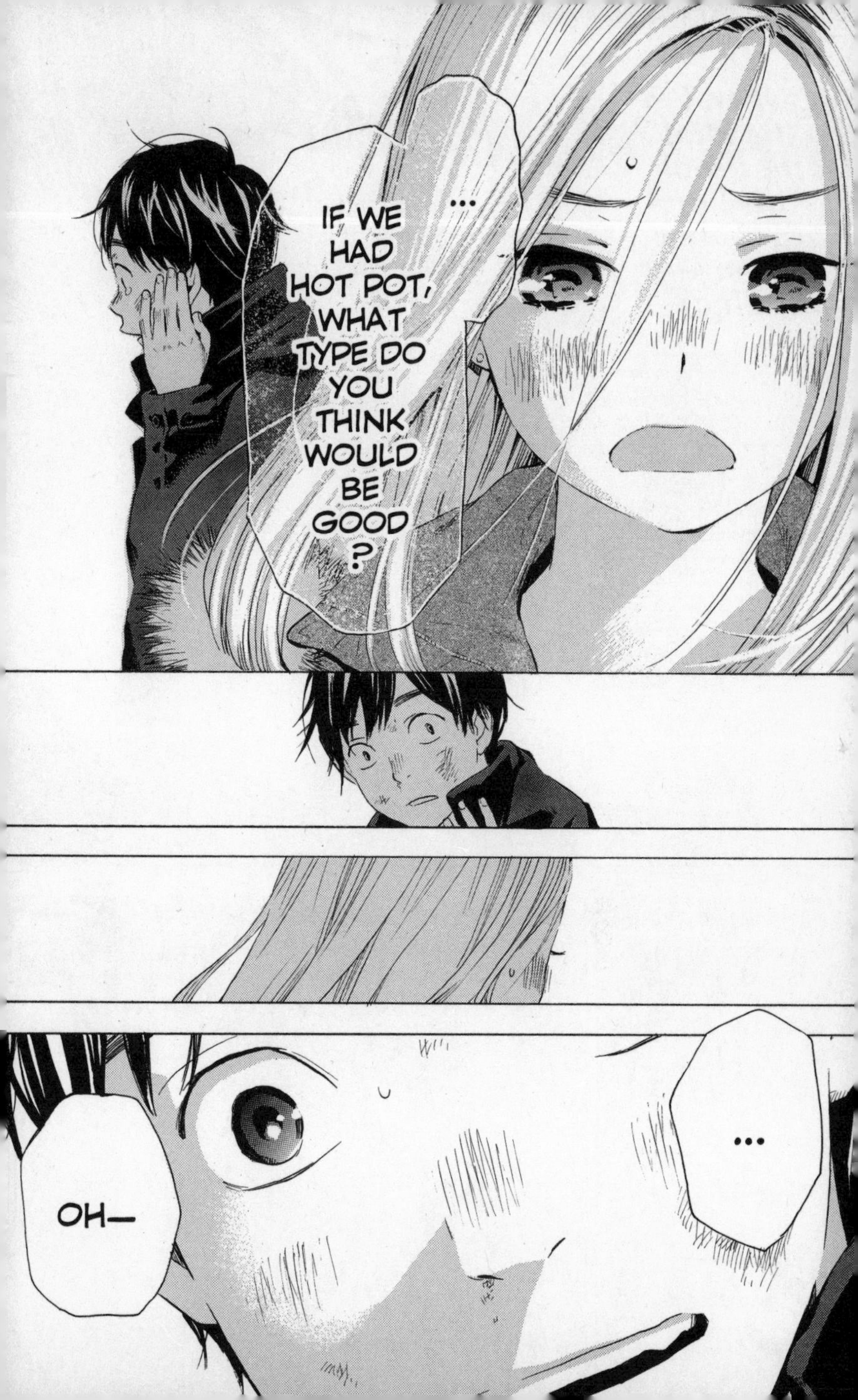
...
IF WE HAD HOT POT, WHAT TYPE DO YOU THINK WOULD BE GOOD?
...
OH—

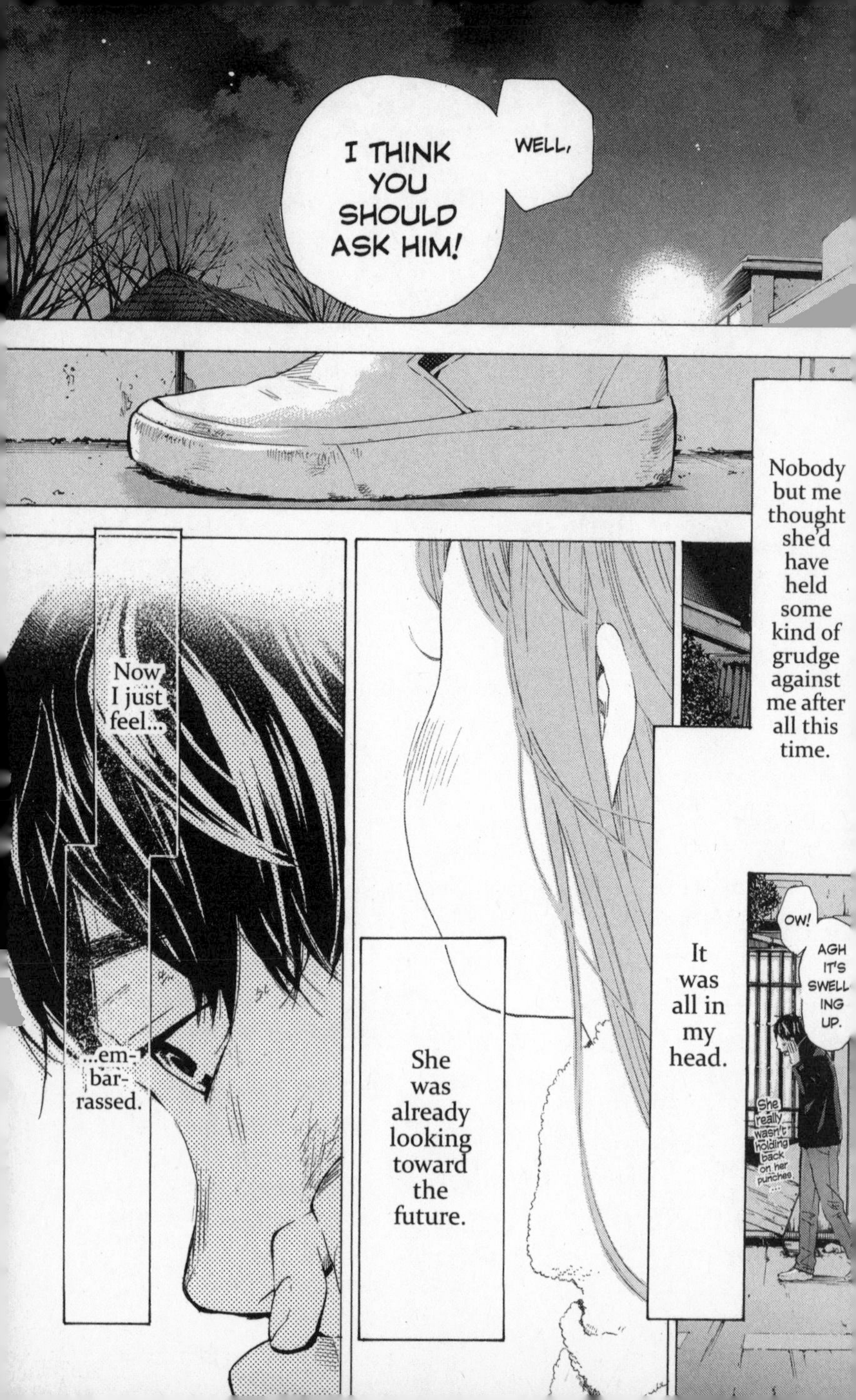
WELL,
I THINK YOU SHOULD ASK HIM!
Nobody but me thought she'd have held some kind of grudge against me after all this time.
It was all in my head.
OW!
AGH IT'S SWELL ING UP.
She really wasn't holding back on her punches...
She was already looking toward the future.
Now I just feel...
...em- bar- rassed.

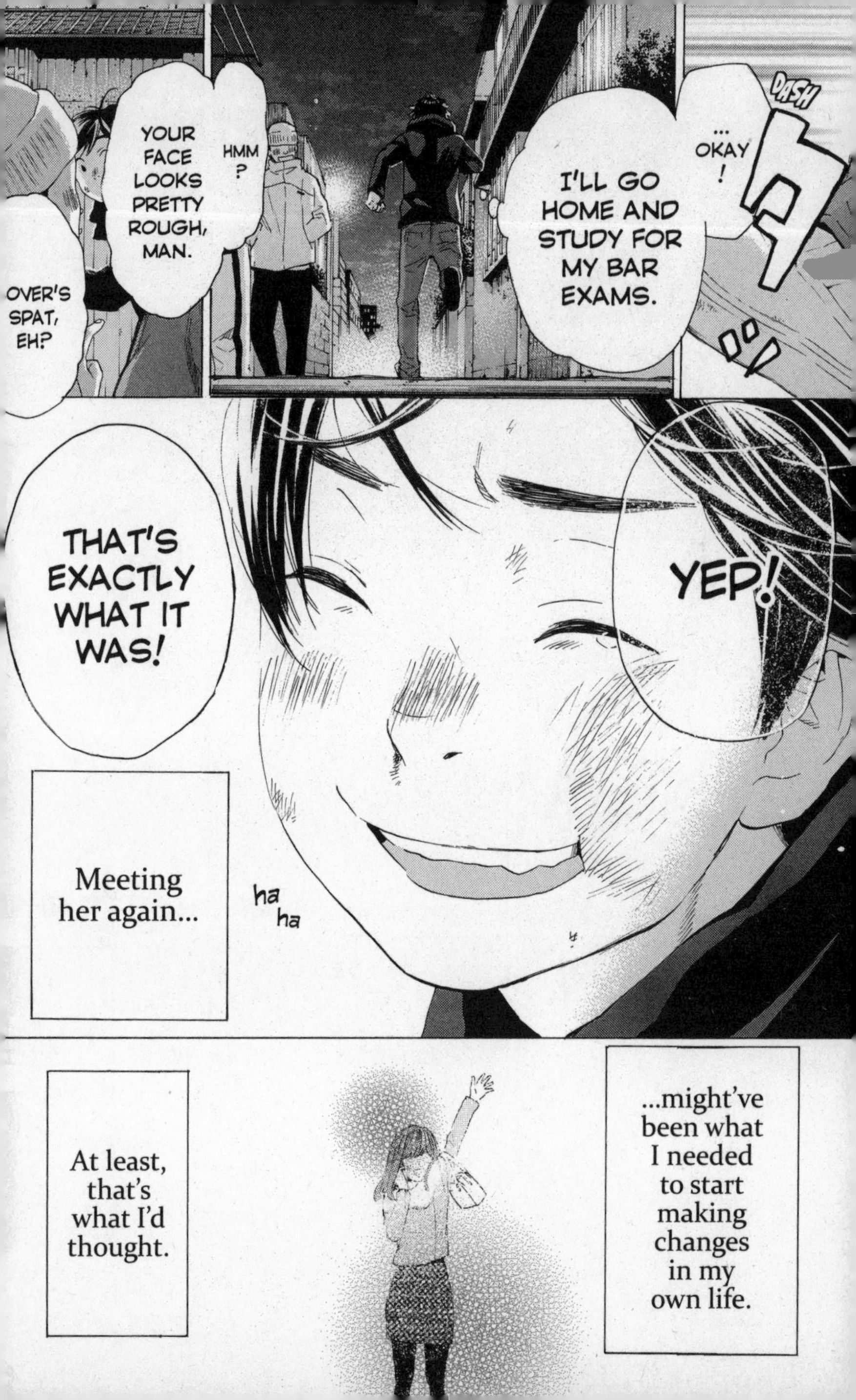
DASH
...OKAY!
I'LL GO HOME AND STUDY FOR MY BAR EXAMS.
HMM?
YOUR FACE LOOKS PRETTY ROUGH, MAN.
OVER'S SPAT, EH?
YEP!
THAT'S EXACTLY WHAT IT WAS!
ha ha
Meeting her again...
...might've been what I needed to start making changes in my own life.
At least, that's what I'd thought.

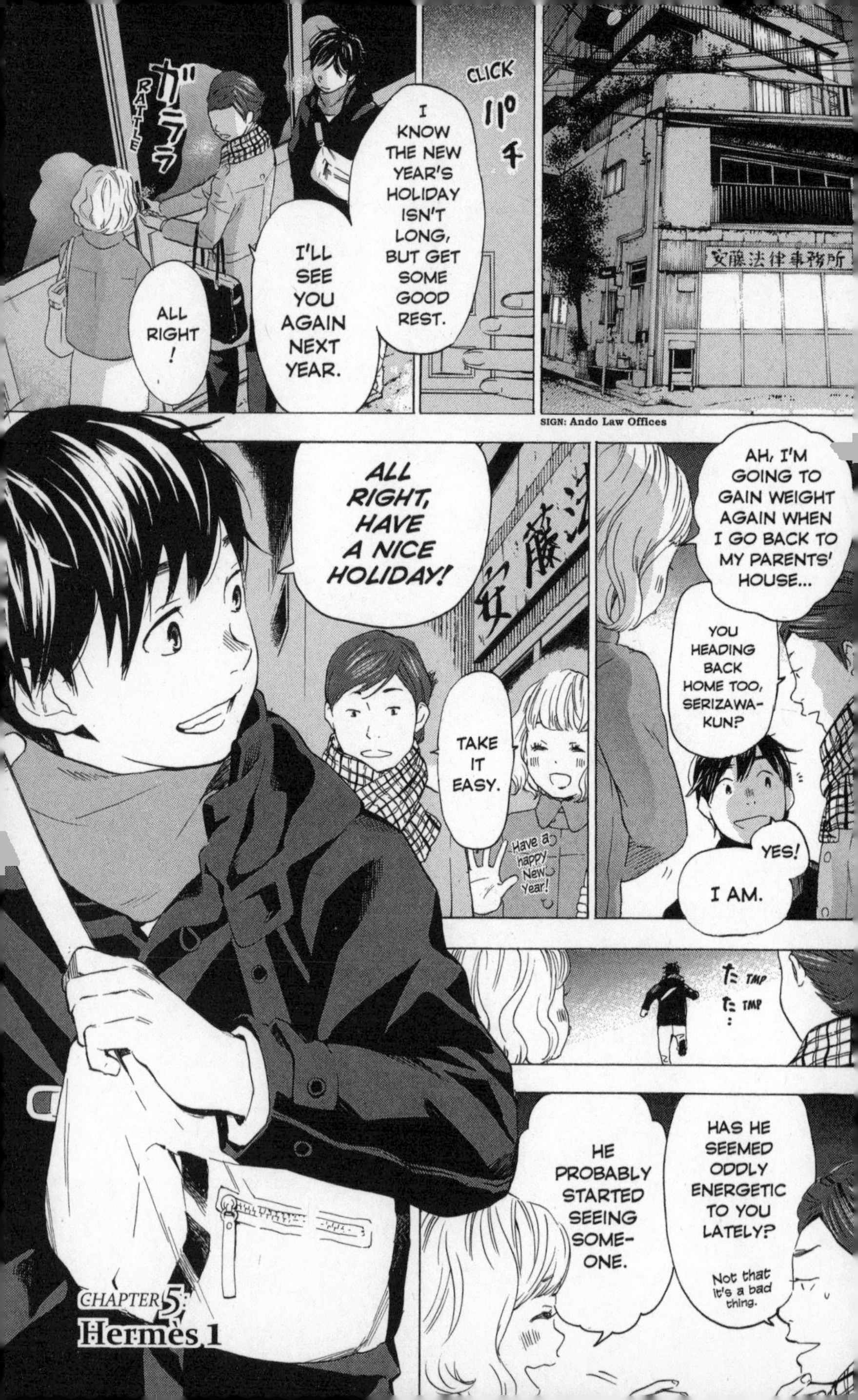
安藤法律事務所
SIGN: Ando Law Offices
CLICK
パチ
I KNOW THE NEW YEAR'S HOLIDAY ISN'T LONG, BUT GET SOME GOOD REST.
I'LL SEE YOU AGAIN NEXT YEAR.
ALL RIGHT!
ガラ
RATTLE
AH, I'M GOING TO GAIN WEIGHT AGAIN WHEN I GO BACK TO MY PARENTS' HOUSE...
YOU HEADING BACK HOME TOO, SERIZAWA-KUN?
YES!
I AM.
ALL RIGHT, HAVE A NICE HOLIDAY!
TAKE IT EASY.
Have a happy New Year!
た TMP
た TMP
HAS HE SEEMED ODDLY ENERGETIC TO YOU LATELY?
Not that it's a bad thing.
HE PROBABLY STARTED SEEING SOME-ONE.
CHAPTER 5: Hermes 1

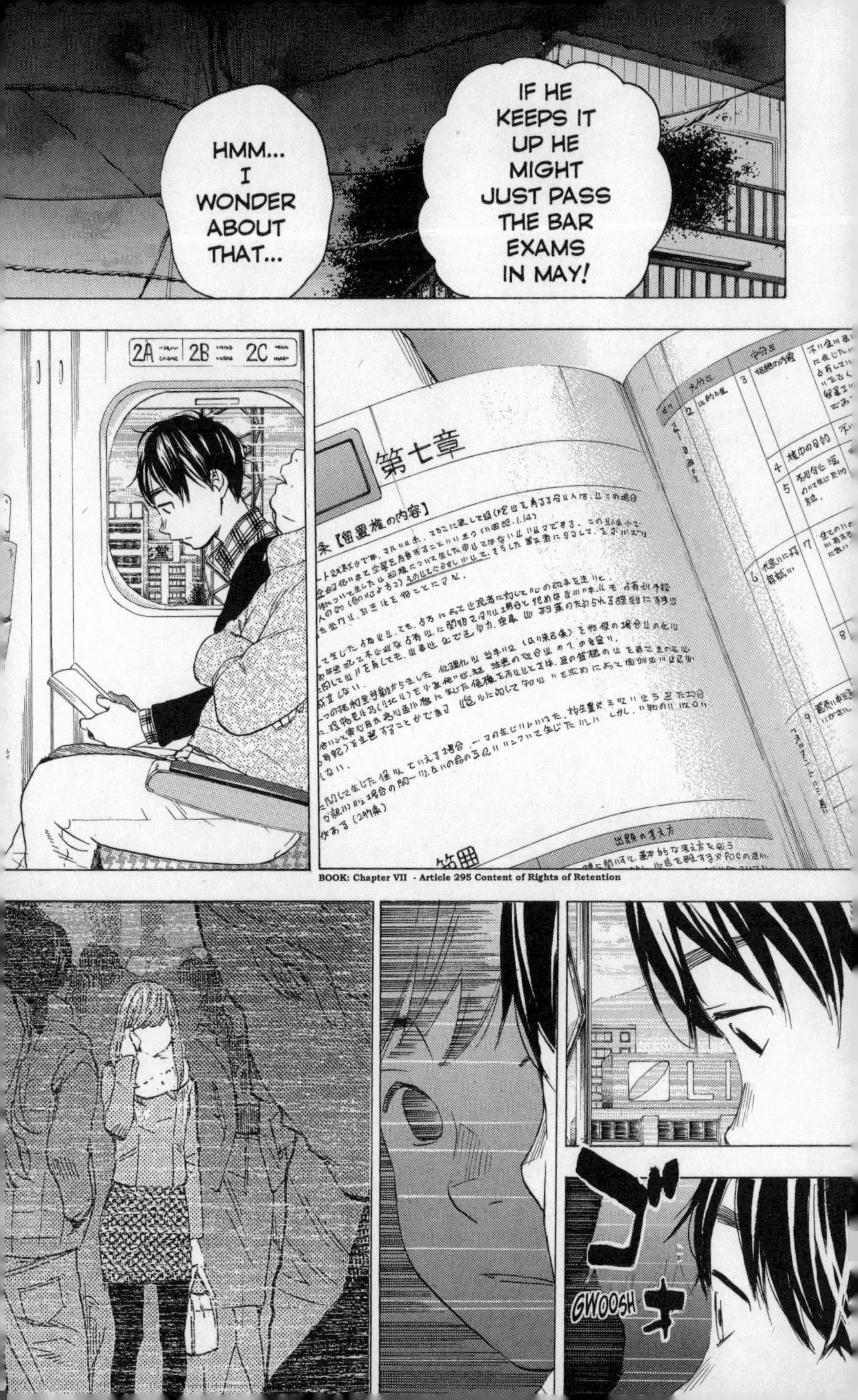
IF HE KEEPS IT UP HE MIGHT JUST PASS THE BAR EXAMS IN MAY!
HMM... I WONDER ABOUT THAT...
第七章
条【留置権の内容】
BOOK: Chapter VII - Article 295 Content of Rights of Retention
2A
2B
2C
GWOOSH

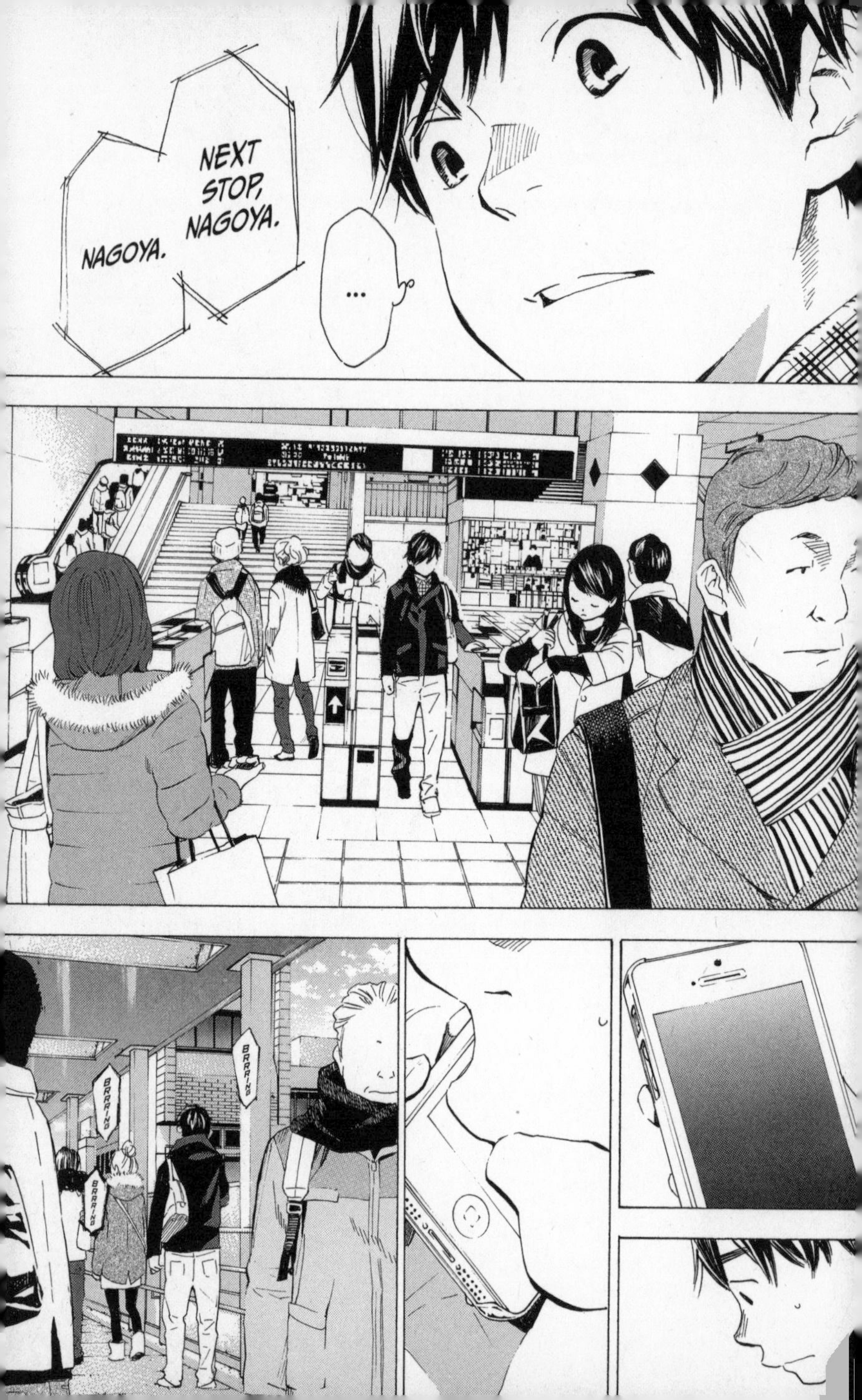
NEXT STOP, NAGOYA.
NAGOYA.
...
BRRRING
BRRRING
BRRRING

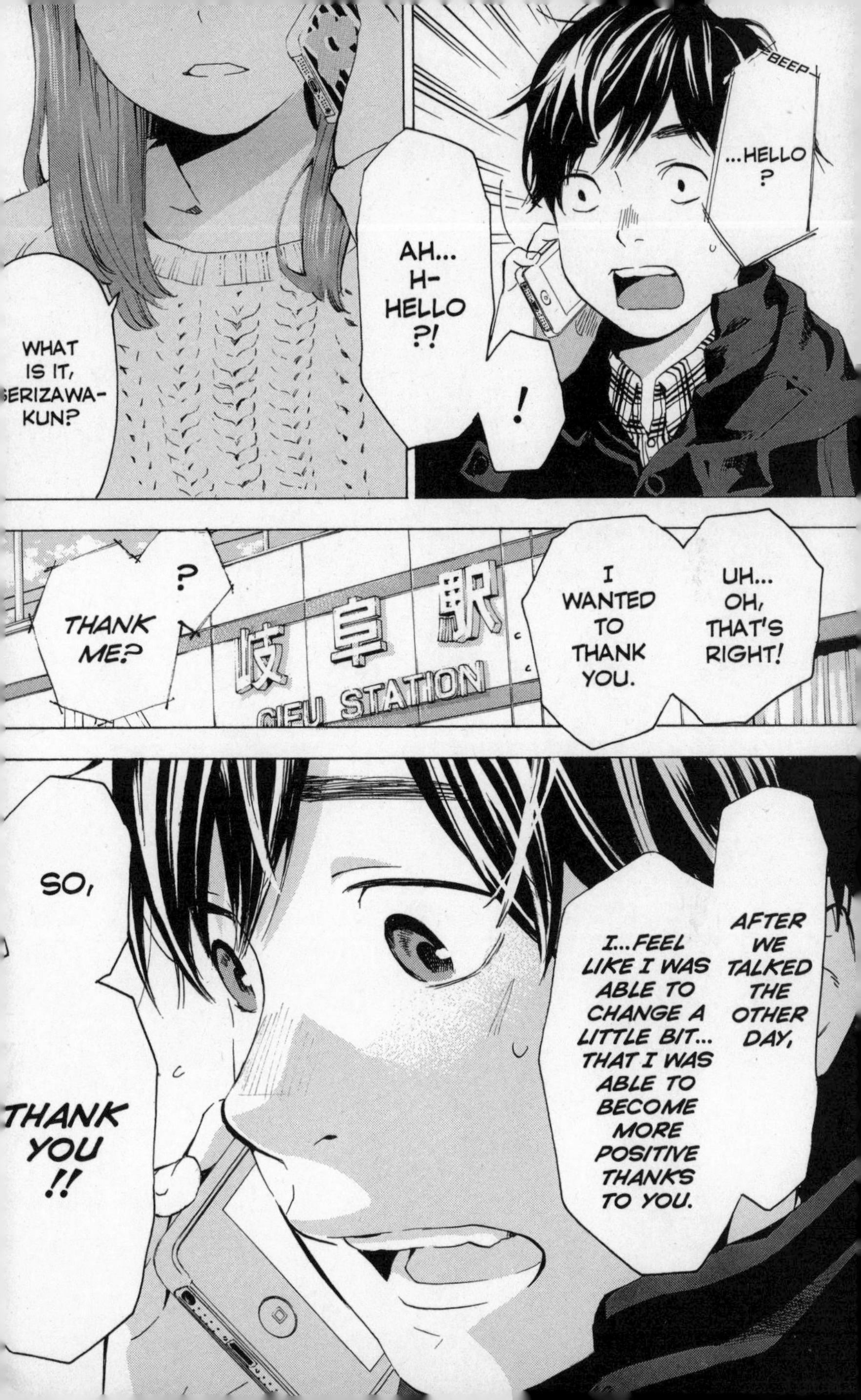
BEEP
...HELLO?
AH... H-HELLO?!
!
WHAT IS IT, ERIZAWA-KUN?
UH... OH, THAT'S RIGHT!
I WANTED TO THANK YOU.
岐阜駅
GIFU STATION
?
THANK ME?
AFTER WE TALKED THE OTHER DAY,
I...FEEL LIKE I WAS ABLE TO CHANGE A LITTLE BIT... THAT I WAS ABLE TO BECOME MORE POSITIVE THANKS TO YOU.
SO,
THANK YOU!!

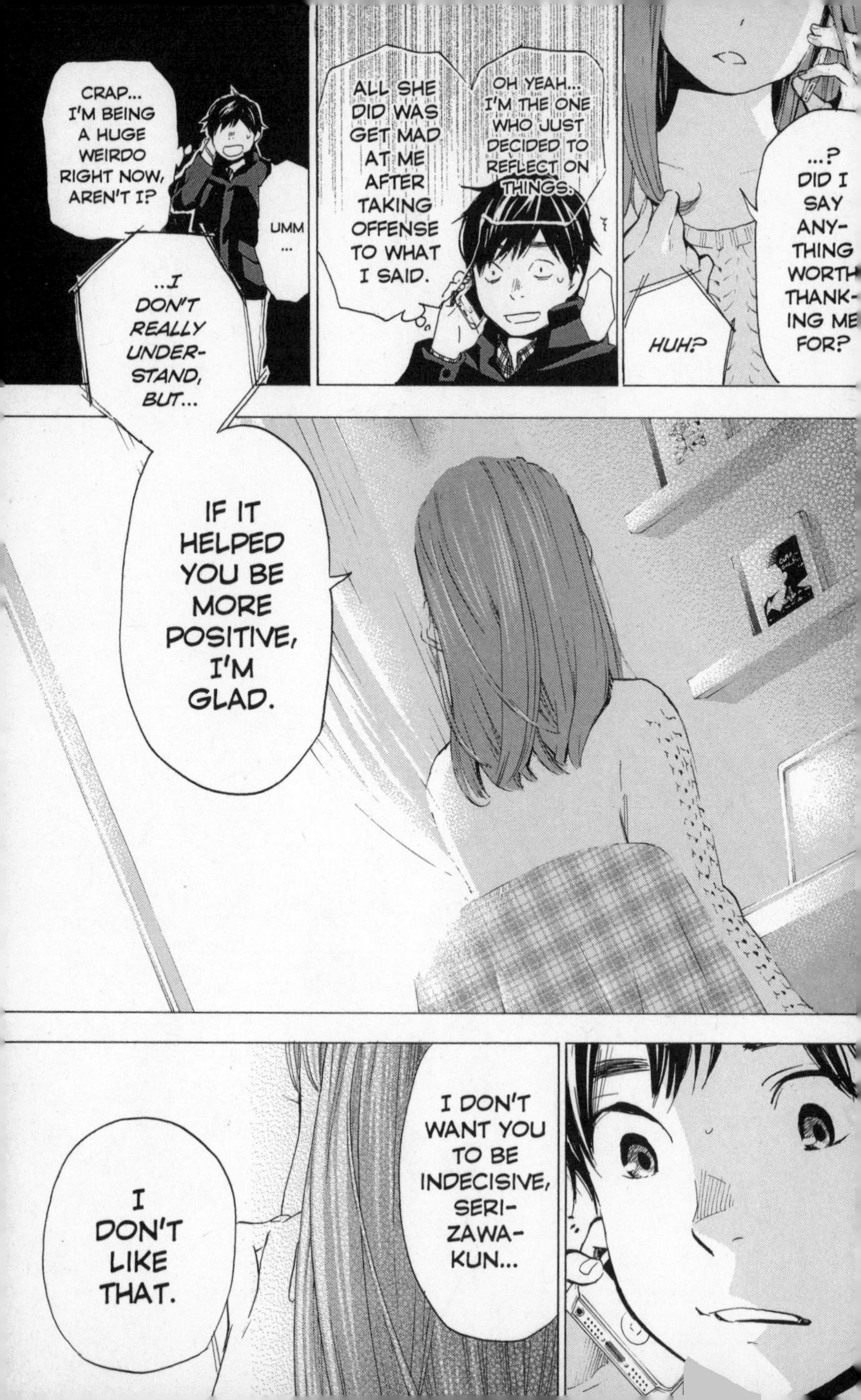
...? DID I SAY ANYTHING WORTH THANKING ME FOR?
HUH?
OH YEAH... I'M THE ONE WHO JUST DECIDED TO REFLECT ON THINGS.
ALL SHE DID WAS GET MAD AT ME AFTER TAKING OFFENSE TO WHAT I SAID.
CRAP... I'M BEING A HUGE WEIRDO RIGHT NOW, AREN'T I?
UMM ...
...I DON'T REALLY UNDER-STAND, BUT...
IF IT HELPED YOU BE MORE POSITIVE, I'M GLAD.
I DON'T WANT YOU TO BE INDECISIVE, SERI-ZAWA-KUN...
I DON'T LIKE THAT.

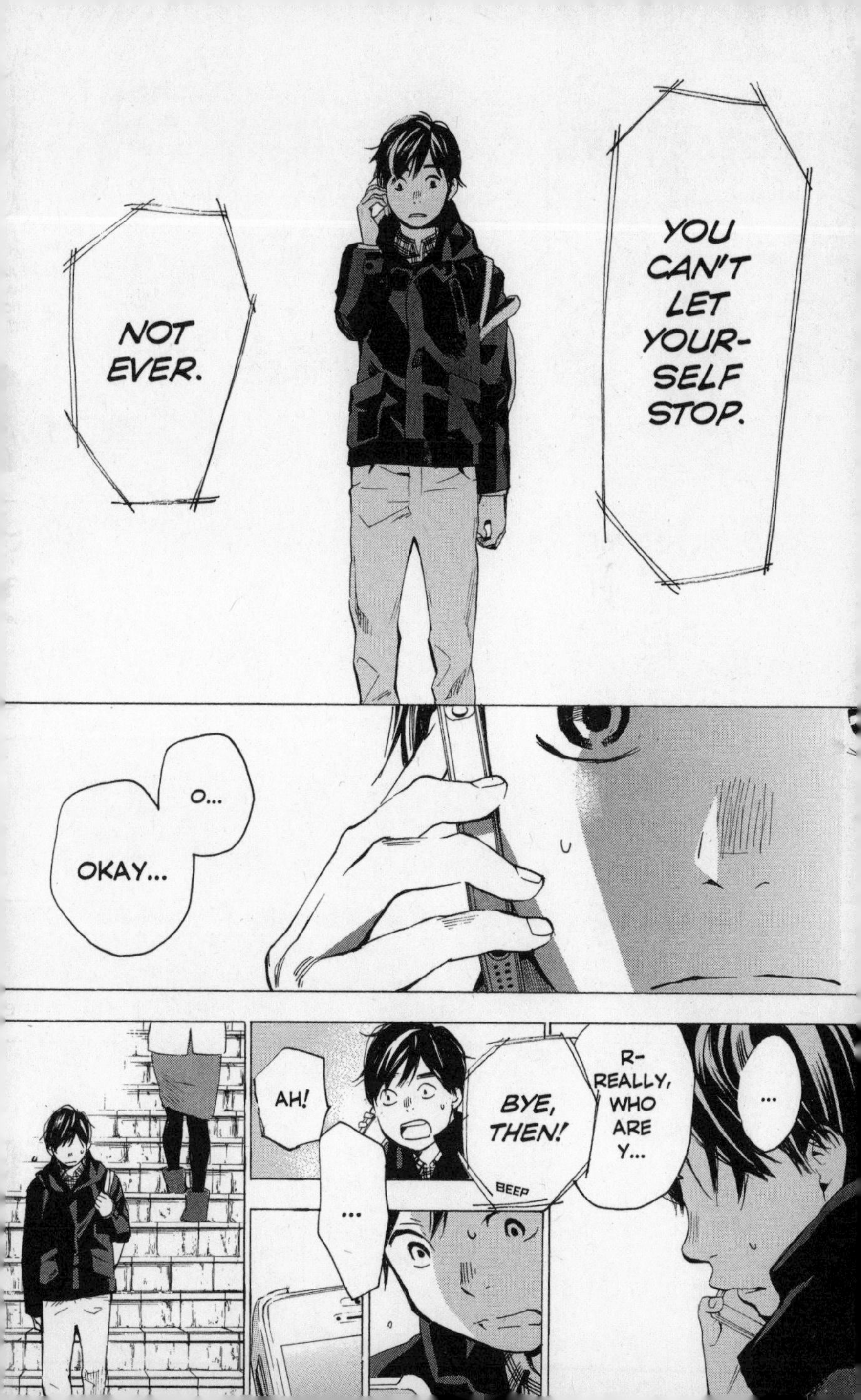
YOU CAN'T LET YOUR-SELF STOP.
NOT EVER.
O...
OKAY...
...
R-REALLY, WHO ARE Y...
BYE, THEN!
BEEP
AH!
...

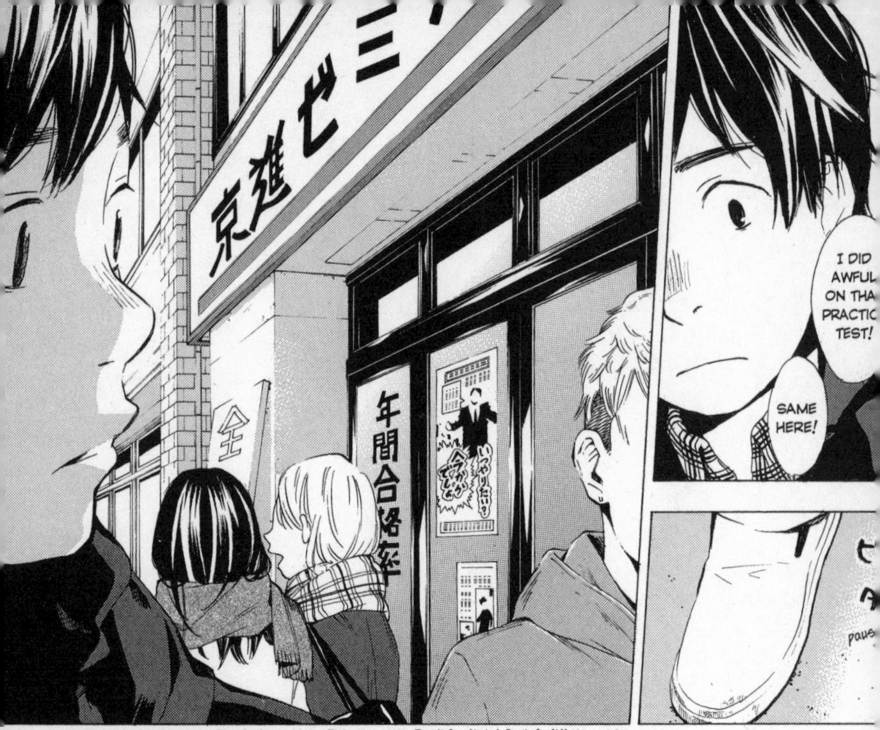
I DID AWFUL ON THA PRACTIC TEST!
SAME HERE!
pause
京進ゼミ
年間合格率

SIGNS: Kyoshin Seminar (top), Yearly Acceptance Rate (door, left), Don't hesitate! Just do it!! (door, right)

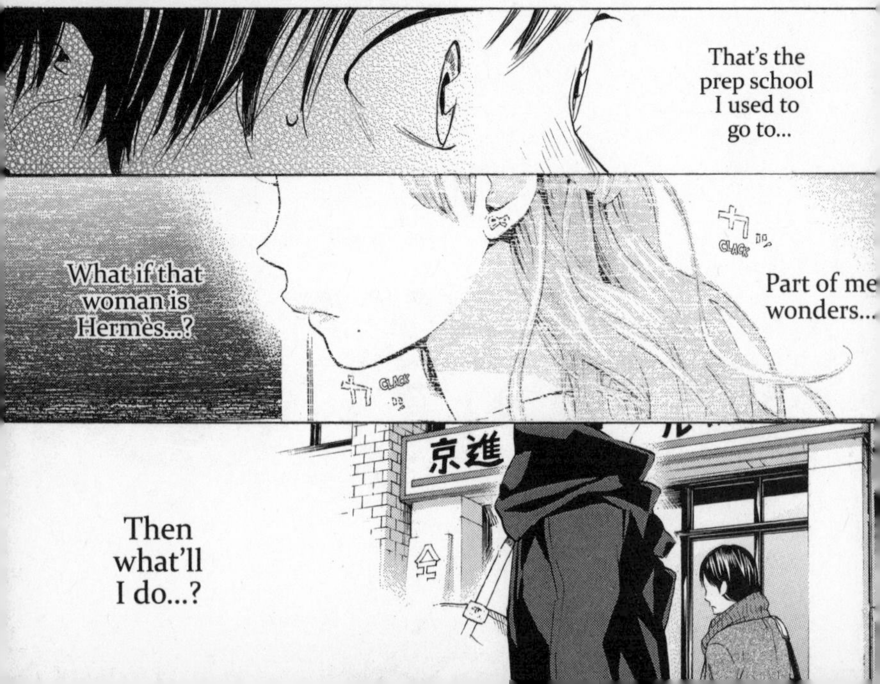
That's the prep school I used to go to...
CLACK
Part of me wonders...
What if that woman is Hermès...?
CLACK
京進
Then what'll I do...?

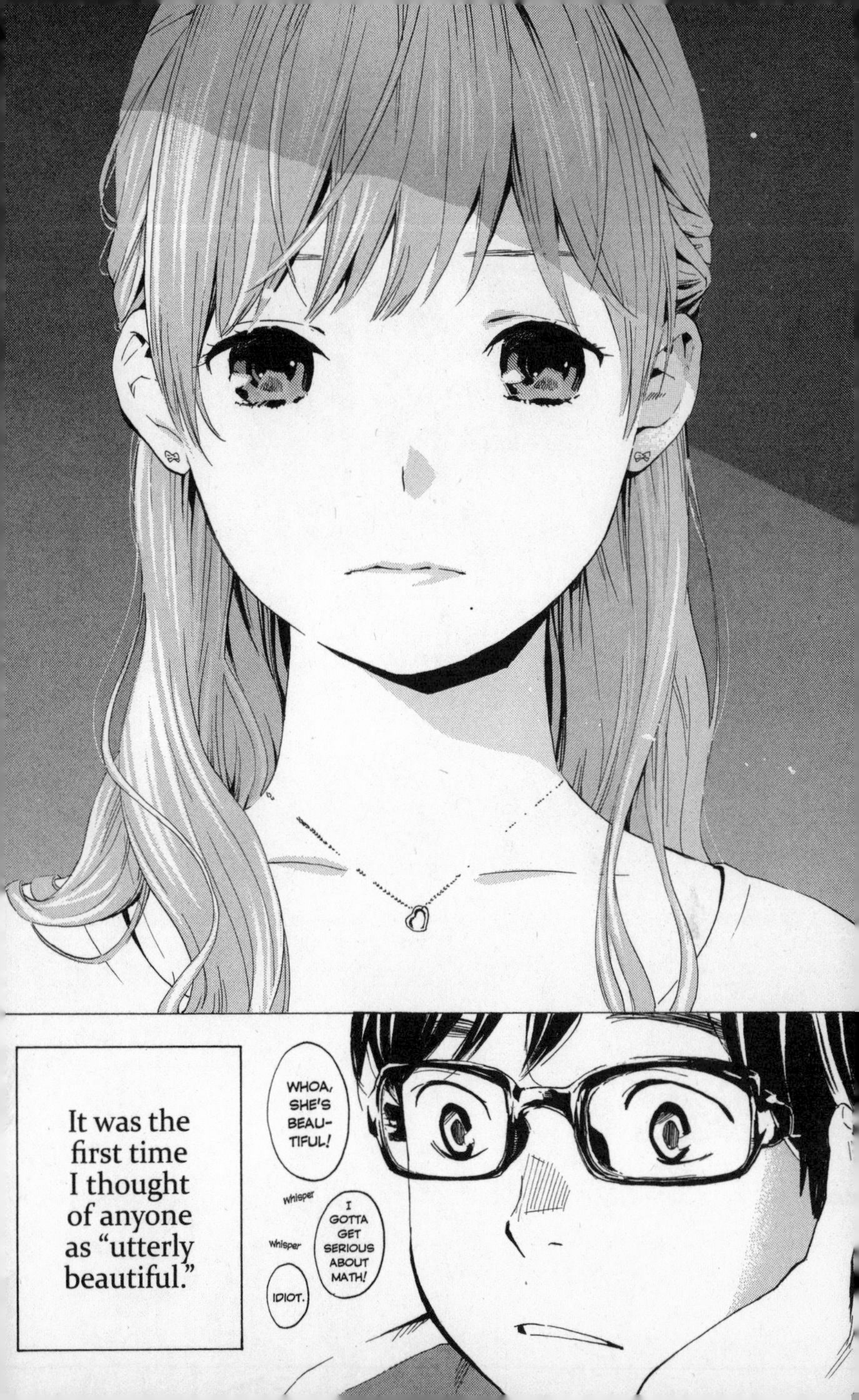
WHOA, SHE'S BEAU-TIFUL!
Whisper
I GOTTA GET SERIOUS ABOUT MATH!
Whisper
IDIOT.
It was the first time I thought of anyone as "utterly beautiful."

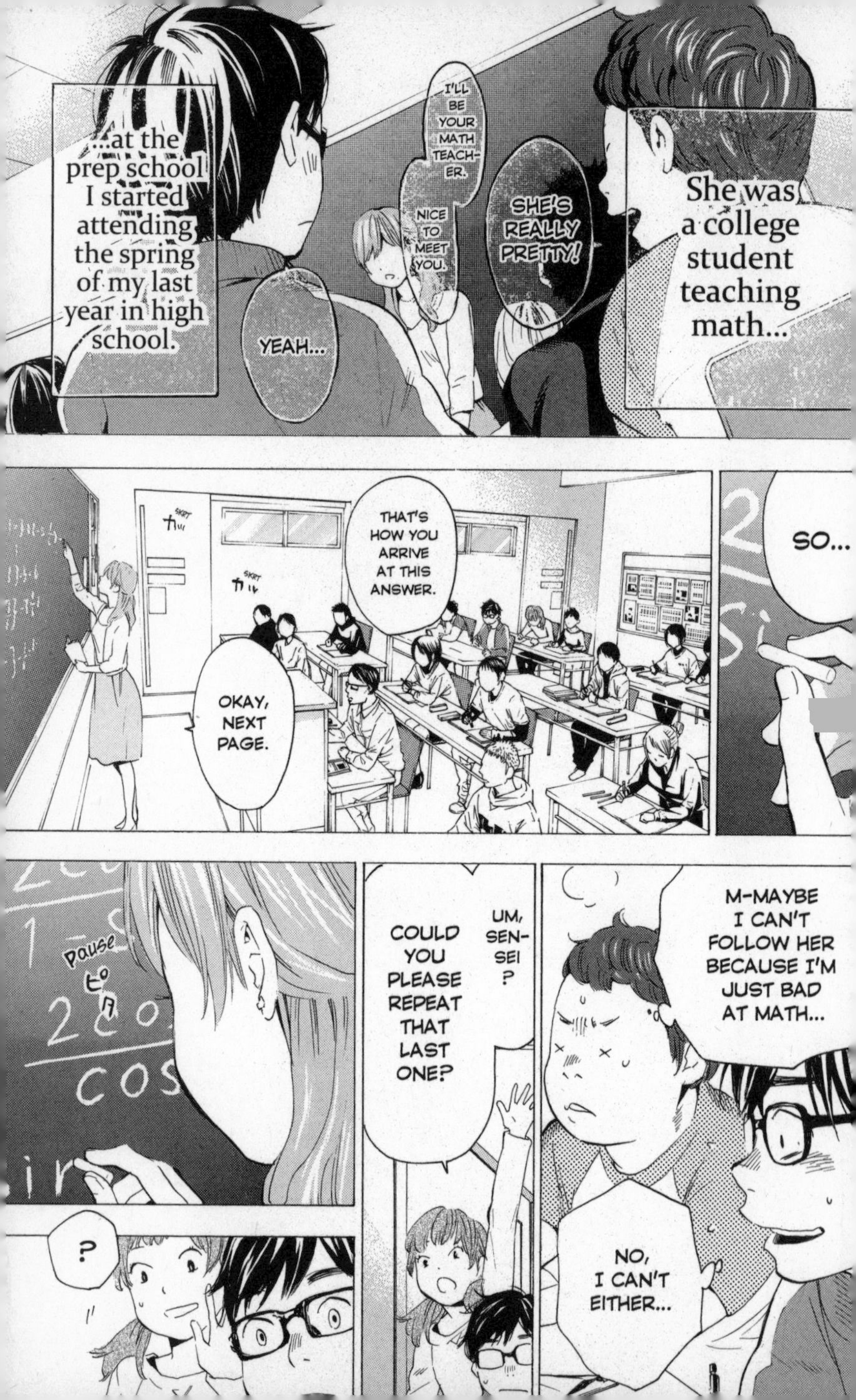
She was a college student teaching math...
SHE'S REALLY PRETTY!
I'LL BE YOUR MATH TEACHER.
NICE TO MEET YOU.
YEAH...
...at the prep school I started attending the spring of my last year in high school.
SO...
THAT'S HOW YOU ARRIVE AT THIS ANSWER.
SKRT
SKRT
OKAY, NEXT PAGE.
M-MAYBE I CAN'T FOLLOW HER BECAUSE I'M JUST BAD AT MATH...
NO, I CAN'T EITHER...
UM, SENSEI?
COULD YOU PLEASE REPEAT THAT LAST ONE?
pause
?

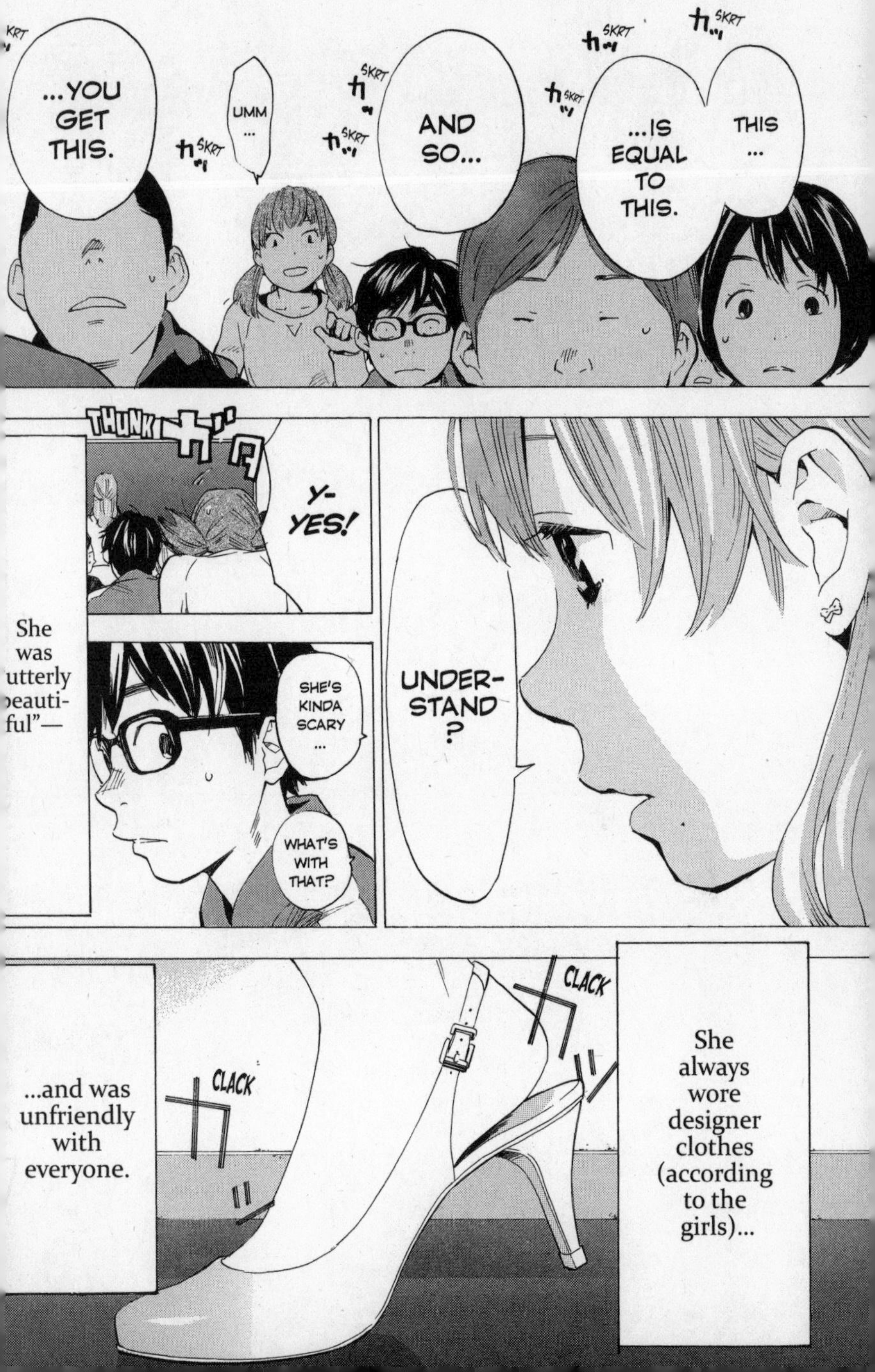
SKRT
THIS ...
...IS EQUAL TO THIS.
SKRT
SKRT
AND SO...
SKRT
SKRT
UMM ...
SKRT
...YOU GET THIS.
UNDER-STAND?
THUNK
Y-YES!
SHE'S KINDA SCARY ...
WHAT'S WITH THAT?
She was utterly beauti-ful"—
She always wore designer clothes (according to the girls)...
CLACK
CLACK
...and was unfriendly with everyone.

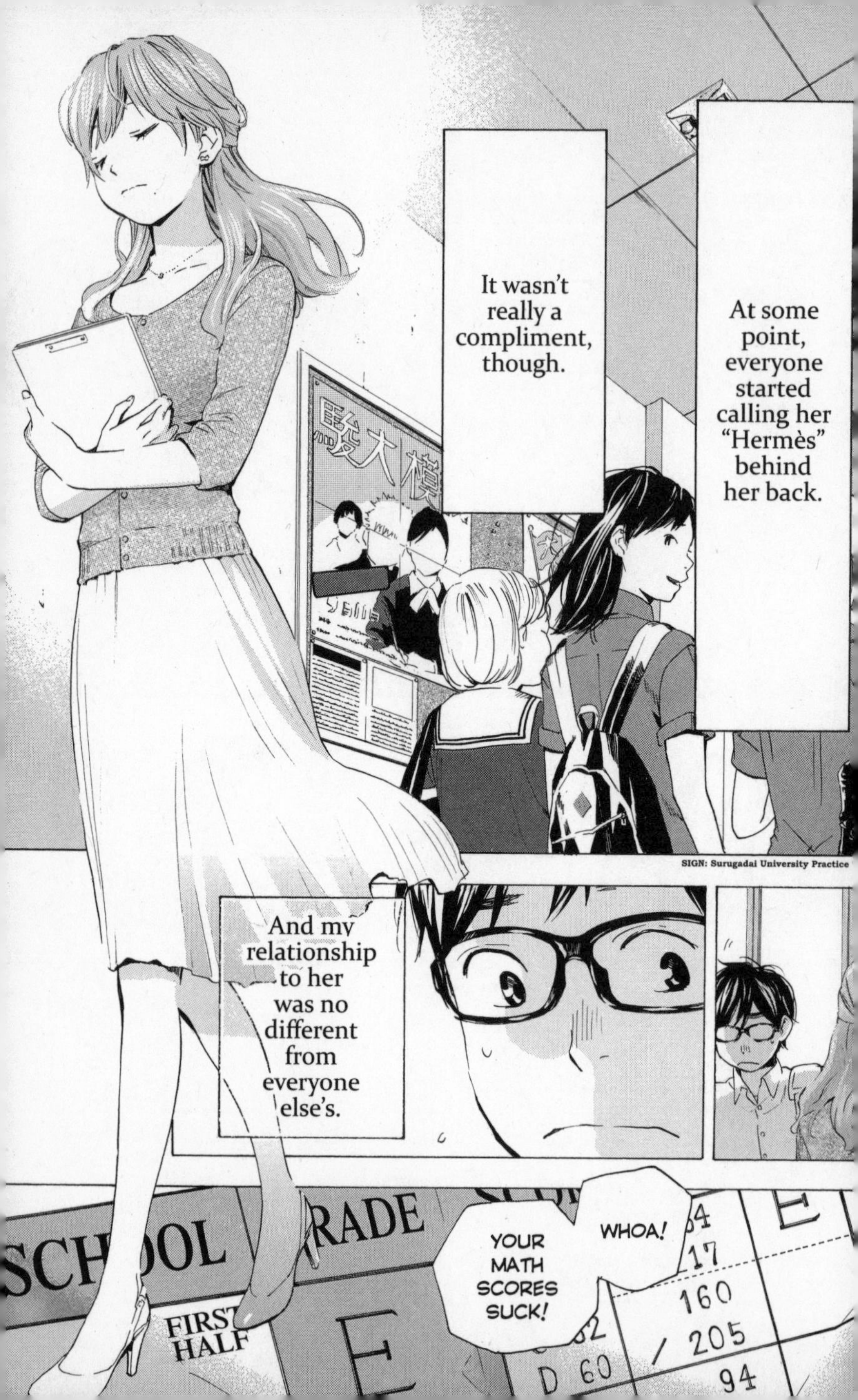

At some point, everyone started calling her "Hermès" behind her back.
It wasn't really a compliment, though.
SIGN: Surugadai University Practice
And my relationship to her was no different from everyone else's.
WHOA!
YOUR MATH SCORES SUCK!
SCHOOL
FIRST HALF
17
160
/ 205
D 60
94

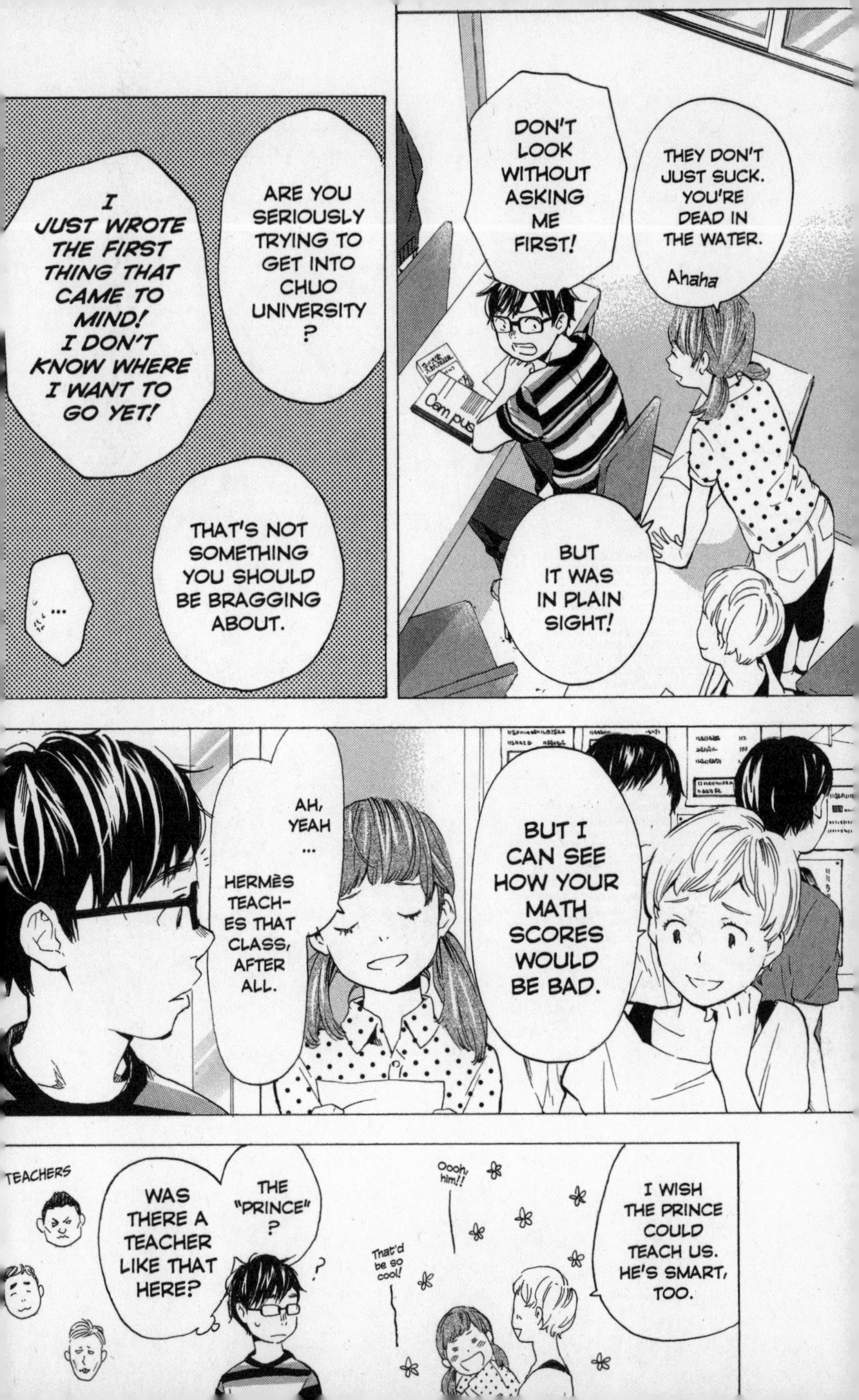
THEY DON'T JUST SUCK. YOU'RE DEAD IN THE WATER.
Ahaha
DON'T LOOK WITHOUT ASKING ME FIRST!
BUT IT WAS IN PLAIN SIGHT!
ARE YOU SERIOUSLY TRYING TO GET INTO CHUO UNIVERSITY?
I JUST WROTE THE FIRST THING THAT CAME TO MIND! I DON'T KNOW WHERE I WANT TO GO YET!
THAT'S NOT SOMETHING YOU SHOULD BE BRAGGING ABOUT.
...
BUT I CAN SEE HOW YOUR MATH SCORES WOULD BE BAD.
AH, YEAH... HERMÈS TEACHES THAT CLASS, AFTER ALL.
I WISH THE PRINCE COULD TEACH US. HE'S SMART, TOO.
Oooh, him!!
That'd be so cool!
THE "PRINCE"?
WAS THERE A TEACHER LIKE THAT HERE?
TEACHERS

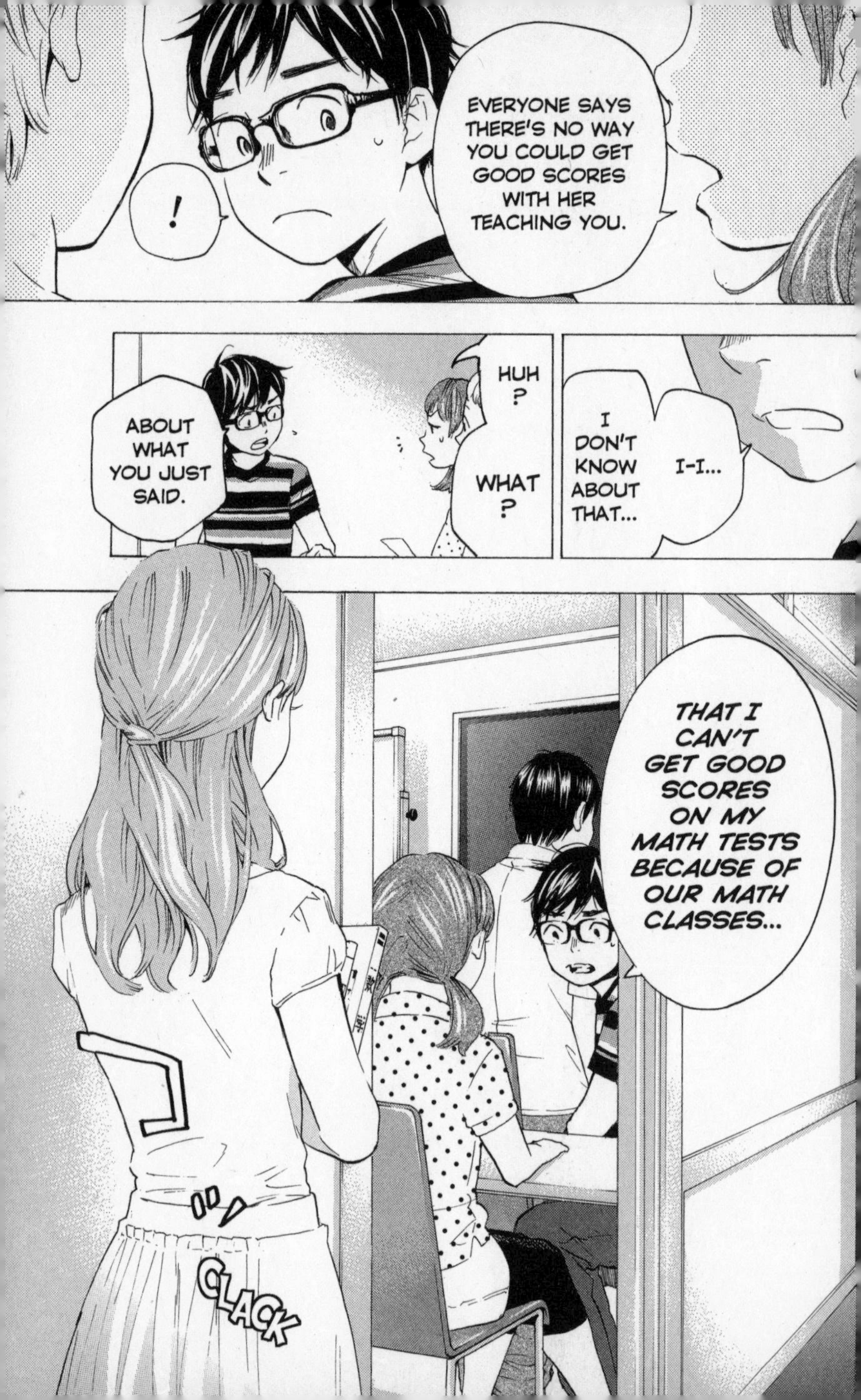
EVERYONE SAYS THERE'S NO WAY YOU COULD GET GOOD SCORES WITH HER TEACHING YOU.
!
I-I...
I DON'T KNOW ABOUT THAT...
HUH?
WHAT?
ABOUT WHAT YOU JUST SAID.
THAT I CAN'T GET GOOD SCORES ON MY MATH TESTS BECAUSE OF OUR MATH CLASSES...
CLACK

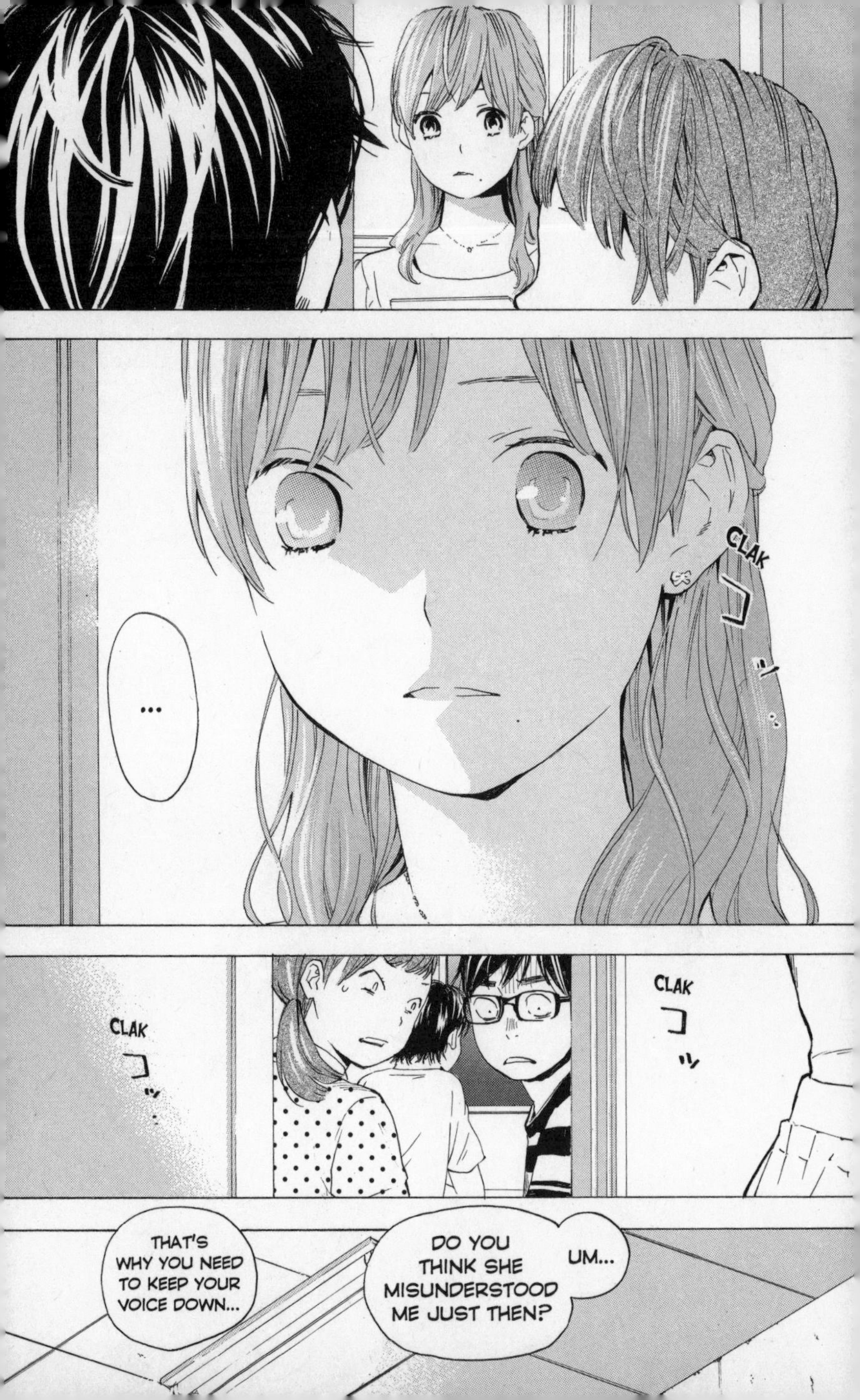
CLAK
コッ
...
CLAK
コッ
CLAK
コッ
UM...
DO YOU THINK SHE MISUNDERSTOOD ME JUST THEN?
THAT'S WHY YOU NEED TO KEEP YOUR VOICE DOWN...

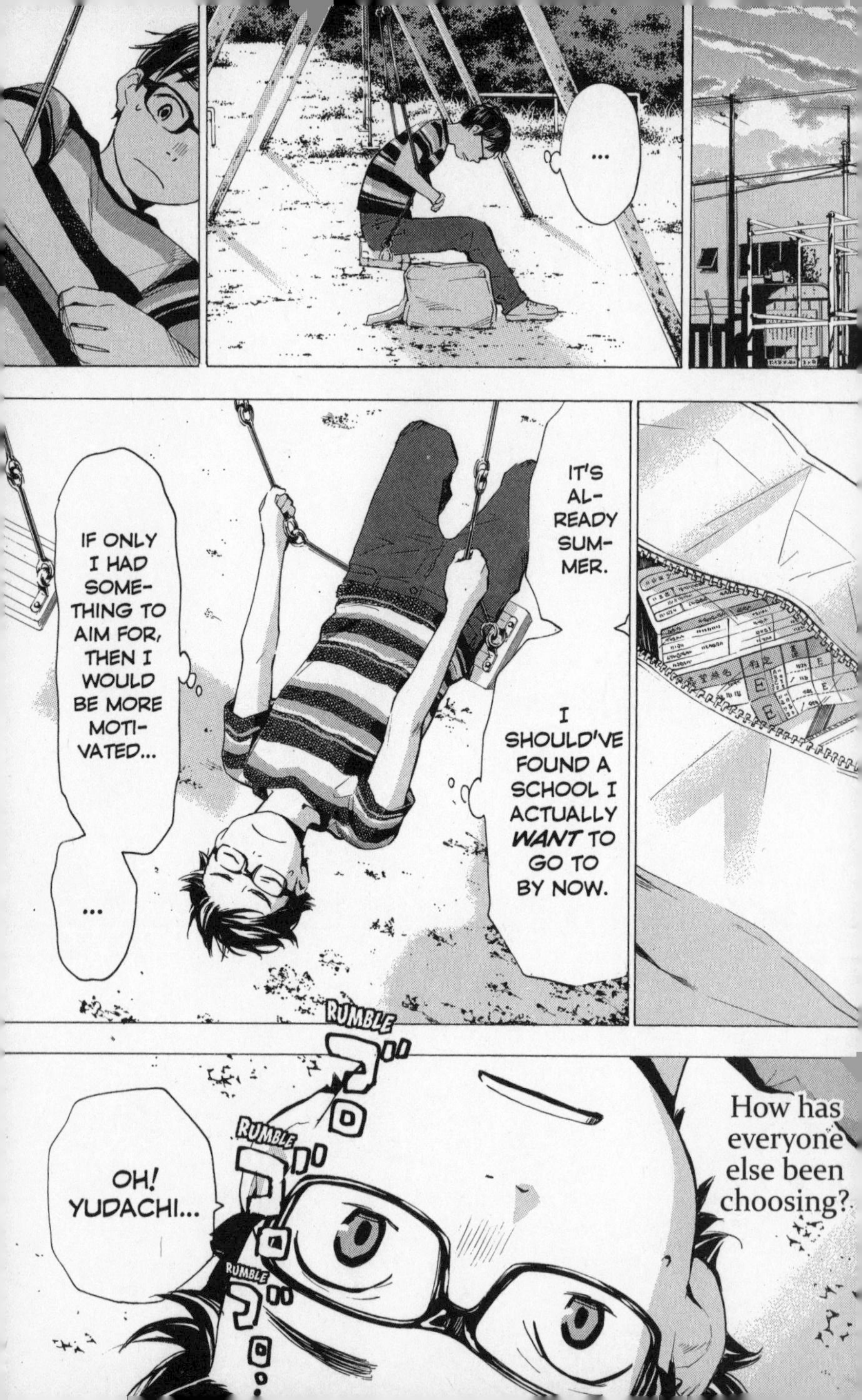
...
IT'S ALREADY SUMMER.
I SHOULD'VE FOUND A SCHOOL I ACTUALLY *WANT* TO GO TO BY NOW.
IF ONLY I HAD SOMETHING TO AIM FOR, THEN I WOULD BE MORE MOTIVATED...
...
How has everyone else been choosing?
RUMBLE
RUMBLE
RUMBLE
OH! YUDACHI...

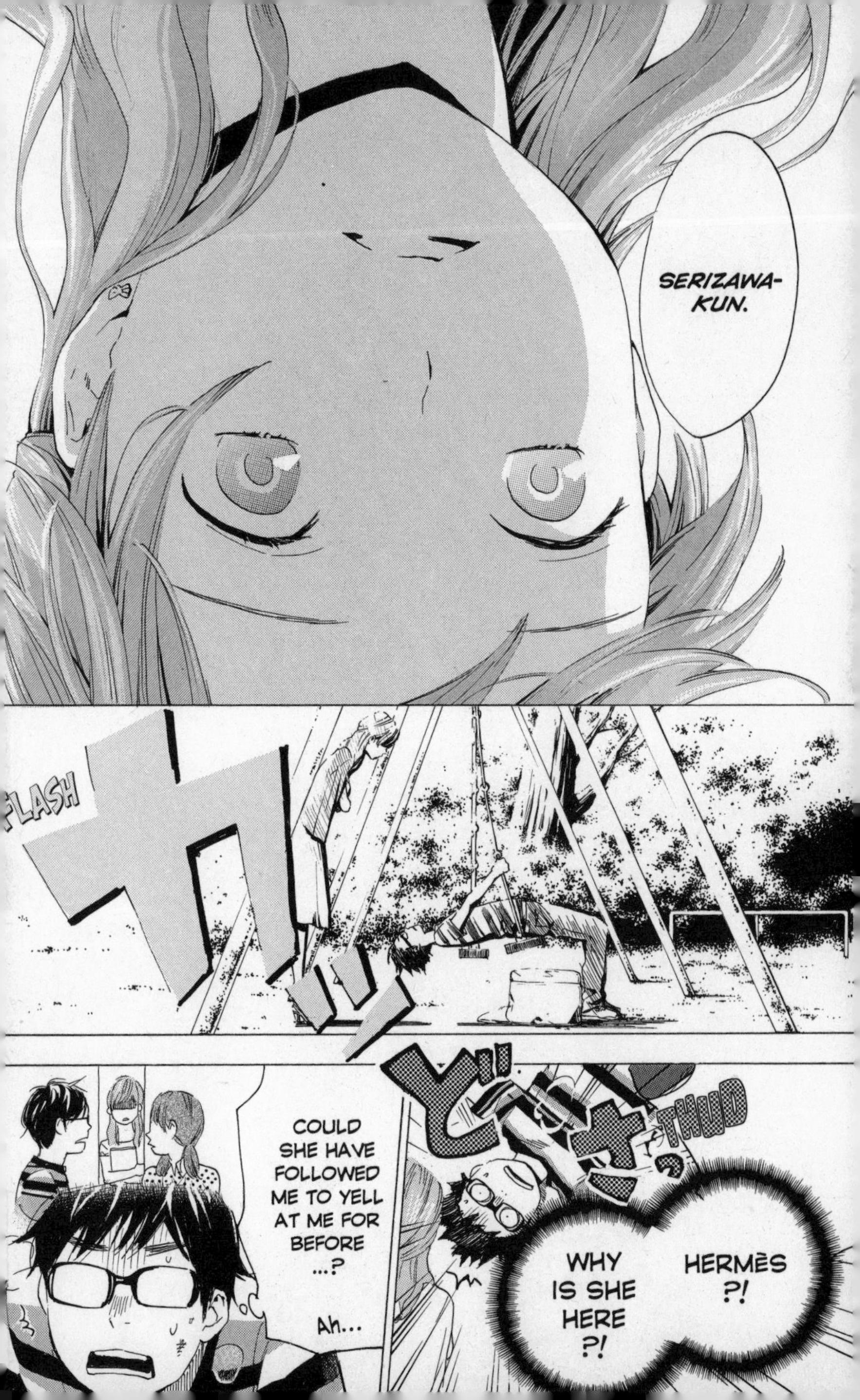
SERIZAWA-KUN.
FLASH
THUD
HERMÈS ?!
WHY IS SHE HERE ?!
COULD SHE HAVE FOLLOWED ME TO YELL AT ME FOR BEFORE ...?
Ah...

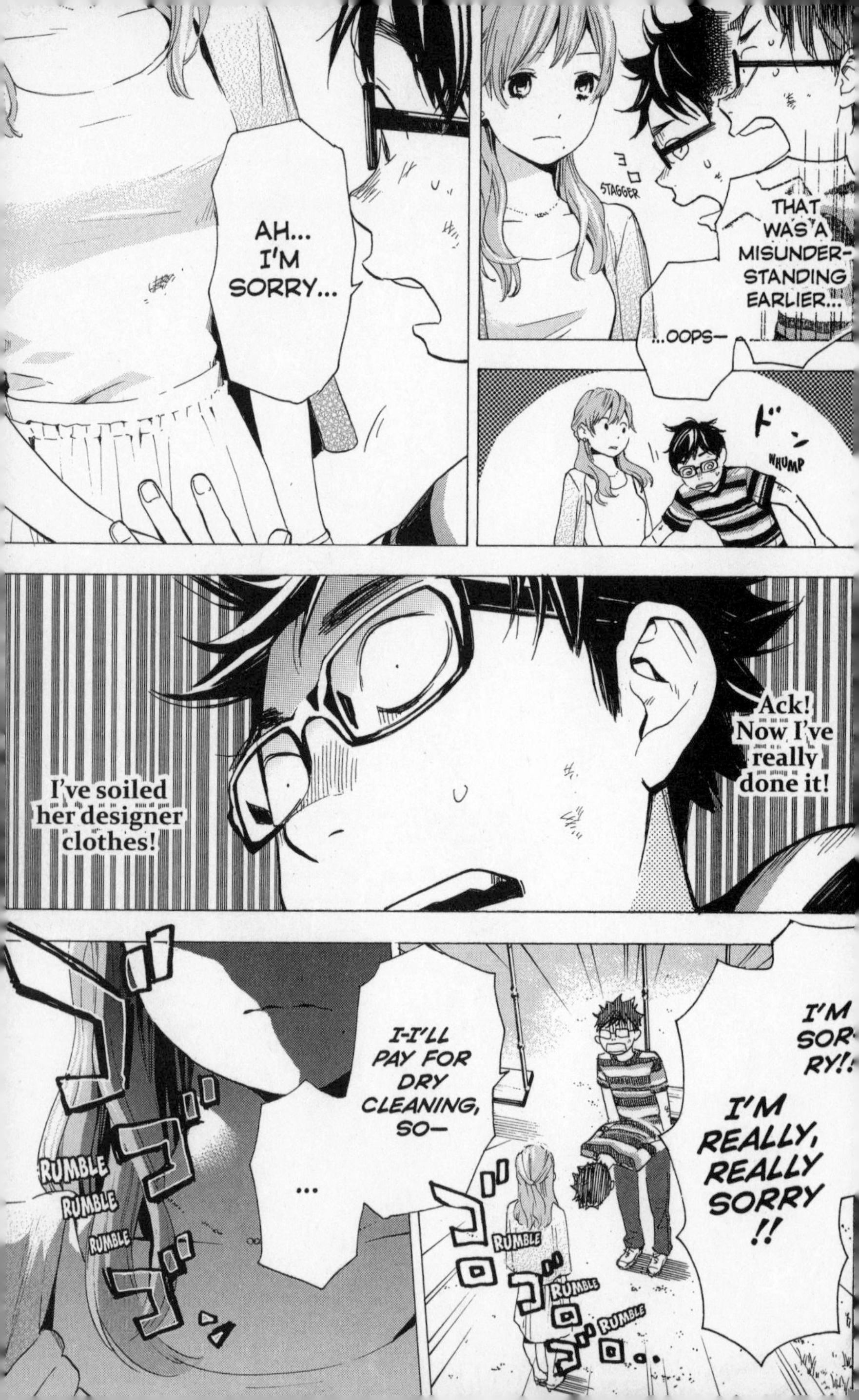
STAGGER
THAT WAS A MISUNDERSTANDING EARLIER...!
...OOPS—
WHUMP
AH... I'M SORRY...
Ack! Now I've really done it!
I've soiled her designer clothes!
I'M SORRY!!
I'M REALLY, REALLY SORRY!!
I-I'LL PAY FOR DRY CLEANING, SO—
RUMBLE
RUMBLE
RUMBLE
RUMBLE
...
RUMBLE
RUMBLE
RUMBLE

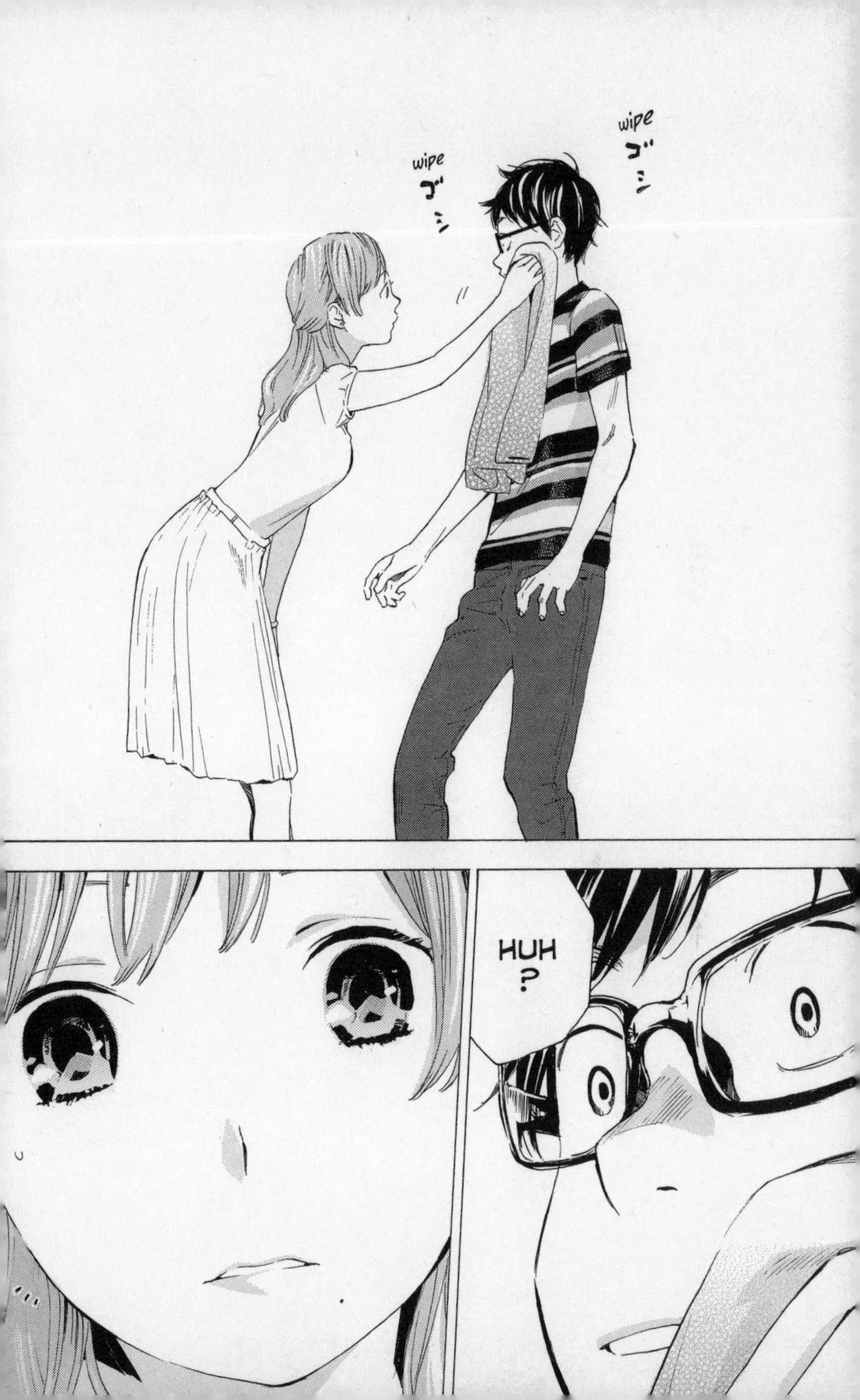
wipe ゴシ
wipe ゴシ
HUH ?

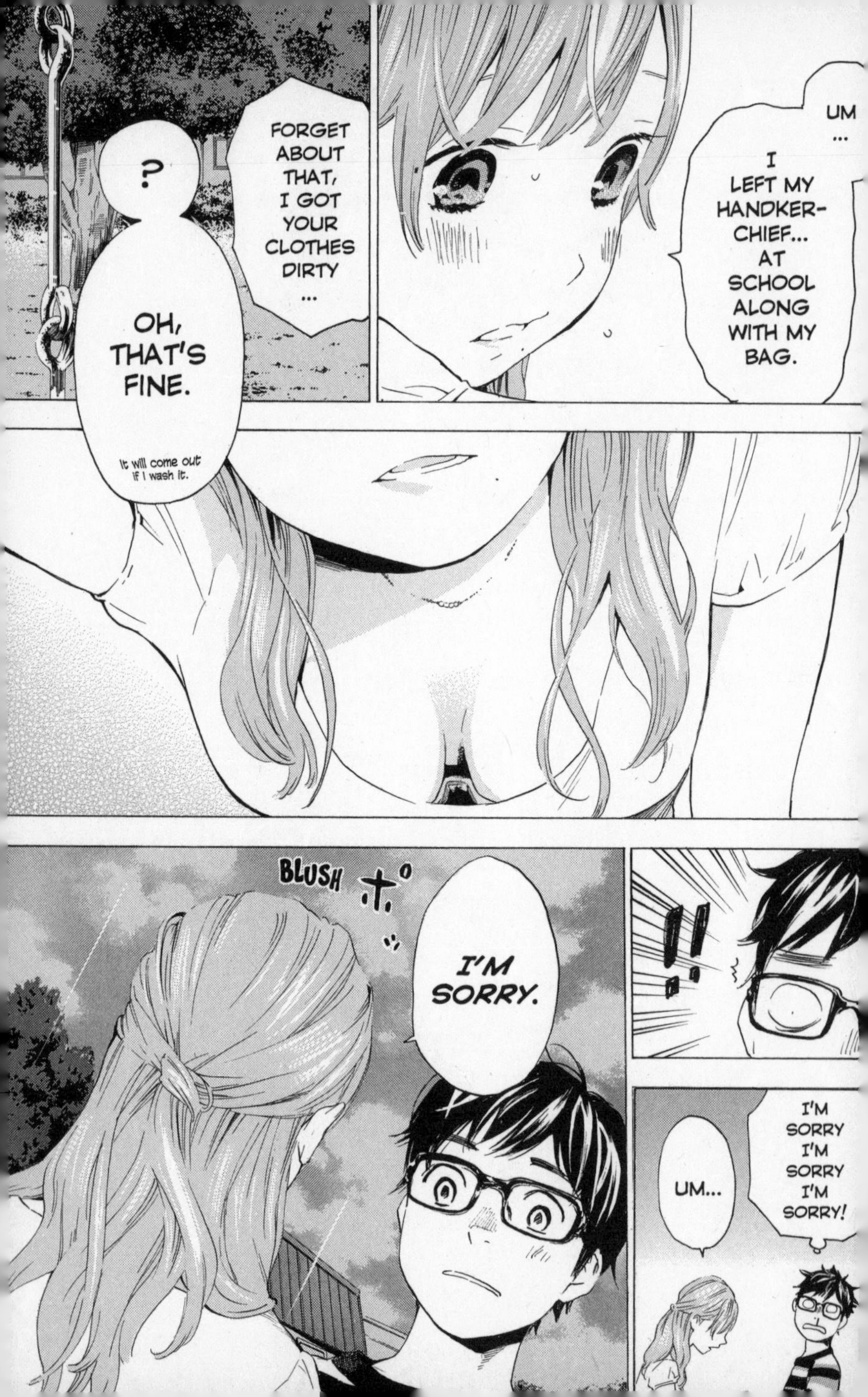
UM ...
I LEFT MY HANDKER-CHIEF... AT SCHOOL ALONG WITH MY BAG.
FORGET ABOUT THAT, I GOT YOUR CLOTHES DIRTY ...
?
OH, THAT'S FINE.
It will come out if I wash it.
!!
I'M SORRY I'M SORRY I'M SORRY!
UM...
BLUSH
I'M SORRY.

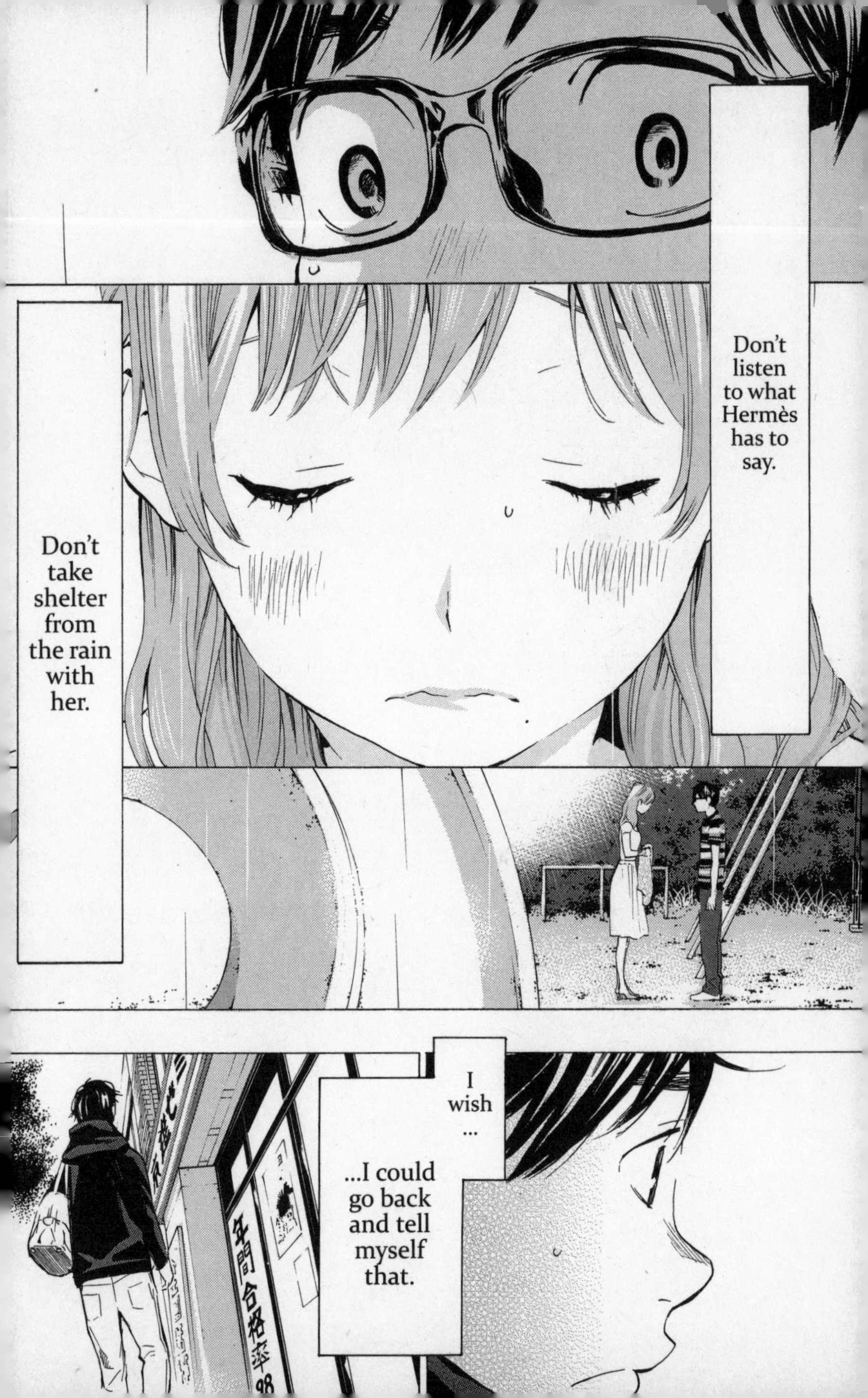

Don't listen to what Hermès has to say.
Don't take shelter from the rain with her.
I wish...
...I could go back and tell myself that.
年間合格率

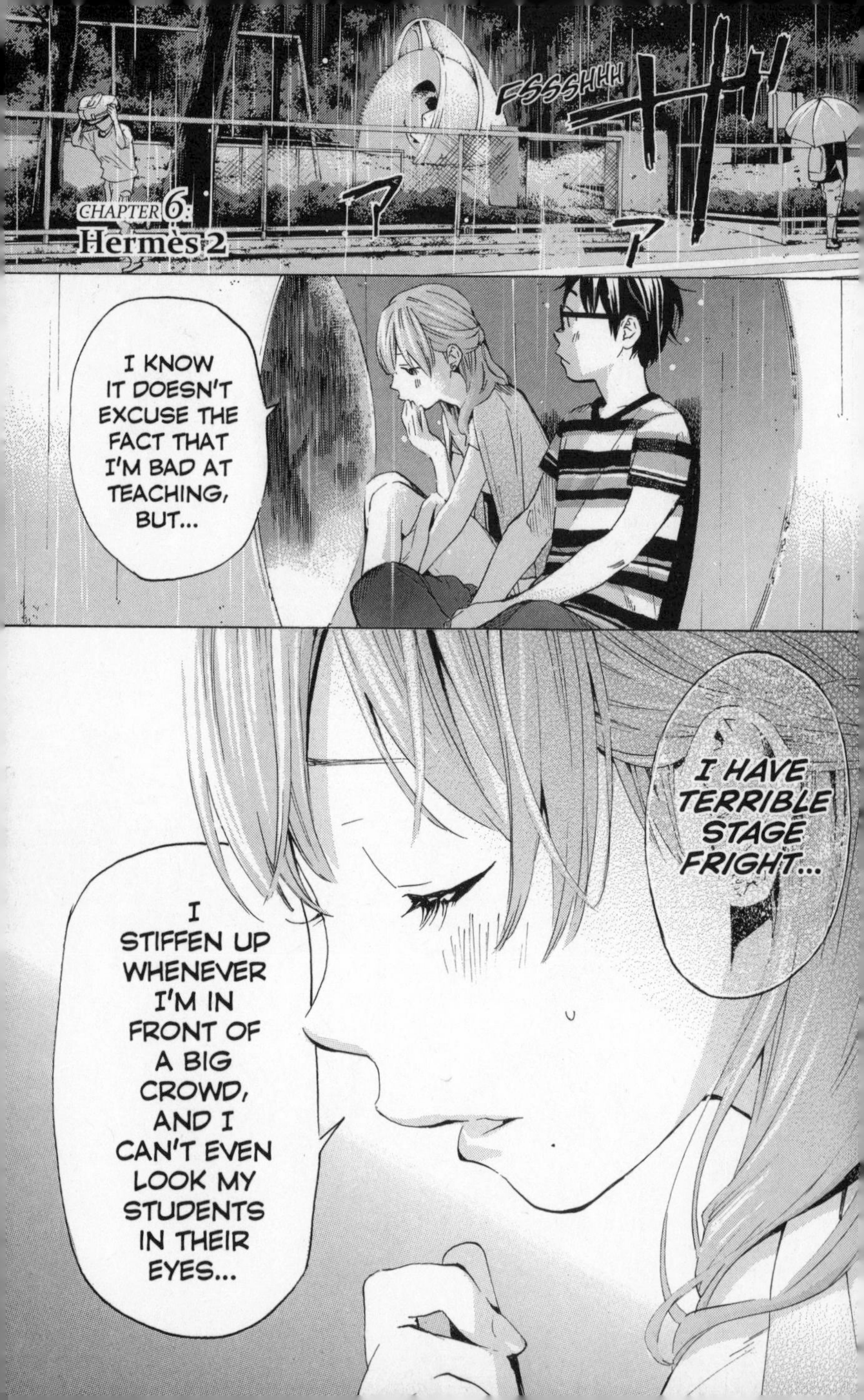
FSSSHHH
CHAPTER 6: Hermès 2
I KNOW IT DOESN'T EXCUSE THE FACT THAT I'M BAD AT TEACHING, BUT...
I HAVE TERRIBLE STAGE FRIGHT...
I STIFFEN UP WHENEVER I'M IN FRONT OF A BIG CROWD, AND I CAN'T EVEN LOOK MY STUDENTS IN THEIR EYES...

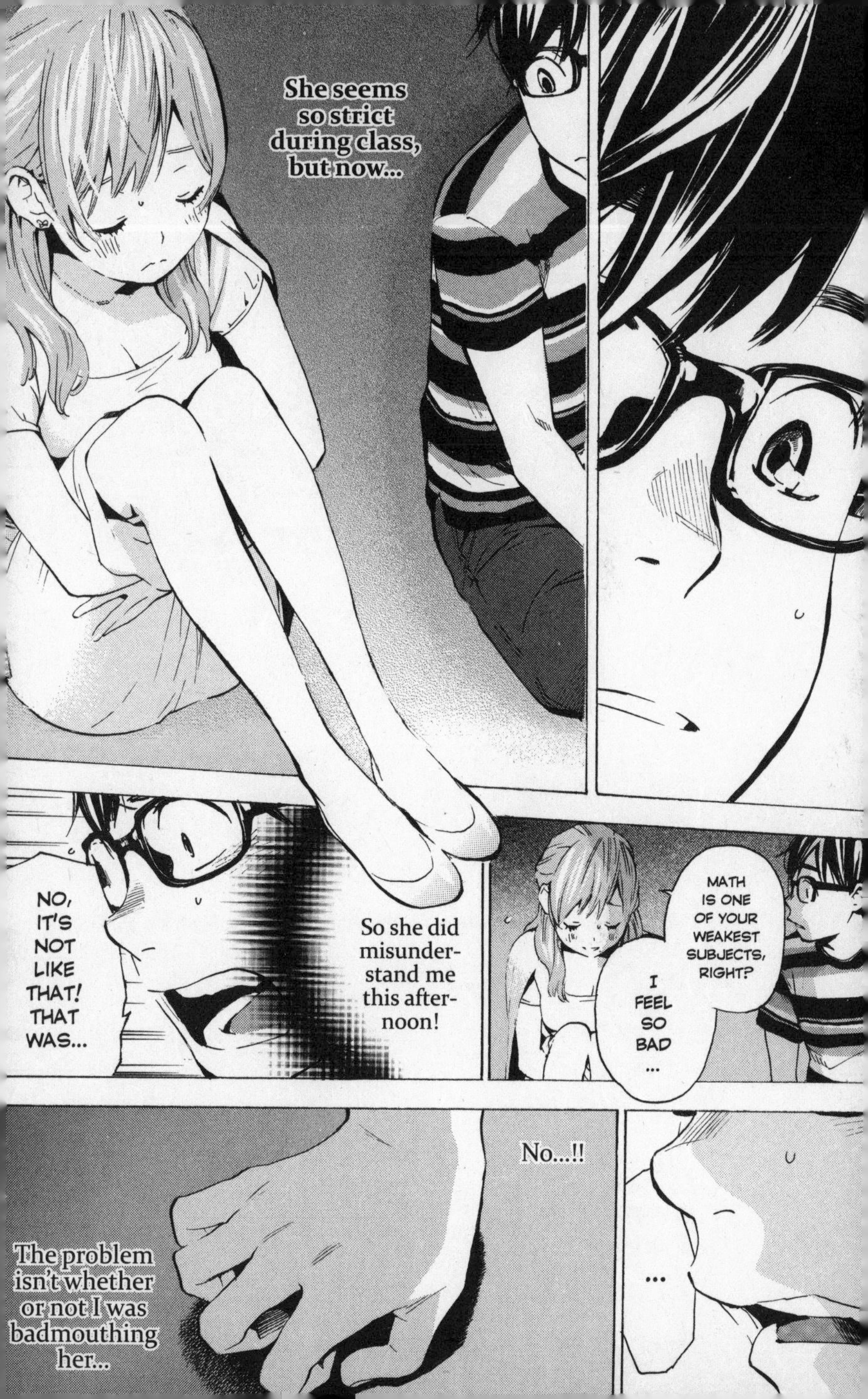
She seems so strict during class, but now...
MATH IS ONE OF YOUR WEAKEST SUBJECTS, RIGHT?
I FEEL SO BAD ...
So she did misunder-stand me this after-noon!
NO, IT'S NOT LIKE THAT! THAT WAS...
...
No...!!
The problem isn't whether or not I was badmouthing her...

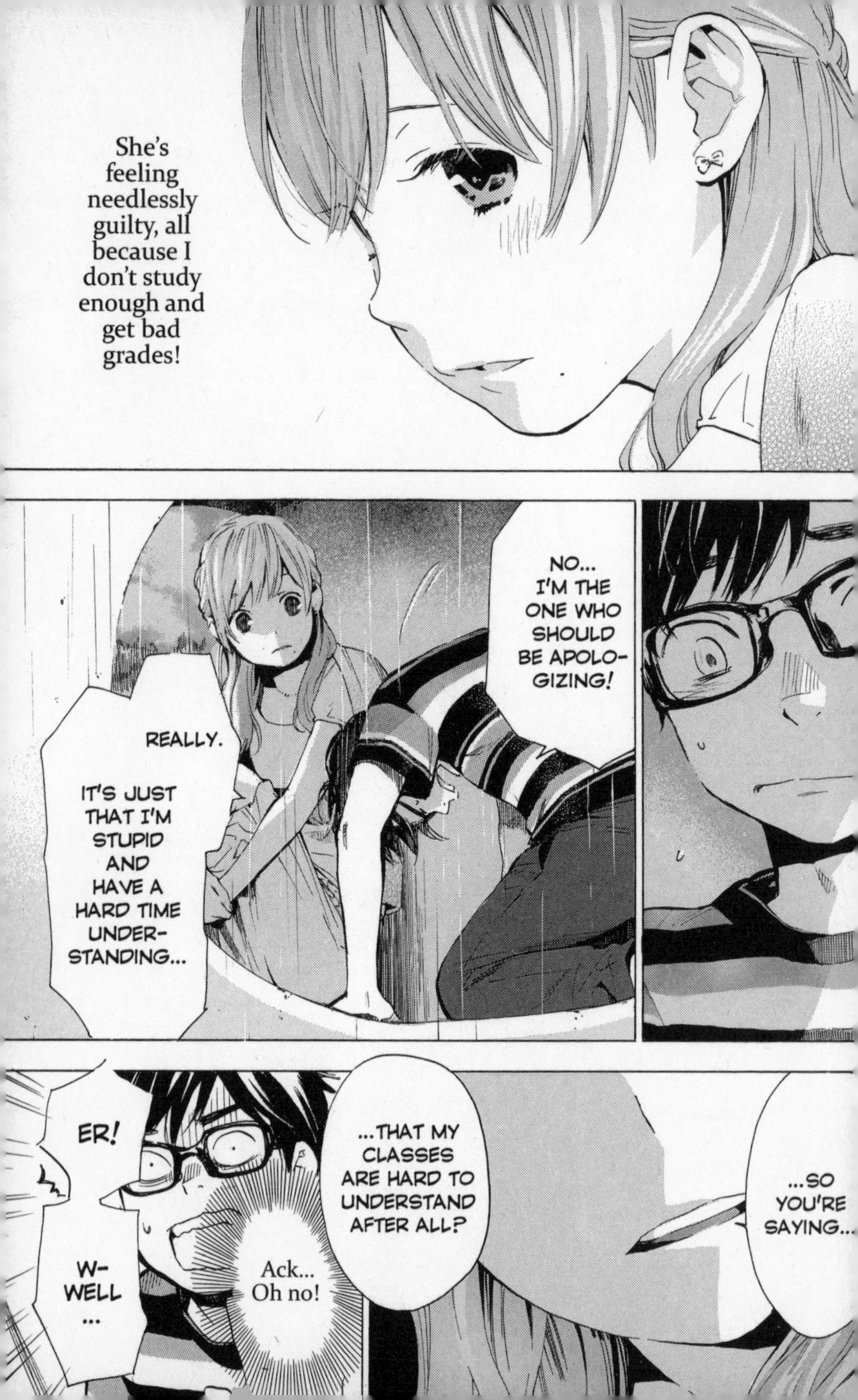
She's feeling needlessly guilty, all because I don't study enough and get bad grades!
NO... I'M THE ONE WHO SHOULD BE APOLO-GIZING!
REALLY.
IT'S JUST THAT I'M STUPID AND HAVE A HARD TIME UNDER-STANDING...
...SO YOU'RE SAYING...
...THAT MY CLASSES ARE HARD TO UNDERSTAND AFTER ALL?
ER!
Ack... Oh no!
W-WELL ...

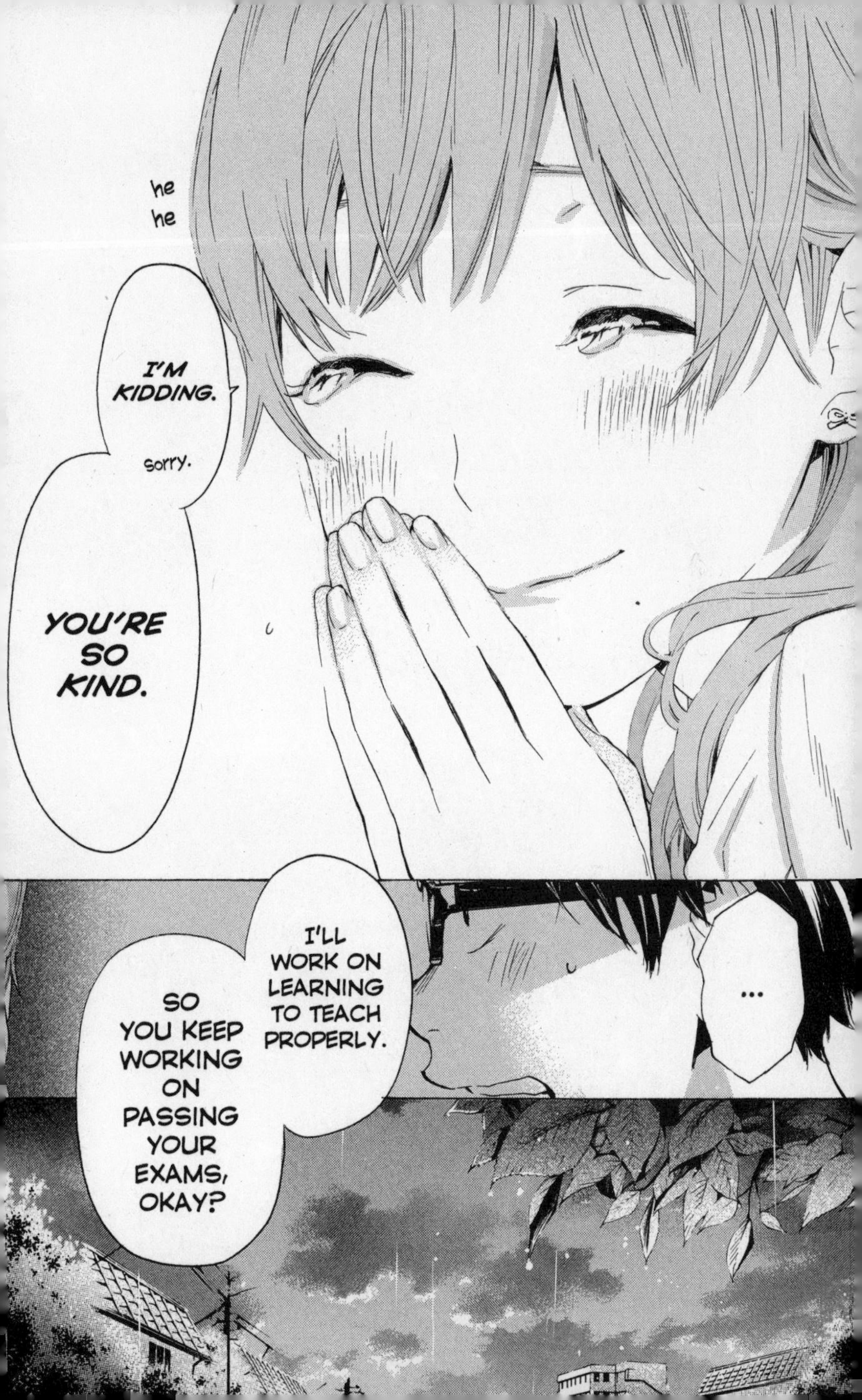
he he
I'M KIDDING.
sorry.
YOU'RE SO KIND.
...
I'LL WORK ON LEARNING TO TEACH PROPERLY.
SO YOU KEEP WORKING ON PASSING YOUR EXAMS, OKAY?

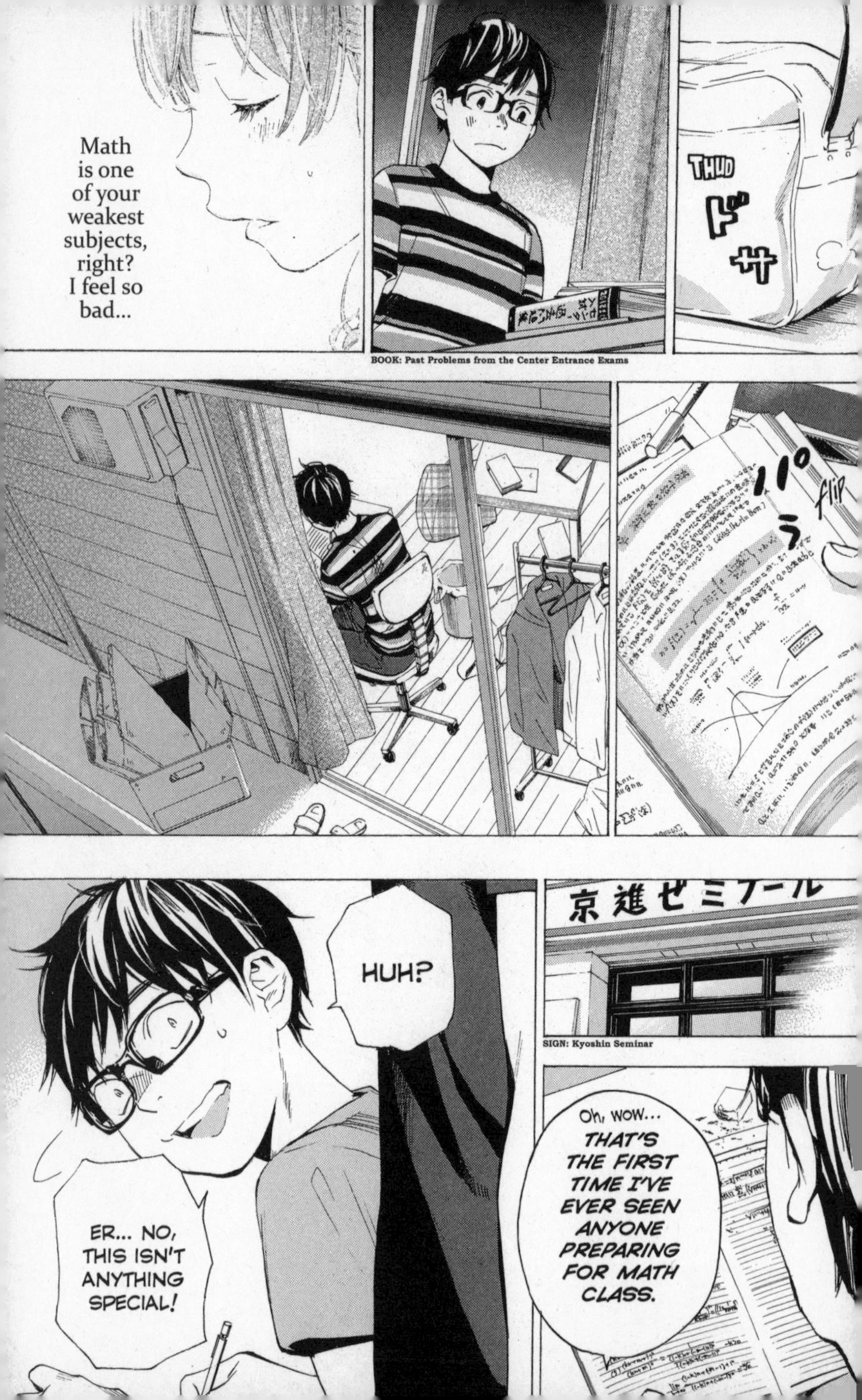
THUD
ドサ
BOOK: Past Problems from the Center Entrance Exams
Math is one of your weakest subjects, right? I feel so bad...
パラ
flip
京進ゼミナール
SIGN: Kyoshin Seminar
Oh, wow... THAT'S THE FIRST TIME I'VE EVER SEEN ANYONE PREPARING FOR MATH CLASS.
HUH?
ER... NO, THIS ISN'T ANYTHING SPECIAL!

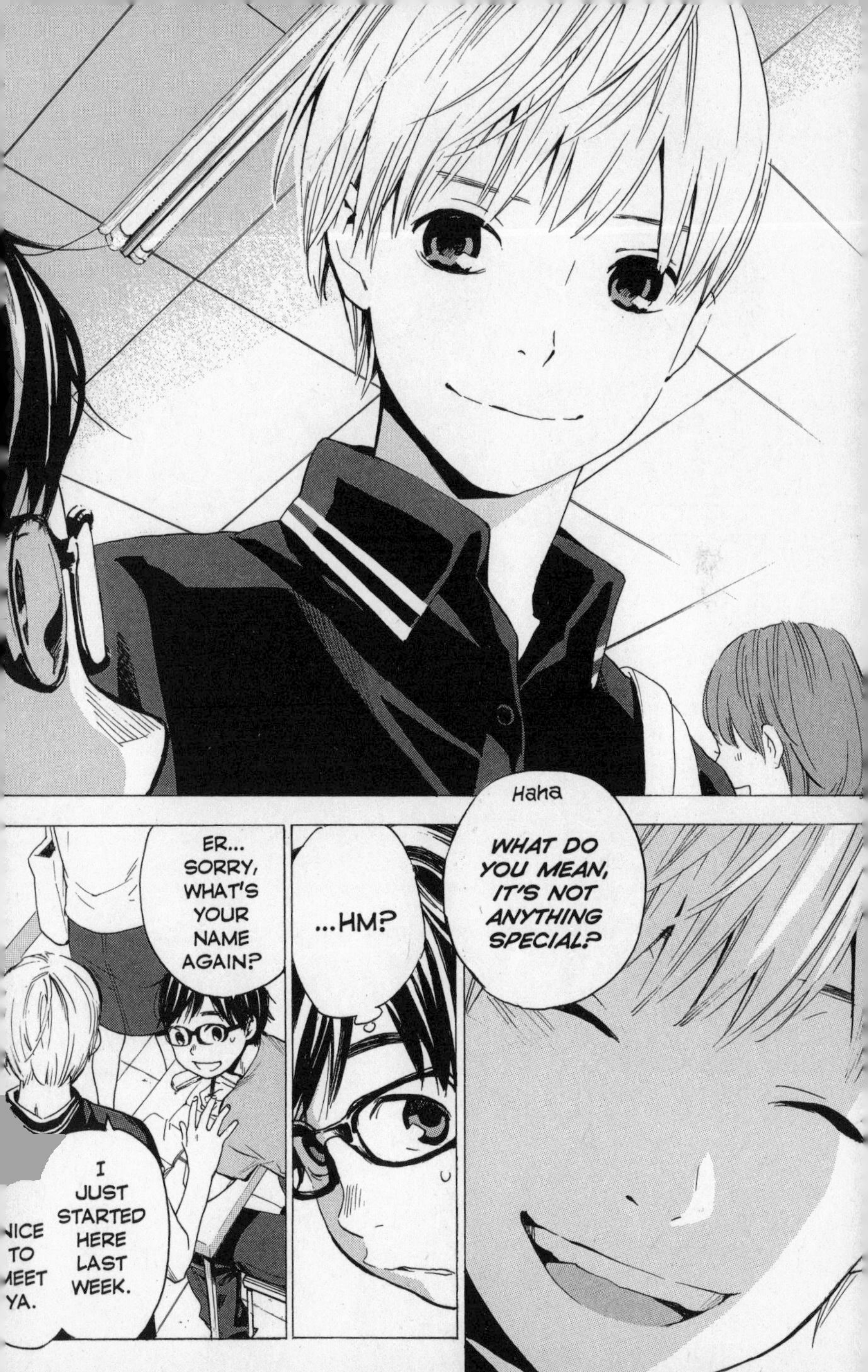
Haha
WHAT DO YOU MEAN, IT'S NOT ANYTHING SPECIAL?
...HM?
ER... SORRY, WHAT'S YOUR NAME AGAIN?
I JUST STARTED HERE LAST WEEK.
NICE TO MEET YA.

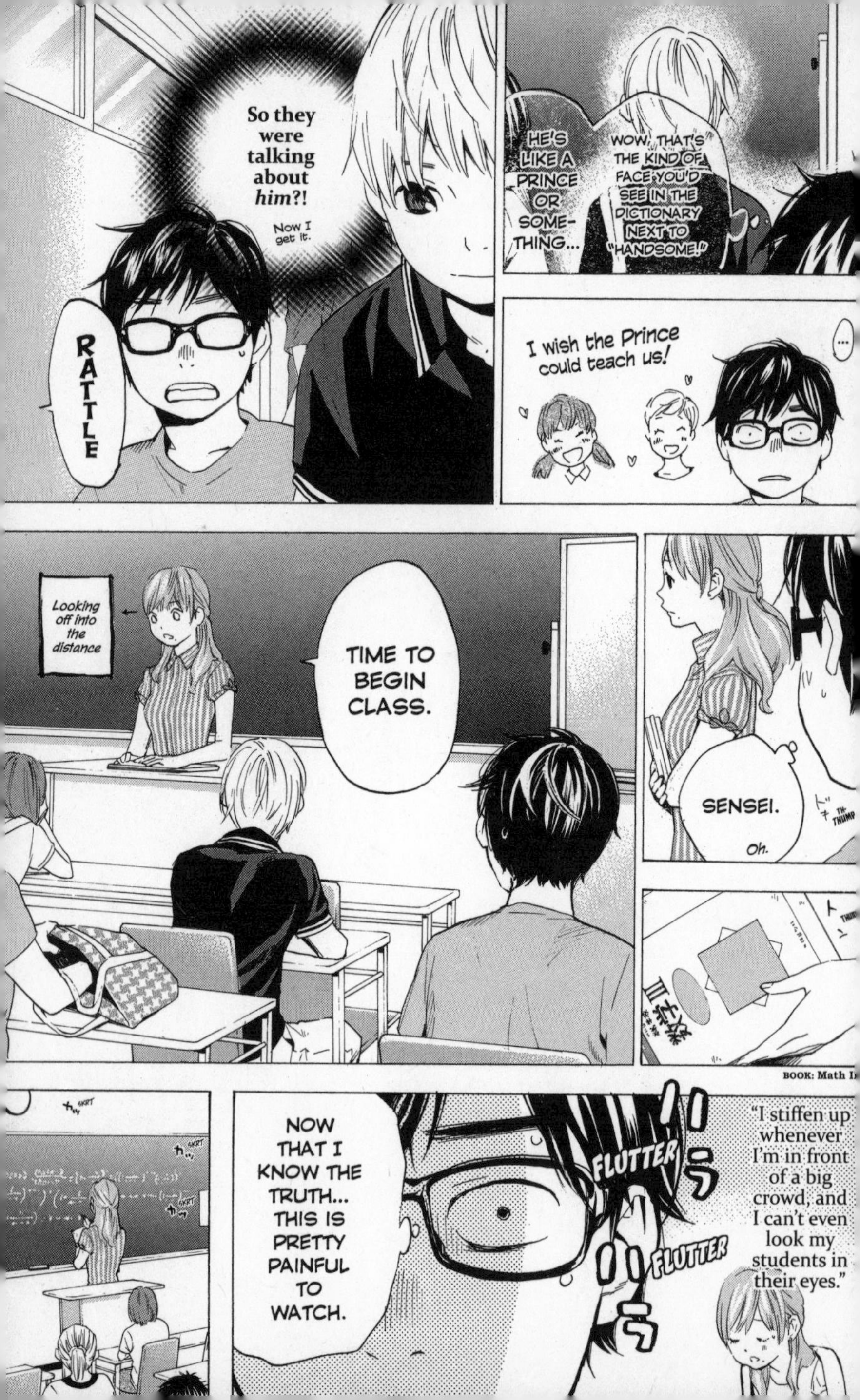
WOW, THAT'S THE KIND OF FACE YOU'D SEE IN THE DICTIONARY NEXT TO "HANDSOME."
HE'S LIKE A PRINCE OR SOME-THING...
...
I wish the Prince could teach us!
So they were talking about *him*?!
Now I get it.
RATTLE
SENSEI.
Oh.
TH-THUMP
THUMP
BOOK: Math I
TIME TO BEGIN CLASS.
Looking off into the distance
"I stiffen up whenever I'm in front of a big crowd, and I can't even look my students in their eyes."
FLUTTER
FLUTTER
NOW THAT I KNOW THE TRUTH... THIS IS PRETTY PAINFUL TO WATCH.
SKRT
SKRT
SKRT

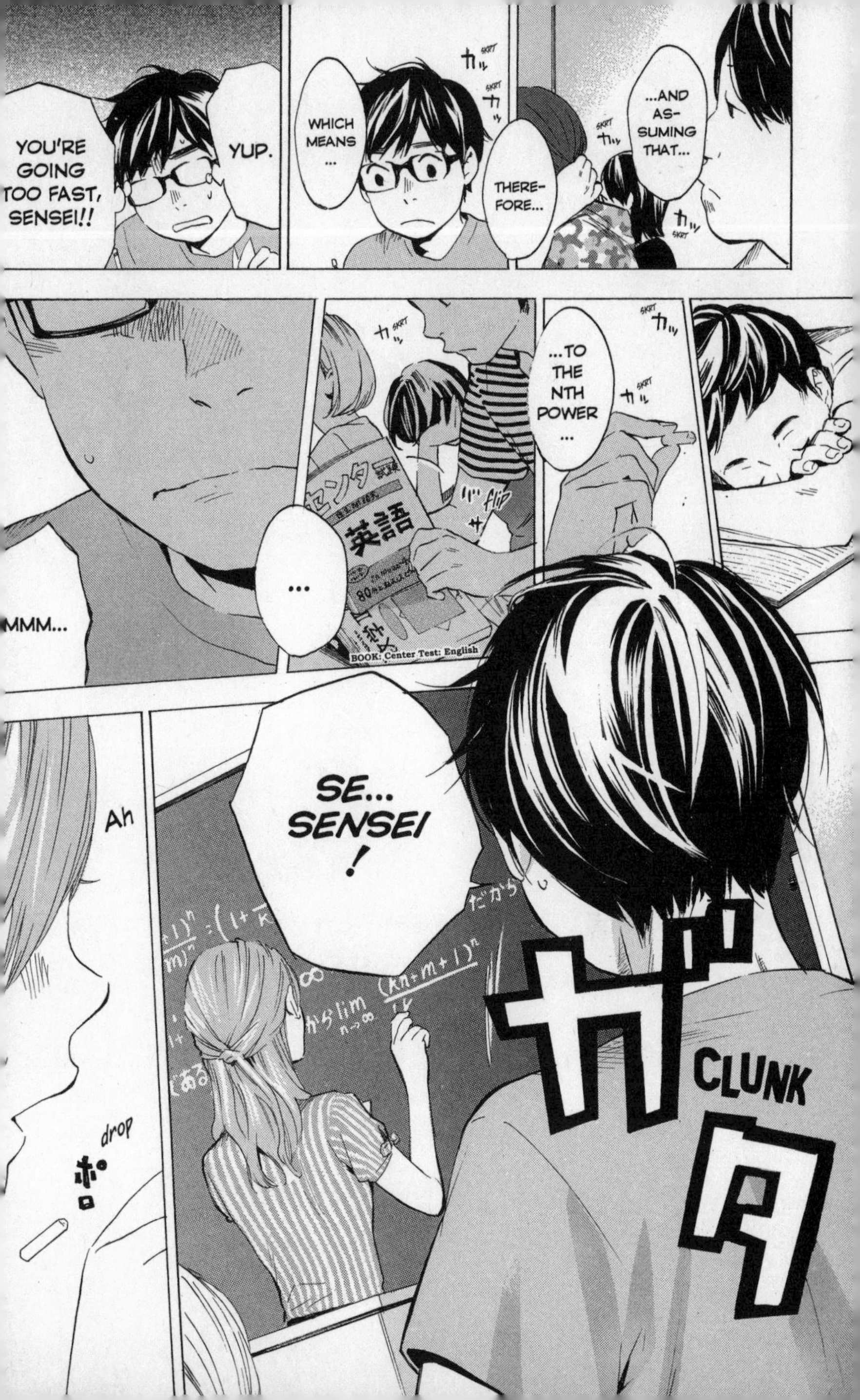

...AND AS-SUMING THAT...
SKRT
THERE-FORE...
WHICH MEANS ...
YUP.
YOU'RE GOING TOO FAST, SENSEI!!
SKRT
...TO THE NTH POWER ...
flip
...
BOOK: Center Test: English
MMM...
SE... SENSEI!
CLUNK
Ah
drop

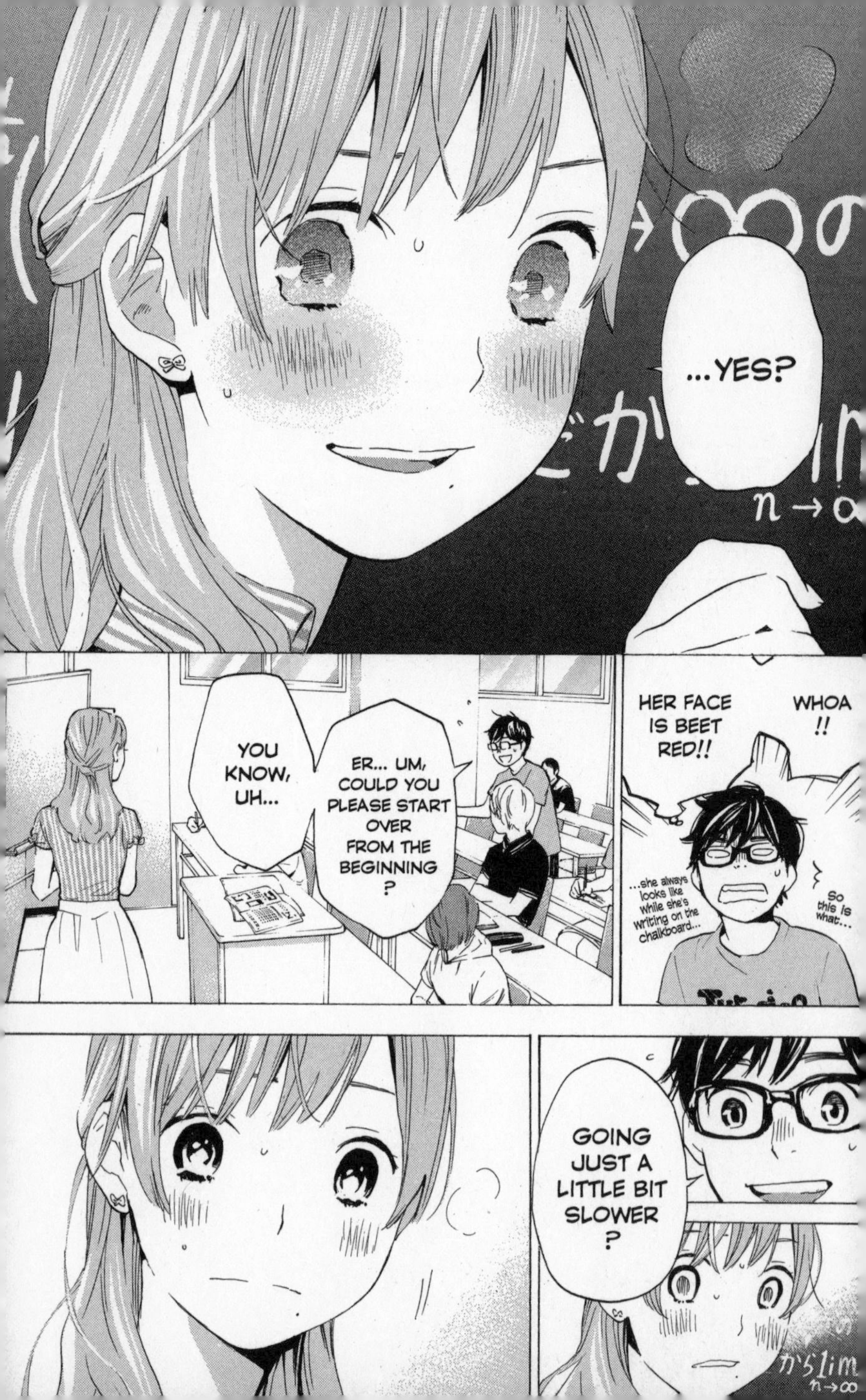
...YES?
WHOA!!
HER FACE IS BEET RED!!
So this is what...
...she always looks like while she's writing on the chalkboard...
ER... UM, COULD YOU PLEASE START OVER FROM THE BEGINNING?
YOU KNOW, UH...
GOING JUST A LITTLE BIT SLOWER?

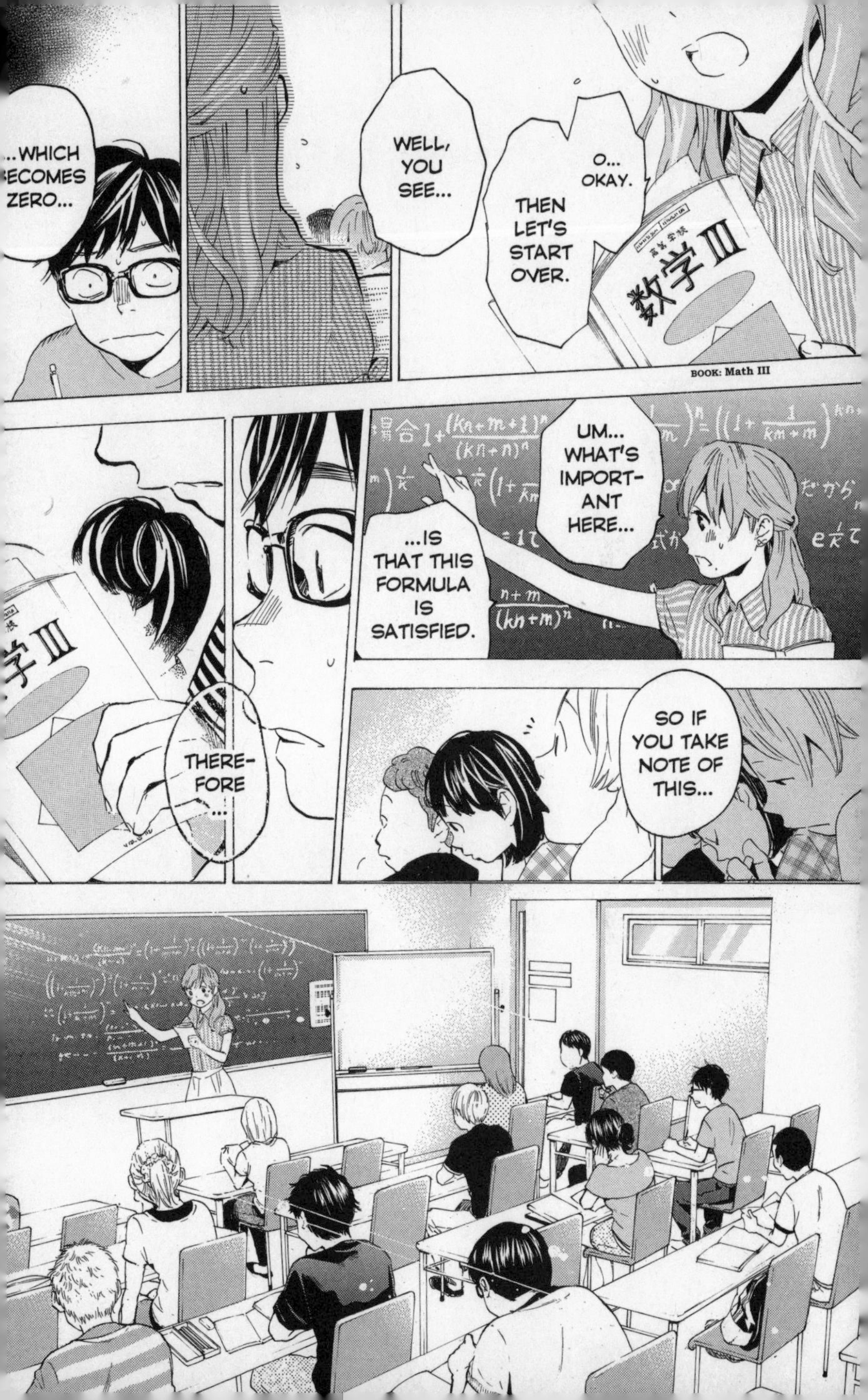
O... OKAY.
THEN LET'S START OVER.
BOOK: Math III
WELL, YOU SEE...
...WHICH ECOMES ZERO...
UM... WHAT'S IMPORT-ANT HERE...
...IS THAT THIS FORMULA IS SATISFIED.
SO IF YOU TAKE NOTE OF THIS...
THERE-FORE ...

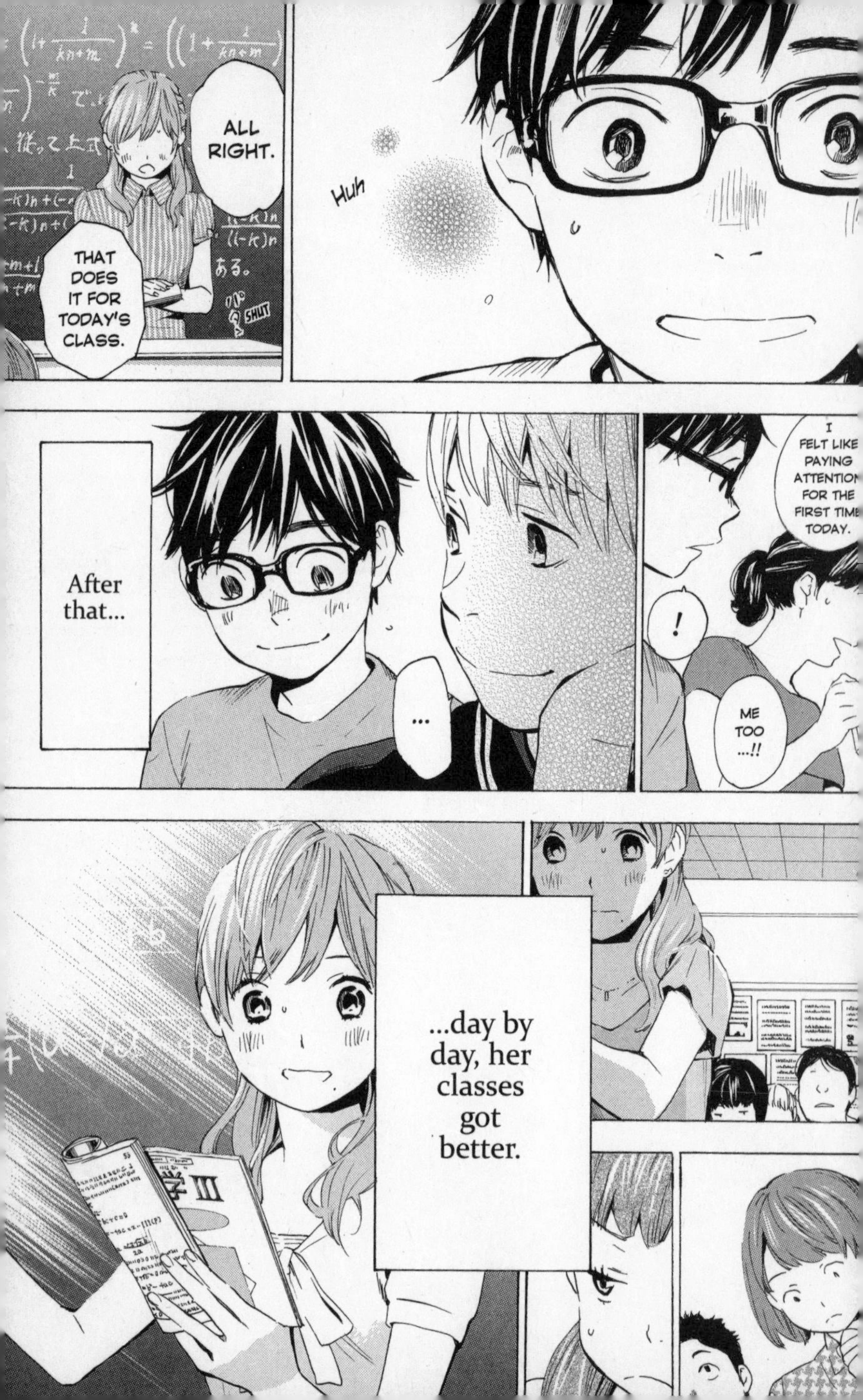
Huh
ALL RIGHT.
THAT DOES IT FOR TODAY'S CLASS.
SHUT
I FELT LIKE PAYING ATTENTION FOR THE FIRST TIME TODAY.
!
ME TOO ...!!
...
After that...
...day by day, her classes got better.

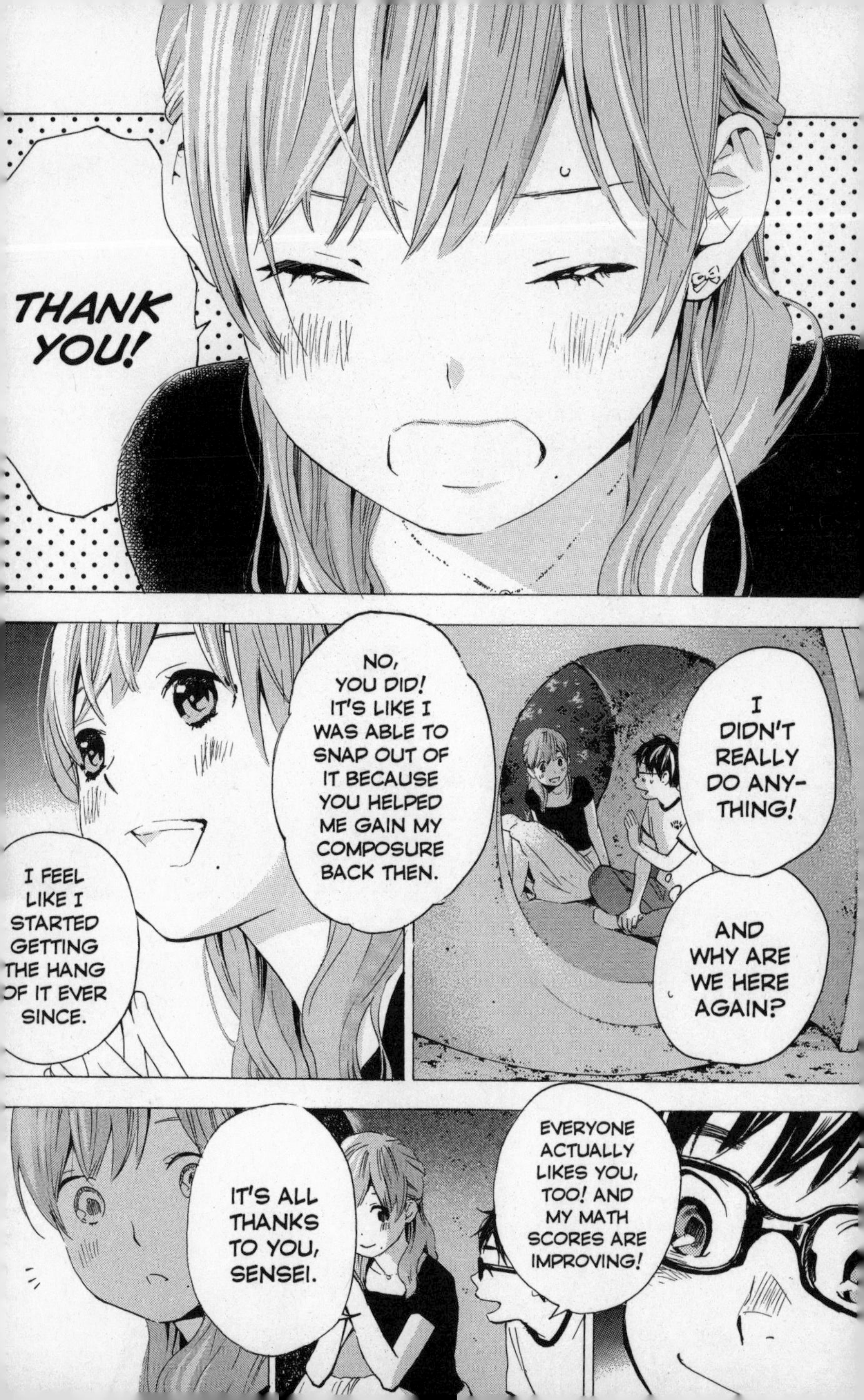
THANK YOU!
I DIDN'T REALLY DO ANYTHING!
AND WHY ARE WE HERE AGAIN?
NO, YOU DID! IT'S LIKE I WAS ABLE TO SNAP OUT OF IT BECAUSE YOU HELPED ME GAIN MY COMPOSURE BACK THEN.
I FEEL LIKE I STARTED GETTING THE HANG OF IT EVER SINCE.
EVERYONE ACTUALLY LIKES YOU, TOO! AND MY MATH SCORES ARE IMPROVING!
IT'S ALL THANKS TO YOU, SENSEI.

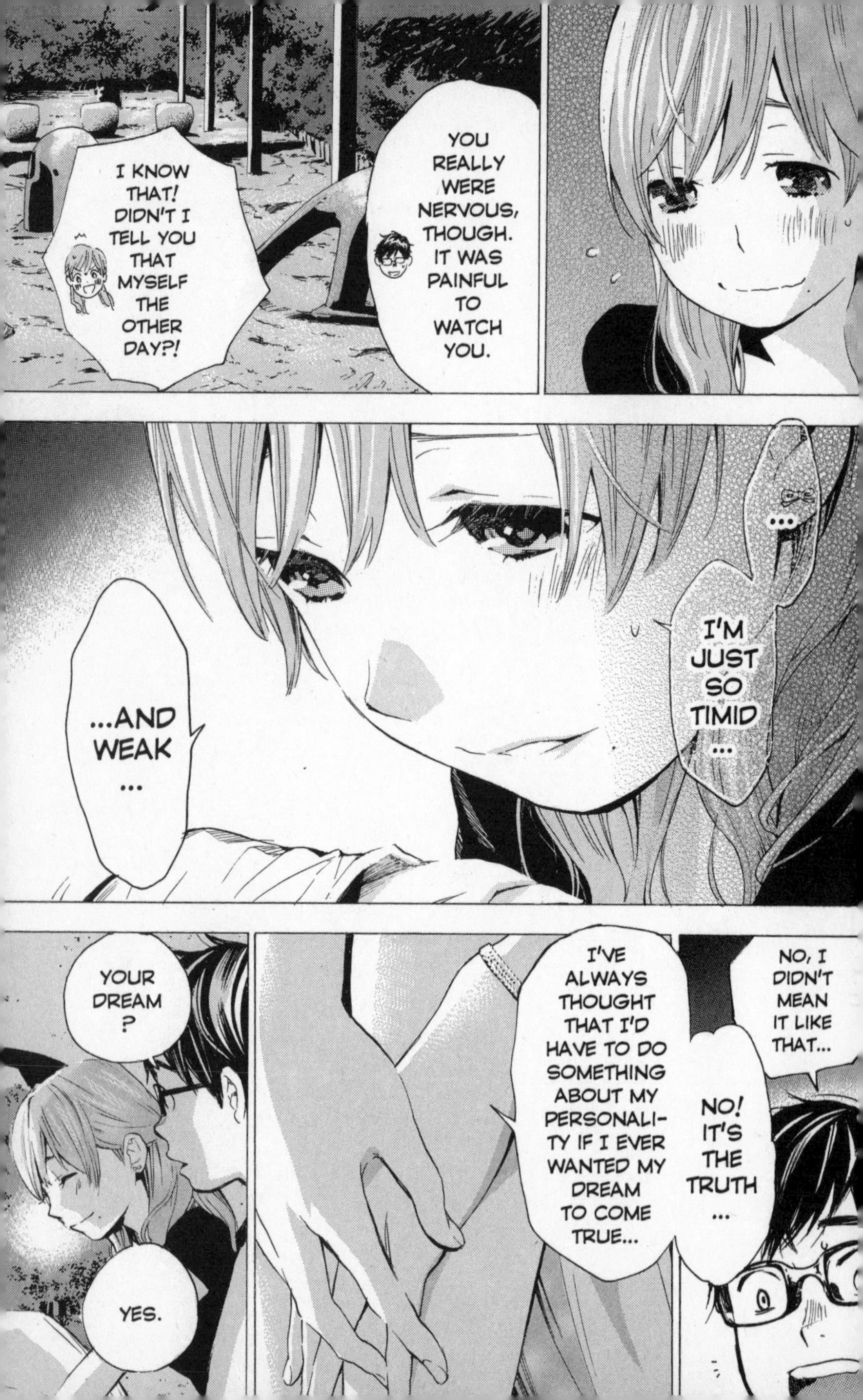
YOU REALLY WERE NERVOUS, THOUGH. IT WAS PAINFUL TO WATCH YOU.
I KNOW THAT! DIDN'T I TELL YOU THAT MYSELF THE OTHER DAY?!
...
I'M JUST SO TIMID ...
...AND WEAK ...
NO, I DIDN'T MEAN IT LIKE THAT...
NO! IT'S THE TRUTH ...
I'VE ALWAYS THOUGHT THAT I'D HAVE TO DO SOMETHING ABOUT MY PERSONALITY IF I EVER WANTED MY DREAM TO COME TRUE...
YOUR DREAM ?
YES.

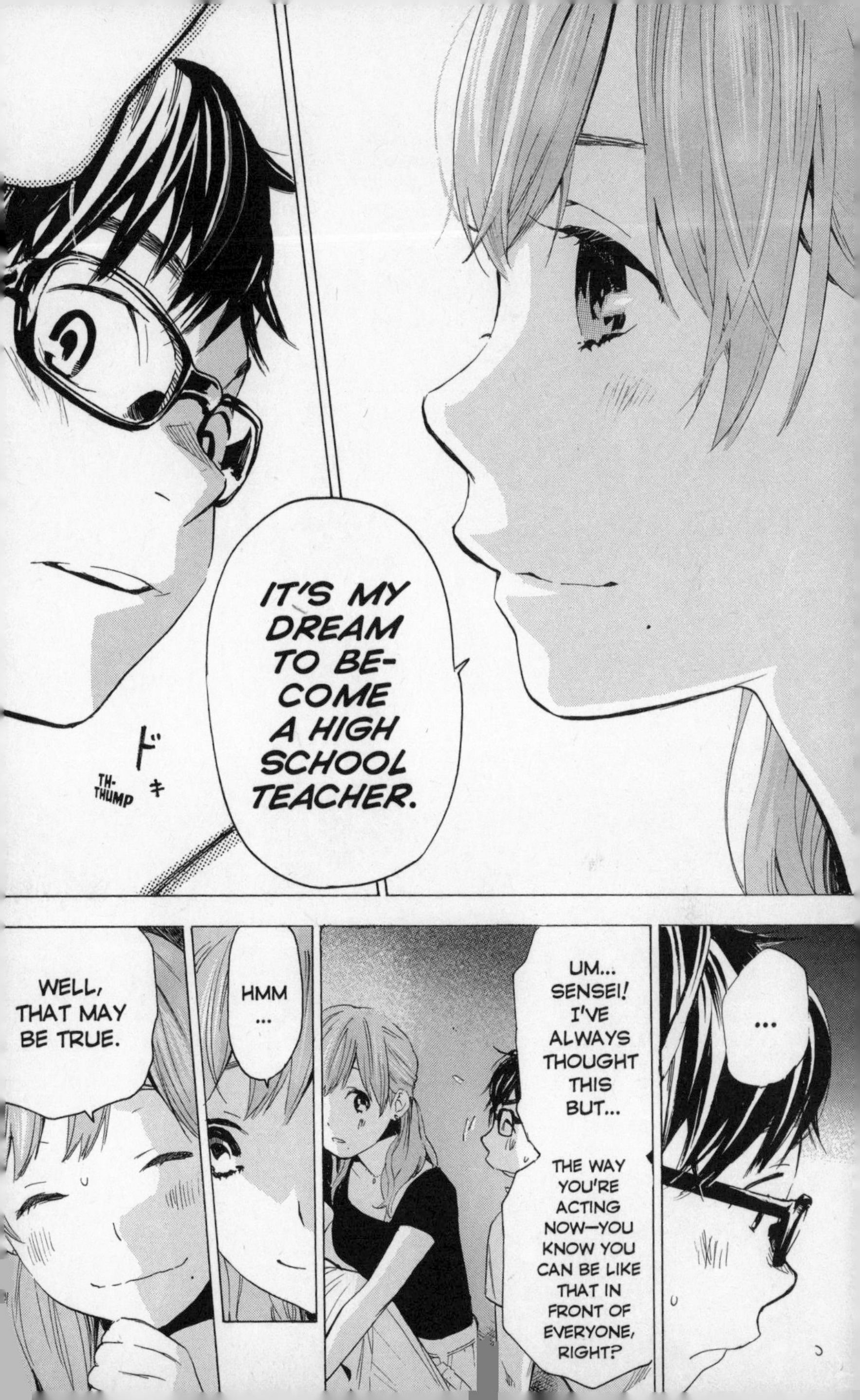
IT'S MY DREAM TO BE-COME A HIGH SCHOOL TEACHER.
ドキ
TH-THUMP
...
UM... SENSEI! I'VE ALWAYS THOUGHT THIS BUT...
THE WAY YOU'RE ACTING NOW—YOU KNOW YOU CAN BE LIKE THAT IN FRONT OF EVERYONE, RIGHT?
HMM ...
WELL, THAT MAY BE TRUE.

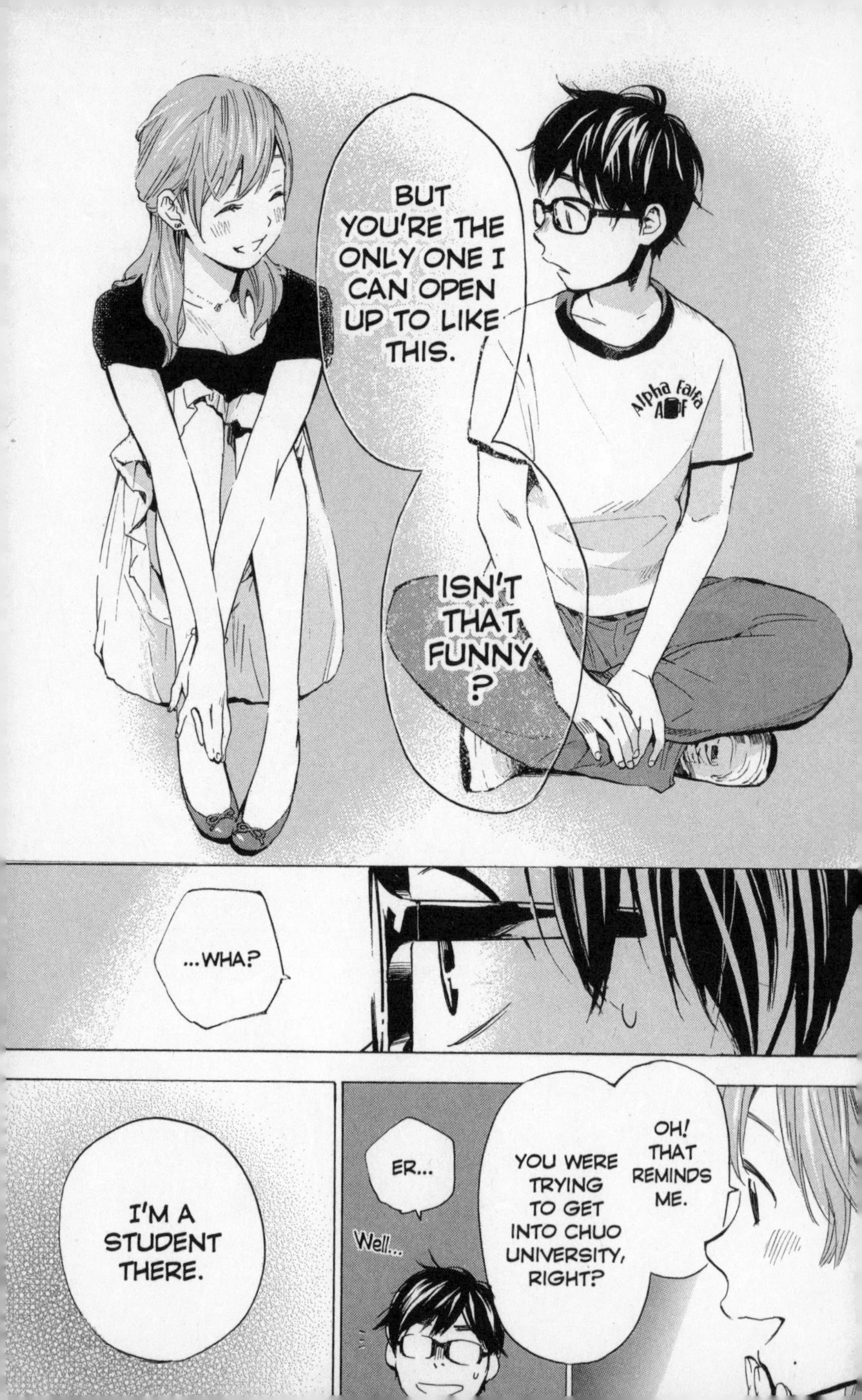
BUT YOU'RE THE ONLY ONE I CAN OPEN UP TO LIKE THIS.
ISN'T THAT FUNNY?
...WHA?
OH! THAT REMINDS ME.
YOU WERE TRYING TO GET INTO CHUO UNIVERSITY, RIGHT?
ER...
Well...
I'M A STUDENT THERE.

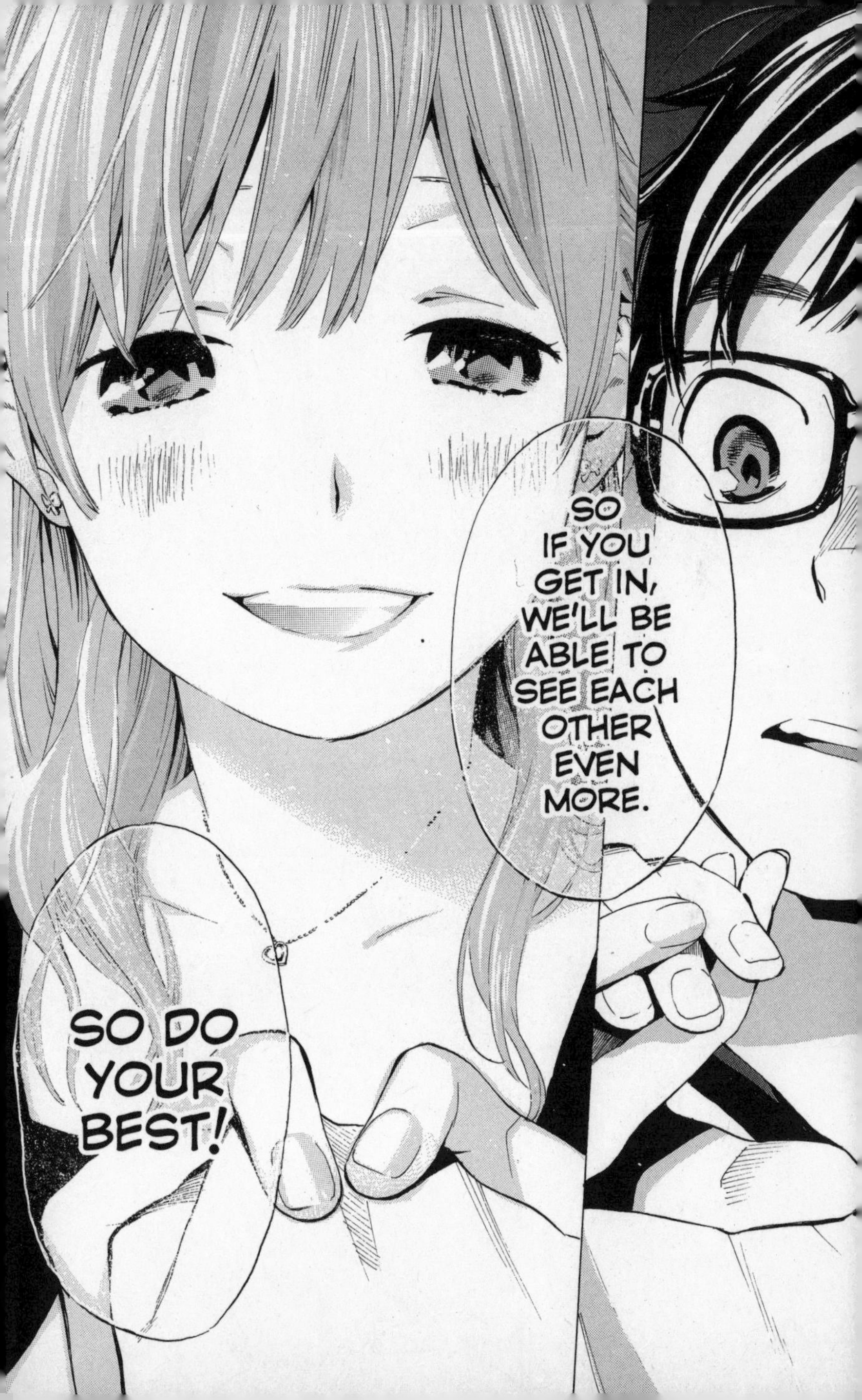
SO IF YOU GET IN, WE'LL BE ABLE TO SEE EACH OTHER EVEN MORE.
SO DO YOUR BEST!

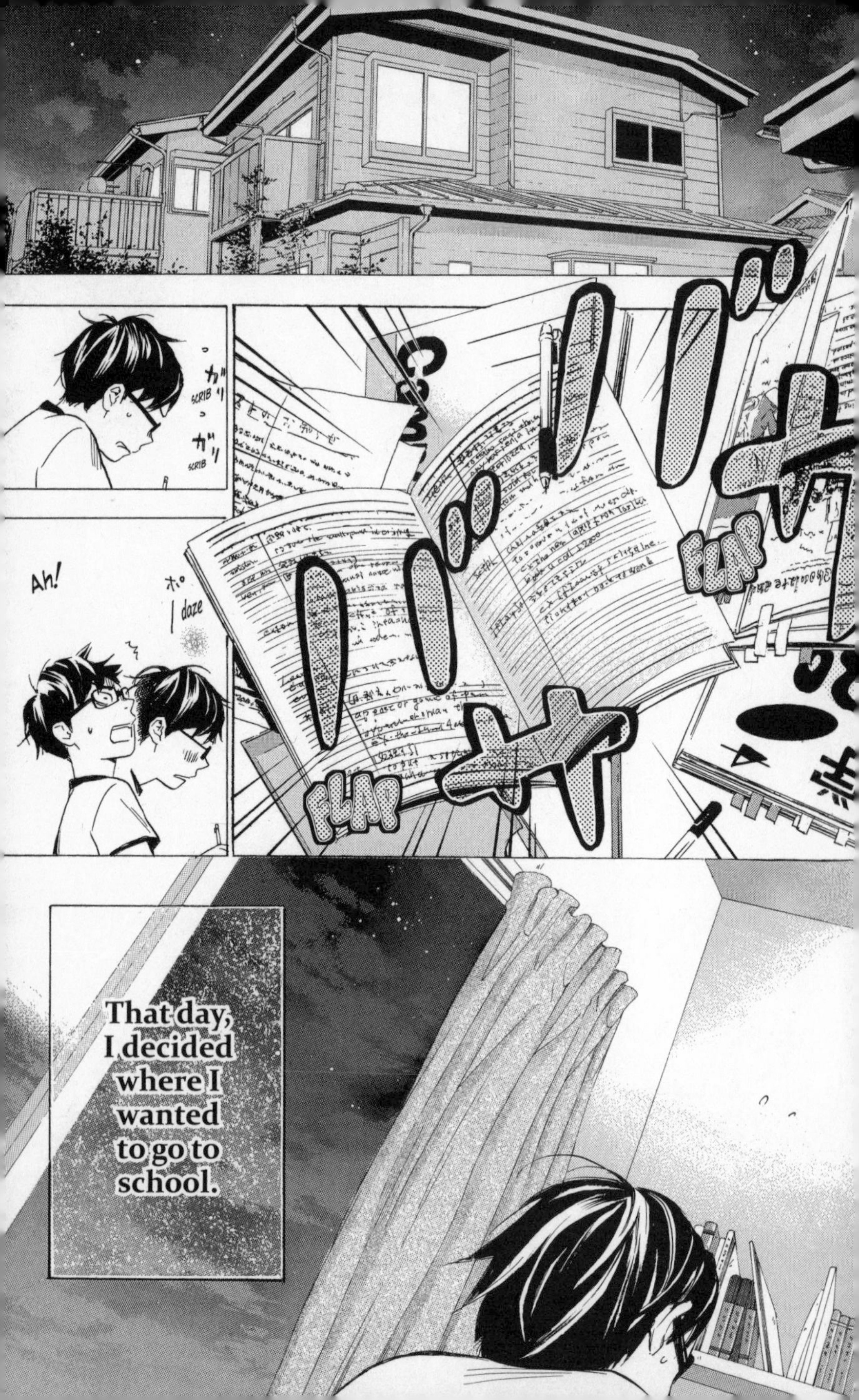
FLAP
FLAP
SCRIB
SCRIB
Ah!
daze
That day, I decided where I wanted to go to school.

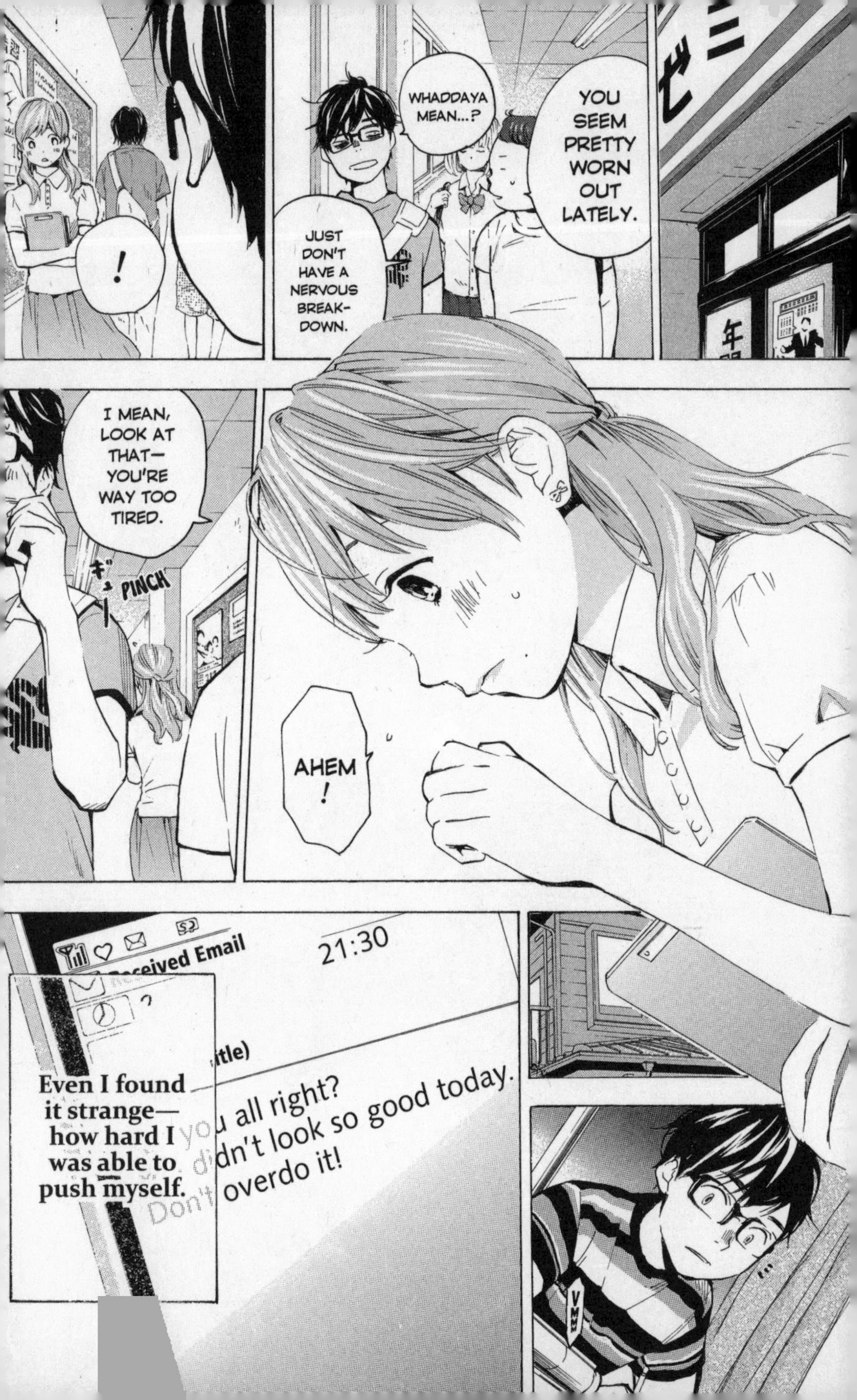
ゼミ
YOU SEEM PRETTY WORN OUT LATELY.
WHADDAYA MEAN...?
JUST DON'T HAVE A NERVOUS BREAKDOWN.
!
AHEM!
I MEAN, LOOK AT THAT— YOU'RE WAY TOO TIRED.
ギュー PINCH
VMM
Received Email
21:30
itle)
you all right?
didn't look so good today.
Don't overdo it!
Even I found it strange— how hard I was able to push myself.

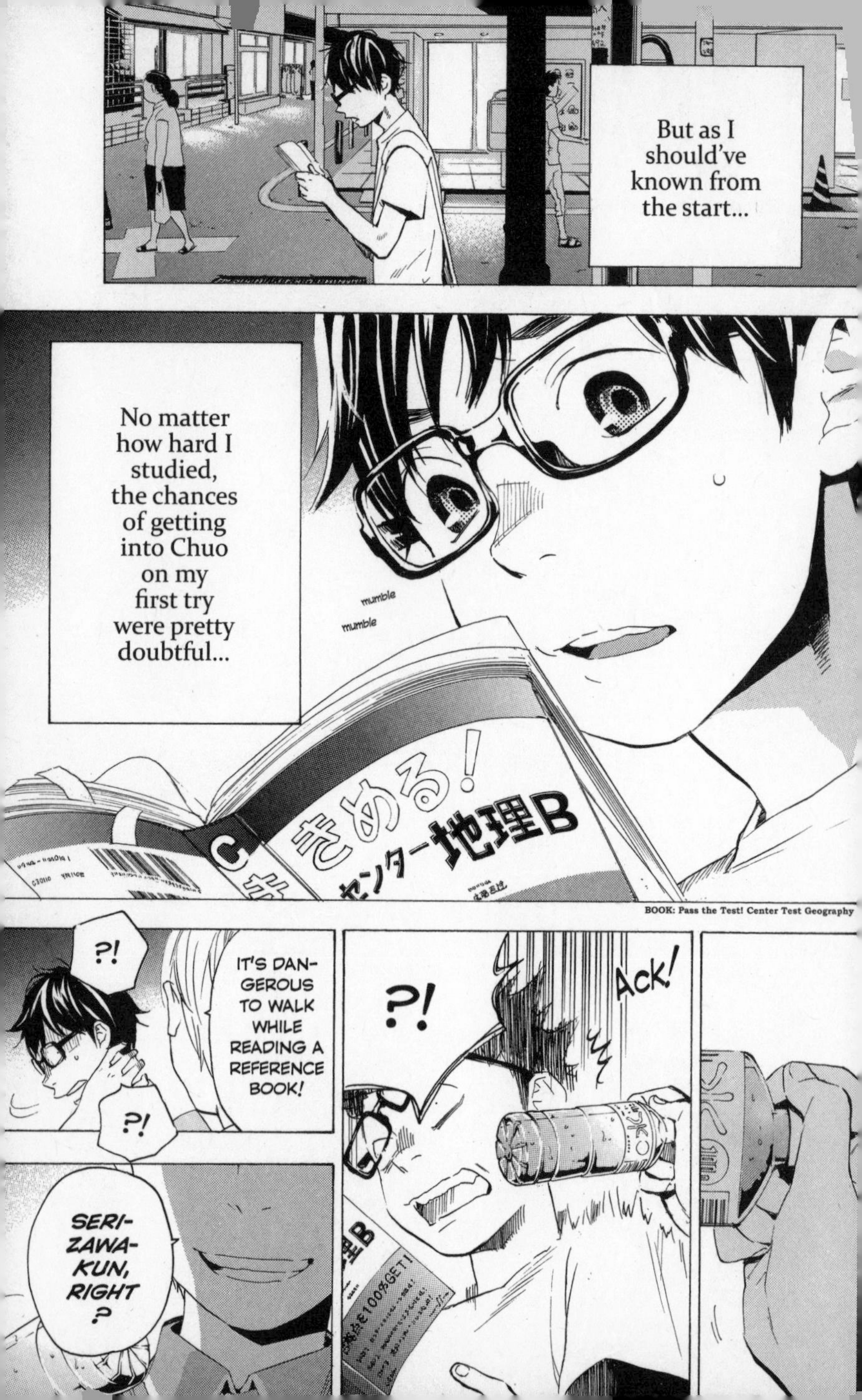
But as I should've known from the start...
No matter how hard I studied, the chances of getting into Chuo on my first try were pretty doubtful...
mumble
mumble
センター地理B
BOOK: Pass the Test! Center Test Geography
?!
ACK!
IT'S DANGEROUS TO WALK WHILE READING A REFERENCE BOOK!
?!
?!
SERIZAWA-KUN, RIGHT?

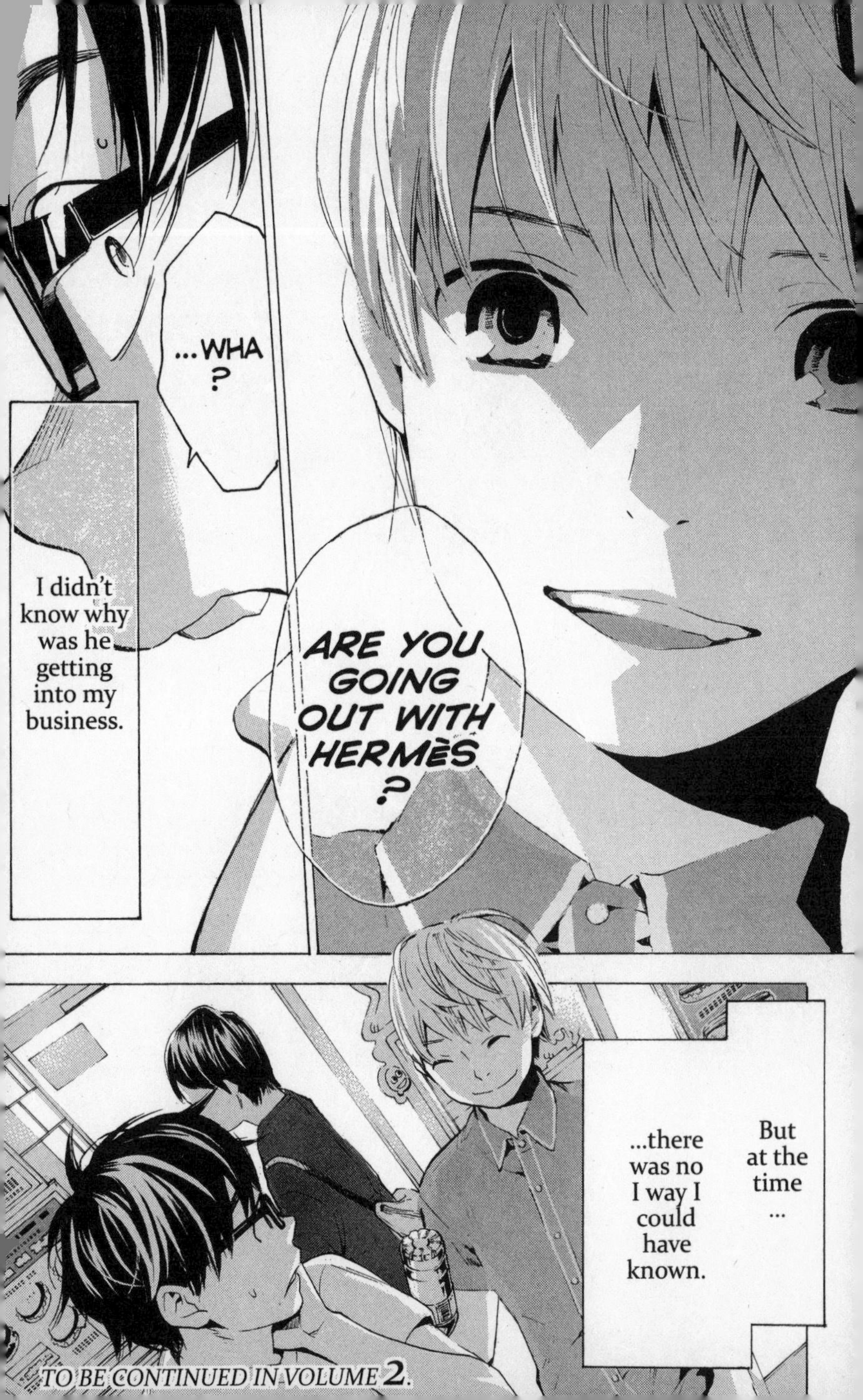
ARE YOU GOING OUT WITH HERMÈS?
...WHA?
I didn't know why was he getting into my business.
But at the time...
...there was no I way I could have known.
TO BE CONTINUED IN VOLUME 2.

STORY:

Mag-san 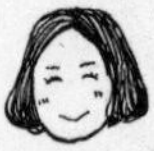

EDITORS:

Suzuki-san 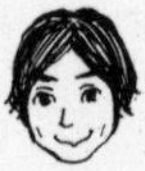 Kawakubo-san 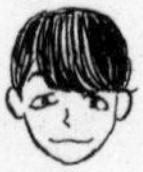

COLLECTED VOLUME:

Nakata-san 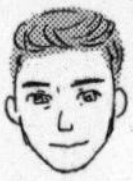 Shimoyama-san Takagi-san

ASSISTANTS:

Ando-san 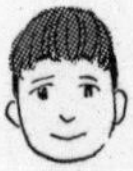

Kanzaki-san 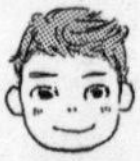

Ogoe-kun 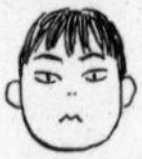

ART:

Emoto 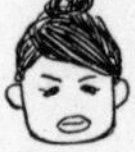

PHOTOGRAPHY & PHOTO PROCESSING:

Hengtong-san 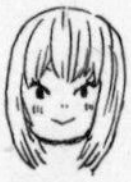

Kodama-kun 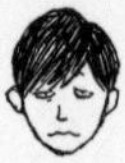

Forget Me Not

—— TRANSLATION NOTES ——

NOBUTA page 10, panel 5

As alluded to by one of the students, this name is taken from the Japanese novel and subsequent television series "Nobuta wo Produce." The series, which was broadcast in 2005, is about a shy girl, nicknamed Nobuta, and the attempts by some of her classmates to make her popular.

MY SASSY GIRL page 58, panel 2

This is the English title of "Yeopgijeogin Geunyeo," a Korean romantic comedy film that was released in Japan as "Ryoukiteki na Kanojo" (My Bizarre Girlfriend) about a man's relationship with a girl whose mood fluctuates wildly. The Japanese title of this film is the same as the title of this chapter.

CONSOLATION MONEY page 130, panel 4

In Japan, consolation money [*isharyo*] is paid out in cases such as traffic accidents, divorces, annulments, and cases of infidelity. The money is supposed to compensate for mental anguish and can start from $200 but can also reach into the hundreds of thousands of dollars depending on how much suffering one party inflicted on the other.

CHUO UNIVERSITY page 160, panel 2

A well-regarded private Japanese university, best known for its law program.

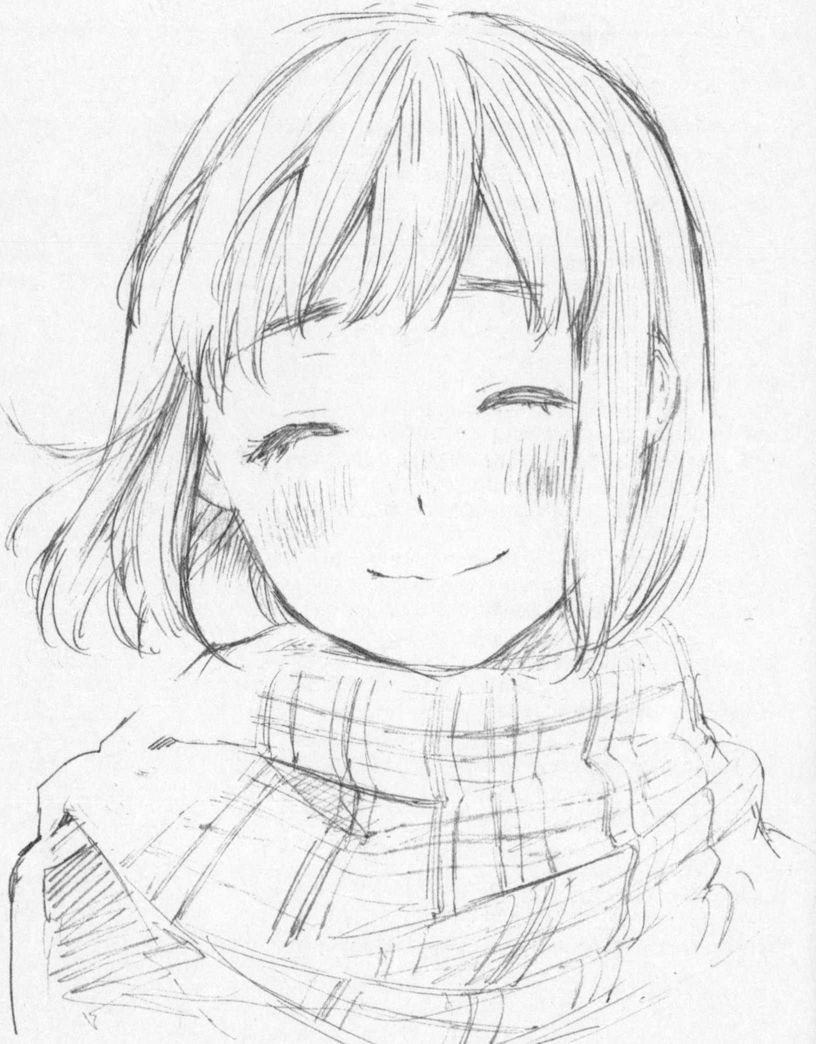

Forget Me Not volume 1 is a work of fiction. Names, characters, places, and incidents are the products of the author's imagination or are used fictitiously. Any resemblance to actual events, locales, or persons, living or dead, is entirely coincidental.

A Kodansha Comics Trade Paperback Original.

Published in the United States by Kodansha Comics,
an imprint of Kodansha USA Publishing, LLC, New York.

Publication rights for this English edition arranged through Kodansha Ltd., Tokyo.

First published in Japan in 2014 by Kodansha Ltd., Tokyo, as *Sore Demo Boku Wa Kimi Ga Suki* volume 1.

ISBN 978-1-63236-280-3

Printed in the United States of America.

www.kodanshacomics.com

9 8 7 6 5 4 3 2 1

Translation: Ko Ransom
Lettering: Evan Hayden
Editing: Ajani Oloye
Kodansha Comics Edition Cover Design: Phil Balsman